Forensic Document Examination in the 21st Century

Forensic Document Examination in the 21st Century

Edited by
Jan Seaman Kelly and Miriam Angel

CRC Press
Taylor & Francis Group
Boca Raton London New York

CRC Press is an imprint of the
Taylor & Francis Group, an **informa** business

First edition published 2021
by CRC Press
2 Park Square, Milton Park, Abingdon, Oxon, OX14 4RN

and by CRC Press
6000 Broken Sound Parkway NW, Suite 300, Boca Raton, FL 33487-2742

CRC Press is an imprint of Informa UK Limited

British Library Cataloguing-in-Publication Data
A catalogue record for this book is available from the British Library

Library of Congress Cataloging-in-Publication Data
Names: Seaman Kelly, Jan, editor. | Angel, Miriam, editor.
Title: Forensic document examination in the 21st century / edited by
Jan Seaman Kelly and Miriam Angel.
Description: First edition. | Boca Raton : CRC Press, 2021. | Includes
bibliographical references and index.
Identifiers: LCCN 2020027214 (print) | LCCN 2020027215 (ebook) |
ISBN 9780367251550 (hardback) | ISBN 9781003112228 (ebook)
Subjects: LCSH: Forensic sciences–History–21st century. | Criminal
investigation–History–21st century.
Classification: LCC HV8073 .F5633 2021 (print) | LCC HV8073 (ebook) |
DDC 363.25/65–dc23
LC record available at https://lccn.loc.gov/2020027214
LC ebook record available at https://lccn.loc.gov/2020027215

ISBN: 978-0-367-25155-0 (hbk)
ISBN: 978-1-003-11222-8 (ebk)

Typeset in Kepler
by codeMantra

For the love you had for Questioned Documents.

For your vast intelligence, boundless enthusiasm, and quick wit.

For the knowledge you shared and contributions you made.

For all the lively discussions.

For inspiration, encouragement, and kind words you gave.

For all the fond memories we will always have of you.

For Peter Tytell.

Contents

Preface

Considerable changes have occurred in the field of forensic document examination since Albert S. Osborn published *Questioned Documents*, the first in-depth book on the discipline's theory and practice. Technological advancements, calls for improvement in forensics by the scientific and academic communities, and collaboration with academics and researchers have shaped the practice and focus of research, as well as prompted introspection and research on the basis of Forensic Document Examiner (FDE) expertise and underlying theory.

The first section of this book discusses forensic document examination's place in the larger world of forensics, investigations, and court, and how the scientific, academic, and legal communities have helped enrich the field. Collaboration with others outside the forensic document examination discipline has helped us develop a standardized training program and improve our standards. Through discovery of how to apply logical reasoning, balance, and transparency to document evidence interpretation, we hope to strengthen the value of our evaluations and reporting. We have become aware of the influence of human factors on the examination process and are accepting the challenge to balance the need to mitigate possible negative effects of bias while still receiving the information necessary to perform a complete and accurate evaluation of the evidence.

Handwriting is the topic of Section II. Current handwriting theory and research enhances our knowledge of factors to be considered in the evaluation process. Studies on handwriting development and frequency of handwriting features support the individuality of handwriting. The large body of research in FDE proficiency demonstrates the expertise to differentiate handwriting exists.

Section III includes topics related to technology or specialized examinations. FDEs use technology in terms of (1) the evidence received in the form of computer-generated documents or electronic signatures, (2) instrumentation for analyzing evidence, and (3) for demonstrating findings in court. Authors of the chapters in this section share their expertise and knowledge developed through extensive research and experience so that we can be prepared for the future.

It is hoped this book offers the reader theoretical, technical, and practical knowledge on modern forensic document examination practice and theory.

Editors

Jan Seaman Kelly has been an FDE since 1987. She earned her Bachelor of Arts degree in Criminal Justice from the University of Central Oklahoma. She did her formal training in forensic document examination with George Lewis at the US Postal Laboratory in San Bruno, California. Ms. Kelly is a Diplomate of the American Board of Forensic Document Examiners (ABFDE) and a Fellow of the Questioned Document Section in the American Academy of Forensic Sciences (AAFS). She established Forensic Dynamics LLC, a private forensic document examination firm that provides examinations and consultations in civil and criminal cases from government and private sectors.

Ms. Kelly's accomplishments in the field of forensic document examination include serving as Director, Secretary, and President of the ABFDE from 1995 through 2002. She held the offices of Program Chair, Section Secretary and Section Chair of the Questioned Documents Section in AAFS from 2016 to 2020. Ms. Kelly served as Section Chair of the 2020 AAFS Interdisciplinary Symposium. She is a member of the National Institute of Standards and Technology (NIST) Organization of Scientific Area Committees (OSAC) Subcommittee for Forensic Documents and a member of the Academy Standards Board (ASB).

Ms. Kelly received two awards in 2004: the Ordway Hilton Award presented by the Questioned Document Section of the AAFS and named Safety Officer of the Year by the Rotary Clubs of Southern Nevada. The ABFDE presented the Charles C. Scott Award to Ms. Kelly in 2002 for her defense of the forensic document profession as a member of the Daubert Group.

Ms. Kelly is the coeditor and coauthor of several chapters in the second edition of Scientific Examination of Questioned Documents, released by CRC Press in 2006. She is the author of Forensic Examination of Rubber Stamps, released by Charles C. Thomas Publisher in 2002. In 1994, the ABFDE published her 62-page monograph, Significant Dates of Typing Methods. Ms. Kelly has published several articles in professional journals such as the *Journal of Forensic Sciences* and the *Journal of the American Society of Questioned Document Examiners.*

Miriam Angel earned a Bachelor of Science degree in Applied Mathematics from the University of California, Los Angeles (UCLA) and a Master of Science degree in Computer Science from the University of Southern California (USC). She did her training at the Los Angeles Police Department (LAPD) from 1994 to 1996 and continues to work as a Forensic Document Examiner in the LAPD laboratory.

Ms. Angel is a Diplomate of the ABFDE and is currently serving on the ABFDE Board of Directors. She was the Secretary of the ABFDE from 2017 to 2019. She is a member of the American Society of Questioned Document Examiners and the AAFS. She also currently serves on the OSAC Forensic Document Examination Subcommittee.

Ms. Angel has given several presentations and published articles in professional journals on kinematics and signature complexity. Having recently completed an 8-month online course on Essentials of Forensic Interpretation from the University of Lausanne, Switzerland, she has presented the application of logical reasoning to handwriting examination at the AAFS and to colleagues at the LAPD laboratory.

Contributors

Zain M. Bhaloo is an FDE with the Canada Border Services Agency (CBSA) in Ottawa, Canada. He holds a Bachelor of Science Honours degree from Carleton University in Biology and Biotechnology and a Master's degree in Forensic Science with distinction, specializing in Forensic Chemistry from Strathclyde University in Glasgow, Scotland.

Mr. Bhaloo completed his training under the tutelage of the distinguished document examiners at the CBSA. Prior to joining the CBSA, Mr. Bhaloo served in the Royal Canadian Mounted Police's (RCMP) Forensic Laboratory Services in Ottawa in the Forensic Evidence Management Unit, as well as with the National DNA Databank.

In 2009, Mr. Bhaloo was the recipient of The William Donald Dixon Memorial Research and Essay Award from the Canadian Identification Society, and he presented his research on the recovery of finger marks from fired cartridge cases at the CIS conference in 2010. He is currently a member of the AAFS in the Questioned Documents section, the American Society of Questioned Document Examiners (ASQDE), and he has held program co-chair positions with both organizations. He is currently the Chair of the AAFS Young Forensic Scientist's Forum, serves on several other committees, and hopes to remain involved with both organizations in the future.

Carolyne Bird holds the degrees of Bachelor of Technology (Forensic and Analytical Chemistry) and Bachelor of Science (Honours), both from the Flinders University of South Australia, and a Doctor of Philosophy in Human Bioscience from La Trobe University, Melbourne. Her research focused on investigating forensic handwriting examiners' skill in detecting unnatural handwriting processes. She commenced training in forensic document examination at Forensic Science South Australia in 2002, where she is still employed, now in the position of Science Leader – Document Examination. Dr. Bird is a member and current (2018–2021) President of the Australasian Society of Forensic Document Examiners, Inc., a member of the Scientific Working Group for Forensic Document Examination (SWGDOC), an associate member of the European Document Experts Working Group and the European Network of Forensic Handwriting Experts, and a corresponding member of the American Society of Questioned Document Examiners. She was also a member of the NIST/NIJ Expert Working Group for Human Factors in Handwriting Examination.

Brett M. D. Bishop received a Bachelor of Science degree in Chemistry from Eastern Washington University. In 2005, he began his career with the Washington State Patrol Crime Laboratory Division as a Forensic Scientist in the Documents section. He is a member of the American Society of Questioned Document Examiners, the Southwestern Association of Forensic Document Examiners, and the International Association for Identification. He has also been part of the Scientific Working Group for Forensic Document Examination and the National Institute of Standards and Technology (NIST) Organization of Scientific Area Committees (OSAC) Forensic Document Examination subcommittee.

Timothy A. Campbell has an Honours Bachelor of Science degree in Biology and Earth Sciences from the University of Waterloo (1998) and has been employed as an FDE at the Canada Border Services Agency (CBSA) in Ottawa, Ontario since 2008.

Prior to his training, Mr. Campbell held various production and technological positions in a plastic credit and ID card printing company. He began his forensic document examination training at the Centre of Forensic Sciences (CFS) in Toronto, Ontario in 2001 under the supervision of Gregory Dawson. For a period in 2005, Mr. Campbell was temporarily assigned to the CFS Electronics Section where he was trained to examine mobile devices. He was a guest lecturer at the Ontario Police College courses for fraud and homicide investigators and has attended and presented at conferences addressing the interface of artificial intelligence and documents.

Mr. Campbell is a member of the Questioned Document Section of the Canadian Society of Forensic Science (CSFS) and an associate member of the Questioned Document Section of the AAFS. He has been the Secretary for the AAFS ASB Consensus Body for Forensic Document Examination since 2016 and is the Chair of an ASB working group.

Khody R. Detwiler has been involved in the field of forensic document examination since 2008 and is currently a Forensic Document Examiner in private practice with Lesnevich & Detwiler, located in Roaring Spring, Pennsylvania. After receiving a Bachelor of Science degree in Criminal Justice from Penn State University, he completed his formal Forensic Document Examiner training under the tutelage of Gus R. Lesnevich. In addition to being a member of the Questioned Documents Section of the AAFS, Mr. Detwiler is also a member of the American Society of Questioned Document Examiners (ASQDE), the Midwestern Association of Forensic Scientists, Inc. (MAFS), Mid-Atlantic Association of Forensic Scientists (MAAFS), the Northeastern Association of Forensic Scientists (NEAFS), and the International Association for Identification (IAI). Mr. Detwiler is currently serving as the 2020 Questioned Documents Section Chair of MAAFS and has been serving as Vice Chair of the Forensic Document Examination Consensus Body of the AAFS ASB since 2017.

Marie E. Durina has a Bachelor of Business Administration degree from Baruch College, CUNY, New York. She holds a Graduate Certificate of Academic Studies in the Examination of Questioned Documents from Oklahoma State University and a Certificate of Achievement in Administration of Justice/Criminal Investigations from Miramar College in San Diego, CA. In 1990, she began her career in forensics as an evidence technician performing crime scene investigations, and in 2003 began training as a Forensic Document Examiner with the San Diego Sheriff's Department Regional Crime Laboratory under the tutelage of Dr. Linton Mohammed. She was promoted to FDE in 2005 and to Senior FDE in 2010. Ms. Durina retired from this agency in 2015. In 2016, Ms. Durina joined Riley Welch LaPorte & Associates Forensic Laboratories as an FDE and retired from this position in 2019. She is a Diplomate of the ABFDE and served on this organization's Board of Directors from 2010 through 2014 in the capacity of Public Relations Chairperson and as a member of the Recertification Committee. She is a member of the American Society of Questioned Document Examiners (ASQDE), the AAFS Questioned Document Section, the Southeastern Association of Forensic Document Examiners (SAFDE), the Scientific Working Group for Forensic Document Examination (SWGDOC), the OSAC Forensic Document Examination Subcommittee, and the AAFS Standard Board's (ASB) Consensus Body for Forensic Document Examination.

Donna O. Eisenberg earned her Bachelor of Arts degree in Psychology from the University of Maryland in College Park and a Master's of Forensic Science degree from the George Washington University in Washington, D.C. In 1988, she began her professional training in the field of forensic document examination at the Forensic Services Division of the US Secret Service. Ms. Eisenberg currently works in the Questioned Document Section at the US Department of Homeland Security (formerly the Immigration and Naturalization Service) and maintains a private practice in Rockville, Maryland. She is a Diplomate of the ABFDE (serving as Vice President from 2007 to 2010) and an associate member of the Questioned Document Section of the AAFS.

Mark T. Goff has been an FDE for over 10 years. He received forensic document training at the Michigan State Police forensic laboratory in Lansing, Michigan. Detective Lieutenant Goff is a Diplomate of the ABFDE. He has presented numerous workshops on digital examinations of forensic documents for national and regional forensic science organizations. He is a member of the OSAC Forensic Document Examination Subcommittee and the ASB.

Lisa M. Hanson began her forensic career at the Minnesota Bureau of Criminal Apprehension (BCA) Forensic Science Laboratory in the Toxicology Section. In 1999, she transferred to the Questioned Document Section and trained under the direct supervision of Forensic Document Examiner Debra Springer. Ms. Hanson is a Diplomate of the ABFDE. Through a grant funded by the United States Department of Justice, she conducted a longitudinal study in the development of handwriting characteristics of elementary school students. The results of this study were published in the *Journal of Forensic Sciences* in October 2016. She is a member of OSAC, as well as a member of the AAFS Standards Board (ASB), an ANSI-accredited Standards Developing Organization. Ms. Hanson retired from the MNBCA in 2016 to pursue a career as a private consultant/examiner in questioned document examination.

Samiah Ibrahim graduated with a Bachelor of Arts in Political Science and a Bachelor of Science in Biology from Carleton University. After spending several years as an intelligence officer, Ms. Ibrahim received her training in forensic document examination at the Canadian Security Intelligence Service. She manages a team of Forensic Document Examiners, chemists, and other forensic experts at the Canada Border Services Agency. Ms. Ibrahim operates a private practice focused on supporting United Nations capacity development projects in the Middle East, Africa, and Latin America. Ms. Ibrahim is a member of the Canadian Society of Forensic Sciences, the American Society of Questioned Document Examiners (ASQDE), the AAFS, and the Chartered Society of Forensic Scientists (England). She currently serves on the ASQDE Executive Committee, as a member of the International Affairs Committee of the AAFS, and as an associate editor of the *Journal of Forensic Sciences.*

Dr. Mara L. Merlino earned her doctoral and master's degrees from the Interdisciplinary Ph.D. Program in Social Psychology and the University of Nevada, Reno. She is a Full Professor of Psychology and Sociology and Coordinator of the MA Program in Interdisciplinary Behavioral Science at Kentucky State University. She currently serves on the Forensic Document Examination Subcommittee of NIST's OSAC, and formerly served as a contributor on the NIST Expert Working Group on Human Factors in Handwriting Examination. She has directed or supervised research projects under the auspices of organizations such as the Federal Judicial Center, The National Judicial College, the State Justice Institute, and the National Council of

Juvenile and Family Court Judges. Her current research contributes to the extant knowledge about the nature of expertise related to forensic document examination, the evaluation and interpretation of the salient features of signature specimens, and the social influences inherent in the context of forensic document examination.

Linda L. Mitchell holds a Bachelor of Science degree in Criminal Justice Administration from the University of Phoenix. She received her training from Manny Gonzales. Ms. Mitchell is a private practitioner who established Forensic QDE Lab, LLC in 2001. Her practice includes forensic document examinations in criminal and civil matters. Ms. Mitchell is a Diplomate of the ABFDE, a member of the American Society of Questioned Document Examiners, a Fellow in the Questioned Documents Section of the AAFS, and a member of the Southwestern Association of Forensic Document Examiners.

Kathleen Annunziata Nicolaides is an FDE with Associated Forensic Laboratory, LLC in Phoenix, Arizona. She received her Bachelor of Arts degree from State University of New York at Binghamton (now Binghamton University). Before opening her own private laboratory in July 2019, Ms. Nicolaides worked at Affiliated Forensic Laboratory, Inc. (AFL). It was there she began her professional training in 1998 through a 3-year apprenticeship with William J. Flynn. She worked at AFL until it closed in June 2019. Ms. Nicolaides is a Diplomate of the ABFDE. She is an associate member of the Questioned Document Section of the AAFS, a regular member of the American Society of Questioned Document Examiners, and a member of the Southwestern Association of Forensic Document Examiners.

Larry A. Olson is an FDE/Ink Chemist at the Internal Revenue Service National Forensic Laboratory in Chicago and has been a practitioner of forensic documents for 37 years. He earned a Bachelor's degree in Chemistry from the United States Naval Academy, Annapolis, Maryland, and a Master's degree in Forensic Science from George Washington University in Washington, District of Columbia. He began document training at the Immigration and Naturalization Forensic Document Laboratory in McLean, Virginia, received training in ink analysis from the Bureau of Alcohol, Tobacco, and Firearms Laboratory in Rockville, Maryland, and completed his training at the Internal Revenue Service National Forensic Laboratory in Chicago.

He is a member of the American Society of Questioned Document Examiners, the Questioned Document Section of the AAFS, the Southwestern Association of Forensic Document Examiners, and a member and Past-President of the Midwestern Association of Forensic Scientists. Mr. Olson is also a Diplomate of the ABFDE.

R. Brent Ostrum graduated in 1984 from Carleton University with a Bachelor of Arts Honours degree (summa cum laude) in Psychology. He also has a Certificate of Advanced Studies in "Statistics and the Evaluation of Forensic Evidence" from the University of Lausanne, Switzerland (2011).

Mr. Ostrum completed his training in forensic document examination at the Royal Canadian Mounted Police Forensic Laboratory (Regina, Canada) in 1985, and stayed at that laboratory until 2002. Since then, he has worked as a Senior FDE with the Canada Border Services Agency's (CBSA) Science and Engineering Directorate in Ottawa, Ontario.

Mr. Ostrum is a Diplomate of the ABFDE and has served as chairman of the Document Section of the Canadian Society of Forensic Science for many years. He is also a volunteer member on the Executive Council for St2ar (Skill-Task Training Assessment & Research, Inc.) and has been active in standards and methods development with both SWGDOC and NIST-OSAC. He was a member of the NIST/NIJ project, "Forensic Handwriting Examination and Human Factors: Improving the Practice Through a Systems Approach" (the Report of the Expert Working Group for Human Factors in Handwriting Examination). He has also served on the Program Committee for "International Workshop on Computational Forensics" (IWCF) meetings.

Mr. Ostrum has been a guest speaker/presenter at various events including the Centre of Forensic Science's "Evaluative Reporting Symposium" (2019), the NIST Measurement Science and Standards in Forensic Handwriting Analysis Conference (2013), and POMA (2013). He was invited to write a chapter in the textbook, *Forensic Examination of Signatures*, 1st Ed. (2019). He has presented tutorials/workshops on a variety of topics including "Logical Inference and Evidence Evaluation," "Proficiency Testing and Competency," "Admissibility of FDE Evidence under R. v. Mohan," "Forensic Handwriting Identification: A Canadian Perspective on the Admissibility of (Expert) Handwriting Evidence," and "A Canadian Perspective on Forensic Science versus Pseudoscience," among others.

Lucinda Risi, ACP, has enjoyed a career in law that spans more than 40 years. She has worked as a paralegal in a district attorney's office, a mid-sized litigation firm, and a large general practice law firm. Ms. Risi obtained a paralegal certificate from the University of Oklahoma Department of Legal Assistant Education and is a certified paralegal through the National Association of Legal Assistants (NALA). In addition, she has obtained advanced certifications in civil litigation and discovery. She is a past president of the Central Oklahoma Association of Legal Assistants. Ms. Risi serves as a judicial assistant to a United States District Court judge and is an instructor in the University of Oklahoma Law Center's Department of Legal Assistant Education.

Tobin Tanaka received his Bachelor of Science degree in Physics and diploma in Meteorology from the University of British Columbia. He has been an FDE with the Government of Canada since 1993. He received his training (1993–1996) and worked as an FDE at the Canadian Security Intelligence Service between 1993 and 2000.

In 2000, he commenced working as an FDE for the Canada Customs & Revenue Agency, which was transferred to his current employment at the Canada Border Services Agency in December 2003. He has been a part-time instructor at the British Columbia Institute of Technology for the Questioned Document Examination course for forensic science students.

His professional memberships include the Document Section of the Canadian Society of Forensic Science, regular member of the American Society of Questioned Document Examiners, member of the Questioned Document Section of the AAFS, member of the Chartered Society of Forensic Sciences, and corresponding member of the Australasian Society of Forensic Document Examiners Inc. He is also a Diplomate of the ABFDE.

Mr. Tanaka was also editor of the *Journal of the American Society of Questioned Document Examiners* (2014–2018), and he is currently on the roster of Justice Rapid Response, a global entity that provides specialized justice experts to assist with international investigations.

Peter Tytell studied the examination of documents with his parents, Forensic Document Examiners Pearl and Martin Tytell, both of whom had been licensed by the University of the State of New York to teach Questioned Document Examination and Identification. He pursued additional relevant studies at Georgetown University's Institute of Advanced Analytical Chemistry and the Institute for Criminal Law and Procedure, Rensselaer Polytechnic Institute, the Institute of Paper Chemistry, and the Rochester Institute of Technology as well as numerous specialized courses and workshops. He also holds a Bachelor of Arts degree in Criminal Justice from John Jay College of the City University of New York (*summa cum laude*).

His many areas of research include the history, differentiation, dating, and classification of typewriter and printing type styles; typewriters; and other business imaging equipment. In addition to being raised and working in the family typewriter shop, he conducted on-site observation at producers of paper and papermaking equipment, typewriters, typewriter type and elements, ribbons, carbon paper, digital typestyles in the United States and other countries, as well as the development and production of specialized overlay plates for the examination of typewritten and other machine generated documents (in use internationally by private and government document examiners). This research has been part of his extensive lecturing and teaching to fellow examiners, investigators, and attorneys in the public and private sectors.

Mr. Tytell is a Diplomate of the ABFDE. He is a member of the Questioned Documents Section of the AAFS and is a recipient of the section's Ordway Hilton Award. He is a member of the Committee on Forensic Sciences of the American Society for Testing and Materials (ASTM) and is a recipient of the ASTM Forensic Sciences Award, the ASTM Award of Merit, and he is an ASTM Fellow. Mr. Tytell is a member of the American Society of Questioned Document Examiners and a recipient of the Albert S. Osborn Award of Excellence. He is a member of the Chartered Society Forensic Sciences (UK) and a recipient of the Long-Term Service Award. He has been an active participant in the work of the FBI-sponsored Scientific Working Group for Forensic Document Examination (SWGDOC), was a founding member of the editorial board of the *International Journal of Forensic Document Examiners*, and currently serves on the Forensic Document Examination Subcommittee of the NIST-sponsored OSAC. He received the Distinguished Individual Service Award for his work in OSAC. He is also a member of the Forensic Document Examination Consensus Body of the AAFS ASB.

Mr. Tytell has worked on document cases submitted by courts, prosecutors, public defenders and legal aid societies, law firms, government crime laboratories, other document examiners, private individuals, banks, insurance companies, and corporations. Since 1971 he has appeared as an expert witness on handwriting, typewriting, typography, and other forensic document problems in State and Federal courts, as well as other venues in the United States and in other countries.

Mr. Tytell provided a basic concept and outline for the chapter on typography that was enhanced and completed by Zain Bhaloo and Tobin Tanaka.

Rigo Vargas holds a Bachelor of Arts degree in Biology with a minor in Chemistry from Indiana University. He received his forensic document examination training at the Mississippi Crime Laboratory from 1998 to 2000. In 2004, he accepted a position as a Forensic Document Analyst with the US Department of Treasury, Internal Revenue Service in Chicago. Mr. Vargas was appointed as the Questioned Documents Section Chief at the Mississippi Forensics Laboratory in Biloxi in 2010. He is the past chairman of both the E30.02 Questioned Documents subcommittee of the American Society of Testing and Materials International (ASTM) and the Forensic Document Examination subcommittee of the OSAC. Mr. Vargas is a member of the American Society of Questioned Document Examiners, the Southeastern Association of Forensic Document Examiners, and the Questioned Documents Section of the AAFS. He is a Diplomate of the ABFDE.

Thomas W. Vastrick has been an FDE since 1977. He holds a Bachelor of Science degree in Forensic Science from California State University at Sacramento. Mr. Vastrick received his training in forensic document examination from the US Postal Inspection Service in Washington DC.

He is a Diplomate of the ABFDE. Mr. Vastrick is a Retired Fellow with the AAFS where he has held several offices to include Questioned Document Section Chair and Director on the AAFS's Board of Directors. In addition, he is a Life Member of the American Society of Questioned Document Examiners, where he has also served as an executive officer.

Mr. Vastrick has an extensive history of published articles and research that include a database of mechanical checkwriter impressions that is a standard reference for Forensic Document Examiners. Mr. Vastrick has authored one book and has been a contributing author to two other textbooks and an Internal Report for the NIST for the US Department of Commerce. He has also published 19 papers in various publications to include the *Journal of Forensic Sciences*, *The Journal of the American Society of Questioned Document Examiners*, and *Forensic Science International*. Mr. Vastrick has also dedicated many years of his career to the establishment of standards within forensic document examination by his active membership and involvement in Scientific Working Groups and with the ASB, an American National Standards Developer (ANSI) accredited Standards Development Organization. Mr. Vastrick has a long history of supporting the Forensic Science curriculum at the University of Central Florida through regular lecturing and sponsoring summer internships. Mr. Vastrick and a team of statisticians were awarded a National Institute of Justice grant to research frequency of proportion databases in handwriting, hand-printing, and handwritten numerals.

Elaine X. Wooton earned her Bachelor of Arts degree in Political Science from the University of Wisconsin-Madison and a Master of Forensic Science degree from the George Washington University in Washington, D.C. In 1991, she began her professional training in the field of forensic document examination at the Questioned Document Section of the US Immigration & Naturalization Service Forensic Document Laboratory. Ms. Wooton continues to work in the Questioned Document Section at the US Department of Homeland Security (which was formerly the Immigration and Naturalization Service). She is a Diplomate of the ABFDE and a member of the Southeastern Association of Forensic Document Examiners.

Section I

Modern Standards, Theory, and Practices

Chapter 1

Forensic Document Examiner Training

Brett M. D. Bishop

CONTENTS

The training of a forensic document examiner (FDE) is the foundation on which the expertise is built. A good training program will cover the various aspects of the discipline that are necessary to do the job. The Scientific Working Group for Forensic Document Examination (SWGDOC) standard[1] covers the criteria and the various topics that are necessary for someone to train in the discipline.

Two key elements of a good training program are the curriculum and the qualifications of the trainer. The curriculum should incorporate challenging problems, including those where the ground truth answer is known. Feedback is vital for trainees to learn and to improve the accuracy of their conclusions. The trainer must have successfully completed an FDE training program that meets published standards; have the knowledge, skills, and abilities (KSAs) as they relate to forensic document examination; and have at least five years of post-training experience. The trainer should also have good instruction skills; completing a course in instructor development would be helpful. Until a standard training program is developed, a trainer must develop lessons, tests, and evaluations, with clearly defined learning objectives and outcomes.

1.1 SKILLS AND APTITUDE OF THE TRAINEE

It is advisable that the trainee have a scientific background. Areas of interest include:

- Science, technology, engineering, and mathematics (STEM), specifically physics, chemistry, and biology. These types of degrees ensure the trainee has the foundation, background, and focus needed in forensic document examination. The trainee should also have a solid foundation in research methodology to understand published studies and to properly conduct and publish his or her own research.

- Cognitive skills. It is critical the trainee be able to observe and discern fine and subtle details and differentiate patterns. This ability should be demonstrated by successful completion of several form-blindness tests. Trainees must also be able to concentrate for long periods of time and have critical thinking skills to properly analyze and evaluate evidence and form judgments.
- Literacy skills, such as reading comprehension and clear oral and written communication skills. The successful trainee will be able to demonstrate the basis for his or her conclusions and clearly articulate those conclusions, along with any limitations present. The trainee will need to describe complex processes such as how an electrostatic detection device works and how various light sources and filters can affect inks or other writing materials.
- Probability and statistics. These provide the trainee with a greater understanding of logical reasoning and the value of various research projects.
- Computer and technology skills. Photography, the ability to use graphics software, and familiarity with typography are desired skills.

1.2 FOUNDATION OF TRAINING

Apprenticeship training has been integral in many trades and disciplines for thousands of years. Skills, crafts, techniques, and knowledge are taught by working side by side with an experienced trainer. Many professional industries primarily use the apprenticeship training style as the foundation of a career. These include professions such as architect, bank teller, carpenter, computer programmer, electrician, farmer, machinist, mechanic, pharmacy assistant, and plumber.

FDE training begins as an apprenticeship. This apprenticeship should last approximately 4,000 hours and include face-to-face meetings. The academic portion of training includes reading literature and research papers on forensic document theory; proper evidence handling; studying the scientific method, historical foundation of the forensic document examination field, copybook styles, and ethics; and presenting court testimony. The majority of the training program consists of practical experience in thousands of inter-writer comparisons, with the trainee receiving feedback from the trainer based on discussion of the results. This helps the trainee build the required knowledge and judgment needed to properly evaluate evidence. Thus, in-person, timely, one-on-one instruction is a vital component to a successful training program.

Ericsson and Pool's book[2] discusses the 10,000 hours it takes to become an expert. They studied many different fields and found that a great many hours of hard work were spent by individuals meticulously refining their craft. It is not just about the amount of time that is spent but the intentionality that makes the difference. It involves the complex nature of "deliberate practice."

Deliberate practice comprises two components: feedback and modification of the effort in response to that feedback. Trainers closely monitor progress, identify problems, and assist with solutions to the problems at the beginning stage of the training. As the training progresses, trainees learn how to solve similar problems themselves. This self-monitoring can only be done with realistic mental representations. For example, in moot court exercises, the trainee describes his or her case examination and defends his or her observations and conclusions. This exercise provides the trainee with exposure to answering various questions he or she can be asked in court. The trainee improves because of the necessary adjustments that are made through feedback that is received.

Training and experience in handwriting examination is particularly essential. Because there is some similarity in everyone's handwriting, trainees initially tend to see all similarities as significant and may ignore differences. After seeing numerous samples of writing, reading the literature, and conferring with experienced examiners, they begin to develop the ability to observe differences beyond the obvious pictorial divergences. Only then can the trainee effectively evaluate the significance and balance of similarities and differences in natural writing. The trainee also will be introduced to the fact that as handwriting is the result of a motor program, it can change, either intentionally or not. A simulation (imitation written by someone else) will have similarities to the writing it is imitating. Disguised writing will exhibit differences compared to a person's normal writing. External factors (such as illness or unusual writing conditions) may also introduce differences. The trainee must learn to consider handwriting complexity and line quality, along with similarities and differences.

Because all cases involve a unique set of circumstances, there is no precise recipe that can be taught and followed for every examination. Trainees must be able to learn from the feedback received and extrapolate that information to apply it to a new case with different features but where their previous experience can be used. For example, the difference in direction of stroke of a particular letter may be important in differentiating two writing samples in one case. The trainee may remember to look at the direction of stroke for that letter in a later case but must also do so for other letters. They should eventually realize that significantly divergent letter construction can be a differentiating factor in general.

The training program is only the beginning of the FDE's career. After successful completion of a training program, continuing education is needed. Attending professional conferences and workshops, engaging in research, publishing in journals, and presenting novel research at conferences allow FDEs to keep abreast of current techniques and continue to enhance their knowledge and expertise. There are also opportunities for FDEs to pursue additional training at universities, but this should supplement, not replace, initial training.

1.3 COMPONENTS OF A TRAINING PLAN

The traditional FDE training program outline includes modules on the following:

- Introduction to Forensic Document Examination
- Evidence Procedures
- Bias, Conclusions, and Statistics
- Scientific Instrumentation
- Handwriting
- Indented Impressions
- Ink and Writing Instruments
- Paper
- Physical Matches
- Printing Processes
- Alterations, Fabrications, and Obliterations
- Typewriters and Mechanical Devices
- Miscellaneous Examinations
- Courtroom Procedures and Testimony

The trained examiner must have enough knowledge, skill, and ability in the various topics of forensic document examination to know his or her limitations and to ensure that evidence is not compromised, or conclusions misrepresented to the trier of fact. Forensic examiners must also realize that they are advocates for the evidence and not for one side or the other.

A good training program is designed with five key stages: introduction, foundation, reinforcement, consolidation, and reporting. Each of the stages should increase the KSAs of the trainee. At various points along the way, learning objectives should be defined along with the assessment method and criteria for success. The training plan, tasks, and accomplishments must be documented in detail. In the introduction stage, the emphasis may be on laboratory protocol such as evidence handling, safety and personal protective equipment, and chain of custody. The foundation stage may include instruction on theory, instrumentation, and methodology. The trainee puts the knowledge into practice in the reinforcement stage. The trainee works through various exercises and problems while receiving direct one-on-one feedback, improving his or her skill. In the consolidation stage, the topics already learned are combined, and the trainee can interrelate the complex components. The final stage of reporting means the trainee can communicate, explain, and demonstrate his or her KSAs to others.

Competency tests must be successfully completed after each module. Challenging and comprehensive competency tests demonstrate that the trainee has the KSAs to accurately interpret evidence and report results in forensic document examination. Pursuing certification would be the next step in demonstrating minimum competency as an FDE.

1.4 CONCLUSION

Training has a profound effect on the qualifications of the FDE. Proper training allows the examiner to acquire and preserve expertise and should provide the foundation to minimize human error in the examination process.

REFERENCES

1. "Standard for Minimum Training Requirements for Forensic Document Examiners" SWGDOC, accessed January 2020, https://www.swgdoc.org/documents/SWGDOC%20Standard%20for%20Minimum%20Training%20Requirements%20for%20Forensic%20Document%20Examiners.pdf.
2. K. Anders Ericsson and R. Pool, *Peak: Secrets from the New Science of Expertise* (Boston: Houghton Mifflin Harcourt, 2016).

Chapter 2

Standards in Forensic Document Examination

Rigo Vargas

Standards are a necessity in many fields. From healthcare and safety to construction and engineering, standards provide procedures and best practices in order to establish and ensure consistency, accuracy, and reliability. Forensic document examiners (FDEs) use standards for compliance and to align the field under common best practices relating to examinations, conclusion terminology, and training. Standards provide transparency and basic information for investigators, academics, and laypersons. They are of paramount importance when challenges in court arise. They assist judges and attorneys in determining the qualifications of expert witnesses and help establish the validity of the science. The forensic document examination field was one of the first forensic disciplines to be challenged in court by Daubert, and one of the first to have an examiner's testimony restricted or entirely excluded. Although few, these court decisions were disconcerting and highlighted the importance of having standards. At that time the forensic document examination field had only a few standards on the books.

The first document examination standard (Guide for Scope of Work of Forensic Document Examiners) was published in 1972, with four additional standards published between 1972 and 1997. The original standards were promulgated by ASTM International and vetted through their subcommittee E30.02 on Questioned Documents. In 1997, the Department of Justice (DOJ) established and funded several Scientific Working Groups (SWGs) to address the standards needs of the forensic community. Disciplines such as firearms, latent prints, and drug analysis all received SWG groups; thus, the Scientific Working Group for Forensic Document Examination (SWGDOC) was born. Utilizing bi-annual face-to-face meetings, SWGDOC took over the majority of the writing, revising, and vetting of the forensic document examination standards navigating the publication process. During the 15 years SWGDOC was in operation, the forensic document examination field published over 20 standards. Currently, these standards can be found on the SWGDOC website free of charge.

In 2012 the E30.02 subcommittee was dissolved, and a year later the DOJ defunded the SWGs. The National Institute of Standards and Technology (NIST) picked up where the SWGs left off in 2015 by establishing the Organization of Scientific Area Committees (OSAC), which represents a larger portion of the forensic disciplines. OSAC membership includes not only forensic practitioners but also academics, lawyers, judges, statisticians, and individuals with specialized knowledge. Chairpersons from one forensic subcommittee are involved in the discussions and approval of work products from another. Members from different disciplines are encouraged to discuss issues together as well. Experts who are not members of OSAC may attend meetings as guests. Guests are invited when they possess specialized knowledge in a particular area. Once completed, OSAC standards are submitted to a standardization development organization (SDO) for publishing. The SDO chosen by the forensic document examination community and many other forensic disciplines is the Academy Standards Board (ASB).

The ASB was established by the American Academy of Forensic Sciences to develop documentary standards for forensics. Accredited by the American National Standards Institute (ANSI), the ASB publishes consensus standards, best practice recommendations, and technical reports via a consensus-based development process. The ASB accepts standards submitted by OSAC, created within the ASB, or received from an outside submitter not affiliated with either organization. Members from OSAC and individuals with specialized knowledge are often invited to join ASB working groups and attend ASB meetings. Doing so helps expedite the writing and vetting process and is crucial when addressing public comments. Once a document has completed the ASB development process, it becomes an American National Standard (ANS) and is published within 6 months of its approval. Published standards may be submitted to OSAC for placement on the OSAC Registry. At the time of this writing, the original SWGDOC standards are either being revised in OSAC or have advanced to the ASB. The ASB and OSAC maintain a synergistic relationship designed to strengthen forensic standards through research and collaboration.

Standards are of the upmost importance in any field. They encourage the sharing of knowledge, facilitate innovation, maintain transparency, and ensure consistency. Standards are not stagnant; they are dynamic documents, always evolving and changing. Advancements can come from new technology, new research, or even a paradigm shift. With the help of organizations like OSAC and the ASB, FDE standards will continue to advance and strengthen the field of forensic document examination for years to come.

Chapter 3

The Logical Approach to Evidence Evaluation

R. Brent Ostrum

CONTENTS

3.1 INTRODUCTION

This chapter presents information, both theoretical and practical, about the logical approach to evidence evaluation, primarily in reference to forensic document examination. This section provides introductory information and terminology, including some discussion of the history of the approach and reasons why this approach can be of great benefit to forensic document examiners (FDEs). Subsequent sections discuss inference and reasoning in general, key concepts such as probability and the other fundamentals, practical elements of the logical approach specific to forensic document examination work, options for conclusion wording including reporting and testimony, and, finally, some discussion of challenges and concerns when using the logical approach.

The role of any expert witness is to provide the court, and more specifically the trier, with a proper understanding of evidence that falls within that examiner's scope of expertise. To fulfill this role, the forensic examiner must be able to evaluate evidence in terms of the matter at hand in a fair, balanced, and objective manner. Only through proper evaluation of the evidence can an examiner fulfill their responsibility to the court. Evidence evaluation is key to the core function of the forensic examiner and arguably the most important aspect of the entire process. Evaluation is the focus of this chapter and, briefly, it refers to any assessment of examination results aimed at determining what those results mean to a trier of fact.

In a judicial setting, the trier of fact, or simply the *trier*, refers to a judge, jury, or both. Other parties will function as the trier for other types of proceedings, e.g., board members for a regulatory body or arbitrator of a tribunal. It is the trier's responsibility to reach decisions about guilt, innocence, or liability as it may apply in a given matter.

The results of many forensic evaluations never make it to court and, hence, a judge or jury is never involved. In those instances, other parties use the information to assess the situation and reach some decision. For example, the "building of a case" involves many different parties who must decide, for themselves, what has (likely) happened (based on all available information) and what the forensic science information means to them.

Through this process, the results of a forensic evaluation may influence a number of different parties, each of whom reaches some decision about the matter. From the perspective of the examiner, the purpose remains the same: the evaluation is done to assist *some other party* in fully understanding what the findings mean for *that party's* overall assessment of the matter at hand. In this context, "Findings are the result of observations, measurements and classification that are made on items of interest. They can be qualitative (nominal or ordinal) or quantitative (discrete or continuous). No result is also a finding."[1] However, it is not the examiner's place to make decisions about what happened or may have happened; their role should be to explain the meaning of the evidence, or findings, so that someone else can make such decisions. As Robertson, et al. put it, "Clearly, such issues and decisions are not up to the forensic scientist but rather the trier of fact. The role of the forensic scientist is not to decide the issue, but to describe what the evidence is worth."[2]

Additionally, while this chapter discusses the logical approach to evidence evaluation, it is important to note that forensic examiners perform a variety of functions for different clients, some of which may not require or involve an evaluative assessment. The European Network of Forensic Science Institutes (ENFSI) guideline for evaluative reporting distinguishes four report types, only one of which is an *evaluative report*.[3] The other report types include intelligence, investigative, and technical (factual) reports, none of which must necessarily conform to the principles of evaluation reflected in an evaluative report.

Most of the time forensic examiners will, in fact, perform an evaluation of findings intended to address the issues of concern to their client and the courts. The end-result of such an evaluative process is an *evaluative report* which provides "... an assessment of the strength to be attached to the findings in the context of alleged circumstances."[4] In brief, the process involves consideration of the findings in terms of two or more competing propositions with the goal being the determination of some form of likelihood ratio (*LR*) while conforming to proper principles of evaluation. An evaluative report is the product of the logical approach to evidence evaluation which refers to a process of evaluation, i.e., assessment or reasoning, conforming to the rules of proper and coherent logic.[5] This approach is scientifically sound and provides a logically defensible way to deal with uncertainty in the reasoning process. This will be discussed at length later in the chapter.

Technical (or factual) reports often precede one of the other types of reports. Technical reports amount to a purely descriptive rendering of the findings and may lead, in some instances, to the assignment of an object to a class (i.e., classification). For example, a statement to the effect that "the observations of the questioned document indicate it was produced using an electrophotographic, dry-toner device" is a technical or factual comment. It serves to delimit the pool of devices an investigator would need to consider further. Similarly, a technical report might present the results from an examination for latent indentations by showing images of the developed indentations, or by presenting the examiner's interpretation of those indentations.

An *investigative report* is similar to a technical report, but it generally goes further by presenting one or more potential explanations for the findings. This can be valuable in an investigation when a meaningful set of competing propositions cannot be formulated due to insufficient information being presently available, e.g., in the early stages of an investigation when there is no theory to be tested. An evaluative report, in contrast, does not explain how evidence may have come into existence. Rather, an evaluative report must be based on an assessment of the findings in terms of arguments being made by someone else and, most importantly, incorporating at least two competing theories.

Finally, an *intelligence report* is one that provides indicators or linkages between cases, events, or activities based upon the findings. The focus for this type of report is an assessment of trends to assist in formulating a strategy for further operational or investigative measures. While this type of report may have elements of an evaluative report, it often takes a form closer to an investigative report.

It should be noted that any given report may consist of more than one of the above types. When that is the case, the different elements should be clearly marked as such.

Evaluation intended for forensic purposes should be balanced, robust, transparent, and logical.[6] To achieve *balance*, an evaluation requires at least two competing propositions, ideally those that reflect the different arguments being made by the parties. *Robust* evaluation means the basis of the opinion is able to withstand scrutiny and review. To that end, an opinion must derive from sound and reliable knowledge. *Transparency* means the process and reasoning must be demonstrable. This point relates to issues of disclosure but basically means the examiner must present all relevant information forming the basis of the opinion – e.g., the specific propositions considered, the observations made (or test results), any background/framework information provided, among other things. This is much easier to achieve when the process and reasoning conform to the logical approach. Finally, *logical* reasoning in this context means the examiner must focus on the probability of the evidence given the propositions plus relevant background information, rather than expressing any belief about the probability of the propositions themselves.

The concept of the proposition is fundamental to this process. A proposition is a statement that is either true or false, and which reflects the position/argument of a party in the matter. For balance in the evaluation, it is necessary to have at least two competing propositions. It has also been noted that "It is logically meaningless to suggest that any evidence has value in itself as support for any particular hypothesis in isolation," and further the "...value [of the findings] depends entirely upon its ability to discriminate between one hypothesis and another."[7–9] As a result, propositions are usually formulated in sets of mutually-exclusive and competing pairs. However, the propositions utilized by the examiner will not be those considered by the trier. Forensic examiners consider propositions relating to sub-source, source, or activity, rather than propositions set at the offence level.[10] Nonetheless, whatever working propositions are used should relate to the ultimate issue in some clear way.

Expert evidence, by its nature and the way people generally view expertise, always runs the risk of usurping the authority of the court, though the precise effect of forensic science evidence on the trier is not very clear. However, as Page et al. put it,

> "The forensic expert's role is not to individualize or even to identify, based solely on the forensic evidence presented to them—it is to provide the trier of fact with additional probative information, within the bounds of their expertise, that may strengthen or weaken the likelihood of guilt. Experts should not usurp the trier of fact's role by drawing prejudicial and unsupportable conclusions such as 'to the exclusion of all others' or other thinly veiled metaphors for the uniqueness proposition."[11]

This position, however, is not held by every court. Some have ruled that it is acceptable for an expert to opine on the ultimate issue in select situations.[12]

The key legal aspect that matters is the requirement that an expert remain within the scope of his or her expertise. One outcome of using the logical approach is it helps to ensure that the examiner stays within scope. From the perspective of the logical approach, extending testimony to provide statements about the propositions demands that the examiner go beyond the scope of his or her expertise. Regardless of any court's position on the matter, statements about propositions require information, or assumptions about that information, that fall outside the expert's domain.

3.2 HISTORY

Some people believe the logical approach is novel, but it is not. As Aitken and Taroni explained, elements of this approach can be seen in the writings of Jewish scholars from over 18 centuries ago.[13] In the 1800s and early 1900s, Bertillon and Locard, both eminent forensic scientists, advocated an approach perfectly aligned with the logical approach.[14] Indeed, the former applied the logical approach to document examination problems in 1898 making him "the first Bayesian forensic scientist."[15] In North America, the pioneering forensic scientist Wilmer Souder, who worked at the National Bureau of Standards (now National Institute of Standards and Technology), conducted examinations in various disciplines, including forensic document examination. He examined both handwriting and typewriting, among other things.[16] Souder, in the 1930s, suggested the use of the likelihood ratio to assess typewritten evidence.[17]

These individuals were not unique or unusual in their day. However, subsequent decades saw the logical approach fall out of use. It is difficult to know precisely why this happened, but two factors seem to make sense. First, there is a strong desire to answer the question posed by the client and, almost always, those questions are posed in terms of the proposition(s). As various laboratory systems developed and the number of practitioners increased, the level of understanding of the underlying logic may well have declined. Second, public forensic laboratories were almost-exclusively developed and managed by police agencies during that period. Those laboratories were motivated to be maximally useful for their client base and to provide testimony as definitively as possible. One of the few exceptions to this general trend was, and remains, the Institute of Police Science at the University of Lausanne, founded in 1909 and still operating.[18] This institution has always endorsed and promoted the logical approach to evidence evaluation throughout its history.

3.3 INFERENCE AND REASONING

When applying the logical approach, an examiner must focus on the probability of the findings, given the competing propositions. Examiners are subject-matter experts with the knowledge, skill, and ability to assess what particular findings mean in a given context or scenario. As the saying goes, "they speak for the evidence" or, alternatively, "they speak for the findings." It is the expert's job to explain to the trier what, in the expert's opinion, those findings mean in a clearly specified context, as defined by whatever propositions were considered.

Any trial is a process of belief updating. The trier begins with some belief about the key propositions of guilt, innocence, or liability. Various types of information are presented to the trier and that information shifts their belief in favor of one of the arguments being made. Once all the information is presented, the trier must reach a decision on the matter.

$$\underbrace{\frac{p(H_1|E,I)}{p(H_2|E,I)}}_{Posterior\ Odds} = \underbrace{\frac{p(E|H_1,I)}{p(E|H_2,I)}}_{Likelihood\ Ratio\ (LR)} \bullet \underbrace{\frac{p(H_1|I)}{p(H_2|I)}}_{Prior\ Odds}$$

Figure 3.1 *Odds* form of Bayes' Theorem.

There are no rules for how such deliberations should be made. However, Bayes' Theorem does provide a logically sound view of the process of belief updating. For this purpose, the so-called *odds* form of the theorem is often presented for reasoning with forensic evidence, as shown in Figure 3.1.

The process begins with prior odds (at the far right) which reflect a decision-maker's belief about the situation prior to receiving new information. New information, or evidence in a court setting, is represented by *E* with its effect encoded in terms of the *LR* (in the middle). The end-effect of adding information is a new state of belief reflected in the posterior odds (left side of equation). The formula indicates that the *LR* has a multiplicative effect on the prior odds. Note that the *odds* in each term are relative in nature, not absolute, so these are not strict odds in the mathematical sense. This is due, in part, to the fact that the set of propositions does not have to be exhaustive in nature; rather it will reflect the competing positions of interest. The formula also shows that prior odds are required in order to use the *LR* to determine posterior odds. An opinion like "the known writer probably wrote the questioned material" is a statement about the proposition that the writer of the specimen samples wrote the questioned material, and such a statement relates to the posterior odds of the proposition. In order to make such statements, consideration must also be given to the prior odds, which are the odds the known writer did/did not write the questioned material before the handwriting evidence is examined.

In the context of a trial, the prior odds and posterior odds both relate to the belief held by the trier, since that party is the decision-maker. The *LR* component corresponds to the testimony of any witness, including an expert accepted by the court. It is *generally accepted* that the findings can best be evaluated and reported in terms of a likelihood ratio or a similar construct serving the same fundamental purpose. As will be discussed, a verbal convention may also be used in situations where a numerical *LR* does not suffice.

It should be noted that "from a mathematical point of view, Bayes' Theorem is universally accepted as correct"[19] and, further, this use of Bayes' Theorem is well established in forensic interpretation, in general.

At the same time, the *LR* does not require invocation of Bayes' Theorem even though it is often presented in terms of the theorem. The latter is unfortunate since the *LR* has value and applicability independent of the theorem. More important, it can be assessed without consideration of the other terms in the theorem. In other words, there is no requirement to consider prior odds or posterior odds that might apply to the propositions.

An examiner's opinion will be informed by various types of information, either quantitative or qualitative in nature, that relate to the findings and the probability of occurrence under each of the competing propositions. This has always been the case and does not change when using the logical approach versus any other option. As Robertson, Vignaux, and Berger observed, "Applying this logic does not require that databases and numerical data be available. Forensic experts should report the evidential value of their findings in the form of a likelihood ratio, whether qualitatively in verbal terms, or, better, quantitatively."[20] They also stated, "The logical approach applies to all types of evidence, even if for some disciplines it is easier to move toward measurement-based likelihood ratios than for others." Similarly, the Association of Forensic

Service Providers wrote, "Probability assignments may be qualitative. In such cases the likelihood ratio may also be expressed in qualitative terms provided this can be justified."[21]

The core function of a true expert is the assessment of the findings in order to say precisely what those findings mean in a given context and, ultimately, to assign a probability that reflects the uncertainty in that assessment.

There is no doubt that quantification of belief, though difficult to achieve, can help understanding and comprehension. The process of quantification gives the recipient of information a better (more precise) understanding of what the examiner is trying to communicate. This is true even in those instances where the examiner is expressing his or her personal belief about the matter. Consider the following two statements by way of an example:

1. "There is a strong probability of X", and
2. "I assign a probability of 95% to X".

The first statement conveys a level of probability that the examiner considers "strong." However, "strong" is ill-defined and its meaning may differ from person to person. It may be possible, through careful explanation, to give an audience a better understanding as to the level of certainty intended, but an accurate or precise understanding is unlikely unless one resorts to some numerical example.

The second statement, in contrast, gives a relatively precise indication of the probability that the examiner has in mind; they have assigned a value of 95%. Undisputedly, this figure would still require explanation and contextualization, but the actual magnitude of belief, i.e., the level of strength assigned by the examiner, will be clear to most people with a rudimentary understanding of probability. It is true that many people have an imperfect understanding of probability, especially when the values discussed are either extremely large or small, but figures like the one given above are relatively easy to grasp and understand.

For this reason alone, quantification of probability via a numeric value has a tremendous advantage over any verbal descriptor that might be used in its stead. There is no doubt that the average person has a more accurate and precise understanding of what *95% probability* means, as compared to the term *strong probability*. As Köller et al. state, "Numerical estimates help avoid misunderstandings resulting from confusing or divergent terminology, especially in cases in which different examiners use the same verbal expressions to mean different things."[22]

In addition, the practical ability of the examiner to express his or her belief in numeric terms is beneficial as it permits a formal calculation of an *LR* that can be used to determine an appropriate final opinion. The *LR* is a ratio of two conditional probabilities as shown in Figure 3.2.

The composite probabilities in the numerator and denominator of the *LR* represent the probability of observing the evidence, *E*, given each of the specific propositions under consideration, H_1 or H_2, respectively, together with the framework information, *I*. As Biedermann et al. explain, "The main point with these numerical assignments is that they allow one to fully specify a probabilistic evaluation procedure, to do computations and to keep track of numerical results."[23]

On the other hand, it is not strictly necessary that an examiner address the composite probabilities that comprise the *LR* directly. The Australia-New Zealand NIFS guideline, for example, states, "Alternatively, practitioners may avoid formal expression of a numeric probability, and

$$Likelihood\ Ratio\ (LR) = \frac{p(E|H_1, I)}{p(E|H_2, I)}$$

Figure 3.2 Likelihood ratio (*LR*) formula.

subjectively select a verbal qualifier to express the degree of support provided by the findings."[24] This suggests that, whether or not the examiner assigns composite probabilities, they can determine and express their belief about the balance of support provided by the findings for the competing propositions.

Still, while such an approach may be considered valid, it is critical to realize that the underlying probabilities exist, even if they have not been elicited, stated, or assigned. Most importantly, there is clear benefit in having some understanding of the probabilities involved, or at least their magnitude. This is particularly important when both of the probabilities are small, yet one is relatively larger than the other with the end result being a large *LR* favoring one proposition over the other. In that situation simply reporting the *LR* might be insufficient because the fact that both probabilities are small implies there may be some other proposition, not yet considered, that would be better supported. It has been suggested that this factor be disclosed to the trier so that they understand this potential.

It is indisputable that conditional probabilities for the evidence are the basis for every opinion. This is true whether or not the examiner expressly assigns numeric probabilities but doing so enhances the evaluation and permits a more meaningful discussion of the evaluation process.

Numeric probabilities assigned by an examiner and informed in some appropriate manner that the examiner can disclose and discuss should be the underlying basis for that examiner's opinion. When empirical data is used to inform the probabilities, the examiner must be prepared to explain how the data was obtained, explain why it was chosen, and disclose any limits of the data in terms of its direct applicability to the case at hand. When personal knowledge is the basis of the assigned probabilities, the examiner must explain why they believe their assigned probabilities are justified and appropriate. Or, alternatively, why the verbal qualifier they are using is appropriate. Of course, the latter is essentially what examiners have always done in their work (though expressed in terms of posterior odds), so the prospect of explaining the process should not be overly daunting.

In summary, an examiner's belief may be based entirely on subjective/personal training and experience, on quantitative/empirical data, or through some combination of the two.[25] The latter is common in other disciplines, though not much in forensic document evaluations.

3.4 KEY CONCEPTS

The logical approach is a system of reasoning. The result of its application is a statement that provides "... an assessment of the strength to be attached to the findings in the context of alleged circumstances."[26] In other words, the outcome of the process will be a statement that conveys the examiner's belief about the *weight of the evidence* as determined by that examiner. This is done in order to inform some different party about the contextualized value of the findings/evidence. As such, it applies to any type of information – or evidence.

However, knowledge is always incomplete and limited. This means that every evaluation of a forensic nature will necessarily be uncertain to a degree. Every evaluation involves an assessment of that uncertainty, and the examiner must ensure the degree of uncertainty is properly conveyed in the end result. Lindley, citing Laplace, observed that "probability is the language of uncertainty,"[27] which means examiners must understand the concept of probability and how it applies to their work. At its most basic level, probability is a matter of how likely something is to happen. More specifically, "probability is a rational measure of one's degree of belief in the truth of a proposition based on information."[28] This is a subjectivist view of probability with two key traits. First, probability is unique to the person holding the belief. In other words, it is personal and subjective. Second, probability is conditional. It is based on the information known to the belief holder at a given point in time.

The knowledge examiners draw upon in a forensic context to assign probabilities is based on different, yet compatible, types of information. Specifically, their belief may be informed by empirical data, or personal knowledge, or both. At present, FDE opinions derive primarily from the individual examiner's training, knowledge, and experience, with few exceptions. In this view of probability, "the term 'assignment' is central ... because it emphasizes that probability is not taken as a property of an event as such, but as an individual's appraisal, depending on the body of knowledge that this individual has."[29] Further, it is important to understand that this view "... does not render probabilities as degrees of belief a more arbitrary and a less accessible concept. On the contrary, an individual's degree of belief can be elicited and investigated empirically."[30]

Köller et al. discussed the issue of subjective probability stating, "One of the biggest problems facing an examiner in his attempt to form a more precise individual opinion by assigning it a subjective numerical degree of probability is his subjective impression that such precision is impossible to attain."[31] Some examiners feel uncomfortable with the idea of subjective assignment, particularly when a specific value is required. However, "It is also important to understand that the choice of a specified numerical value is fundamental to the basic concept of subjective probability. Subjective/personal probability is defined through the process of selecting a specific value which appears most reasonable."[22]

It is important to appreciate that such assignments are estimates and not intended to be exact. They are ultimately a matter of personal opinion which makes no particular claim to exactness. Such numeric assignment serves to describe the examiner's subjective degree of belief, or "conviction" in Köller et al.'s terminology.[22] As they put it, "A numerical estimate that is clearly identified as a numerical estimate does not claim a higher degree of exactness. The use of numerical estimates simply requires a more precise assessment by the examiner, and it increases the degree to which the meaning of the statement can be determined inter-subjectively."[22]

When expressed numerically, probability is assigned a value from 0 to 1. The probability would be assigned 0 when the event or proposition is impossible and assigned 1 when the event is certain. Values in between those extremes reflect varying degrees of belief.

Overall, the logical approach is aimed at helping the examiner assign probabilities that describe how well the evidence conforms to their expectations under each of the competing propositions while taking into account relevant background information, thereby contextualizing the evaluation to the matter at hand. To achieve this, the examiner's evaluation should conform to three simple principles all encapsulated in the likelihood ratio, as shown in Figure 3.2 above:

1. All evaluation occurs in a framework of circumstances and information,
2. Evaluation requires two or more competing propositions, and
3. The examiner must evaluate the probability of the evidence (findings), and not the probability of the propositions.

The logical approach helps ensure proper consideration of conditionality in the evaluation. As noted earlier, the *LR* is a ratio of two conditional probabilities, where the probability of observing the evidence, E, is dependent upon the specific proposition under consideration, H_1 or H_2, as well as the framework information, I. In other words, in the case of forensic evidence the relevant probabilities assigned by the examiner depend upon two things: a framework of relevant information, and the competing propositions being considered. The task of the examiner is to simply express his or her belief about the probability of observing the evidence under the pertinent conditions that apply.

The importance of conditionality cannot be overstated. All too often people make probabilistic statements without reference to the relevant conditions that apply. Many of the issues that arise, both in interpretation and in understanding of evidence, come from an inadequate consideration of conditionality. As Lindley put it, "[p]robability ... depends on two arguments: the element whose uncertainty is being described and the knowledge on which that uncertainty is based. The omission of the conditioning argument often leads to confusion."[32]

The term *framework*, designated *I*, refers to *relevant* information about the situation that may impact the evaluation process.[33] Framework or background information is independent of the propositions under consideration, and separate from the evidence/findings; it is necessary for the proper evaluation of the findings. There is *always* a framework in which the evaluation occurs – it is unavoidable. Even a process that eliminates all extraneous information from a submission results in a particular framework, one which may not give the most accurate or reliable results for the trier. Still, a key concern when considering the framework, and what information should be given to the examiner, is the potential for that information to bias the results in some negative way.[34] Put bluntly, there is always a risk that contextual framework information may expose an examiner to biasing information. See Chapter 4 for further discussion of bias.

The most critical factor is a determination of task-relevancy.[35–37] Task-relevant information is information required by the forensic expert to perform a proper and complete evaluation. It is not a trivial thing to determine precisely what information is task-relevant. For example, FDE work involves many different types of examinations and "...information that might be relevant for one task will not be relevant for another."[38] This is one factor that makes any process intended to control information based upon task-relevancy very difficult.

In general, if information is task-relevant then it should be made available, whether or not it has biasing potential. A general framework to decide what action should be taken is reflected in Table 3.1.[39]

The issue of how an examiner can be shielded from task-irrelevant information is complex. The most common recommendation is some form of Contextual Information Management (CIM) solution that aims "...to minimize task-irrelevant information while maximizing the task-relevant information that reaches the examiner."[40–42]

Forensic document examination presents particular challenges in this regard as will be discussed in the next section of this chapter. However, there is one option always available to any examiner which, though less than ideal, may mitigate some concerns relating to this issue. That option is proper and complete disclosure, something generally required anyway. In their disclosure, examiners must explain any information provided to them and its relevance to their evaluation, as well as its effects from their point-of-view. This ensures that the presence of any potentially biasing information is known to the trier and that any issues can be discussed and explored.[43,44]

While disclosure does not address the issue of bias directly, as a minimum it provides an opportunity for assessment of the potential effect it may have on the evaluation. The logical approach is well suited to this pursuit as it demands express consideration of all relevant

TABLE 3.1 FACTORS RELATING TO BIAS VERSUS TASK-RELEVANCY

	Task-Relevant Information	Task-Irrelevant Information
Biasing	Keep, but take measures	Shield examiner from this information
Nonbiasing	Use	Shield if possible and efficient. Not strictly necessary since it is not biasing.

conditioning factors, including framework information. Making those elements that matter an overt part of the process simultaneously makes them subject to disclosure.

As noted earlier, it is important that evaluation be balanced and fair. To assist the trier, the examiner must provide an assessment of the findings in terms of the different arguments being made to the trier by the parties. This balance is shown in the formula by the presence of the competing propositions, H_1 and H_2, in the numerator and denominator, respectively. Of course, there is no need to have only two propositions, but that is the minimum to achieve balance. As Jackson explained many years ago, "We need to consider at least two competing propositions or views. Frequently, the prosecution view is relatively clearly defined; the defense view, on the other hand, may be less so. To be clear about the propositions that we are addressing gives us a real focus and a clear purpose to the work that we do and allows our customers also to be clear about what it is we are trying to test."[45]

In general, propositions are based on the framework information provided and the questions asked of the examiner. This presents a challenge because, on the one hand, the examiner must try to avoid exposure to unnecessary biasing information. On the other hand, clients do not usually understand what can be done in their case (or what is needed to do the work). Trying to obtain the necessary information required to set the propositions (and to do the evaluation), while also avoiding unnecessary information, can be particularly problematic for sole practitioners.

It is especially critical to understand that the propositions to be used in the evaluation must be set *prior* to any evaluation or examination. This is difficult, but it should be done as much as possible. Examples of proposition sets applicable to forensic document examination are discussed in the next section.

As noted earlier, the *LR* formula exposes a key element of forensic evaluation that can be overlooked – conditionality. In forensic science, conditionality is important because it means the opinion *depends* entirely on the applicable conditioning factors, i.e., the specific propositions and relevant framework information known to the examiner. Any change to those conditioning factors may result in a different outcome. Thus, no opinion can be considered absolute, or "carved in stone."

This is another reason why thorough disclosure is critical. It ensures all parties understand the:

1. Specific propositions considered, and
2. Elements of the framework that were known to the examiner and which influenced the opinion.

The likelihood ratio lies at the heart of the logical approach. At its simplest, a likelihood ratio is a value of the relative strength of support provided by a set of findings for one proposition versus some declared alternative. Likelihood ratios are *not* probabilities. Rather, each likelihood ratio is a scalar value that consists of the ratio of two conditional probabilities. That is, a likelihood ratio is the ratio of two probabilities, each of which can range in value from 0 to 1. As a result, the likelihood ratio will range from 0 to infinity with a "balance point" at 1, where it consists of two probabilities of equal value.

When the likelihood ratio is equal to 1, it means that both propositions are equally supported by the findings. In other words, the findings do not differentiate between the propositions and are not particularly useful for assisting the trier in their assessment of the propositions. Such an outcome is, in a sense, uninformative. However, it is important to understand that such "inconclusive" results are not *completely* uninformative. While it will not assist the trier in their assessment of the propositions, it is a very important indication that the material at hand is inadequate for comparison purposes and should not be used by anyone to assess writership. In that way, it is still informative and valuable as there is a tendency for laypersons to assess handwriting on their own, with no appreciation of any limitations that may be present. This outcome is an indication that such a process should not be undertaken.

Likelihood ratio values above 1 favor the numerator (meaning the findings provide more support for that proposition over the other). Values below 1 favor the denominator (meaning the findings provide more support for that proposition over the other). More specifically, a likelihood ratio value of X can be interpreted as meaning that it is X times more likely that the findings would be observed if proposition H_1 is true, than if proposition H_2 is true. Thus, very large values for the likelihood ratio favor the proposition in the numerator over the one in the denominator, while very small values for the likelihood ratio function in the reverse.

The examiner's opinion about the findings can be expressed directly as a likelihood ratio value but, more often, a verbal scale of equivalent terms is used. Whatever verbal scale is used must be clearly defined and should be based upon the value of the likelihood ratio. The ENFSI guide directs that "The [examiner's] conclusion should express the degree of support provided by the forensic findings for one proposition versus the specified alternative(s) depending upon the magnitude of the likelihood ratio (*LR*)."[46] One approach expresses the *degree of support* provided by the findings on an ordinal scale with the levels on the scale defined in terms of the logarithm of the likelihood ratio; i.e., $\log_{10}(LR)$.[47,48] An example scale is discussed later in section 3.5.6.

Any practitioner interested in applying the logical approach in their work should review the guidance documents produced by various forensic, legal, and statistical bodies as those documents address the various theoretical and practical issues that arise in its application. The most noteworthy is the ENFSI "Guideline for evaluative reporting in forensic science" referenced throughout this chapter. It is a general guideline that addresses all of the common forensic science disciplines. The National Institute of Forensic Science Australia-New Zealand has produced a cross-discipline "Introductory Guide to Evaluative Reporting."[49] Finally, other excellent resources are the guides endorsed by the Royal Statistical Society (RSS) UK: "Fundamentals of probability and statistical evidence in criminal proceedings" (November 2010), "The logic of forensic proof: inferential reasoning in criminal evidence and forensic science" (May 2014), and "Case assessment and interpretation of expert evidence" (January 2015).[50]

3.5 ELEMENTS OF THE LOGICAL APPROACH SPECIFIC TO FDE WORK

Almost every type of criminal or civil matter can involve questioned documents. As a result, the type of questions addressed by FDEs vary a great deal. FDEs will assess handwriting for potential writership, assess a potential source of typewriting and other impressions and marks, assess genuineness or non-genuineness, and reveal or decipher alterations, additions, erasures, or deletions. FDE cases involve a number of different situations (i.e., frameworks) and different propositions.

3.5.1 Consider the Framework

Framework information is usually provided with a submission or during initial discussions with a client. For handwriting cases, information about the environment, the age of the writer, physical health of the writer, medications taken, and so on, may be relevant and important. As clients do not understand the significance of such elements, the examiner must explore the matter to determine whether this type of relevant information applies to the case at hand. At the same time, examiners must try to avoid soliciting any extraneous and irrelevant information from the client. Ideally, some sort of CIM system should be used but, in lieu of one being in place, examiners must record and report whatever information is provided to them.

3.5.2 Set the Propositions

The propositions to be used for the evaluation must be determined prior to the examination. The set of competing propositions, which ideally reflect the arguments to be made by the opposing parties, should be delimited based upon the framework and beliefs of the parties while avoiding unnecessary exposure to potentially biasing information. If the set cannot be delimited, then the examiner will have to consider a broad range of potentialities in the proposition set.

The setting of propositions is often the most challenging aspect of an examination. First, clients usually pose the issues in the form of questions about the matter. Alternatively, they may provide a statement of their belief about what happened. The latter is beneficial as it can often be used directly as one of the propositions in the set to be used. When the matter is posed as a question, such as "Did my client write the signature?," the examiner must rephrase the statement as a proposition like "The writer of the specimen samples (the client) wrote the questioned signature." Propositions are statements that are either true or false; not questions or suppositions. Second, clients may not know the position to be taken by the other side in the matter. When the other position is not known, the examiner can utilize the negation of the main proposition written in a positive frame, in order to provide a balanced view of the evidence. For example, "Someone other than the writer of the specimen samples wrote the questioned signature."

It is also important that the examiner not adjust the propositions to fit the observations. In the traditional evaluation method, examiners may assign a *cause* to *explain* the evidence. In fact, examiners have been taught to explain what is seen in the evidence by assigning a probability to the proposition(s) based upon the evidence. In other words, examiners try to figure out the best explanation (i.e., proposition) through their examination of the material. When viewed in the context of the logical framework, this means that examiners are literally trained to equate the probability of the evidence to the probability of a proposition; a process which may unintentionally result in painting a target around the arrow, also known as the "Texas Sharpshooter" fallacy.[51,52] To help avoid this issue, propositions should be set before any examination or comparison work is done.

Balance in the evaluation process is ensured through the requirement of having at least two competing propositions. Traditionally, most examiners consider at least one alternative in their evaluation, but this is not usually explicitly done. For example, many examiners consider their client's request with phrases like "to determine whether or not..." which incorporates the negative as a type of proposition. But that does not permit other types of alternatives – by default it considers only the negation of the main proposition, which may or may not be appropriate.

The following are examples of common sets of propositions that might be used in FDE casework. This set could be used for specific source assessment, when a particular suspect is known:

> H_1: The writer of the specimen samples wrote the questioned signature.
> H_2: Someone other than the writer of the specimen samples wrote the questioned signature.

The following set could be used for a common source assessment, when no suspect exists, and the issue is one of *common authorship* of entirely questioned material:

H_1: The questioned signatures were written by one writer.
H_2: The questioned signatures were written by two (or more) different writers.

The following set might be appropriate for a closed set of multiple suspects:

H_1: The writer of the specimen samples K1, the husband, wrote the questioned signature.
H_2: The writer of the specimen samples K2, the wife, wrote the questioned signature.
H_3: One of the other 2 employees, and not the husband or wife, wrote the questioned signature.

Note in the example immediately above that (1) the *population* of potential writers is limited to only those four persons, and (2) specimen samples are obtained only from the husband and wife but not the employees. If, instead, specimen samples were obtained from all involved parties, including employees, the following might be used:

H_1: The writer of the specimen samples K1, the husband, wrote the questioned signature.
H_2: The writer of the specimen samples K2, the wife, wrote the questioned signature.
H_3: The writer of the specimen samples K3, employee A, wrote the questioned signature.
H_4: The writer of the specimen samples K4, employee B, wrote the questioned signature.

Or, for an open set:

H_1: The writer of the specimen samples K1, the husband, wrote the questioned signature.
H_2: The writer of the specimen samples K2, the wife, wrote the questioned signature.
H_3: The writer of the specimen samples K3, employee A, wrote the questioned signature.
H_4: The writer of the specimen samples K4, employee B, wrote the questioned signature.
H_5: Someone other than the writers of the specimen samples, K1 through K4, wrote the questioned signature.

The above are examples of sets of main-level propositions that might be considered in any given case depending upon the information available to the examiner or the questions asked by the client.

When setting propositions, it is important to take note of the following:

1. The set of propositions used should be based upon the questions asked by the client and the framework of relevant information provided to the examiner;
2. The information and samples required to perform the assessment may differ for each of these sets of propositions; and
3. The concept of the *LR* as a ratio of only two probabilities does not apply directly for sets involving multiple propositions or sub-propositions. Sub-propositions are derived from a main-level proposition when different types of writing are considered. For example, sub-propositions of a main-level proposition, "The writer of the specimen samples wrote the questioned signature" might include "The writer of the specimen samples wrote the questioned signature in a normal manner" and "The writer of the specimen samples wrote the questioned signature under unusual circumstances." Evaluation that involves multiple propositions or sub-propositions is a nontrivial process, as discussed in Section 3.6.

3.5.3 Declare Expectations

One of the benefits when propositions are predeclared is that it permits *expectations* to also be predeclared. Examiners are trained to know what can be expected from different types of writing. This is what distinguishes an expert examiner from the layperson. Any true expert will be able to explain his or her expectations under any given (sub)proposition. The inability to do this would be a clear indicator that the individual is not actually an expert as they lack the requisite knowledge for proper and complete evaluation.

Expectations are statements about the future; they are whatever the examiner expects to be observed in the actual examination and comparison. For example, if the examiner is considering the proposition that the specimen writer wrote the questioned material, their expectations may include conformity in all writing habits displayed in both the questioned and specimen samples, i.e., both samples will display similar skill, line quality, size, slant, arrangement, alignment, master allographic design as well as range of variation, etc. In other words, the examiner would expect to observe similarities, with no significant differences, in handwriting habit.

Ultimately, whatever is actually observed in the examination (i.e., the findings of that process) will either fit the expectations or they will not. In general, evaluation is a process of determining the significance of the findings in terms of the propositions at play in a given matter but, in practical terms, evaluation is the process of determining how well the actual findings conform to previously-stated expectations *under each of the propositions.*

As much as possible, expectations should be outlined *prior* to any review or examination of submitted material. They should not be modified after-the-fact. If expectations are changed based on knowledge of the evidence, then they are no longer expectations.

The idea of outlining expectations beforehand may seem strange, but it serves two important purposes. First, by outlining expectations before any formal examination of the submitted material, the examiner cannot be accused of fitting the findings to conform to a particular proposition. The prospect of painting the target around the arrow, whether intentional or not, is greatly reduced or eliminated. Second, doing this demonstrates clear expertise and knowledge of the domain. This should be done for *every* proposition the examiner will address. The expression of expectations can be difficult and complicated, particularly when the proposition set is extended.

As a rule, examiners will be able to draw on their basic training to express expectations. In some situations, however, a literature search or specific research may also be beneficial or required. In general, expectations are detailed extensively in the FDE literature. As a result, it is possible to formulate standard or predetermined expectations based on the literature; however, this has not yet been done in any standardized fashion.

A trained examiner should be able to outline an extensive set of features that might reasonably be expected when dealing with disguised, simulated, traced, spurious, genuine/natural writings, or any type of writing in other scenarios and propositions. This is, after all, routine knowledge for a properly trained examiner. The examiner has knowledge, as well as skills and abilities, developed through their training and experience that are akin to a personal knowledge base the examiner consults to perform their evaluation. Generally, such knowledge is qualitative in nature though there may be quantitative elements as well. The latter might relate to the results of experimentation or feedback about discipline or personal performance on skill-task testing. However, most examiners perform the evaluation in a purely qualitative manner.

It is reasonable to ask "why must the examiner go to the trouble of outlining *specific* expectations beforehand in any given case when it is possible to have a set of *predetermined* standard expectations derived from the literature?" The reason is that the actual propositions of interest in a case will be specific to the case. Hence, the expectations will likely differ from the standard set in some manner that reflects those propositions. In essence, the examiner must express expectations that are appropriate to the matter at hand; specifically, for the proposition set being used.

When the examiner explains beforehand what they expect to see in the findings should either proposition be true, then the explanation of the resulting evaluation becomes easy and straightforward and there can be no claim that the findings were driven by the observations. Most important, it helps to make the examiner's reasoning clear and transparent to everyone involved.

3.5.4 Conduct the Examination

The determination of the findings involves a detailed analysis of the submitted items and an inter-comparison to determine what features and underlying habits are similar, divergent, or not able to be assessed. In other words, the findings from this type of comparison process consist, first, of the set of features observed by the examiner and, second, the set of habitual motor processes that produced those features as inferred by the examiner from the visible writing trace. The examination and comparison aspects of FDE work need not change when applying the logical approach.

3.5.5 Evaluate Findings in Terms of the Propositions

The process of evaluation leads to a formal assignment of probabilities and, based upon those values, a subsequent determination of the degree of differential support provided by the findings for each of the competing propositions. The outcome of the evaluation is a likelihood ratio though some parties prefer the term *Bayes Factor* (BF).[53] These two terms operate according to the same underlying logic and function equivalently as a result. In mathematic terms, the BF is a ratio of two probability densities whereas the *LR* is a ratio of two probabilities; in addition, the latter can be considered a special case of the former.[54,55] However, whether or not the result of an evaluation is a *LR*, BF, or some other less rigorous construct that serves the same purpose, *LR* is the term used in most of the literature and in this chapter. This is appropriate when the evaluation considers the sum of the findings as a whole and when the probability is assigned by the examiner based on their subjective assessment.

The assignment of probability for the findings, taken as a whole, corresponds to how well those findings conform to expectations under *each of the propositions*, while taking into account sources of uncertainty in the evaluation, e.g., limitations in the materials. The examiner must remember several things when assigning such probabilities. First, the evaluation basis will vary depending upon which specific proposition is being considered. Second, the evaluation of the numerator and denominator is done independently. Third, limitations in the material must be taken into account. When present, limitations introduce uncertainty into the evaluation with the end effect of producing a probability closer to the indeterminate state. Finally, limitations may have a different effect under different propositions.

To understand what the process involves in the practical sense, consider an assessment where no limitations are present. In that situation, when the observed findings conform perfectly to previously stated expectations, the probability assigned to the findings will be very close to 1.0. When the findings do not conform at all to those expectations, the assigned probability will be essentially zero. Finally, if the matter is unclear such that the result falls midway between those two outcomes, then the assigned probability should be roughly 0.5. That value represents a balance between conformity and nonconformity of the findings to the expectations. In that sense, it is the point of least certainty. Such will be the case when the findings are unclear or indistinct, and that is most likely to occur if the examination material is limited in some manner.

Speaking procedurally, the examiner considers first one proposition, then the other, when assigning the necessary probabilities to the findings. To do this, the examiner must first assume that one of the propositions is true and then determine how well the observed findings fit with the expectations previously set forth. Based upon this and conditioned by the framework information, while taking into account limitations in the material, the examiner then assigns a probability. Once that is done, the examiner assumes the second proposition to be true and repeats the process, determining how well the findings conform to expectations under that proposition to assign the second probability. Once the findings have been assessed under all propositions, the examiner proceeds to determine the relative support provided by the findings for one proposition over the other, and reports an opinion reflecting that degree of relative support. The latter aspect of the process is discussed in the next subsection of the chapter.

Ideally, the examiner will begin by assessing the questioned material without considering the specimen samples so as to conform to the concept of sequential unmasking.[56] In terms of the logical approach, this means the examiner should consider the findings under the alternative proposition, H_2, before considering H_1. This is because an assessment of the findings under H_1 requires the comparison of the questioned and specimen samples, whereas the assessment of findings under H_2 does not. For handwriting comparisons, under H_2, the examiner is ultimately concerned with the probability of observing the findings as depicted in the questioned sample if it were written by someone other than the specimen writer, and that someone is drawn from the relevant population of potential writers. As such, the specimen samples do NOT matter directly in the evaluation. Instead, the evaluation under H_2 must be based on the examiner's expert knowledge of writing, in general.

A preliminary consideration of the findings under H_2 is possible without any reference to the specimen material; however, it will be limited. When considering the questioned material on its own, the examiner can only tentatively assign a probability that ultimately depends upon whether or not the specimen and questioned samples display the same set of writing habits. The specimen samples still have value in that they represent a model or master that might be copied or simulated by a perpetrator. As such, the samples may assist in the consideration of simulation, tracing, or some other form of copying. That issue cannot be fully addressed until the specimen samples have been incorporated, which is why the evaluation under H_2 can only be finalized after all the findings are available. The complete assessment and assignment of probability cannot be finalized until the complete findings are available and that only occurs post comparison.

When considering the findings under H_1 the specimen writer *is* the suspect writer, so the specimen samples become critically important as they are representative of that particular writer's habits and range of variation. The examiner is primarily concerned with how well the specimen and questioned samples conform to one another in terms of the underlying writing habits, *as described in the expectations*, taking into account limitations. As noted earlier, when significant limitations are present, the probability to be assigned should be closer to the indeterminate point.

Following a preliminary evaluation of the questioned sample in terms of H_2, the specimen samples can be examined and compared to produce the complete findings. At that point, the findings must be assessed under H_1 and then finalized for H_2.

One option for examiners is to express their belief in numeric terms using the following guidelines:

- Probability assigned to the findings is 0.9999+ (approximately 1) when perfect conformity is observed between the findings and expectations under H_x. In other words, the examiner believes that the findings are what he or she expects to observe 100% of the time when H_x is true.
- Probability assigned to the findings is <0.0001 (approximately 0) when perfect nonconformity is observed between the findings and expectations under H_x. Equivalently, the examiner believes the findings are what is expected to be observed 0% of the time when H_x is true.

TABLE 3.2 FINDINGS VS EXPECTATIONS AND RESULTING PROBABILITIES

If the Findings Are...	Assigned Probability...	Verbal Expression...
Exactly as expected	Above 0.9999	Extremely high probability
Almost exactly as expected	0.999–0.9999	Very high probability
Largely as expected	0.99–0.999	Moderately high probability
Moderately as expected	0.9–0.99	Slightly high probability
Somewhat as expected	0.6–0.9	Very slightly high probability
Inconclusive or indeterminate	0.4–0.6	Balanced probability
Somewhat divergent	0.1–0.4	Very slightly low probability
Moderately divergent	0.1–0.01	Slightly low probability
Largely divergent	0.01–0.001	Moderately low probability
Almost completely divergent	0.001–0.0001	Very low probability
Completely divergent	Below 0.0001	Extremely low probability

- Intermediate values of probability are assigned to the findings in accordance with Table 3.2. So, for example, the assigned probability would be 0.5 whenever the findings neither conform nor do not conform to expectations under H_x. This is considered to be an *indeterminate* point where the findings are inconclusive.

The above conditions are analogous to saying, for the former, "If H_x is true, I (the examiner) *always* expect to see these findings (thus, assigned probability is ~ 1.0)" and, for the latter, "If H_x is true I *never* expect to see these findings (thus, assigned probability is ~ 0.0)." Intermediate steps between those extremes reflect examiner belief about *how often* they expect to see the findings, if/when H_x is true.

Table 3.2 provides example probabilities, based on binned values, that could be assigned according to the degree of conformity observed in the findings, taken as a whole, relative to the expectations and in the absence of limitations. This would be done for each of the propositions considered in the matter.

However, often there are limitations in casework material such that more extreme probabilities might not be warranted. Handwriting cases that involve serious limitations, for example, are unlikely to produce extreme probabilities, while other types of evidence might produce probabilities that fall beyond either end of the scale, with extreme values simply being binned into the end categories.

In general, when limitations are present, the assigned probability shifts toward the middle levels of the scale, into the range of 0.1–0.9. The most indeterminate probability in this range is at 0.5, which is the point where the findings are considered to be neither consistent with nor divergent from the expectations. When submitted material is limited, a condition not all that unusual in handwriting cases, the resulting probabilities often fall in this range.

Above all else, the examiner must be able to explain, in his or her own words, the criteria they personally apply when assigning any probability; in particular, how the findings fulfill, or do not fulfill, the expectations, plus the effects of any limitations that may be present. Ideally, such scales would be calibrated to some objective standard but that is not the case at present. This is, ultimately, a personal scale. In situations where the examiner is not able to express very large or very small probabilities shown in the table, the scale must be adjusted for his or her use.

It is also critical to note that the examiner does *not* assign their probabilities with the goal of obtaining a particular *LR*. The assignment of probabilities must be according to the examiner's belief about the evidence and not some desired *LR* value. It is not a matter of back-engineering to get a particular *LR*. The *LR* is whatever comes out once the examiner has assigned the probabilities.

Finally, it is important to understand that an examiner's probability assignment is neither arbitrary nor random in nature. Rather it is representative of their personal belief about the findings and is based upon their knowledge, training, and experience. The examiner provides any such numeric values to help the trier understand more precisely what their opinion and testimony means.

3.5.6 Determine the Opinion

The evaluation process outlined above produces two conditional probabilities. The opinion is a statement about the relationship between those two values; specifically, expressed in the form of the *LR*. One of the most appealing aspects of the logical approach is the fact that the examiner's opinion flows logically and directly out of the evaluation process. Further, the opinion is a relatively straight-forward restatement of the evaluation outcome. However, as shall be seen, it can be complicated in practice because of (1) the need for a clear explanation of the conditioning elements that apply for any given opinion, and (2) the number of different ways the process can be done. As noted earlier, the ENFSI guide states that opinions may be expressed as a value of the likelihood ratio or by using a verbal scale based upon the magnitude of the likelihood ratio.

The first option is most appropriate if the information informing the outcome is quantitative in nature (i.e., it derives from appropriate empirical data). The likelihood ratio itself can be provided to the trier by explaining that "the likelihood ratio of the findings is X" meaning that "the findings are X times more likely to be observed if one proposition is true than if the alternative proposition is true." There are, of course, many different ways this could be stated.

When expressing any quantitative form of *LR*, it is important to fully disclose any elements of a subjective/personal nature that affect the assessment process. This includes the specific metric(s) used, the reason for choosing the metric(s), how sampling was done, any data processing applied to the metric(s), limitations that may affect generalization of the data beyond its original intent, application to a specific case scenario, and so on.

The second option is to express the opinion using a verbal equivalent. At this time there is no standardized scale for this purpose, and it is challenging to formulate a proper scale. To that end, the ENFSI guide provides an example scale derived, in part, from the work of the Association of Forensic Science Providers.[21] As noted earlier, the verbal degree of support should ideally relate to the magnitude of the likelihood ratio in some clear manner. A common approach defines support in terms of the *logarithm* of the likelihood ratio, i.e., $\log_{10}(LR)$. In other words, relative support can be represented by a logarithmic function centered on zero and extending to infinity in either direction, depending upon which of the two propositions is favored.

The ranges in the scale represent a continuum of expression for the strength of support, rather than being discrete and separate bins. In general, each level on the scale covers a range of binned *LR* values, and the support expressed is considered the same for any *LR* falling within the range. However, it is important to recognize the continuous nature of the scale. There is little difference between the top of one level and the bottom of the next.

The choice of descriptive terms and the number/size of the steps may vary between laboratories or examiners; however, a scale should be applied consistently within a laboratory. Additionally, it is essential that whatever scale is used should be disclosed in full so that the result expressed in a given report has contextual meaning. Verbal modifiers may be subject to misunderstanding,

TABLE 3.3 OPINION SCALE USING VERBAL TERMS

Likelihood Ratio Values	Opinion Wording – from Evaluation of Evidence[a]
>100,000	Evidence provides extremely strong support for proposition X over proposition Y.
10,000–100,000	Evidence provides very strong support for proposition X over proposition Y.
1,000–10,000	Evidence provides strong support for proposition X over proposition Y.
100–1,000	Evidence provides moderately strong support for proposition X over proposition Y.
10–100	Evidence provides moderate support for proposition X over proposition Y.
2–10	Evidence provides more support for proposition X than for proposition Y and the level of support, while stronger for X than for Y, is limited/weak.[b]
1	Evidence provides roughly equal support for proposition X and proposition Y.

[a] Either proposition may be presented first in the conclusion wording to reflect whichever is supported more than the other by the evidence.

[b] This wording for evidence that does not strongly differentiate between propositions is necessary to avoid or minimize any *weak evidence effect*. See Martire et al. (2014) for further discussion.

which leads to the need for definition of those terms and, hence, some predefined concordance scheme such as that outlined in Table 3.3.

So, for example, an $LR=1$ results whenever there is equal support for both propositions. Alternatively, one might state that the findings provide no more support for one proposition than the other. In terms of the constituent probabilities assigned by the examiner, a result of $LR=1$ occurs when both probabilities are equal, regardless of the size of those probabilities. It was noted earlier that probabilities in the range of 0.1–0.9 often result when limitations are present or when the findings display limited correspondence to the expectations. If both of the assigned probabilities fall within that range, the resulting LR will be either 1.0, i.e., indeterminate, or less than 10. In other words, the largest possible LR in that situation is 10. Such findings indicate there is more support for the first proposition than for the second with the level of support being limited/weak. As a side note, it is important to pay attention to the wording for this level of opinion. Care must be taken in the selection of descriptors to avoid, for example, the *weak evidence effect*.[57,58]

In summary, probabilities are assigned to the findings by the examiner, conditioned by both the propositions and framework information. The resulting LR reflects the relative strength of the findings under competing propositions. The appropriate level on the verbal scale derives from the underlying LR value and its constituent probabilities. The constituent probabilities are important; particularly in instances where both are assigned relatively small values.

When reporting the opinion, it is critical to disclose all of the relevant factors that affect or influence the opinion. Most importantly, there should be a clear admission and acknowledgment of the *conditionality* that affects the opinion. To this end it is recommended that every report include a caveat or disclaimer similar to the following:

Please note that all opinions expressed in a report are based upon relevant background information and specific exhibits provided to the examiner, as well as the proposition set utilized in the evaluation and as laid out in the report. Should the information, exhibit material, or propositions change, the opinion may also change. In particular, if different propositions are of interest, please contact the examiner to discuss the matter further.

3.6 SUB-PROPOSITIONS AND MULTIPLE PROPOSITIONS

The process outlined to this point considered the evaluation of the findings in terms of main-level propositions. However, a proper and complete evaluation may require consideration of component sub-propositions that make up the main-level propositions. In practical terms, the purpose of such a decomposition is to formally address the various ways in which writing might be produced as a series of sub-propositions falling under one or both of the main-level propositions.

FDEs routinely consider the prospect of different types of writing in their assessments including, for example, disguised writing, attempts at simulation/tracing, the effect of alcohol or drugs, and so on. Decomposition of the main propositions into sub-propositions formalizes the evaluation process in a detailed manner. This idea was previously explored by Köller et al.[59] (in terms of sub-hypotheses) and later by Biedermann et al.[23] The basic idea should be familiar to any qualified examiner. When the evaluation addresses well-specified sub-propositions, the process also becomes simpler because such sub-propositions tend to have well-defined expectations, meaning there is *separation* from the expectations of other sub-propositions.

A very basic decomposition for the standard specific-source set of propositions might go as follows:

H_{1a}: The writer of the specimen samples wrote the questioned handwriting *in a normal and natural manner*

H_{1b}: The writer of the specimen samples wrote the questioned handwriting as some type of unnatural writing

Versus

H_{2a}: Someone other than the writer of the specimen samples wrote the questioned handwriting writing naturally with no attempt to mimic the suspect (i.e., a spurious writing)

H_{2b}: Someone other than the writer of the specimen samples wrote the questioned handwriting attempting to mimic the writing of the suspect

Each sub-proposition represents a type of writing and, more importantly, a potential scenario under which the questioned sample *may* have been produced. Whenever the main-level propositions are broadly defined, decomposition into various sub-propositions helps to ensure the evaluation process is complete, clear, and transparent.

In mathematical terms, the *LR* can become quite complex when sub-propositions are included. To do this, consideration must be given to the prior likelihood of each sub-proposition. This is done in terms of a *likelihood function* where each sub-proposition is evaluated in a weighted manner with the weights reflecting the prior likelihood of each sub-proposition.[23] Note that these are not prior probabilities or odds for the propositions but, rather, priors inherent to the structure of the likelihood ratio. However, as for any prior, the examiner has no direct knowledge of what values are appropriate.

In non-mathematical terms, the examiner must evaluate the findings in terms of each component sub-proposition and express a final opinion while ensuring the conditionality at play is fully explained. To do this, the examiner must express expectations for each sub-proposition and then consider the probability of the findings under each of the sub-propositions (for one main proposition). This process results in a series of probabilities that must be consolidated to form the probability of the findings given that main proposition. The process of consolidation is not necessarily trivial and entails additional consideration beyond what can be detailed in this chapter.

However, it is fortunate that the majority of handwriting comparisons fall in to one of two categories wherein the consolidation can be relatively straightforward:

1. The probability of the findings given one sub-proposition may be far higher than the probability of the findings given any of the others. In that situation, the probability of the findings under that particular sub-proposition can be substituted and used for the probability of the findings given the main proposition.
2. In some cases, the findings given each of the sub-propositions will be assigned the same probability. In that situation any weights that might be relevant to the prior likelihood function become irrelevant, and the probability can be substituted and used as the probability of the findings given the main proposition.

Regardless of the manner in which the examiner consolidates sub-propositions and formulates the probability for the main-level proposition, it is important that they be able to explain the process that was used.

The following should be noted when decomposing main-level propositions into sub-propositions. First, possibilities may exist other than those listed above or those considered by the examiner. The examples provided do not represent all the different ways in which handwriting might occur, nor which may apply in a given situation. As any testifying examiner knows, it is the job of opposing counsel to present counterarguments and theories to explain the evidence. In that process, counsel is really providing different propositions, or sub-propositions, for consideration. The examiner should do their best to consider all such possibilities beforehand in order to provide appropriate testimony should they be challenged. The real key to this is disclosure – letting all parties, including the trier, know what propositions were, or were not, considered in their evaluation. Second, the decomposition process may result in competing sub-propositions, but not always. The key requirement is that the set of sub-propositions must collectively describe the types of writing that fall under the top-level category. Third, these concepts are not new or unexpected. Examiners have always given consideration to these factors in their work; however, rarely has it been done with complete transparency. When using the logical approach, this aspect is made explicit as part of the overall process of evaluation to aid in disclosure and understanding of the process.

Whenever possible, it is important to delimit the proposition set as much as possible. For example, it may be possible that one or more of the sub-propositions can *be excluded based upon information known to the submitter or client.* The examiner might become aware of some exclusions based on the framework information if, for example, that information indicates only certain sub-propositions are of interest (e.g., the suspect may make specific claims about the writing, the conditions under which it occurred, or some aspect of how it came to be). When that is the case, the examiner need only address those specific sub-propositions without concern for others that can be excluded. Please note that this does not mean the examiner should arbitrarily delimit the proposition set based on the framework as that remains an issue for whoever is responsible for setting the propositions. Any such delimiting should be disclosed, together with the reasons for doing so.

The removal of any sub-proposition, when justified, serves to reduce uncertainty in the overall evaluation process. Uncertainty in any facet of the matter at hand increases the overall complexity and greatly complicates both the evaluation process and reporting of the end result. If uncertainty can be reduced by delimiting the set of propositions, the evaluation will be better focused on the key issues of interest and the opinion rendered as a result should be more focused, valuable, and meaningful to the client. This is not a particularly contentious issue; but it is something examiners need to understand, implement, disclose, and explain to the trier.

An example where this might apply is a questioned signature on a will. Although it is possible that a purported writer might disguise his or her signature, it is not a scenario that makes sense in the case of a legitimate will. After all, disguise is done to hide one's identity. If a will is genuine and intended to be acted upon, then why would the writer disguise his or her signature? It does *not* fall within the examiner's domain to decide if the argument is valid, but it is something that counsel or the investigator should consider. And, if that argument is acceptable, then removing the sub-proposition involving disguise by the suspect writer from the evaluation would be perfectly sensible and acceptable.

The concepts introduced in this section also apply when dealing with multiple main-level propositions. Consider the following set of propositions:

H_1: The writer of the specimen sample K1 wrote the questioned material.
H_2: The writer of the specimen sample K2 wrote the questioned material.
H_3: The writer of the specimen sample K3 wrote the questioned material.
H_4: Someone other than the writers of K1, K2, and K3, wrote the questioned material.

One approach for this might be to split these pairwise, addressing each pair of propositions by reporting the degree of relative support within each pair; however, that option is likely to lead to a convoluted and confusing set of opinions. Typically, as is the case with sub-propositions, one main proposition will often be clearly supported more than the others. In that situation, it is possible to treat the "unsupported" propositions as a group and report the result accordingly. That is, the evidence provides <modifier> support for H_1, rather than H_2, H_3, and/or H_4.

In instances where more than one proposition is supported by the findings, it may be best to provide a conditional, multi-part opinion that addresses the conditionality involved. For example, the examiner might provide two or more opinion(s), each of which would result if a particular main level proposition is deemed most important to the matter. Decisions about which is "most important" must reside with the trier and be based upon other information in the case. Presenting the opinion in this manner can be very complicated but it should provide the most complete information about the findings and what they mean in the matter at hand.

It should be understood that this type of issue exists regardless of whether the examiner is using the traditional method of evaluation or the logical approach. However, the logical approach exposes such issues and forces the examiner to address them.

3.7 CHALLENGES AND CONCERNS

It is fair to say that acceptance of the logical approach, when presented overtly to the court, has been somewhat mixed.[60,61] To a proponent for the logical approach, these rulings are troubling as they represent significant misunderstanding by the courts.

One issue raised is the concern that the examiner might be applying Bayes' Theorem in its full form or suggesting that the trier use the theorem for their determinations. Both of these would be inappropriate, and there is absolutely no need for either. Trying to apply the theorem in full would be an extension beyond the more constrained expression of the *LR*, as is advocated in the logical approach. So long as examiners express only their belief about the findings in terms of the propositions, they cannot be accused of overstepping the bounds of their expertise or their responsibility to the court. Nor can they be accused of applying the full theorem or of suggesting that the court do so. The examiner is simply providing the trier with exactly the information they require to make their own deliberations in the matter.

Confusion has also arisen from concerns about metrics and database suitability, or from a misunderstanding of the bases for probability assignment. When the opinion is based upon quantitative data from empirical studies, that type of concern may be legitimate, however proper court presentation should mitigate those concerns. When the opinion is based upon the examiner's subjective belief about the findings, that fact should be disclosed so that the matter can be explored more fully. One option is to include a statement in the report such as the following:

> Please note that this evaluation process is based upon a personal assessment by the examiner of the relevant probabilities that apply in a given situation with that assessment deriving from the examiner's training, ongoing professional development, and experience, including proficiency testing of related skills.

It is noteworthy that judicial disapproval of this approach runs contrary to the recommendations of various academic, scientific, and legal bodies. Almost unanimously, these bodies have recommended this approach as being significantly better than the traditional wording and reasoning used by many examiners.

One thing is clear. There is a tremendous need for better awareness, education, and more research, particularly with respect to terminology and explanation to be provided to laypersons. All of these issues are important and challenging. As has been recognized both by ENFSI and the Australia-New Zealand NIFS, proper implementation of this approach, particularly in an adversarial justice system, requires much concerted effort by several parties.

Despite these challenges, there is no doubt an examiner can go into court and explain what was done using this approach without any particular challenge or issue. Courts do not, as a rule, place constraints on forensic evidence, the form or substance of testimony, or what can or should be said in court. There are exceptions, of course, but most of the time an examiner is expected to explain the conclusion scale that was used (if any) together with the basis or reasons for their opinion. Courts do not generally restrict an examiner in how they go about doing this.

The most significant challenge is adoption by examiners themselves. In general, this relates directly to a given examiner's level of understanding of the logical approach. Presently in the US and Canada, both understanding and adoption are limited, though that is changing. There is certainly more use of this approach in other jurisdictions (e.g., Europe, UK, Australia, etc.) but, even there, adoption has been sporadic and piece-meal. Examiner concerns are a reflection of trepidation and uncertainty about the value of this approach, how to apply it, and what is actually gained through its use.

3.8 CONCLUSION

Forensic document examiners must be able to explain complex and complicated issues to laypersons. That is a part of the job and has always been fundamental to it. It is true that some elements of the logical approach can be challenging, even complex, but consider the most basic form of opinion that results from this approach is "The findings support belief A more than they do belief B" with some explanation regarding the strength of that support. That is neither difficult to explain nor to understand.

The logical approach is a system of reasoning that involves and requires the correct application of logic in the evaluation process. That underlying logic is well-established, fundamentally sound, and has been accepted in all areas of science and philosophy. Beyond this, existing validation for the procedures used by FDEs remains broadly applicable when using the logical approach. The underlying basis of the conclusion is the same as it has always been, though it is expressed more clearly in probabilistic terms. In terms of the practical examination itself, there is no change in how analysis or comparison is done. The key change is in the evaluation element of the process, which is a matter of reasoning, as noted above. Finally, while additional research into inter-examiner consistency and calibration of opinions is definitely warranted, that aspect of the situation is the same as it has always been.

REFERENCES

1. "ENFSI Guideline for Evaluative Reporting in Forensic Science," approved version 3.0, published March 2015, http://enfsi.eu/wp-content/uploads/2016/09/m1_guideline.pdf, 20.
2. B. Robertson, G.A. Vignaux, and Charles E.H. Berger, *Interpreting Evidence: Evaluating Forensic Science in the Courtroom*, 2nd Ed (Hoboken: John Wiley & Sons, Ltd., 2016), 1–3.
3. "ENFSI Guideline for Evaluative Reporting in Forensic Science," approved version 3.0, published March 2015, http://enfsi.eu/wp-content/uploads/2016/09/m1_guideline.pdf, 6.
4. "ENFSI Guideline for Evaluative Reporting in Forensic Science," approved version 3.0, published March 2015, http://enfsi.eu/wp-content/uploads/2016/09/m1_guideline.pdf, 5.
5. Dennis V. Lindley, *Understanding Uncertainty* (Hoboken: John Wiley & Sons, Ltd., 2006), 65.
6. Association of Forensic Service Providers, "Standards for the formulation of evaluative forensic science expert opinion," *Science & Justice*, vol. 49, no. 3 (September 2009): 161–164.
7. B. Robertson, G.A. Vignaux, and Charles E.H. Berger, *Interpreting Evidence: Evaluating Forensic Science in the Courtroom*, 2nd Ed (Hoboken: John Wiley & Sons, Ltd., 2016), Chapter 3.
8. "ENFSI Guideline for Evaluative Reporting in Forensic Science," approved version 3.0, published March 2015, http://enfsi.eu/wp-content/uploads/2016/09/m1_guideline.pdf, 24.
9. Ian W. Evett et al., "More on the hierarchy of propositions: Exploring the distinction between explanations and propositions," *Science & Justice*, vol. 40, no. 1 (January 2000): 3–10.
10. R. Cook et al., "A hierarchy of propositions: Deciding which level to address in casework", *Sci. Justice*, vol. 38, no. 4 (October 1998): 231–239.
11. M. Page et al., "Uniqueness in the forensic identification sciences—Fact or fiction?" *Forensic Science International*, vol. 206, nos. 1–3 (March 2011): 12–18.
12. David H. Kaye, "The ultimate opinion rule and forensic science identification," *Jurimetrics: The Journal of Law, Science and Technology*, vol. 60, no. 2 (Winter 2020): 175–185.
13. C. Aitken and F. Taroni, *Statistics and the Evaluation of Forensic Evidence for Forensic Scientists*, 2nd Ed (Hoboken: John Wiley & Sons, Ltd., 2004), 119.
14. F. Taroni et al., "Forerunners of Bayesianism in early forensic science," *Jurimetrics*, vol. 38, no. 2 (Winter 1998): 183–200.
15. F. Taroni et al., "Forerunners of Bayesianism in early forensic science," *Jurimetrics*, vol. 38, no. 2 (Winter 1998): 14.
16. Rich Press, "Who Was Detective X?" accessed October 28, 2019, https://www.nist.gov/featured-stories/who-was-detective-x.
17. F. Taroni et al., "Forerunners of Bayesianism in early forensic science," *Jurimetrics*, vol. 38, no. 2 (Winter 1998): 15.

18. Margot, P., and Quinche, N., "The institute of police science of the University of Lausanne celebrates its 100 year anniversary (1909–2009)," *Revue Internationale de Criminologie et de Police Technique et Scientifique*, vol. 62, no. 2 (March 2009): 4–16.
19. A. Biedermann, "The role of the subjectivist position in the probabilization of forensic science," *Journal of Forensic Science and Medicine*, vol. 1, no. 2 (December 2014): 140–148.
20. B. Robertson, G.A. Vignaux, and Charles E.H. Berger, *Interpreting Evidence: Evaluating Forensic Science in the Courtroom*, 2nd Ed (Hoboken: John Wiley & Sons, Ltd., 2016), Chapter 8.
21. Association of Forensic Service Providers, "Standards for the formulation of evaluative forensic science expert opinion," *Science & Justice*, vol. 49, no. 3 (September 2009): 163.
22. N. Köller et al., "Probabilistische Schlussfolgerungen in Schriftgutachten (Probability Conclusions in Expert Opinions on Handwriting)," Luchterhand, Munchen (2004). https://www.bka.de/SharedDocs/Downloads/DE/Publikationen/Publikationsreihen/PolizeiUndForschung/1_26_ProbabilistischeSchlussfolgerungenSchriftgutachten.html, 98.
23. A. Biedermann et al., "Learning about Bayesian networks for forensic interpretation: An example based on the 'the problem of multiple propositions,'" *Science & Justice*, vol. 52, no. 3 (August 2012): 191–198.
24. National Institute of Forensic Sciences Australia-New Zealand, "An introductory guide to evaluative reporting," June 2017, http://www.anzpaa.org.au/forensic-science/our-work/projects/evaluative-reporting, 9.
25. A. Biedermann et al., "The meaning of justified subjectivism and its role in the reconciliation of recent disagreements over forensic probabilism," *Science & Justice*, vol. 57, no. 6 (November 2017): 477–483.
26. "ENFSI Guideline for Evaluative Reporting in Forensic Science," approved version 3.0, published March 2015, http://enfsi.eu/wp-content/uploads/2016/09/m1_guideline.pdf, 4.
27. Dennis V. Lindley, Letter to the editor in *Teaching Statistics*, vol. 24, no. 1 (March 2002).
28. B. Robertson, G.A. Vignaux, and Charles E.H. Berger, *Interpreting Evidence: Evaluating Forensic Science in the Courtroom*, 2nd Ed (Hoboken: John Wiley & Sons, Ltd., 2016), Section 2.1.3
29. A. Biedermann et al., "The subjectivist interpretation of probability and the problem of individualisation in forensic science," *Science & Justice*, vol. 53, no. 2 (June 2013): 192–200.
30. A. Biedermann et al., "The subjectivist interpretation of probability and the problem of individualisation in forensic science," *Science & Justice*, vol. 53, no. 2 (June 2013): 194.
31. N. Köller et al., "Probabilistische Schlussfolgerungen in Schriftgutachten (Probability Conclusions in Expert Opinions on Handwriting)," Luchterhand, Munchen (2004). https://www.bka.de/SharedDocs/Downloads/DE/Publikationen/Publikationsreihen/PolizeiUndForschung/1_26_ProbabilistischeSchlussfolgerungenSchriftgutachten.html, 97.
32. Dennis V. Lindley, "The philosophy of statistics," *Journal of the Royal Statistical Society. Series D (The Statistician)*, vol. 49, no. 3 (September 2000): 302.
33. B. Robertson, G.A. Vignaux, and Charles E.H. Berger, *Interpreting Evidence: Evaluating Forensic Science in the Courtroom*, 2nd Ed (Hoboken: John Wiley & Sons, Ltd., 2016), Section 11.5.
34. D. Michael Risinger et al., "The *Daubert/Kumho* implications of observer effects in forensic science: Hidden problems of expectation and suggestion," *California Law Review*, vol. 90, no. 1 (2002): 1–56.
35. N. Osborne et al., "Determining the Relevance of Contextual Information in Forensic Handwriting Examinations," *paper presented at the International Association of Forensic Sciences (IAFS)*, August 21–25, 2017 in Toronto, Canada.
36. N. Osborne et al., "Write or Wrong? Bias, Decision-Making, and the Role of Contextual Information in Forensic Handwriting Examinations," *workshop presented at the American Society of Questioned Document Examiners meeting*, San Diego, CA, August 28–September 1, 2017.
37. M.K.J. Kouwenhoven, "Focus on the Task at Hand: Contextual Bias in the Forensic Examination of Handwriting," (PhD Thesis, Otaga University, 2018).
38. Expert Working Group for Human Factors in Handwriting Examination, "Forensic Handwriting Examination and Human Factors," accessed May 13, 2020, https://doi.org/10.6028/NIST.IR.8282, 40.
39. Expert Working Group for Human Factors in Handwriting Examination, "Forensic Handwriting Examination and Human Factors," accessed May 13, 2020, https://doi.org/10.6028/NIST.IR.8282, 42.

40. E.J.A.T Mattijssen et al., "Implementing context information management in forensic casework: Minimizing contextual bias in firearms examination." *Science & Justice*, vol. 56, no. 2 (March 2016): 113–122.
41. B. Found et al., "The management of domain irrelevant context information in forensic handwriting examination casework," *Science & Justice*, vol. 53, no.2 (June 2013): 154–158.
42. William C. Thompson, "Developing Effective Methods for Addressing Contextual Bias in Forensic Science," https://www.ncjrs.gov/pdffiles1/nij/grants/252784.pdf, (April 2019).
43. Mohammed A. Almazrouei et al., "The Forensic Disclosure Model: What Should be Disclosed *To*, and *By*, Forensic Experts?" *International Journal of Law, Crime and Justice*, vol. 59 (December 2019): 1–14.
44. Charles E.H. Berger et al., "Response to 'A study of the perception of verbal expressions of the strength of evidence,'" (Letter to the editor), *Science & Justice*, vol. 58, no. 1 (2018): 76–77.
45. G. Jackson, "The scientist and the Scales of Justice," *Science & Justice*, vol. 40, no. 2 (2000): 81–85.
46. "ENFSI Guideline for Evaluative Reporting in Forensic Science," approved version 3.0, published March 2015, http://enfsi.eu/wp-content/uploads/2016/09/m1_guideline.pdf, 16.
47. A. Nordgaard et al., "The likelihood ratio as value of evidence—more than a question of numbers," *Law, Probability and Risk*, vol. 11, no. 4 (July 2012): 303–315.
48. A. Nordgaard et al., "Scales of conclusions for the value of evidence," *Law, Probability and Risk*, vol. 11, no. 1 (March 2012): 1–24.
49. National Institute of Forensic Science, "An introductory guide to evaluative reporting," June 2017, http://www.anzpaa.org.au/forensic-science/our-work/projects/evaluative-reporting.
50. https://rss.org.uk/news-publication/publications/our-research/.
51. E. Wagenmakers, "Origin of the Texas Sharpshooter" posted January 11, 2018, accessed March 4, 2019, https://www.bayesianspectacles.org/origin-of-the-texas-sharpshooter/.
52. William C. Thompson, "Painting the target around the matching profile: The Texas sharpshooter fallacy in forensic DNA interpretation," *Law, Probability and Risk*, vol. 8, no. 3 (September 2009): 257–276.
53. Danica M. Ommen et al., "Reconciling the Bayes Factor and Likelihood Ratio for Two Non-Nested Model Selection Problems," arXiv:1901.09798v1 [math.ST], (2019).
54. A. Nordgaard et al., "The likelihood ratio as value of evidence—More than a question of numbers," *Law, Probability and Risk*, vol. 11, no. 4 (July 2012): 308.
55. F. Taroni et al., "Bayes factor for investigative assessment of selected handwriting features," *Forensic Science International*, vol. 242 (September 2014): 266–273.
56. N. Osborne, "Forensic handwriting examination and cognitive bias: Recommendations from the NIST expert working group on human factors," *Australian Journal of Forensic Sciences*, DOI: 10.1080/00450618.2019.1568552 (February 2019).
57. R. Marquis et al., "Discussion on how to implement a verbal scale in a forensic laboratory: Benefits, pitfalls and suggestions to avoid misunderstandings", *Science & Justice*, vol. 56, no. 5 (May 2016): 364–370.
58. K.A. Martire et al., "On the interpretation of likelihood ratios in forensic science evidence: Presentation formats and the weak evidence effect," *Forensic Science International*, vol. 240 (July 2014): 61–68.
59. N. Köller et al., "Probabilistische Schlussfolgerungen in Schriftgutachten (Probability Conclusions in Expert Opinions on Handwriting)," Luchterhand, Munchen (2004), https://www.bka.de/SharedDocs/Downloads/DE/Publikationen/Publikationsreihen/PolizeiUndForschung/1_26_ProbabilistischeSchlussfolgerungenSchriftgutachten.html, 104.
60. *R v. T,* [2010] EWCA Crim 2439.
61. *R.v. Adams, D.J.* Court of Appeal, Criminal Division, Transcript, April 26, 1996.

Chapter 4

Cognitive Bias and Handwriting Examination

Concepts, Current Knowledge, and Future Practice

Mara L. Merlino

CONTENTS

4.1 INTRODUCTION

Cognitive bias refers to systematic errors in thinking that depart from the rules of formal logic or accepted norms. In the context of forensic science and practice, the term *cognitive bias* elicits a proverbial Pandora's box of controversy which contains information and misinformation, strong emotions, elements of advocacy, implications of both good and bad intention, and other challenging concepts. The word *bias* is linked in our minds with negative concepts such as prejudice, unfairness, and discrimination. This unfortunate association exists not only among forensic document examiners (FDEs) but also among members of other pattern and physics examination areas such as bloodstain pattern analysis, firearms and toolmarks analysis, footwear and tire analysis, and friction ridge analysis, as well as in all 20 of the additional forensic fields identified by the National Institute of Standards and Technology (NIST) Organization of Scientific Area Committees for Forensic Science (OSAC).

We may like to think of ourselves as rational and bias-free, but we are all susceptible to cognitive bias, which takes many forms. Cognitive bias is neither conscious nor intentional; rather, it results from nonconscious cognitive "trade-offs" that allow humans to quickly and efficiently process greater amounts of information.[1] As humans, we are evolutionarily predisposed to save mental effort by using cognitive shortcuts such as heuristics, which are mental "rules of thumb" that allow us to solve problems with minimal cognitive effort, and algorithms, or operations or procedures used to solve specific problem sets. Some forms of cognitive bias are due simply to the normal functioning of the human brain within the context of the environment.

In 1980, Anthony Greenwald argued that our ego (self) is an organization of self-knowledge, ruled by cognitive biases that allow us to fabricate and reconstruct our personal histories so that they are self-oriented (egocentric). According to Greenwald, we are inclined to represent ourselves as responsible for desirable (but not undesirable) events, and resistive to cognitive change.[2] As Greenwald's research suggests, none of us wants to think of ourselves as biased—and yet every single one of us, every human being, and even some animals—function effectively within our environment precisely because of our cognitive biases.

The purpose of this chapter is, first, to offer some insights about what cognitive bias is (and is not). Understanding cognitive bias requires some background knowledge of cognitive processes that contribute to how humans receive and interpret perceptual information, how we learn and how we develop expertise, and how expertise shapes the processes we use to solve classes of problems. Knowledge of both the nature and the sources of cognitive bias is critically important to any discussion of mitigating its impact.

Next, this chapter will describe key findings from several studies of cognitive bias as they relate to forensic practice. An extensive body of research conducted over the past 50 years describes approximately 180 sources of cognitive bias, memory distortion, information processing shortcuts, logical fallacies, and other phenomena that have been empirically demonstrated to impact human problem solving and decision making.

A comprehensive review of this vast literature is beyond the scope of this chapter; nevertheless, drawing the reader's attention to this extensive body of research illustrates an important point: Cognitive bias is a well-established psychological phenomenon. It has been empirically observed across time, among many different populations both outside and within forensic practice, in studies using multiple research methods, and in a wide range of circumstances. Although acknowledging and investigating factors which may lead to misleading opinions is sensitive and uncomfortable for forensic scientists and practitioners in all fields, these discussions are vital to help ensure that the best possible outcomes are achieved for all parties in legal disputes.

Finally, to help address the need to understand sources of error and bias in forensic science, the National Institute of Justice (NIJ) Office of Investigative and Forensic Sciences (OIFS) and the NIST Special Programs Office planned a series of expert working groups, each charged with investigating how human factors arise among forensic science disciplines. In 2012, NIST published the findings of the first working group in a report titled "Latent Print Examination and Human Factors: Improving the Practice through a Systems Approach."[3] In June 2015, NIJ and NIST convened the Expert Working Group for Human Factors in Handwriting Examination.[4] The charge of this international working group was to conduct "a scientific assessment of the effects of human factors on forensic handwriting examination with the goal of recommending strategies and approaches to improve its practice and reduce the likelihood of errors."[5]

The working group members were selected for their expertise in handwriting examination, law, forensic sciences, human factors principles, education and training, handwriting evidence in the courtroom, and statistics. The group included document examiners from both government and private laboratories in the US and abroad, legal scholars and professionals, members of professional organizations, and academicians from cognitive and behavioral science, statistics, and forensics.

In February 2020, NIST published the findings of the expert working group in a report titled "Forensic Handwriting Examination and Human Factors: The Report of the Expert Working Group for Human Factors in Handwriting Examination" (Human Factors Report). This chapter will present selected findings and recommendations from the Human Factors Report related to the mitigation and prevention of cognitive bias. The chapter will also discuss how future research can help to reduce the potential impact of cognitive and environmental factors on FDE decision making.

4.2 THE COGNITIVE ORGANIZATION OF CONCEPTUAL KNOWLEDGE

Although an extensive discussion of models of human memory and cognitive functioning are beyond the scope of this chapter, several cognitive psychological concepts related to human cognition are relevant to any discussion of the formation and mitigation of bias.[6] One such process is the formation and revision of cognitive schemas.

Schemas are hypothetical knowledge structures that are created through experience in our environment. We experience the world in terms of what we know, and we make sense of the stimuli that constantly bombard us both within and outside of our conscious awareness by creating cognitive structures into which we "slot" information about the attributes, or characteristics, of the concept. In other words, schemas are created through learning. In turn, schemas influence how we learn, interpret, and remember information.

Learning occurs in three stages. The first stage, encoding, involves the initial learning of information, or the creation of the schema. The second stage, storage, involves acting on the information in some way so that it remains in memory for an extended period. The movement of information from encoding to storage often involves associating the new information with previously existing schemas. The third stage, retrieval, refers to the ability to later access the stored information contained in the schema.[7]

In the early stages of development, schemas are rudimentary classifications of information. For example, a child in the early stages of language development may learn the word "cat," and correctly use the word to refer to a family pet. Her simple schema for cat contains several attribute slots such as legs (how many?), tail (has a tail/does not have a tail), fur (what color?). Among other preliminary assessments, the examiner evaluates the type of writing and range of variation of characteristics within the questioned writing. By learning the characteristics of the writing, FDEs create similar schematic knowledge structures upon first encountering writings. Thus, the preliminary assessment forms the basis for the attribute slots in the examiner's cognitive schema.

The child's schema develops from her experience with the environment, and changes with additional experience. In other words, upon seeing a dog, she might recognize that the dog has some of the attributes in the existing cat schema (the appropriate number of legs and a tail). Having no "dog schema," she may call the animal a cat based on the information in her existing schema. Once she learns that cats say "meow" and dogs say "woof," this new knowledge results in a revised cat schema (cats say meow). The new knowledge also differentiates between cats and dogs and creates a dog schema, which is linked to the cat schema through the associated attribute nodes about legs, tails, and fur. Both dog schema and cat schema will eventually be incorporated into a higher order "animal schema" as the child encounters other creatures with similar attributes.[7]

Similarly, FDEs update schematic knowledge based on new information learned from the subsequent examination, identifying attributes of the writing that indicate inclusion in the existing schema, as well as those that distinguish the writing from it. For example, when FDEs intra-compare known writings to establish the natural writing habits of the writer (range of variation), they are noting similarities and dissimilarities and slotting these attributes within the previously developed known writing schema. According to the Human Factors Report, the initial stage of the process of screening known writings is to check their internal consistency to determine whether the writing was produced by one writer or multiple writers.[5] As the examiner encounters the presence or absence of attributes, links are created between the writings based on their similarities. As new information is added to the existing schema, the examiner may find that the two sets of writing are significantly different and establish additional schemas, indicating that multiple writers are involved.

4.3 SCHEMAS AND EXPERTISE

Schematic knowledge also forms the basis of all forms of expertise. Expertise development involves three stages of skill acquisition. The first is termed the *cognitive stage*, during which examiner trainees acquire "declarative knowledge" by memorizing and rehearsing facts relevant to conducting a handwriting examination. These facts are incorporated into the trainee's existing schematic knowledge about the mechanics of writing, the system of allographs or symbols and how they are created by the writer, and other fundamental knowledge learned by being a member of the local culture.

During this stage, trainees rely largely on central cognition, or effortfully pairing factual declarative knowledge and procedural knowledge. In the same way that most people learn to drive a car, trainees initially take a step-by-step approach to their tasks, rehearsing the factual schematic knowledge about what to do as they perform the actions. At this stage, *tactical* learning, or the process by which trainees learn specific procedures to address specific problems, takes place.[7] Tactical knowledge may vary depending on the information imparted by the individual trainer or the laboratory environment in which the trainee learns.

The second stage of developing expertise is referred to as the *associative stage*. At this stage, the tactics developed during the cognitive stage are employed to solve specific problems and "strategic" learning occurs. The declarative, factual knowledge acquired in the cognitive stage develops into procedural skill. Repeated pairings of knowledge and process enable trainees to identify and correct errors in both thinking and practice as schematic knowledge is repeatedly accessed and revised. Practice reduces the need to think explicitly about the steps of the examination (central processing) as the tasks become more automatic. This is referred to as "proceduralization." With extended practice, trainees learn to recognize classes of problems, and they are then able to apply proper strategies and proceed through examinations with less effortful pairing of fact and procedure.[7]

The third stage of skill acquisition is the *autonomous stage*. As knowledge and skill increase, trainees rely more and more heavily on their previously acquired schematic knowledge and the organization of categories of information, methods, and solutions. Central cognition is significantly reduced as trainee skill increases. Trained examiners recognize classes of problems and deploy problem solving strategies without the need to revisit each step, making complex skills more automatic.

By its very nature, however, schematic knowledge may impact the document examination process in several ways. Consider, for example, how we are taught to read and write. As children, we discover that the sounds we make can be represented by symbols (letters, or in linguistic terms, allographs). We encode and store this information in memory. Once we grasp this essential schematic knowledge about the symbolic nature of language, we are then able to retrieve it from memory and update it as we are taught that we can combine symbols into meaningful units to represent words. We then learn that we can generate infinite combinations of these units and represent them all using the symbol systems we are taught, and that we, and other people who know our symbol system, can correctly interpret our written communications. Each newly learned concept is added to the existing schema by the process of encoding and storage, and the knowledge is retrieved from memory when we need it. Every new document examiner trainee brings this fundamental schematic knowledge into the training environment, and subsequently expands on it by slotting new information acquired from training into existing schematic structures.

4.4 HUMAN COGNITION: COGNITIVE MISERS AND MOTIVATED TACTICIANS

In 2016, Haselton, Nettle, and Murray wrote "Evolutionary psychologists explain cognitive bias as 'a necessary by-product of processing limitations—because information processing time and ability are limited, humans must use shortcuts or rules of thumb that are prone to breakdown in systematic ways.'"[8] In 1974, Daniel Kahneman and Amos Tversky published their early research about how humans process information, describing how the human brain tends to use cognitive shortcuts to preserve cognitive resources.[9] According to Tversky and Kahneman, "People rely on a limited number of heuristic principles which reduce the complex tasks of assessing probabilities and predicting values to simpler judgmental operations."[10] They identified several heuristics that can be applied to various classes of problems. Their work inspired a large and robust series of theories and research studies about heuristics, algorithms, and the forms of bias which may result from the conservation of cognitive effort.

Ten years after Tversky and Kahneman's seminal 1974 publication, Susan Fiske and Shelly Taylor coined the term *cognitive miser* to refer to this tendency for the human brain to seek cognitively simple, effortless ways to reach solutions to problems rather than engaging in more effortful and complex cognitive strategies. Because our brains tend toward conserving cognitive resources—in other words, because we are cognitive misers—humans rely on these shortcuts to make sense out of information which may be limited, received under time constraints, or received under other circumstances of cognitive limitation, such as those described in the Human Factors Report and elsewhere in this book.

Fiske and Taylor later revised their model of cognitive processing to include the idea of the *motivated tactician*. This term is used to denote those instances in which people engage in effortful processing and actively seek out the greatest amount of information prior to reaching a decision, as FDEs do during examinations.[11] Still, while FDEs behave as conscious motivated tacticians during examinations, the nonconscious cognitive miser remains active and susceptible to the influence of factors that occur outside of conscious awareness.

Training in forensic document examination prepares trainees to become motivated tacticians. Nevertheless, even motivated tacticians who have developed complex skills, and who appropriately apply their expertise to specific classes of problems, rely on cognitive shortcuts and are susceptible to various cognitive flaws associated with heuristics and algorithms. Table 4.1 presents just a few of the sources of cognitive bias that have been identified since Kahneman and Tversky's early work in this area.

TABLE 4.1 COGNITIVE HEURISTICS AND BIASES

Heuristic/Bias	Definition
Priming effects	Ideas tend to prompt later ideas without conscious awareness. This occurs when activation of a node in a cognitive network (schema) leads to later activation of a related node. Example: a person who is primed with the word "eat" will later fill in the missing letter in "SO_P" with the letter U (SOUP) instead of the letter A (SOAP). In forensic document examination, knowing the name of the person who writes using text-based or stylized writing may prime the examiner to look for and interpret the characteristics of the writing differently than if the name were unknown.
Repetition priming	These effects are demonstrated by improvements in performance such as time or accuracy due to repeated exposure to the stimulus. Example: fully qualified FDEs were exposed to a series of six signature sets consisting of one questioned signature and four known signatures for comparison. The questioned signature differed in each comparison, but the known signatures were the same in all six sets. The time taken to complete comparison of the sixth set was less than the time taken to complete the first set due to prior experience with the set of known signatures.[12]
Associative priming	A word or idea that has been consistently paired with an associated concept will be more quickly activated than will a word or idea less frequently paired. Example: due to the more frequent association between police officers and crimes, an FDE who works in a crime laboratory will more quickly pair the word "cop" with "robber" than with "car." Likewise, the frequent pairing of the word "robbery" and "crime" in the experience of an FDE creates an association pair that may be unconsciously activated when an examiner is required to evaluate the source of a robbery note.
Anchoring	Also known as *focalism*, this form of bias occurs when one focuses, or anchors, on initial information when making subsequent judgments. Example: a 2001 study published in the Cornell Law Review investigated the effect of several forms of cognitive bias on judicial decision making.[13] Judges were assigned to either an *anchor* or *no anchor* condition. Those in the no anchor condition read a scenario and were asked to assign an award for compensatory damages, with no additional information given. Those in the anchor condition were first asked to rule on a meritless motion which argued that the case did not meet the jurisdictional minimum of $75,000, and then asked to assign compensatory damages. As the anchoring effect predicted, judges in the anchor condition assigned an average award of $882,000, while those in the no anchor condition assigned an average of $1.25 million.
Representative heuristic	This cognitive shortcut leads us to make decisions about a specific object or idea based on its similarity to a prototype that already exists in our minds. Example: attorneys will often recommend that their clients wear clothing in court that covers their tattoos. In the context of the courtroom, tattoos may activate the prototype of a criminal. In forensic document examination, certain features of writing (e.g., accidental or extraneous features occurring in a questioned signature) may activate prototypes of a certain class of examinations, leading the examiner to weigh those features more heavily than the remaining features when making decisions.

(Continued)

TABLE 4.1 (*Continued*) COGNITIVE HEURISTICS AND BIASES	
Heuristic/Bias	**Definition**
Confirmation bias	Confirmation bias is the tendency to interpret or search for new information that is consistent with one's own perceptions, and to avoid information that conflicts with them. Example: In forensic document examination, an examiner may form an impression about the characteristics of a questioned signature early in the evidence preparation process (e.g., the questioned signature demonstrates blunt beginning and ending strokes, and appears to be written slowly, suggesting that the signature may have been drawn or copied from a genuine signature). In the subsequent examination, the examiner may unconsciously place more weight on characteristics that confirm the earlier impression and fail to consider evidence that supports a conclusion that the signature is naturally written.
Contextual bias	Contextual bias, or context effects, occur when task-irrelevant information from the surrounding environment interferes with judgment or decision-making. Example: if an examiner receives information about three DUI convictions for one of the parties in a contested will case, the examiner might be influenced to erroneously attribute lack of fluency in the writing samples to intoxication rather than to some underlying physical condition.

For a more extensive discussion of sources of cognitive bias, the reader is encouraged to review Chapter 2 of the Human Factors Report, which provides an in-depth treatment of confirmation bias and contextual bias, including methods for reducing or eliminating their effects. The chapter includes references for selected studies from the substantial body of research describing various sources of bias in a variety of contexts. A brief overview of two of the most frequently mentioned sources of bias—confirmation bias and contextual bias—is presented below.

4.5 CONFIRMATION BIAS

Confirmation bias is the tendency to interpret or search for new information that is consistent with one's own perceptions, and to avoid information that conflicts with them. Table 4.2 presents a brief description of circumstances which may elicit instances of cognitive bias.

TABLE 4.2 CIRCUMSTANCES THAT ELICIT CONFIRMATION BIAS	
Cognitive Bias Source	**Description**
Cognitive dissonance	Cognitive dissonance occurs when a person's actions and beliefs conflict. This condition may trigger selective attention or selective information seeking in which the person discounts information contrary to prior beliefs.
Heightened commitment	Higher levels of commitment to a course of action elicits greater confirmation bias.
Information source	Confirmation bias is greater when information comes from an expert source.
	(*Continued*)

TABLE 4.2 (*Continued*) CIRCUMSTANCES THAT ELICIT CONFIRMATION BIAS

Cognitive Bias Source	Description
Finality	Confirmation bias is more likely if the decision is irreversible.
Anxiety	Anxious people are more likely to experience confirmation bias.
Costs	Confirmation bias increases if additional resources or monetary costs are associated with a more in-depth information search.
Time pressure	Heavy workload or time-critical cases may limit the person's ability to test alternative interpretations of information.
Problem complexity	High complexity is more likely to elicit the use of cognitive shortcuts.
Opinion strength	People with strong opinions are more likely to find supporting evidence more credible than evidence that conflicts with their opinions.
Accountability	Those who are required to justify their decisions may disproportionately seek supporting information to bolster the impression they make.

4.6 CONTEXTUAL BIAS

Recall that contextual bias, or context effects, occur when task-irrelevant information from the surrounding environment interferes with judgment or decision-making. In 2017, Dror presented a seven-level model of sources of task-relevant information that examiners encounter when forming opinions.[14] The components of the model are presented in Table 4.3. It should be noted that many potential sources of cognitive bias are subconscious, implicit, and outside the examiner's direct control. Lower levels of the model indicate that the source of bias resides within the examination materials, and higher levels indicate that the source of bias lies farther away from the materials in question.[5]

TABLE 4.3 SEVEN-LEVEL MODEL OF CONTEXTUAL BIAS SOURCES

Level	Sources of Bias	Examples
1	Case evidence (features of the questioned handwriting).	The semantic content of the questioned writing (such as a ransom note) may contain biasing information that is irrelevant to the examination. If possible, irrelevant biasing information should be removed prior to the examination.
2	Reference materials (features of the known writing).	Course of business writing or documents; other characteristics unrelated to the features of the known samples. Although this information may be contained within the writings, it provides information extraneous to the actual examination of the writing features.
3	Irrelevant case information (information unrelated to the characteristics of the questioned or known writings).	Information from communications such as written reports, oral discussion, or other information obtained from outside sources or parties.

(*Continued*)

TABLE 4.3 (*Continued*) SEVEN-LEVEL MODEL OF CONTEXTUAL BIAS SOURCES

Level	Sources of Bias	Examples
4	Base-rate expectations (based on past experience with other cases).	Expectations due to regularities in how case materials are usually selected for the examination; information about which party is submitting the materials; any information based on the examiner's past experience that activates prototypes or stereotypical assumptions about the current case. FDE training using counter examples which contradict base-rate expectations may reduce base-rate expectations.
5	Factors related to the lab culture and organization.	Laboratory affiliation with government or law enforcement agencies; interactions with colleagues and supervisors that may create pressure to conform; heavy caseloads or insufficient staffing that may lead to time pressure; laboratory procedures and protocols that may insufficiently control for the presence or effect of extraneous information; error correction practices that create culture of blame versus a culture of improvement.
6	Biases introduced during examiner training and examiner motivation.	Bias based on the trainer's past experience or skill may be unconsciously introduced into training. Bias may be positively motivated (using cognitive heuristics such as base-rate expectations to meet high caseload demands) or negatively motivated (unconscious bias based on whether the prosecution or defense requests the examination). FDE training about cognitive bias should reduce the impact of these factors.
7	Cognitive functioning and the functioning of the human brain.	All intrinsic factors involving sensation or perception that affect how humans experience and interpret information from the environment.

This model demonstrates the broad scope of the factors to which FDEs are exposed in everyday practice, and some of the ways in which the sources can convey potentially biasing information. The preceding information is intended to acquaint the reader with some of the key concepts and issues related to cognitive bias, and to refer the reader to additional sources of information about the variety of biases and heuristics, their sources, and their extensive impact on our thinking and decision making. The next section will discuss trends in forensic document examination research and provide two brief research examples demonstrating the effects of cognitive biases and heuristics.

4.7 COGNITIVE HUMAN FACTORS RESEARCH: CURRENT KNOWLEDGE AND FUTURE DIRECTIONS FOR FORENSIC DOCUMENT EXAMINATION STUDIES

In 2016, this author analyzed a substantial body of currently available information about handwriting examination to inform the activities of the Expert Working Group for Human Factors in Handwriting Examination. The purpose of this analysis was to identify extant studies about human factors in handwriting examination, and to investigate research trends and knowledge gaps in the field.[15] Many more sources of information about forensic document examination are available, but the scope of this analysis was confined to information about handwriting examinations.

The literature search identified 1,093 topics of discussion published in 458 information sources of various types, including professional and academic journals, book chapters, books, published conference proceedings, research reports, academic dissertations and theses, and presentations at various professional and academic venues. The topical information fell into 11 broad areas, encompassing the entire spectrum of possible sources of cognitive bias identified in the seven-level model. Of these information sources, only 11 were specifically related to human factors, although studies in other areas touched on factors that influenced examiner decision making. Table 4.4 presents topic categories and what types of information are included within each category.

Source content also varied according to the time period in which the information was made public (publication or presentation date). The earliest source, *Ames on Forgery: Its Detection and Illustration with Numerous Causes Celebres,* was published in 1900, and the most recent sources

TABLE 4.4 LITERATURE SEARCH RESULTS BY TOPIC CATEGORY

Topic Category	Topics
Writing characteristics (382 studies)	Discussions of writing complexity, foreign or unfamiliar writing systems, the frequency of occurrence of features or characteristics, the type of writing, line quality, spatial characteristics, signature type and complexity, and other writing characteristics.
Examination process (196 studies)	Deployment of visual attention, various methods of reaching opinions about the authenticity of writing, the identification of class characteristics, conducting comparisons, methods of distinguishing between disguised, genuine, traced, and simulated signatures, and various methods of weighting features in the examination process.
Writer characteristics (144 studies)	The effects of factors such as writer age, race, and sex, cognitive or physical impairment, the influence of impediments such as writing posture, alcohol or drug induced writing performance, handedness, hereditary or genetic factors, and writer skill.
Human factors (11 studies)	Various sources of cognitive bias, such as confirmation bias, context and training effects, and irrelevant information.
Standardization (6 studies)	The extent of agreement among examiners about the importance or meaning of writing features, and methods for determining and presenting the extent of confidence expressed in examiner opinions.
Writing development (26 studies)	Writing learning and development, writing education, the development of motor programs for writing, and perceptual and proprioceptive aspects of writing development.
Writing dynamics (75 studies)	Dynamic measurements of writing including writing speed, biometrics, stroke acceleration and deceleration, neuromotor programs and motor control, and creating writing profiles based on the kinematic aspects of writing.

(Continued)

TABLE 4.4 (*Continued*) LITERATURE SEARCH RESULTS BY TOPIC CATEGORY

Topic Category	Topics
Statistical models (72 studies)	Quantifying aspects of the examination process, such as applying Bayesian models to decision making and reporting, applying various statistical techniques such as principle components analysis, structural equation modeling, or other methods of quantifying certainty or measurement.
Examination automation (54 studies)	Computerized search and comparison capabilities, the development of databases, or other digital methods of working with writing.
Examiner proficiency (41 studies)	Examiner performance, such as examiner accuracy, expertise, and proficiency.
Legal issues (51 studies)	Legal factors relating to forensic document examination, such as the social construction of the admissibility of expert testimony, relevant court decisions, and other areas at the intersection of law and forensic science.

reported here were published in 2016, spanning a period of 116 years. Over time, the focus of the body of literature has changed, reflecting the contextual influences of advances in scientific discovery, practice innovations, and the demands of the legal system. For example, an examination of the distribution of published information across time reveals a pattern of responsiveness to factors in the practice environment.

Table 4.5 demonstrates shifts in the focus of information which appear to correspond to impactful events in the legal arena. The time periods represent time frames between major events that may have influenced discourse about the intersection between forensic practice and law, and subsequently the content of available information:

- Period 1 (1900–1975): information produced prior to the 1975 revision of Federal Rule of Evidence (FRE) 702
- Period 2 (1976–1993): information produced between the 1975 revision of FRE 702 and the 1993 U.S. Supreme Court decision *Daubert v. Merrell Dow Pharmaceuticals, Inc.,* 509 U.S. 579 (1993)
- Period 3 (1994–1997): information produced between *Daubert* and the subsequent 1997 U.S. Supreme Court decision *General Electric Co. v. Joiner,* 522 U.S. 136. 143 (1997)
- Period 4 (1998–1999): information produced between *Joiner* and the 1999 U.S. Supreme Court decision *Kumho Tire Co. v. Carmichael,* 526 U.S. 137 (1999)
- Period 5 (2000–2009): information produced between *Kumho* and the 2009 publication of the National Academy of Sciences report *Strengthening Forensic Science in the United States: A Path Forward*
- Period 6 (2010–2016): information produced in the period following the 2009 NAS publication to 2016

Readers should note that information about writing characteristics, writer characteristics, and the examination process have garnered much of the attention of scholars and practitioners across time periods. Examiner proficiency, automation of the examination process, statistical modeling, writing dynamics, standardization, human factors, writing development, and research design have received far less attention. These findings indicate that knowledge gaps exist in these areas, and these should be addressed in future studies.

TABLE 4.5 LITERATURE CONTENT BY TIME PERIOD

Publication and Presentation Content	1900–1975	1976–1993	1994–1997	1998–1999	2000–2009	2010–2016	Total
Legal issues	3	4	6	3	30	5	51
Writing characteristics	31	84	60	25	102	80	382
Examiner proficiency	1	3	3	4	17	13	41
Writer characteristics	21	53	4	5	31	30	144
Examination automation	1	1	11	4	16	21	54
Statistical models	1	10	6	6	25	24	72
Writing dynamics	7	26	5	5	10	22	75
Examination process	22	36	19	12	57	50	196
Standardization	0	2	0	2	2	0	6
Human factors	0	0	1	0	3	7	11
Writing development	6	9	2	1	3	5	26
Research design	3	5	6	0	9	9	32
Total	96	233	123	67	305	266	1,090

Given these data, the Human Factors Report indicated that the amount of research specifically addressing cognitive bias in handwriting examination is limited. This may be due in part to acrimonious discussions occurring within the legal and forensic communities about the reliability and validity of scientific evidence and other expert testimony following the revision of the Federal Rules of Evidence in 1975, and subsequent challenges to the admissibility of expert testimony in many forensic fields following *Daubert v. Merrell Dow Pharmaceuticals, Inc.*, 509 U.S. 579 (1993), *General Electric v. Joiner,* 522 U.S. 136, 148 (1997), and *Kumho Tire Co. v. Carmichael,* 526 U.S.137 (1999).

An unfortunate consequence of the adversarial context of these initial discussions is that forensic practitioners in many fields have been hesitant to participate in studies conducted by well-qualified researchers, even though these studies are a vital source of evidence for the extent of the reliability and validity of forensic methods and procedures. Moving beyond the adversarial system is vital if questions about possible sources of bias are to be answered by empirical knowledge about the nature and extent of the factors that influence human perception and interpretation of information during forensic examinations.[16]

Although FDEs conduct examinations in a laboratory environment, where they have access to instrumentation, the time necessary to complete the examination, and review of results before a conclusion is issued, lack of control of the forensic lab environment makes the FDE's laboratory generally unsuitable for the purposes of experimental research. When considering experimental research addressing the methods and procedures of forensic scientists generally, it is important to note that experimentation requires careful control of factors such as the testing environment and standardization of experimental methods and procedures. While this may be considered a limitation of all experimental studies, control of the experimental situation is extremely important because lack of standardization and control of the experimental environment reduces the experiment's ability to reveal meaningful similarities or differences in behavior.

Properly conducted and reported research in any field acknowledges study design limitations and addresses the generalizability of the findings to the population of interest—in other words, researchers should address the internal and external validity of the study. An unbiased discussion of any body of research requires a thoughtful critique of the strengths and weaknesses of the studies, as well as what may reasonably be concluded given both the evidence provided by the findings and the limitations of the study designs and procedures. It should also be noted that a single study on any topic is not conclusive. Reliable findings require multiple studies to ensure that the outcome of a seminal piece of research did not occur by chance.

Critiques of existing research on cognitive bias in forensic document examination have pointed out important limitations such as small sample sizes, and the use of partially trained examiners, students with no document examiner training, or lay individuals as participants.[17] Other limitations include constraints to normal document examiner practice that naturally occur in any controlled experimental environment.[18]

Study limitations such as those described above may constrain the research findings to certain groups or circumstances, but the limitations do not negate study results. Even though the idea of cognitive bias may create some discomfort among members of the field, much more research is needed to understand the sources and consequences of cognitive bias in forensic document examination. As the Human Factors Report stated, "...human cognition plays a critical role in the judgments and performance of FDEs and other examiners. For example, in latent print examination (LPE), not only is there inter-examiner variability in the analysis, interpretation, and conclusion on the same prints, but the same LPE may reach a different conclusion upon reexamination of the same prints. There is no manifest reason not to assume that the same type of variation is likely to hold true among FDEs."[19] Examples of research demonstrating two of the concepts previously introduced in Table 4.1 are presented below.

4.7.1 Direct Priming

Recall that direct priming results in easier and more rapid access to related information within the schematic knowledge of the information receiver.[20] This effect was demonstrated by Merlino and colleagues, who conducted experimental research using eye tracking technology to study the relationship between simultaneous or sequential presentation of signatures and examiner decision making accuracy. Figure 4.1 demonstrates examples of how the stimuli were presented.

The study revealed that when four single signatures were presented sequentially, both the average number of gaze fixations (fixation count) and the average total length of time the examiners spent looking at the signatures (fixation duration) were significantly greater for the first signature in the sequence compared to the remaining three signatures.

When the same four signatures were presented simultaneously to a different group of examiners, the fixation count and fixation duration were both significantly lower for the first signature in the simultaneous presentation condition than for the same signature in the sequential presentation condition. In both presentation conditions, the fixation count and fixation duration decreased for signatures two, three, and four, although fixation counts and durations were all

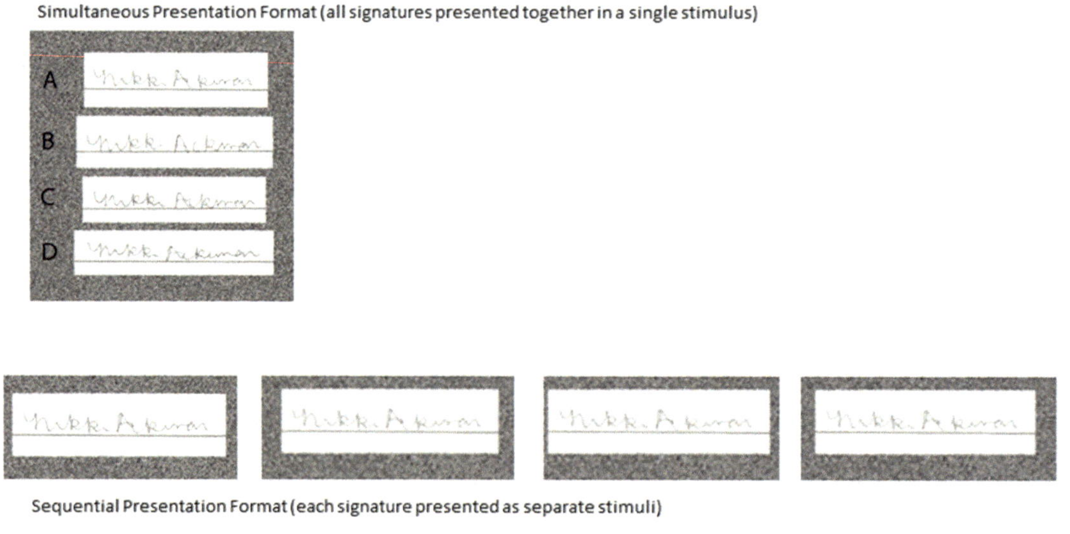

Figure 4.1 The top image is an example of a typical stimulus examiners viewed in the simultaneous presentation format. All four writing samples were viewed at the same time. After comparing the writing samples, examiners were asked whether the writing was produced by one person or by more than one person. The series of four images at the bottom represent the sequential presentation format. FDEs examined each writing sample singly. After viewing the final image, examiners were asked whether the series of writings was produced by one person or more than one person. All eye tracking protocols were conducted with Tobii binocular eye tracker systems with 17" TFT, 1280×1024 pixel displays (Tobii Technology, Stockholm, Sweden) and Tobii Studio software (version 3.4.5). Dell model Precision 7710 laptop computers with Intel Core i7-6820HQ CPUs at 2.7GHz, 8GB RAM and 64-bit Windows 7 operating systems were used with all eye tracking units.

lower for signatures viewed sequentially compared to those viewed simultaneously. Figure 4.2 presents the mean fixation durations by signature and presentation format. Evidence of cognitive priming is suggested by the lower fixation durations and fixation counts observed in the sequential condition, which indicate more efficient cognitive access to the previously learned signature features.[21]

4.7.2 The Representative Heuristic

The *representative heuristic* is commonly used by people who are attempting to determine the extent of similarities between a stimulus and a representative member of a category (i.e., standard), or the similarities between an event and a process.[22] When determining whether a novel object such as a questioned signature fits within an existing group of objects (known signatures), examiners make judgments about whether the observed features of the writing are similar enough to be included or dissimilar enough to be excluded from the group.

These judgments are based on salient characteristics, but they may be unduly influenced by highly salient characteristics. For example, examiners are taught and trained that certain strategies are often used by people who are trying to disguise their signatures. Among these are changing the slant of their writing or the form of allographs so that they are obviously different from the disguiser's natural writing.[5]

Bird, Found, and Rogers studied the extent to which FDEs were successful in distinguishing between naturally written and disguised writing. They reported in a 2012 publication that FDEs in their sample had greater difficulty in correctly identifying the writing process used to produce the written samples when the writing was disguised (29.9% accurate) than when the writing was genuine (65.1% accurate).[23] Later research by Bird, Found, and Rogers investigated what features FDEs felt were diagnostic of simulation or disguise. They found in a 2013 study that the FDEs in their sample identified differences in the slant or slope of the writing as an indicator

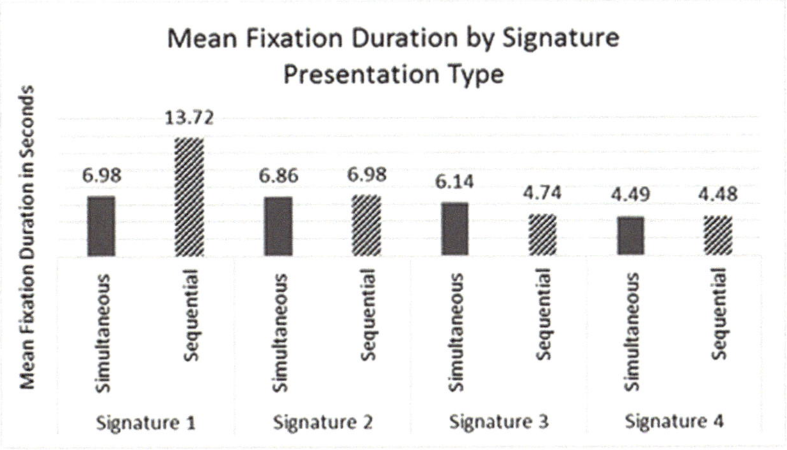

Figure 4.2 The more extensive examination of the first signature in the sequential condition indicates that greater cognitive effort was expended when examiners were required to encode and store information about the first signature so it could be retrieved when viewing the subsequent three signatures. This is an example of a Level 1 contextual effect.

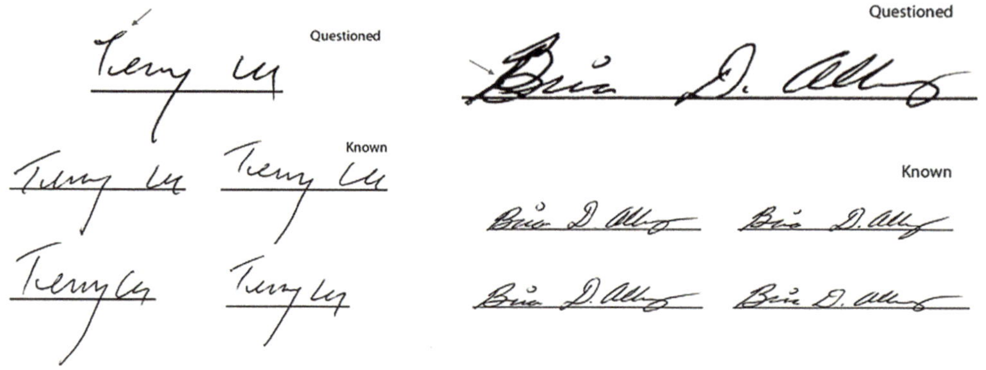

Figure 4.3 The Lu and Albury signature comparison stimuli presented here each contain genuine questioned signatures with accidental features. Many FDEs commented that these features might be indicators of disguised writing. This is an example of a Level 6 contextual effect.

of disguise, while differences in line quality or the formation of writing features were indicators of simulation.[24]

Merlino and colleagues similarly asked fully qualified FDEs to perform a series of 66 comparisons of questioned and known signatures. The examiners were asked to determine whether the questioned signatures were genuine, disguised, or simulated. The findings closely replicated those of Bird and colleagues, with examiners accurately identifying disguised writing in 30.8% of comparisons and genuine writing in 62.7% of comparisons.

Bird and colleagues concluded that their results might be due in part to the strong resemblance between the disguised samples and the writer's natural writing behavior, suggesting that the disguise strategies used did not provide adequate evidence of disguise. Results reported by Merlino and colleagues added to current knowledge about indicators of disguise by revealing that the most challenging signatures for FDEs in their sample were genuine signatures containing "accidental" or extraneous features.[25]

Examples of comparisons containing extraneous features are presented in Figure 4.3. These features were interpreted by examiners to be indicators (in other words, representative) of disguise, even though the remaining writing in the comparisons demonstrated only variations attributable to the writer's range of variation.

4.8 SUMMARY

An extensive body of research addresses the causes and consequences of cognitive bias. Human beings are by nature cognitive misers who conserve mental resources by relying on nonconscious cognitive shortcuts such as heuristics, problem solving algorithms, and other ways of minimizing the cognitive effort it takes to interact with the environment. In the sense that we all experience systematic departures from rational and logical thinking, cognitive biases are a normal part of thinking. Even though we can function as motivated tacticians, cognitive bias remains pervasive because many of the cognitive processes involved occur outside consciousness.

Cognitive bias can be elicited by mere exposure to stimuli in the environment, and bias impacts how information is encoded, stored, and retrieved from memory. Interactions with police and attorneys, other laboratory staff members, or the evidence itself may impact the outcome of a forensic examination. Even training during the development of expertise may predispose fully qualified examiners to incorrectly interpret the evidence they are evaluating.

Managing bias is critical in all forensic disciplines. Fortunately, research also demonstrates that cognitive bias can be successfully mitigated by using either general techniques or techniques that are bias specific. Some suggested techniques involve changes at the institutional or case management level, but even small-scale techniques can make important impacts.

4.8.1 Confirmation Bias

Found and Ganas described contextual bias in the forensic sciences as the effect of extraneous or potentially biasing information received by examiners while working a case.[26] One example of potentially biasing information is prior knowledge of the outcome of an examination conducted by a fellow FDE. Some have argued that the most direct measure of the reliability of an expert's opinion is the analysis of another expert,[27] but others have countered that the technical peer review process is highly susceptible to both contextual bias and confirmation bias.[28]

4.8.2 Reducing the Impact of Extraneous and Potentially Biasing Information

Bryan Found and John Ganas identified potential sources of bias relevant to all areas of pattern evidence science, including the examination context, case intake documentation, and communications with investigators, attorneys, or other examiners who may be working on the same case.[29] Correcting cognitive bias, even at the level of international systems, depends heavily on direct action taken by individuals. The first and most important step at the individual level is realizing that a biasing event has occurred, and then recognizing and acknowledging the resulting cognitive bias. Once the decision to correct the bias has been reached, the extent and impact of the bias should be considered so that the proper debiasing techniques can be employed. Decisions made prior to the debiasing process may then be revisited once the bias has been mitigated.

Selection of a debiasing technique should include consideration of several factors. One is the demonstrated effectiveness of a technique in combating specific forms of bias. Some mitigation methods work only with very specific forms of bias, while other methods reduce a wide variety of biases. For example, Found and Ganas described a case management system implemented by the Victoria Police Forensic Services Department (VPFSD). The system was designed to mitigate biases caused by agency procedures for requesting lab services, such as communication with attorneys or investigators involved in the case, or extraneous information included on case intake forms or service requests.[30] The practice of removing this biasing information is referred to as *linear sequential unmasking*.[31–36]

Other important considerations include the skill and training needed to implement the bias mitigation strategy, as well as the cost and effort required. Implementing a case management system for bias mitigation in a large government laboratory might be relatively easier and less costly than would implementing an equivalent system in a private practice or sole practitioner document examination laboratory, where resources are likely to be more limited.[37] Sequential unmasking procedures have been initiated in some government forensic laboratories, but this technique may be too costly for some laboratories to sustain, and it has been argued that sequential unmasking may not be feasible for examiners in private practice.

In contrast to the broad bias mitigation system used by VPFSD, teaching a new trainee the importance of seeking not only evidence that supports, but also evidence that refutes the proposition that two writing samples were created by the same person, requires a different implementation strategy because it involves altering individual thought processes. Reducing internal sources of bias, such as confirmation bias, may require several different techniques. Suggested methods include standardizing the decision-making process to include debiasing techniques and reducing time pressure on examiners by slowing down the decision-making process.

Creating psychological distance between the self and the examination decision, as well as psychological self-distance from how one believes he is viewed by others, has been demonstrated to improve decision making. Maintaining psychological and physical distance from cognitive priming stimuli such as police uniforms, laboratory supervisors, or even from document examiner colleagues when examiners perform technical reviews, are also simple and effective debiasing strategies.

When determining which bias mitigation techniques to use, it is important to remember that change is most likely to occur in work environments where laboratory supervisors are trained to address sources of error, while at the same time avoiding punitive consequences for laboratory personnel. When error due to cognitive bias is discovered, feedback and correction should be positive, constructive, professional, and designed to help examiners recognize the specific form of bias and learn techniques to reduce its impact.

Chapter 2 of the Human Factors Report offers a series of recommendations for reducing the sources and consequences of cognitive bias through Contextual Information Management (CIM). The summary below is not exhaustive, but provides some methods to help mitigate possible bias:

- Whenever possible, remove or mask sources of biasing information from Level 1 contexts. Whether or how this is accomplished should follow careful consideration of whether the mitigation technique compromises the amount of task-relevant evidence available for examination.
- In Level 2 contexts, examiners should identify relevant features from the evidence (questioned information) before being exposed to the reference material (known information).
- To the greatest extent possible, avoid task-irrelevant communications in Level 3 contexts by using a context manager to screen evidence submissions for potentially biasing information.
- Level 4 contexts should incorporate *blind review* cases into the examiner's workflow to create an expectation that both exculpatory and inculpatory submissions are a regular part of the examiner's workload.
- In Level 5 contexts, document examination laboratories should implement a quality management system including casework reviews, monitoring of reports and testimony, competency training, proficiency testing, and other methods for ensuring the quality of ongoing practices and procedures.
- In Level 6 contexts, all FDEs who conduct examinations should be certified by a certification body accredited to ISO/IEC 17024. Certified examiners should undertake ongoing education and recertification.
- Level 7 contexts such as visual acuity, the effects of stress, anxiety or medication, or other physical, cognitive, or mental states are connected to all other human factor issues. These must be considered on a case-by-case basis.

Chapter 7 of the Human Factors Report presents a summary list of all the recommendations of the Expert Working Group for Human Factors in Handwriting Examination. Ongoing research to evaluate the efficacy of these recommended practices, and to better understand the extent and effects of cognitive human factors in forensic document examination is needed. Continued collaboration among FDEs, academicians and researchers, statisticians, legal professionals, and organizations such as NIST and NIJ should be encouraged to help foster ongoing improvement and excellence in the field.

REFERENCES

1. McClelland, J., & Rumelhart, D. (1981). An interactive activation model of context effects in letter perception: Part 1. An account of basic findings. *Psychological Review, 88*(5), 375–407. doi:10.1037/0033-295X.88.5.375
2. Wilson, T. D., & Brekke, N. (1994). Mental contamination and mental correction: Unwanted influences on judgments and evaluations. Psychological Bulletin, *116*(1), 117–142. doi:10.1037/0033-2909.116.1.117
3. Greenwald, A.G. (1980). The totalitarian ego: Fabrication and revision of personal history. *American Psychologist, 35*(7), 603–618.
4. Expert Working Group on Human Factors in Latent Print Analysis. Latent Print Examination and Human Factors: Improving the Practice through a Systems Approach. U.S. Department of Commerce, National Institute of Standards and Technology. 2012.
5. Expert Working Group for Human Factors in Handwriting Examination. Forensic Handwriting Examination and Human Factors: Improving the Practice through a Systems Approach. U.S. Department of Commerce, National Institute of Standards and Technology. 2020. NISTIR 8282, p. 30. https://nvlpubs.nist.gov/nistpubs/ir/2020/NIST.IR.8282.pdf
6. Expert Working Group for Human Factors in Handwriting Examination. Forensic Handwriting Examination and Human Factors: Improving the Practice Through a Systems Approach. U.S. Department of Commerce, National Institute of Standards and Technology. 2020. NISTIR 8282, p. ix. https://nvlpubs.nist.gov/nistpubs/ir/2020/NIST.IR.8282.pdf
7. Revlin, R. *Cognition: Theory and Practice*. New York: Worth Publishers, 2012.
8. Anderson, John R. *Cognitive Psychology and Its Implications*. New York: Worth Publishers, 2015.
9. Haselton, M.G., Nettle, D., & Murray, D.R. (2016). The evolution of cognitive bias. In Buss, D. (Ed.), *Handbook of Evolutionary Psychology* (2nd Ed.), (pp. 968–987). Hoboken: John Wiley & Sons.
10. Tversky, A., & Kahneman, D. (1974). Judgment under uncertainty: Heuristics and biases. *Science, 185*(4157), 1124–1131.
11. https://www.alleydog.com/glossary/definition.php?term=Cognitive+Miser
12. Merlino, M.L., Freeman, T.M., Springer, V., Dahir, V., Hammond, D., Dyer, A.D., Found, B.J., Smith, L., & Duvall, I. (November 29, 2014). Final report for the National Institute of Justice grant titled "Validity, Reliability, Accuracy, and Bias in Forensic Signature Identification." Submitted to Gerry LaPorte, National Institute of Justice, Washington, DC. https://www.ncjrs.gov/pdffiles1/nij/grants/248565.pdf
13. Guthrie, C., Rachlinski, J.J., & Wistrich, A.J. (2001). Inside the judicial mind. *Cornell Law Review, 86,* 91 p. Available at SSRN: https://ssrn.com/abstract=257634 or http://dx.doi.org/10.2139/ssrn.257634
14. Dror, I.E. (2017). Human expert performance in forensic decision making: Seven different sources of bias. *Australian Journal of Forensic Sciences, 49*(5), 1–7.
15. This information was collected to inform the research recommendations presented in the Human Factors Report. The reference list of source materials and an annotated bibliography are available from the author at mlmerlinophd@gmail.com.
16. Merlino, M.L., & Springer, V. (2009). Context and controversy: Why questions of validity and reliability are seldom resolved in an adversarial setting. *Tulsa Law Review, 45,* 133–145.

17. Miller, L.S. (1987). Procedural bias in forensic examination of human hair. *Law and Human Behavior, 11*(2), 157–163.
18. Miller, L.S. (1984). Bias among forensic document examiners: A need for procedural change. Journal of Police Science and Administration, 12(4), 407–411.
19. Kukucka, J., & Kassin, S. (2014). Do confessions taint perceptions of handwriting evidence? An empirical test of the forensic confirmation bias. Law and Human Behavior, *38*(3), 256 –270.
20. Dyer, A.G., Found, B., & Rogers, D. (2008). An insight into forensic document examiner expertise for discriminating between forged and disguised signatures. Journal of Forensic Sciences, 53(5), 1154–1159.
21. Dyer, A.G., Found, B., & Rogers, D. (2006). Visual attention and expertise for forensic signature analysis. Journal of Forensic Sciences, *51*(6), 1397–1404.
22. Forster, K.I., & Davis, C. (1984). Repetition priming and frequency attenuation. *Journal of Experimental Psychology: Learning, Memory, and Cognition, 10*(4), 680–698. doi:10.1037/0278-7393.10.4.680
23. Merlino, M.L., Dahir, V., Hammond, D.L., Al Namer, C.D., Al Namer, T.A., Edwards, C., & Smith, L.R. (October 3, 2019). Final report for the National Institute of Justice grant titled "Cognitive Human Factors and Forensic Document Examiner Methods and Procedures." Submitted to Theodore Robinson, National Institute of Justice, Washington, DC.
24. Kahneman, D., & Tversky, A. (1972). Subjective probability: A judgment of representativeness. *Cognitive Psychology, 3*(3), 430–454. doi:10.1016/0010-0285(72)90016-3
25. Bird, C., Found, B., & Rogers, D. (2012). Forensic document examiners' skill in distinguishing between natural and disguised handwriting behaviors. *Journal of Forensic Document Examination, 22,* 15–23.
26. Bird, C., Found, B., & Rogers, D. (2013). Predictors of disguised and simulated handwritten text. *Journal of the American Society of Questioned Document Examiners, 16,* 13–18.
27. Found, B., & Ganas, J. (2013). The management of domain irrelevant context information in forensic handwriting examination casework. *Science and Justice, 53,* 154–158.
28. Harmon, R., & Budowle, B. (2006). Questions about forensic science. *Science, 311,* 607.
29. Saks, M.J., Risinger, D.M., Rosenthal, R., & Thompson, W.C. (2003). Context effects in forensic science: A review and application of the science of science to crime laboratory practice in the United States. *Science & Justice, 2,* 77–90.
30. Found, B., & Ganas, J. (2013). The management of domain irrelevant context information in forensic handwriting examination casework. *Science and Justice, 53,* 154–158.
31. Found, B., & Ganas, J. (2013). The management of domain irrelevant context information in forensic handwriting examination casework. *Science and Justice, 53,* 154–158.
32. Dror, I.E. (2011). The paradox of human expertise: Why experts can get it wrong. In N. Kapur (Ed.), *The Paradoxical Brain* (pp. 177–188). Cambridge, UK: Cambridge University Press.
33. Dror, I.E., & Charton, D. (2006). Why experts make error. *Journal of Forensic Identification*, 56(4), 600–616.
34. Dror, I.E., Charlton, D., & Peron, A.E. (2006). Contextual information renders experts vulnerable to making erroneous identifications. *Forensic Science International*, 156, 74–78.
35. Dror, I.E., & Cole, S. (2010). The vision in 'blind' justice: Expert perception, judgment and visual cognition in forensic pattern recognition. *Psychonomic Bulletin & Review*, 17(2), 161–167.
36. Dror, I.E., & Mnookin, J. (2010). The use of technology in human expert domains: Challenges and risks arising from the use of automated fingerprint identification systems in forensics. *Law, Probability and Risk*, 9(1), 47–67.
37. A good, brief summary of cognitive bias and debiasing may be found at https://effectiviology.com/cognitive-debiasing-how-to-debias/#Bias-specific_debiasing_techniques.

Chapter 5

Forensic Intelligence

Samiah Ibrahim

Intelligence is the end result of the collection and subsequent analysis of information assembled from myriad sources. The purpose of gathering intelligence directly relates to the directive or mandate of the organization collecting the information.

Worldwide, intelligence-gathering agencies draw upon the gamut of their resources in order to render a more complete model during investigations. The use of science, and in particular forensic science, has long been part of these resources; however, this does not preclude other organizations from employing forensic analyses in the development of their intelligence product. In fact, the use has, in certain countries and areas of investigation, become almost mainstream.

Forensic document examination, its product and expertise, has long been used to feed into the intelligence cycle. Although it has been decades since we have welcomed the digital age, the fact is that based on paper consumption[1] worldwide, there are more and more documents created now than at any previous time in human history. The ubiquitous nature of documents for all reasons of business, education, influence, entertainment, culture, law, politics, trade, etc., means that we do not automatically think of documents' evidentiary value except when confronted by the classic storied examples from crime novels or traditional forensic scenes of crime. And while documents such as ransom notes, counterfeit currency, or forged wills are direct tools of crime, because of their pervasiveness, documents and their components can also be silent witnesses to crimes of all sort.

It should be emphasized that not all forensic science comes under the purview of the crime laboratory, and certainly forensic document examination does not always begin with a crime scene. Forensic document examination has greater application apart from the traditional crime laboratory housed within law enforcement. In effect, the result of forensic document examination is often used to determine if a crime has been committed. Forensic document examination has applicability in criminal cases, in the civil realm, and in regulatory and administrative matters as well.

The classic forensic science parable is that evidence is submitted to a laboratory for forensic examination in order to conduct appropriate analyses, provide findings in an unbiased manner, and objectively resolve matters that are before the courts. After some time, the case is completed and the forensic report with analysis and conclusions is returned to the client. It has been standard practice in the crime lab as well as in many other forensic laboratories to treat cases uniquely, in isolation of other case data unless specifically requested by the client. Emphasis is placed on avoiding or minimizing bias by not sharing case data outside of those that have strict need-to-know, while ensuring the forensic scientist is not overly influenced by extraneous data before completing his or her analysis.[2] While this practice is undeniably correct, once analyses are completed, there is much to be gained from reevaluating the case data to look for trends or nonobvious linkages. Forensic science is usually thought of as a requirement at the end of an investigation to confirm or refute connections and findings from evidence. But just like any source, forensics can start, progress, or finish investigations to provide a range of inputs and outputs to assist investigations.

This use of forensic data is not new in the intelligence world and has been steadily gaining acceptance in mainstream law enforcement and security. Intelligence-led policing,[3] created in the United Kingdom[4] has been promoted to assist in all areas of policing, including decision-making, planning, strategic targeting, and crime prevention. In this model, intelligence, as analyzed information, is collated from traditional sources such as surveillance, informants, and undercover operations. There is significant information to be obtained from the analysis of crime, such as where crimes occur geographically, time information from when crimes occur, behavioral data of the suspects or victims, and evidential analysis. Other information can be obtained from analysis of crime networks and target profiles and from threat and risk assessments.[5–7] A much more complete intelligence product is available once all the information from these data sources is compiled (Figure 5.1). Forensic data and the results and findings of forensic analyses feed into each of these labels. The concept of forensic intelligence is now gaining popularity as a field unto itself. Forensic intelligence has been defined in the literature as the "accurate, timely and useful product of logically processing forensic case data for investigation and intelligence purposes.[8]

Forensic intelligence may identify investigative or information gaps. It may provide profiles of suspects or criminal activity. In support of strategic analysis, it may be used to define modus operandi and other trends and patterns.[9] And it may define emerging threats, including identifying how external factors, such as technological innovations like 3-D printers impact security issues.[10] By applying an analytical process to all intelligence sources available, a more complete understanding emerges; conversely, by not utilizing all resources available, law enforcement and

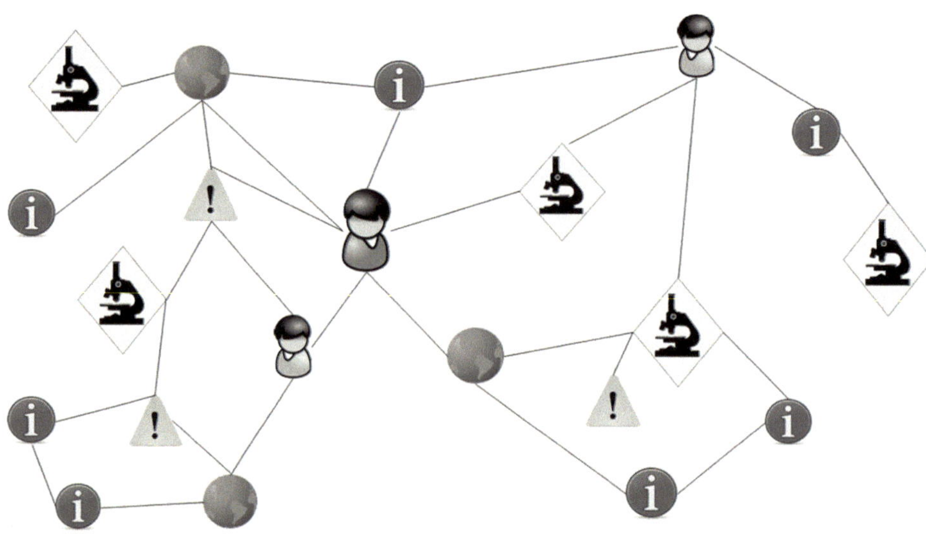

Figure 5.1 Rudimentary relationship graph showing linkages between information, people, places, and laboratory analysis.

intelligence agencies, as well as other agencies with regulatory and administrative functions, are working and making decisions with incomplete data.[11,12]

Computerized databases have been developed in forensic science to provide intelligence for the investigator, such as with fingerprint or DNA data (Automated Fingerprint Identification System, Combined DNA Index System).[13,14] The compilation of certain forensic case data combined with other investigative information, perhaps including threat and risk assessments, may yield intelligence through inferences. This does not necessarily require the implementation of complex computer systems but rather the systematic application of the data as a criminal analysis method and as an investigative tool.[15]

Within many law enforcement agencies, there is access to much more powerful analytical tools to view data. By applying rigorous data analytics to these compiled datasets, invaluable trends that otherwise go unnoticed may be revealed, such as a series of potentially linked events.[16]

Predictive analytics uses historical data to anticipate future events by building mathematical models using data, then applying this predictive model on current data to suggest outcomes.[17] These models are generated without human intervention, so the patterns are data driven; there are no assumptions about which variables are important. Already used in fraud detection, there are other forensic opportunities to assist law enforcement and the security and intelligence world using predictive analytics. Data from disparate document examination casefiles could feed into these models and ultimately link casework. Information about adhesive type, or the peculiar positioning of adhesives on envelope flaps, the ink composition of entry or exit stamps on passports, the specific printer defects from physical examinations of commercial documents or packaging, and perhaps other data that has not yet even been considered, could all be substantive in a predictive model.

Forensic document examiners (FDEs) are familiar with the examination of anonymous letters to determine any links the documentary evidence may reveal, whether there is suspect writing or a suspect machine to compare against. Some public laboratories compile information gleaned from examining those letters into databases in order to establish the author or sender of those communications. Information from postal markings, envelope dimensions, seemingly extraneous markings, class of handwriting, and printing processes from the many and varied ransom letters, hold-up notes, and threatening letters, are categorized and the data saved in order to compare against other similar communications should they surface. When a first note or document is received, it is not necessarily known how widespread other similar or related documents may be or when another may be retrieved or sent for analysis. This data-basing of information is a step toward gathering forensic intelligence.

Taking this example further, by analyzing the other investigative elements surrounding these communications, such as sending and receiving locations, content of letters, identifying or distinguishing information from the document examination, or other case data from the investigation, and evaluating it in combination with the forensic data, the resultant findings could imply or prove links between events, persons, or source material.

The use of forensic intelligence within the classical model of intelligence only serves to strengthen the quality of the information, and in turn, the decisions made based on this information. Essentially, the intelligence cycle consists of collection, processing, analyzing, dissemination, feedback, and then direction of information.[18] Ultimately, the role of intelligence is to:

- assist law enforcement officers, policy makers, or decision makers in dealing more effectively with uncertainty and new challenges;
- provide timely warning of threats; and
- support operational activities and complex investigations.

In essence, the goal is to detect, disrupt, and dismantle criminal or intelligence networks.

Forensics, as an independent lens, offers another layer of intelligence and can link across great spans of time and distance what would not otherwise be linked. Forensic document examination is a multifaceted discipline that can be of significant aid to the investigation as well as to the courts and trier-of-fact. Handwriting and signature examinations help resolve who did or did not write something. During an examination of documents to determine how they were produced, the FDE can identify the components of the documents, that is, the mix of materials used in the production, such as the make-up of the paper or other substrate, and the chemical constituents of the inks or toners used to print the document. This examination can possibly infer where the documents were produced, what are the possible sources of the components, and even when they were produced. Examination of documents may also result in determining what were the occurrences to the documents that resulted in why a document appears a certain way or how it came to have the observed features. Answers to these questions, all from basic document examination, are particularly useful during an investigation and in determining scope of a crime as well.

Casework is routinely submitted to forensic laboratories from crime-scene investigators, prosecutors and others from the judiciary, law enforcement officers, and other investigators for scientific analysis. By far the throughput systems of most of these laboratories instructs that analytical results are provided directly back to the client, within the context of the case or client request. There is little application of the scientific information from this casework to the broader intelligence mandate of the law enforcement organization, the intelligence service, interdisciplinary law enforcement teams, or other clients. If we take, for example, a typical drug analysis submission, there is more forensic data available than the chemical analysis of the suspected-drug material to determine composition. In conjunction with this analysis, the forensic document examination of packaging materials can provide important investigative leads for operations, and useful evidential information to link a suspected trafficker to other cases or to investigations involving organized crime at the national or international level.

Similarly, human and asset smuggling operations and terrorist groups develop recognizable modus operandi in the types of documentation used, the methods for alteration or counterfeiting, and the preferred routes used. Forensic examination of the materials seized from seemingly random or disparate instances may identify links between suspects, activities or items, and their involvement in criminal activity.[19] Increasingly, casework is presented within law enforcement that warrants further inquiry using the resultant analyses.

Some larger public laboratories have embraced the interdisciplinary nature of forensic science investigations and have specifically established units to holistically review case data in order to ensure that the appropriate forensic conclusions are given based on the multidisciplinary nature of the submission and the various analyses conducted in the laboratory.[20] This reckoning of data, first within a complex case, is a step toward recognizing and identifying case data that transcends seemingly disparate cases.

The historic cases of Alger Hiss, Alfred Dreyfus, and the Hitler Diaries demonstrate that counter-intelligence practices have included forensic handwriting comparisons.[21] Newer academic research has shown that this aspect of forensic document examination continues to be a valuable means to intelligence product.[22] Keeping with forensic handwriting examinations, several interesting databases have been established to assist in the comparison process. CEDAR-FOX[23] Handwritten Document Analysis System is a computational tool for writer identification/verification. Likewise, SCRIPT,[24,25] FISH,[26] and FLASH-ID[27] are tools developed in Europe and the United States (For more information on these systems, see Chapter 22). The data generated from these systems, used to classify and compare handwriting in traditional forensic document examination casework, can be further refined using computational tools so that the information can be more easily compiled with other case data. By way of example, handwritten postal addresses can be imaged and run through a handwriting classification system.[28,29] The resultant data can then be associated with other investigative information, becoming provisional intelligence, such as revealing the existence of shell companies in international financial fraud or the shipping routes for the movement of illicit goods.

The current international trend to mine all data for myriad reasons seems endless. However, it is foolhardy to ignore the enormous potential to improved law enforcement and intelligence that the analysis of forensic data offers. Forensic Intelligence can also be fed into by those private examiners who conduct work on contract to public organizations and by the many large multinational organizations that conduct their own intelligence and support enforcement activities that also rely upon forensic document examination, such as brand protection, counterfeit deterrence, and insurance fraud. Further, the findings from forensic document examination can be integrated into established data analytics for fraud prevention, policy noncompliance, internal fraud, and insider threat. The findings of data analytics in turn generate inferences; predictive analytics looks for anomalies and similarities to identify patterns, including predictive behaviors, to inform decision making as a proactive tool.[30]

Despite the progressive work underway to strengthen validity and credibility in forensic fields since the US NAS report was published,[31] many governments and other organizations have begun to evaluate forensic science again,[32] with questions like:

- Are we getting more justice as a result of advances in the forensic sciences?
- Is forensic evidence being used as efficiently and effectively as possible in criminal investigations and prosecutions?
- What impact are forensic science advancements having on policies and procedures in the criminal justice system?

Forensic intelligence offers a positive response to these questions because one outcome is proactive, preventative assistance in early investigations.

International organizations that work in the law and security domain understand the need for forensics and have incorporated forensic science into their toolkit. The United Nations Office on Drugs and Crime,[33] INTERPOL,[34] and the International Criminal Court[35,36] all rely upon forensic science, and in particular forensic document examination, in their application of the law. The crimes investigated and prosecuted by these organizations include transnational organized crime, under the umbrella of which resides cybercrime, counterfeit goods, money laundering, environmental and wildlife crimes, drug-related crimes, human trafficking, migrant smuggling, and the trafficking in firearms. And the current trend to combat this crime is the use of forensic intelligence to ensure the entirety of the fraud or the crime has been detected, evaluated, prosecuted, and learned from in order to predict and prevent. For example, the UNODC promotes that forensic science can support proactive and preventive approaches, that solutions need to be collaborative and trans-disciplinary, that all stakeholders need to be involved, and that all aspects of the problem must be considered.

This topic is included in this text to underscore the potential of forensic document examination work outside of the narrow view some take of forensic science and the crime laboratory. By incorporating a forensic intelligence lens into routine forensic document examination, it is possible to identify and exploit the data from analyses and examinations to cross-reference and link people, places, events, and materials; that is, to link suspects or targets, crime scenes, or criminal modus operandi and evidence, maximizing the value of all intelligence and evidence.

REFERENCES

1. Martin, J., and M. Haggith. *The State of the Global Paper Industry.* Environmental Paper Network, 2018.
2. Stoel, R.D., I.E. Dror, and L.S. Miller. "Bias among Forensic Document Examiners: Still a Need for Procedural Changes." *Australian Journal of Forensic Sciences* (2014) 46: 91–97.
3. *Intelligence-Led Policing: The New Intelligence Architecture – Bureau of Justice Assistance,* U.S. Department of Justice, Office of Justice Programs (NCJ 210681) September 2005.
4. Milne, R. 2013. *Forensic Intelligence.* Boca Raton, FL: CRC Press., 1–42.
5. Baechler, S., O. Ribaux, and P. Margot. "2012 Student Paper: Toward a Novel Forensic Intelligence Model: Systematic Profiling of False Identity Documents." *Forensic Science and Policy Management* (2012) 3: 70–84.
6. Baechler, S., V. Terrasse, T. Fritz, J.-P. Pujol, O. Ribaux, and P. Margot. "The Systematic Profiling of False Identity Documents: Method Validation and Performance Evaluation Using Seizures Known to Originate from Common and Different Sources." *Forensic Science International* (2013) 232(1–3): 180–190.
7. Baechler, S., M. Morelato, O. Ribaux, A. Beavis, M. Tahtouh, K.P. Kirkbride, P. Esseiva, P. Margot, and C. Roux. "Forensic Intelligence Framework: Part II: Study of the Main Generic Building Blocks and Challenges through the Examples of Illicit Drugs and False Identity Documents Monitoring." *Forensic Science International* (May 2015) 250: 44–52.
8. Ribaux, O., S.J. Walsh, and P. Margot. "The Contribution of Forensic Science through Crime Analysis and Investigation: Forensic Intelligence." *Forensic Science International* (2006) 156(2–3): 171–181.
9. Bruenisholz, E., S. Prakash, and A. Ross. "*The Intelligent Use of Forensic Data.*" Australia New Zealand Policing Advisory Agency/National Institute of Forensic Science Australia, 2015.
10. Chase, R.J., and G. Laporte. "The Next Generation of Crime Tools and Challenges: 3D Printing." *National Institute of Justice NIJ Journal* No. 279, April 2018. www.NIJ.gov.
11. Legrand, T., and L. Vogel. "Forensic Intelligence." *Australian Research Council Centre for Excellence in Policing and Security.* (2012) 9: 1–6.
12. Ribaux, O., and B. Talbot Wright. "Expanding Forensic Science through Forensic Intelligence." *Science & Justice* (2014) 54(6): 494–501.
13. Rossy, Q., and O. Ribaux. "A Collaborative Approach for Incorporating Forensic Case Data into Crime Investigation Using Criminal Intelligence Analysis and Visualisation." *Science & Justice* (2014) 54(2): 146–153.
14. Rossy, Q., S. Ioset, D. Dessimoz, and O. Ribaux. "Integrating Forensic Information in a Crime Intelligence Database." *Forensic Science International* (2013) 230: 137–146.
15. Ribaux, O., A. Girard, S. Walsh, P. Margot, S. Mizrahi, and V. Clivaz. "Forensic Intelligence and Crime Analysis." *Probability, Law and Risk* (2003) 2(2): 47–60.
16. Geradts, Z. "Digital, Big Data and Computational Forensics." *Forensic Sciences Research* (2018) 3(3): 179–182.
17. Baesens, B., V. Van Vlasselaer, and W. Verbeke. *Fraud Analytics Using Descriptive, Predictive, and Social Network Techniques: A Guide to Data Science for Fraud Detection.* Hoboken, NJ: John Wiley & Sons, Inc., 2015.
18. Bureau of Justice Assistance (NCJ 210681) September 2005.
19. Ribaux, O., P. Margot, R. Julian, and S.F. Kelty. "Forensic Intelligence." In *Professional Issues in Forensic Science,* edited by M. Houck. Oxford: Elsevier, 2015. 127-132.
20. De Koeijer, J.A., M.J. Sjerps, P. Verger, and C.E.H. Berger. "Combining Evidence in Complex Cases – A Practical Approach to Interdisciplinary Casework." *Science & Justice* (2020) 60: 20–29.

21. Mohammed, L. “History of the Forensic Examination of Documents.” In *Encyclopedia of Forensic Sciences Second Edition,* edited by J. Siegel and P. Saukka. San Diego, CA: Elsevier, 2013: 386–394.
22. Agius, A., K. Jones, R. Epple, M. Morelato, S. Moret, S. Chadwick, and C. Roux. “The Use of Handwriting Examinations beyond the Traditional Court Purpose.” *Science and Justice* (2017) 57: 394–400.
23. Srihari, S.N. “Computational Methods for Handwritten Questioned Document Examination: Final Report.” National Institute of Justice. Award Number: 2004-IJ-CX-K050. August 2010.
24. Kroon-Van der Kooij, L. “Computer Supported Analysis of Handwriting: Progress and Results of a NIFO Project.” *Presented at the American Society of Questioned Document Examiners Annual Meeting.* Milwaukee, WI, August 1992.
25. Kroon-Van der Kooij, L. “The NIFO-TNO System ‘SCRIPT’.” *Paper presented at the American Society of Questioned Document Examiners Annual Meeting.* Washington, DC, August 1996.
26. Hecker, M. R., “FISH.” *Paper presented at the American Society of Questioned Document Examiners Annual Meeting.* Savannah, GA, August 1986.
27. Gantz, D.T., and M.A. Walch. “FLASH-ID: Handwriting Derived Biometric Analysis Software.” *Presented at the Measurement Science and Standards in Forensic Handwriting Analysis Conference.* Gaithersburg, 2013.
28. Bulacu, M. L. “Statistical Pattern Recognition for Automatic Writer Identification and Verification.” PhD diss., Rijksuniversiteit Groningen, 2007.
29. Neils, R., L. Vuurpijl, and L. Schomaker. “Automatic Allograph Matching in Forensic Writer Identification.” *International Journal of Pattern Recognition and Artificial Intelligence* (2007) 21(1): 61–81.
30. Rossy, Q., D. Décary-Hétu, O. Delémont, and M. Mulone. *The Routledge International Handbook of Forensic Intelligence and Criminology.* London, UK: Routledge, Taylor & Francis Group, 2017: 136–159.
31. National Research Council. 2009. *Strengthening Forensic Science in the United States: A Path Forward.* Washington, DC: The National Academies Press.
32. Browning, K. “Social Science Research on Forensic Science: The Story Behind One of NIJ’s Newest Research Portfolios.” *National Institute of Justice NIJ Journal* No. 275, September 2015. www.NIJ.gov
33. United Nations Office on Drugs and Crime. “Criminal Intelligence Training Manual: Manual for Analysts.” Vienna: UNODC, 2002. www.unodc.org.
34. *19th INTERPOL Forensic Science Managers Symposium Proceedings*, edited by M. Houck. https://www.sciencedirect.com/journal/forensic-science-international-synergy/special-issue/10QWNF78TVR; www.interpol.int.
35. *International Criminal Court* www.icc-cpi.int; https://www.icc-cpi.int/Pages/item.aspx?name=pr1464.
36. Mehandru, N., and A. Koenig. “Open Source Evidence and the International Criminal Court.” *Harvard Human Rights Journal.* 32 15 April 2019. https://harvardhrj.com/2019/04/open-source-evidence-and-the-international-criminal-court/.

Chapter 6

Expert Testimony

The Path to the Jury

Lucinda Risi

CONTENTS

In the American legal system, there are two sets of issues surrounding every dispute – issues of fact and issues of law. Issues of fact (where, when, how, whose version of the facts is more believable) are the province of the trier of fact – the jury. Issues of law (what standards apply, whether proper procedure was followed, whether a particular piece of evidence or testimony is admissible) are the province of the judge. The jury decides which facts are true and how much weight to give to the testimony, but the judge determines which facts and testimony they can consider. When it comes to expert witnesses, it is the judge who will decide whether an expert is qualified to testify as an expert, and whether his findings and conclusions meet the criteria for admissible evidence. In this chapter, we will examine the rules governing the admissibility of expert testimony and the ways in which the issue of expert testimony comes before the court. As a preliminary matter, an overview of the litigation process, and the expert's role in it, is in order.

Matters to be heard in a court of law fall into two broad categories – civil and criminal. Criminal matters arise when an individual violates the laws of the United States or an individual state. In criminal matters, the government (either the United States or an individual state) is always the plaintiff. The plaintiff always bears the burden of proof; that is, the plaintiff is the one who is responsible for proving that the defendant is guilty of the allegations against him. In civil litigation, a person who believes he has been wronged by the actions or inactions of another may file suit in the state court of the state in which he resides, or in a federal court, if the alleged wrong is a violation of a federal law, such as a violation of constitutional rights.

6.1 STRUCTURE OF THE COURT SYSTEM

All court systems have three main parts: a trial court level, an intermediate appellate court, and a court of last resort. The trial courts are the only ones in which testimony is given and evidence is introduced. Intermediate and "last-resort" appellate courts concern themselves solely with whether the trial court correctly interpreted and applied the law in its rulings, its instructions to the jury, and the conduct of the trial. While the trial court judge makes rulings as an individual, decisions of the appellate courts are made by a panel of three or more judges, and opinions by the highest court are made by all members of that court.

In the federal court system, the trial courts are the United States District Courts located in each state. Every state has at least one of these federal trial courts, and more populous states may have two or more, located in different cities. Federal judges at every level are appointed by the sitting president, subject to confirmation by the United States Senate. Federal judgeships are lifetime appointments. District judges preside over both civil and criminal dockets. Typically, they have one or more law clerks, lawyers who assist the judges in researching the various legal matters that come before them. Because federal courts are courts of limited jurisdiction (that is, only certain cases can be brought there), federal district court dockets are not as crowded as state court trial dockets, and cases tend to proceed through the litigation process more quickly than in state courts.

Individual state court systems have the same basic structure as the federal courts – a trial court, intermediate appellate court, and a court of last resort – although the nomenclature may vary from state to state. The state trial court may be called the district court, superior court, court of common pleas or some other name. Regardless of the name, their function is generally the same – they are the general jurisdiction court where parties can bring just about any matter that arises in that state. In most states, trial court judges are elected in either partisan or non-partisan elections. In some states, after judges are elected, they are subject to retention ballots after a certain period of time. There are some states, however, where judges are appointed by the governor. Depending upon the state, a trial court judge may hear exclusively civil or criminal matters or may hear both. Typically, state court judges have more crowded dockets and do not have law clerks to assist them.

6.2 OVERVIEW OF CIVIL LITIGATION

A person wishing to bring suit against another files a complaint (called a petition in some jurisdictions) in the appropriate trial-level court. Then a copy of that complaint is served upon the defendant, along with a summons from the court advising the defendant that he must answer within a specified period of time. Once the defendant has answered the allegations in the complaint, the case is said to be at issue. At this point, the discovery phase of the litigation begins. During discovery each side issues formal requests to the other side asking for information, relevant documents, the identification of potential witnesses, etc. Courts vary by jurisdiction in the amount of control they exercise over this phase of the litigation. Some courts allow the parties to proceed at their own pace through the discovery phase, other courts issue scheduling orders that prescribe certain deadlines for completing discovery, identifying witnesses, and filing various motions.

Once the parties have identified expert witnesses, there will be a deadline for the party to deliver a copy of the expert's report to the opposing side. Following receipt of the report, the opposing counsel may choose to inquire into the expert's qualifications and opinions through a deposition. During a deposition, the opposing party will ask questions of the expert witness to which the expert must respond under oath. A court reporter records the testimony and copies of the transcript are subsequently delivered to both sides. During the deposition, the attorney may inquire into the opinions expressed in the expert's report, the facts provided to the expert by the client, the bases for the opinions, the expert's qualifications, and the scientific basis of his discipline. If the opposing counsel believes she can in good faith argue that the expert's qualifications, discipline, or opinions do not meet the criteria for admission to a jury, she can file a motion to exclude all or part of the expert's proposed testimony from the trial. Such motions are often referred to as *Daubert* motions, because they rely on criteria for expert testimony set forth in the Supreme Court case *Daubert v. Merrell Dow Pharmaceuticals*, 509 U.S. 579 (1993). *Daubert* criteria will be discussed in further detail below.

The party supporting the expert will file a response, setting out all the reasons why the expert meets the relevant evidence rules and *Daubert* criteria, and the opposing party will be entitled to file a reply. After that, the motion is said to be at issue and will be considered by the Court. Depending upon the judge and the situation, the judge may request oral argument on the motion, or she may rule on the briefs. The Court has the option of allowing the expert to testify, allowing limited testimony on certain points, or completely excluding the expert.

In a state court proceeding, the judge can either announce his decision from the bench in open court, or he may write a very brief, summary-type order. In federal court, it is likely that the judge will issue a written opinion. Either way, the parties and the expert are bound by that decision and must conduct themselves accordingly in the subsequent trial.

During the trial of the matter, each side will present witnesses and elicit testimony from them in a question and answer format. The plaintiff or prosecution will present their case first, and when they have finished, or rested their case, the defendant will present his case. Most lawyers will invoke what is known as "the rule" – a generally accepted practice that allows witnesses to be present in the courtroom only while they are testifying. Each witness will first be questioned by the lawyer who called them. This is called direct testimony. At the completion of direct testimony, the witness will be cross-examined by the opposing attorney. Cross-examination is limited to topics covered in the direct examination. During cross-examination, the lawyer will frequently use what are known as leading questions – questions whose form suggests the answer the lawyer is seeking. Leading questions are generally not permitted during direct testimony. Following cross-examination, the first lawyer may wish to ask some additional questions in redirect examination to clear up issues which were raised in the cross-examination. This can be followed by recross examination, again dealing only with matters discussed in the redirect examination. During any examination, if the opposing lawyer feels the examiner is asking an improper question, he or she may object. The judge will rule on the objection, and the examination will continue. In some instances, the judge may also ask questions of the witness.

After all the witnesses have been examined and all the exhibits have been introduced, the parties will make their closing statements, and the judge will instruct the jury as to the law that applies to the case, after which the jury will retire to deliberate on their verdict. When they have reached a verdict, they return to the courtroom, the verdict is announced, and the trial is completed.

6.3 APPELLATE COURTS

A party who is dissatisfied with the outcome of a jury trial or with the judge's ruling on a dispositive motion (motion that seeks to end the case by asking the judge to declare as a matter of law that one party should prevail over the other) may file an appeal, setting out the areas where he feels the trial court was incorrect in its rulings. In the federal system, the appeal is filed in the Circuit Court of Appeals that is over that particular district court. There are 11 circuit courts of appeals, each one serving a separate geographic area. The Court of Appeals will consider only the disputed matters referred to it. They do not resolve questions of fact; they consider only whether the trial court correctly applied the law. Their review is limited to the record of proceedings in the trial court – the trial transcript and court filings. A panel of three judges will review the briefs submitted and issue a written opinion. They may affirm the decision of the trial court, reverse the decision of the trial court, or reverse the trial court's decision and remand the case to the trial court for additional proceedings consistent with their opinion of how the law should be applied.

The next level of appeal in the federal system is the United States Supreme Court, but only a few cases ever reach that court, as the justices have the power to choose which cases they wish to hear. A party desiring to have its case heard before the Supreme Court files a petition for certiorari, asking the Court to hear its case. At least four of the nine justices must agree to hear the case. If not enough justices agree to hear the case, they will deny certiorari and the case is over. If they do choose to hear the case, all nine justices will consider the case and will vote on the outcome.

Although there may be some procedural differences from one state to the next, state court appellate systems function in much the same way as the federal system.

6.4 OVERVIEW OF CRIMINAL LITIGATION

In many ways, criminal cases mirror the general structure of civil cases, particularly in the trial phase. A criminal case generally begins with the filing of an information or an indictment, which sets forth the charges against the defendant. The defendant is arrested and appears before the judge in an arraignment, where he is advised of the formal charges against him and pleads either guilty or not guilty. If he pleads guilty, the judge can either pronounce sentence at that time, or set a later court appearance for sentencing. If he pleads not guilty, the case will proceed to the discovery phase.

As in civil trials, during discovery the parties can obtain information from one another on the evidence they plan to introduce at trial. As in civil litigation, the goal of discovery is to avoid surprise witnesses or evidence, thus avoiding the "trial by ambush," which has long been a staple of television and movie trials. Often the defense will file pretrial motions to suppress certain evidence, and either party may file motions in limine regarding certain evidence or the scope of examination. After all discovery and motion practice is complete, the case proceeds to trial, which is conducted much like the civil trial discussed above.

6.5 ARBITRATION

A final type of proceeding in which an expert may be called to testify is an arbitration proceeding. Many contracts governing commercial dealings, construction, employment, and consumer issues have clauses that require the parties to the contract to resolve disputes through arbitration, in an effort to avoid the expense of trial.

In an arbitration proceeding, the parties select a neutral third party to serve as the arbitrator, or decision maker. The proceedings are governed by rules promulgated by the American Arbitration Association. There are separate rules for commercial disputes, labor disputes, construction disputes, etc. In general, the rules, procedures, and hearing are more relaxed than in a court setting. An expert who is to be a witness in an arbitration proceeding will typically submit a written report to the parties at a time set by the arbitrator, then appear for hearing before the arbitrator. These hearings are not held in courtrooms, and the testimony is not recorded. Although the rules governing admissibility of expert testimony and *Daubert* factors do not apply as they would in the court system, the expert may still have to satisfy the arbitrator of the reliability of her methodology and findings, and may need to provide background information regarding her discipline.

6.6 RULES RELATING TO EXPERT TESTIMONY – THE EXPERT REPORT

The foundation of the expert's testimony is her report. It is important that the report adhere to the Court's rules governing its content. It is also important that the report be thorough and encompass all the opinions the expert intends to offer. Although the expert may be deposed after the report is submitted, not all courts will allow the expert to offer additional opinions via a deposition or at trial if they are not contained in the expert report. Thus, experts should do everything possible to ensure their reports contain all of the opinions they intend to offer, and all information used to arrive at their opinions. The requirements for expert reports contained in the Federal Rules of Civil Procedure are listed below.

Fed. R. Civ. P. 26(a)(2) **Disclosure of Expert Testimony.**

A. In General. In addition to the disclosures required by Rule 26(a)(1), a party must disclose to the other parties the identity of any witness it may use at trial to present evidence under Federal Rule of Evidence 702, 703, or 705.

B. Witnesses Who Must Provide a Written Report. Unless otherwise stipulated or ordered by the court, this disclosure must be accompanied by a written report – prepared and signed by the witness – if the witness is one retained or specially employed to provide expert testimony in the case or one whose duties as the party's employee regularly involve giving expert testimony. The report must contain:

- i. a complete statement of all opinions the witness will express and the basis and reasons for them;
- ii. the facts or data considered by the witness in forming them;
- iii. any exhibits that will be used to summarize or support them;
- iv. the witness's qualifications, including a list of all publications authored in the previous 10 years;
- v. a list of all other cases in which, during the previous 4 years, the witness testified as an expert at trial or by deposition; and
- vi. a statement of the compensation to be paid for the study and testimony in the case.

D. Time to Disclose Expert Testimony. A party must make these disclosures at the times and in the sequence that the court orders. Absent a stipulation or a court order, the disclosures must be made:

- i. at least 90 days before the date set for trial or for the case to be ready for trial; or
- ii. If the evidence is intended solely to contradict or rebut evidence on the same subject matter identified by another party under Rule 26(a)(2)(B) or (C), within 30 days after the other party's disclosure.

Many state courts do not require that experts produce written reports as part of the discovery process. However, they do allow opposing counsel to inquire into the facts known and opinions held by an expert witness, either through interrogatories (written questions to be answered by the party under oath), or by deposing the expert witness. Opposing counsel may also, through interrogatories, require the party who expects to call the expert witnesses to state the subject matter on which each expert witness is expected to testify; the substance of the facts and opinions to which the expert is expected to testify; and a summary of the grounds for each opinion, as well as additional information such as the qualifications of each expert witness, a list of all publications authored by the expert witness, the compensation to be paid to the expert witness for the testimony and preparation for the testimony; and a listing of any other cases in which the expert witness has testified as an expert at trial or by deposition. If the expert is deposed and develops additional opinions after his deposition, in some jurisdictions he may not be able to offer those opinions at trial.

6.7 THE JUDGE'S ROLE IN THE ADMISSIBILITY OF EXPERT TESTIMONY

Not all information that is obtained during the discovery or investigation process will be given to the jury to consider. The jury is the trier of fact – they will determine which facts are true and what weight is to be given to the testimony they hear. However, it is the judge who determines what evidence is admissible – what evidence the jury can hear. The judge does not make his decision regarding expert testimony in a vacuum. He is guided and constrained by the applicable statutory evidence rules and court opinions interpreting those rules.

In the federal system, the Federal Rules of Evidence control. The rules most applicable to expert testimony are Rules 702, 703, and 705.

Rule 702. Testimony by Expert Witnesses

A witness who is qualified as an expert by knowledge, skill, experience, training, or education may testify in the form of an opinion or otherwise if:

a. the expert's scientific, technical, or other specialized knowledge will help the trier of fact to understand the evidence or to determine a fact in issue;
b. the testimony is based on sufficient facts or data;
c. the testimony is the product of reliable principles and methods; and
d. the expert has reliably applied the principles and methods to the facts of the case.

Rule 703. Bases of an Expert Opinion

An expert may base an opinion on facts or data in the case that the expert has been made aware of or personally observed. If experts in the particular field would reasonably rely on those kinds of facts or data in forming an opinion on the subject, they need not be admissible for the opinion to be admitted. But if the facts or data would otherwise be inadmissible, the proponent of the opinion may disclose them to the jury only if their probative value in helping the jury evaluate the opinion substantially outweighs their prejudicial effect.

Rule 705. Disclosing the Facts or Data Underlying an Expert's Opinion Testimony

Unless the court orders otherwise, an expert may state an opinion – and give the reasons for it – without first testifying to the underlying facts or data. But the expert may be required to disclose those facts or data on cross-examination.

State courts operate under rules of evidence promulgated by their own state legislatures. These rules are generally similar to the federal rules, however, there may be some variance from state to state. Evidence rules for any state can be obtained through a Google search.

6.8 COURT OPINIONS

Trying to craft a rule that would apply to every situation without ambiguity is nearly impossible. Ambiguity in a statute can occur for several reasons: an attempt to draft the rule broadly so as to cover a multitude of situations; deliberate ambiguity as a result of compromise during legislative debate regarding the statute; or ambiguity that arises over the course of time as changes in society and culture create new situations to which old rules must apply. When a situation arises that doesn't fit neatly into the language of a statute, lawyers bring their arguments before the court, which will then issue its opinion as to how and whether the current law applies to the new situation. Over the course of time, court opinions explain the meanings of statutes. Statutes are then subsequently amended to meet the changing demands of the times. Then, a new set of court opinions come out that begin again to explain the statutes.

How do written opinions expounding upon the statutes come about? Using the example of expert testimony, consider the following. In a trial court matter, one side proposes the testimony of an expert witness. The opposing party wants to find a way to prevent the witness from testifying, so he or she examines the language of the statute and compares it to the circumstances surrounding the expert witness (adequately qualified, reliable methodology, etc.). That party then files a motion, called a Motion to Exclude, or a Motion in Limine (before the trial) to exclude the testimony of the expert witness, claiming that, under the evidence code and the decisions interpreting it, the testimony does not meet the criteria necessary to be submitted to the jury. The issue will be briefed by the parties, and in some cases, argued before the presiding judge. After considering the briefs filed and the arguments of counsel, the court will rule on the admissibility of the testimony and either allow or prevent the expert from testifying, or may limit the testimony. In a federal district court (the trial court in the federal system), this will be a written opinion. In the state court, it is more likely to be a ruling from the bench or a summary order.

The party opposed to the court's ruling on expert testimony can appeal the issue. Appellate review of a judge's decision on expert testimony utilizes an abuse of discretion standard; in other words, the appellate court is only looking to see if the judge was within acceptable guidelines when he issued his opinion. The appellate court then issues its opinion, which becomes mandatory authority for the courts below it.

In an attempt to ensure that similar cases are decided in a similar manner, the American legal system long ago adopted the doctrine of *stare decisis*, which states that normally, once a court has decided a particular issue in a particular way, other courts should decide similar cases the same way, unless there is a reason not to do so. Thus, court opinions play an important role in shaping judicial decisions regarding expert testimony. A few of the key decisions affecting expert testimony are discussed below. These cases are all Supreme Court cases, and thus are mandatory authority in all federal courts. Many state courts have adopted some or all of the principles set out in these rulings.

6.9 THE *DAUBERT* TRILOGY

Perhaps the most important case to affect expert testimony is *Daubert v. Merrell Dow Pharmaceuticals*, 509 U.S. 579 (1993). Prior to *Daubert*, the standard for admissibility of expert testimony was a broad "general acceptance in the scientific community" test set out in *Frye v. United States*, 293 F. 1013 (D.C. Cir. 1923). *Daubert* set aside this 70-year-old test, characterized the judge as a "gatekeeper," and required her to perform a two-part analysis when determining whether to admit expert testimony. This analysis required asking the following questions:

1. Is the evidence reliable?
   a. Testimony must be scientific (grounded in the methods and procedures of science);
   b. Testimony must not be speculative (must be derived by the scientific method and supported by appropriate validation).
2. Is the testimony relevant – will it aid the jury in resolving a factual dispute?

Daubert created something of a revolution in the judiciary's thinking regarding expert testimony. However, the decision was vague in outlining how judges were to go about their new gatekeeping duties. Subsequent case law functioned to provide additional guidance to judges on how to evaluate expert testimony for admissibility.

In 1997, the Supreme Court decided *General Electric v. Joiner*, 522 U.S. 136 (1997), which determined that the proper standard of appellate review for a trial judge's decision to admit or exclude expert testimony was the abuse of discretion standard. *Joiner* also noted that a "court may conclude that there is simply too great an analytical gap between the data and the opinion proffered." *Joiner*, 522 U.S. at 146.

Two years later, the Supreme Court decided *Kuhmo Tire Co. v. Carmichael*, 528 U.S. 137 (1999). In *Kuhmo Tire*, the Court held that the *Daubert* two-part test could be expanded to include technical and other types of specialized knowledge. In doing so, it explained that the *Daubert* factors could be flexible, and that all may not be applicable to certain types of knowledge.

In 2000, Rule 702 of the Federal Rules of Evidence was changed to reflect the holdings of *Daubert*.

6.10 CONCLUSION

Expert testimony is an important part of the judicial process. Expert witnesses are used when scientific, technical, or other specialized knowledge will assist the trier of fact. But merely offering an expert opinion does not automatically ensure an expert will be allowed to present his findings to the jury. Expert opinions must initially be disclosed to all parties either via a carefully prepared report, or a deposition, through detailed answers to interrogatories, or a combination of these methods. Further, the expert must be qualified by "knowledge, skill and experience" to offer the opinions, and the expert's methodology and findings must meet the court's standards for reliability, scientific rigor, etc. These standards have been developed over the years through a combination of statutory evidence rules and court opinions interpreting those rules. It is likely that standards for admissibility will continue to evolve, and expert witnesses would do well to keep abreast of the changes in this area of the law as it affects their discipline. An expert should further be prepared to assist the attorney who retains him or her, and the judges before whom he or she testifies, to understand how her particular field of expertise meets the standards for expert testimony set forth in *Daubert* and the rules of evidence appropriate to the court in which she will testify.

Section II

Handwriting Topics and Research

Chapter 7

Development of Habitual Handwriting Characteristics in Elementary School Students

Lisa M. Hanson and Marie E. Durina

CONTENTS

For forensic document examiners (FDEs), the tasks of handwriting examination and comparison are based on the assumption that, given a sufficient amount of writing, no two people are likely to produce the same handwriting in terms of all the writing features. Studying how and when an individual develops his or her own personal writing habits is important in forensic document examination. It is not until the combination of writing patterns becomes stable that an accurate opinion of the source of that writing can be made.

7.1 EARLY FINDINGS ON HANDWRITING DEVELOPMENT

Before beginning the research project discussed in this chapter,[1] several searches were conducted for large-scale studies on the development of personal handwriting characteristics in elementary school students. A few small studies were located; however, their topics were not relevant to handwriting development. Furthermore, no studies were located that were longitudinal in design or contained a large number of subjects. Although there are multiple explanations and descriptions on the development of personal handwriting habits in forensic document examination textbooks and articles, none contain references to supportive empirical data.

7.2 DEVELOPMENT OF HANDWRITING SKILL

Learning to write involves practicing letters, first by mimicking forms from the copybook of the handwriting system taught. Handwriting characteristics common to those who learned using the same copybook are called *class characteristics*. Once the handwriting forms are committed to memory and further practiced, they begin to deviate from the system taught and become personal. How much they diverge depends on numerous features, such as the writer's skill, visual recall of the copybook forms, and personal preference. Practice increases the writer's skill and produces writing that becomes more fluently and rapidly executed as the focus shifts more to the message being written than the physical movements of the writing act itself. Once graphic maturity has been achieved, the act of writing is a habitual neuromuscular act that is performed with ease. At this point, the writing becomes relatively stable and contains many personalized characteristics. Early forensic document examination literature and research asserts that this typically occurs in the late teens or early twenties. The writer's skill level then typically remains relatively stable throughout adulthood.

7.3 DEVELOPMENT OF NON-CLASS CHARACTERISTIC HANDWRITING HABITS OVER TIME

Since the beginning of the 21st century, there have been changes to teaching curriculums in the United States. At the time the study discussed here began, and for several years previously, students were only required to reach a level of writing skills sufficient for others to be able to read their writing. During this same time period (approximately 2004 through 2012), most public schools had also discontinued cursive writing instruction in their curriculums.

Considering these major changes, it was decided research should be conducted to gather empirical data to support, expand upon, and update the body of knowledge available on the topic of handwriting development. This meant the study would need to be conducted on a large scale and over an extended period of time. It was intended that data collected during this study would address the issue of whether or not changes in school handwriting curriculums affected when students began to develop nonclass or personalized characteristic handwriting habits. It also sought to determine if those nonclass characteristic handwriting habits would be stabilized at an earlier age, due to teachers no longer requiring students to adhere to the copybook model. The goal was to gain a higher degree of understanding as to how personalizing handwriting characteristics develop in elementary school students and determine when these characteristics become habitual and stabilized.

Four separate elementary schools in the State of Minnesota's Independent School Districts participated in this handwriting study between 2011 and 2014: Liberty Ridge, Middleton, Red Rock, and Wildwood. All four schools taught their students to write using the Zaner-Bloser method of writing, the most common writing method being taught throughout the United States at that time (see Figure 7.1).

The Zaner-Bloser system of writing was developed in the late 1880s by two master penmen, Lloyd Kelchner and Elmer Ward Bloser, together with Charles Paxton Zaner. The Zaner-Bloser method of handwriting sought to streamline the ornate, but tedious, method of the Spencerian writing system, and it became widely used in the 19th century for business documents as well as personal letters. At the time of this writing, the Zaner-Bloser system of handwriting continues to be taught in many schools throughout the United States.

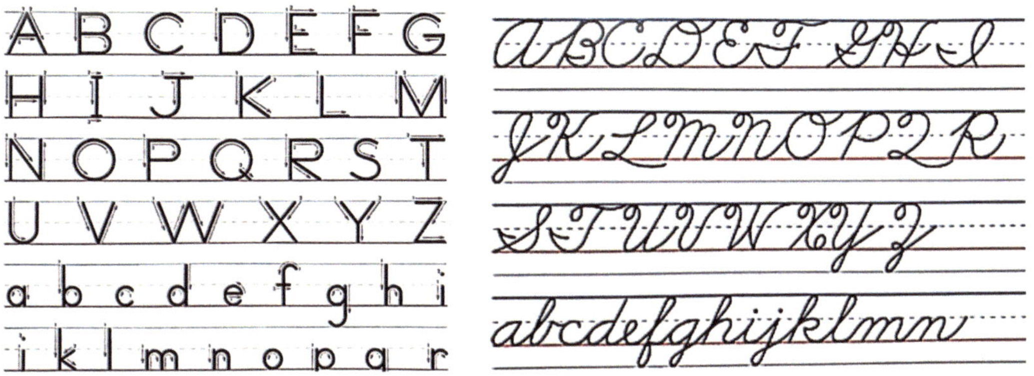

(a) (b)

Figure 7.1 (a) Zaner-Bloser hand-printing copybook and (b) Zaner-Bloser cursive copybook.

Hand-printed and cursive samples were collected from approximately 1,800 students in second grade (about 7 years old), third grade (about 8 years old), and fourth grade (about 9 years old). These groups were selected because writing lessons begin, and then continue to be practiced, during these three grades.

Writing samples were collected each spring season for consistency in data sampling, necessary to document minute changes in hand-printing and cursive writing skills and habits as the students' abilities change over time. The students were asked to write the following ninety-nine-word paragraph four times each year, twice in cursive writing and twice by hand-printing:

> The brown fox went into the barn where he saw the black dog. After a second, the black dog saw the fox too. The brown fox was fast and quick. The black dog was not fast, and he lost the fox. The fox hid in a hole and waited for the black dog to go home. After the black dog went home, the fox was able to go to the hole he called home and saw all the other foxes. The other foxes were glad to see him, and they all asked him to tell them about his day.

All writing samples were collected on the same forms to control variation in document size and format. Each year, the teachers read the same instructions to the students prior to collecting the writing samples. The data-gathering process produced an average of five to ten hand-printed and cursive samples of the word *and* per student. (Note: Cursive writing was not obtained from second graders since they had just begun learning that style.)

7.3.1 First Approach: Analysis of the Word *and*

Two different approaches were used to analyze the students' handwriting samples. In the first approach, the distribution of the characteristics of the letters in the word *and* was studied. The word *and* was selected for analysis because it is one of few words that students write repeatedly in their early writings. Therefore, it was theorized that the development of differentiable handwriting characteristics in the samples would be observed.

As a preliminary step, two FDEs certified by the American Board of Forensic Document Examiners (ABFDE) performed visual examination and intra-comparison of each of the student's writing samples. The FDEs would then choose the appropriate descriptor that best described the student's repetitive habits (see Figure 7.2). Then, each of the descriptors were assigned different numeric values to be used by the statisticians.

The collected data was forwarded to Dr. Srihari of the Center for Excellence in Document Analysis and Recognition for statistical analysis. The resulting data was analyzed first by constructing probabilistic graphical models from which information measures were computed to

# strokes in "a"	one	two	three	uppercase	
formation of "a" staff	tented	retraced	looped	no staff	single down
# strokes in "n"	one	two	three	uppercase	
formation of "n" staff	tented	retraced	looped	no staff	single down
shape of arch of "n"	pointed	rounded			
# strokes in "d"	one	two	three	uppercase	
formation of "d" staff	tented	retraced	looped	no staff	single down
initial stroke of "d"	staff top	bulb			
Unusual formations	formation		symbol		
a-n relationship	a taller	a equal	a smaller		
a-d relationship	a taller	a equal	a smaller		
n-d relationship	n taller	n equal	n smaller		

(a)

Initial stroke of "a"	staff right	staff left	staff center	
Formation of "a" staff	tented	retraced	looped	no staff
Number of "n" arches	one	two		
Shape of "n" arches	pointed	rounded	retracted	combination
Location of "n" mid	above base	below base	at base	
Formation of "d" staff	tented	retraced	looped	
Formation of "d" initial	overhand	underhand	straight across	
Formation of "d" terminal	curved up	straight	curved down	no obvious end stroke
Symbol	unusual		symbol	
a-n relationship	a taller	a equal	a smaller	
a-d relationship	a taller	a equal	a smaller	
n-d relationship	n taller	n equal	n smaller	

(b)

Figure 7.2 Twelve characteristics of the word *and*: (a) handprinted and (b) cursive.

determine the range of variation within each student's writing. The measures represented the extent of changes in the writing samples of the word *and* by the same student between grades. The relative stability of hand-printing between grades 2 and 3 was found to be greater than between grades 3 and 4 and between grades 2 and 4. This is expected because the students adhere more closely to the copybook model through grade 3. However, by grade 4, they begin to diverge from this model and begin to introduce their own personal characteristics into their writing.

7.3.2 Second Approach: Analysis of the Full Sample

In the second approach, the entire writing sample of each student was examined using an automated software system for handwriting comparison, known as CEDAR-FOX. The images of the handwriting were first mapped to a transcript containing the seven sentences the students were asked to copy. Then, based on the recognized characteristics, the system computed three types of features: macro-features, micro-features, and style features, to determine the strength of whether two samples were written by the same writer or not. Examples of macro-features are features like slant and height. Micro-features are handwriting characteristics such as stroke structure, and style features come from pairs of letters, known as *bigrams*.

A total of 2,755 comparisons were made: 1,974 of them for hand-printing and 781 for cursive writing. Results were computed for comparison of writing samples prepared by the same student in different grades, as well as for comparison of writing samples prepared by different students in the same grade.

The findings support an increase in differences between different writers as the students move up to a higher grade (see Figures 7.3 and 7.4).

7.3.3 Study Findings

The analysis of the writing samples collected over the 3-year span led to the following findings:

1. The handwriting of each student contained less variation at the end of second grade, which was expected as this is a new skill, and a time period when students appeared to follow the copybook model. However, many of the student's range of variations became

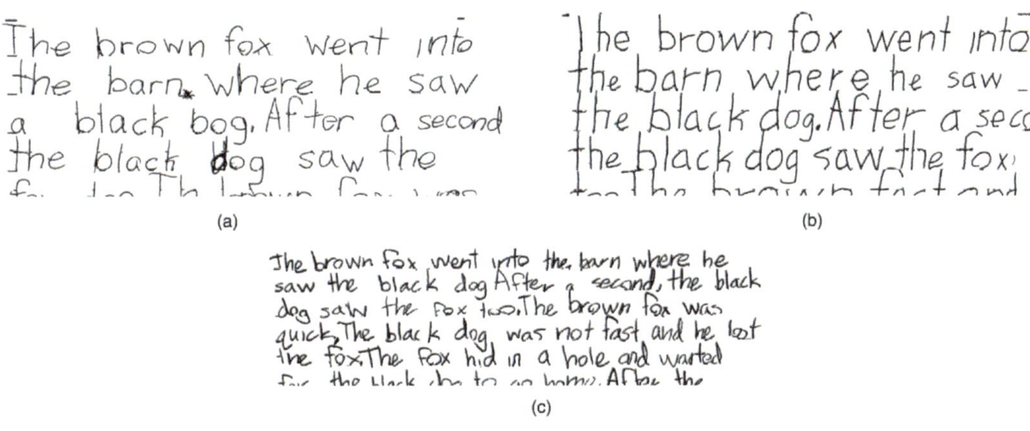

Figure 7.3 Hand-printed samples for the same student in (a) grade 2, (b) grade 3, and (c) grade 4.

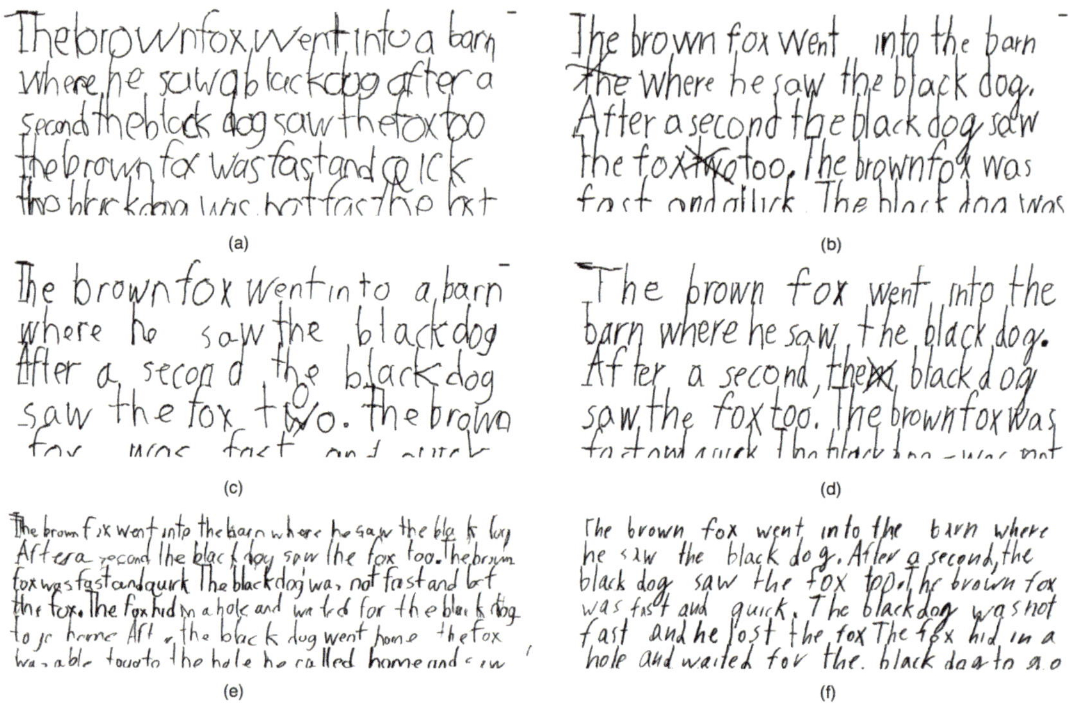

Figure 7.4 Hand-printed samples of two different students: (a, b) in grade 2, (c, d) in grade 3, and (e, f) in grade 4.

markedly wider during third and fourth grade, as the students began to write more from memory and less from copying the copybook handwriting model.

2. The handwriting characteristics present in the samples of students in second grade contained increasing numbers of nonclass characteristic handwriting habits and wider ranges of variation as the students progressed through fourth grade.
3. The students, on average, were developing nonclass characteristic handwriting habits at a younger age than previously discussed in many forensic handwriting examination textbooks and articles. The exact reasons for this phenomenon are not known because the researcher could not speak with the students due to the requirements of the Institution Research Board (IRB) guidelines which governed this research project. However, history and the empirical data gathered in this study supports that it is highly likely for two reasons: First, students are no longer required to master the copybook model as prior students were required to do over the previous eight to ten decades. Secondly, because adherence to the copybook model is no longer strictly enforced, deviations from the model remain so that personal handwriting characteristics are allowed to become habitual.

7.4 CONCLUSIONS

Previous information regarding the development of handwriting in students was gathered from studies that had small numbers of subjects and that were not longitudinal in design. Data from this research provides additional empirical support for the premise that individuals develop and incorporate nonclass characteristic writing habits that personalize their handwriting. Since technological shifts in the 21st century have led the US educational system to place less importance on mastering handwriting skills, the findings of this study also support that the development of personalized handwriting characteristics begins when students are young and just learning to write. Additional data mining from this study from older writers in grades 4–6 would be useful to further understand the factors that affect the development of nonclass characteristic handwriting habits in students as they age, as well as when the habits become stable. This is important in forensic document examination, because the lack of stability in a subject's writing is a limiting factor in a handwriting comparison that can impact a writership conclusion.

REFERENCE

1. Sargur N. Srihari et al., "Development of Individuality in Children's Handwriting." *Journal of Forensic Sciences*, vol. 61, no. 5 (October 2016): 1292–1300.

Chapter 8

Evaluation of Handwriting Evidence

Carolyne Bird

CONTENTS

8.1 INTRODUCTION

The examination of handwriting relies upon observation of the characteristics of the handwriting, a comparison of these features between the samples (typically, questioned and known), and evaluation of the observed similarities and dissimilarities. The logical (or evaluative) approach to evidence interpretation provides a standardized framework for evaluating the observations by explicitly assessing their probability given each of at least two competing propositions and using a likelihood ratio (or verbal equivalent) to express the relative strength of the evidence[1–3] (see also Chapter 3). In a typical handwriting examination, these propositions may be, for example, "The known writer wrote the questioned entries" and "Someone other than the known writer wrote the questioned entries." The evaluation focuses on how well the observations meet the expectations for each proposition (including sub-propositions, if relevant. Under the proposition "The known writer wrote the questioned entries," relevant sub-propositions may be "The known writer wrote the questioned entries naturally" and "The known writer wrote the questioned entries using a disguise"). Observations that are consistent with expectations will be assessed as having high probability under a particular (sub-)proposition while observations that differ from expectations will be considered as having low probability given a particular (sub-) proposition.

This formal approach to evaluating handwriting evidence is currently used in some forensic laboratories, including the School of Criminal Justice at the University of Lausanne and the Swedish National Forensic Center in Europe, and Queensland Police Service Forensic Services Group and Forensic Science SA in Australia. In the United States and other parts of the world, it may be the case that even if the interpretation of evidence is not described in the same way, handwriting examiners are still considering competing propositions when conducting comparisons and assessing observations against their expectations under different scenarios.

Aside from evaluating observations regarding feature similarity or dissimilarity against the expectations for particular propositions, the interpretation of findings must also take into consideration any features of the questioned or known writing that may limit a full examination or affect the examination process itself. As handwriting is a product of human behavior that can be generated under a wide range of circumstances, there are many variables that play a part in its production. The examiner is also restricted to examining the material that is provided by the client, which may take varying forms (e.g. original, non-original, digital) and have been subjected to a variety of environmental conditions. Each of these circumstances may affect the extent of support that the findings provide for one proposition over the competing proposition(s), as well as the examiner's ability to assess this.

For example, in some circumstances, writing will be lacking feature detail or contain additional artifacts resulting from a copying process, damage, or handling after the document was created. These circumstances may arise when the questioned document is non-original, has been subjected to prior chemical testing (such as examination for fingerprints), or when writing has poorly defined ink lines (perhaps due to a faulty writing implement). This can adversely affect the examiner's ability to determine features for comparison and therefore increase the uncertainty in the conclusions, which may potentially decrease the strength of opinion expressed.

This chapter will discuss some of the factors associated with handwriting examinations which may make the significance of findings difficult to determine, such as intentionally unnatural writing in either signatures or handwritten text, unusual writing conditions, handwriting complexity, foreign scripts, legibility, amount of writing, non-original documents, and the nature of known material. Some of these considerations are discussed in detail in other chapters.

8.2 UNNATURAL HANDWRITING

Unnatural handwriting can be defined as any writing that is not typical of the normal writing of an individual and may be the result of (1) a deliberate alteration of usual writing behavior or (2) the influence of some internal or external factor such as intoxication, illness, or underlying writing surface. As such, unnatural handwriting may be either intentional or unintentional.[4] Intentional alteration of handwriting (outside of changes made to handwriting for aesthetic purposes or during the development of handwriting) may be classed as disguise or simulation.

Simulation behavior is an attempt by someone to copy another writer's handwriting features, usually by use of a physical or mental model. This may be achieved via freehand copying, tracing, or machine generation.

Disguise behavior in handwriting is a deliberate attempt to change the appearance of one's handwriting features so that the writing does not resemble the writer's usual, normal writing. Disguise may be used to avoid being linked to the writing and deny writership later.

The overarching strategy employed may depend on whether the recipient of the handwriting is familiar with the writer's normal handwriting. If the recipient is not familiar with the normal handwriting, such as a bank teller receiving a demand note, the writer may use a freeform disguise, trying to change as many features of his or her handwriting as possible. If the recipient of the handwriting is familiar with the writer's usual writing, such as a bank teller receiving a signed check that the writer plans to deny signing later, the signature will need to be sufficiently similar to pass the first check, but different enough to be able to disown later and if subjected to further scrutiny. Auto-simulation is a particular form of disguise where the writer copies or draws his or her own handwriting features in a similar process to another writer attempting to simulate the signature.

In forensic casework, simulation may be more commonly suspected in questioned signatures (e.g. on disputed wills, property, or finance documents) than in handwritten text. Disguise may be more often encountered in specific types of questioned handwritten text, for example threat, nuisance, or ransom letters. This is not to say, however, that the forensic document examiner (FDE) will never be faced with questioned simulated handwritten text or disguised signatures.

Disguise behavior may also be employed by a writer when completing requested known writing samples (both signatures and handwritten text). Although some elements of the natural writing may be present, a disguised known sample can make the evaluation of compared handwriting features extremely difficult and may prevent a meaningful examination from being undertaken.

8.2.1 Handwriting Production

To better understand the production and therefore expected features of disguised and simulated writings, it can be helpful to gain an understanding of how natural, normal handwriting is produced. The act of writing is a complex learned behavior that is the product of cognitive, psychomotor, and biomechanical processes which leave a visual trace on a writing surface. Like other complex movements, learning to write takes place over three relatively distinct phases of movement acquisition. In the initial *cognitive phase,* the construction of letters and symbols is the primary focus. For example, the writer will consider where the implement needs to be put down on the page, what direction to move it, and how long each stroke should be. The high cognitive load associated with having to consider and control every movement means that writing produced during this phase usually displays poor fluency and rhythm. Within this phase, the writer will try different motor strategies and retain those that are successful. The *associative phase* produces writing that is more consistent as the writing movement is more uniform. In this phase the writer typically has an effective strategy for constructing forms and is making only subtle adjustments to improve output. The *autonomous phase* is reached when the writer can produce writing seemingly without attention to the process. This writing is typically fluent and free-flowing, exhibiting graduations in pressure between up and down strokes. Although each writer works toward a similar goal of producing legible handwriting, differences in muscular control, sequence of movements, frequency of writing, and design preferences mean that the movement style of an individual writer may be somewhat characteristic and the motor control "automatic."

Both simulation and disguise behaviors require the writer to suppress his or her usual motor control system while attempting to copy other handwriting features or introduce new features different from his or her own, respectively. Writing generated "automatically," particularly signing one's name, is driven by an open loop mode of movement control, where a message is sent from the brain to execute a movement or string of movements which proceeds autonomously, largely without peripheral feedback. Compared to this usual open loop system of motor control that a reasonably skilled writer utilizes when writing normally, simulation and disguise (depending on the strategy) rely on a closed loop system. The feedback-dependent closed loop mode of movement control means the movement is interrupted or paused so the writer can monitor progress and allow adjustments to the movement as deemed necessary; visual feedback on how the writing is progressing is relied upon to effect the formation of the resultant writing.

The higher level of sensory input and corresponding increased cognitive load means that simulated writing movements are generally slower and less fluent than natural handwriting movements, as the writer stops to check progress against the model. The slower movements and dependence on visual feedback are likely to be reflected in the static handwriting trace in terms of features that can be readily observed by the FDE, including a lack of fluency, pauses, and retouches, as well as internal inconsistencies in pen direction, letter construction, or connectivity. Simulators are also likely to focus on the more obvious structural features of the model handwriting while more subtle features such as proportions and spacing are unlikely to be faithfully copied. If attention is given to fairly representing the fluency of a moderate to complex sample of writing, then it is likely that the representation of structural elements will suffer. Depending on the skill of the simulator, simulation behavior is expected to result in handwriting that displays both similarities and dissimilarities when compared to the target writing.

Two usual methods of simulation by tracing, the transmitted-light process and the carbon outline method, have been described in the literature.[5] If employing either of these tracing methods, the writer will typically need to slow down their usual writing speed to be able to accurately follow the guidelines. The resultant traced writing is likely to be pictorially similar to the model writing, but the reduced speed is likely to be evidenced in the handwriting trace as a lack of fluency, including hesitations, interruptions,[6] abrupt changes in direction, and a uniformly heavy stroke.[5] However, a more fluent tracing may be attempted utilizing transmitted light, where the writer trades accuracy of form for increased speed and fluency.[7]

There may be evidence on a questioned document that a tracing process has been employed, for example, remnants of a carbon copy, pencil, or indented guideline. Evidence may also be associated with a known document if the model happens to have been submitted for examination, for example, superimposition of the questioned and known model writing or indentations of the questioned writing on the model document. The features that may provide evidence of a tracing process have been described in detail elsewhere.[8] However, any evidence of tracing visible on the questioned or known document will not provide information about who made the tracing; a tracing could equally have been carried out by the known writer or someone else. Therefore, an opinion may reasonably be offered that the questioned writing was traced, but no opinion can be made on writership.

Like the act of simulation, disguise behavior requires additional cognitive function to execute, and therefore, disguised writings often display poor fluency, rhythm, and line quality when compared to natural writing. Many writers find it difficult to create altered forms of their writing, particularly if they need to maintain the disguise over extended writing. In addition, people are not generally aware of the characteristics of their own writing and therefore may introduce ineffective disguise. The forensic document examination literature generally reports that any disguise (of handwritten text) is rarely consistent over more than a few lines[9] and that most strategies are relatively simple and focus on obvious features[10,11] like change in size or slant.[12,13] There is also consensus that subtle features such as punctuation and arrangement on the page are rarely disguised.[14]

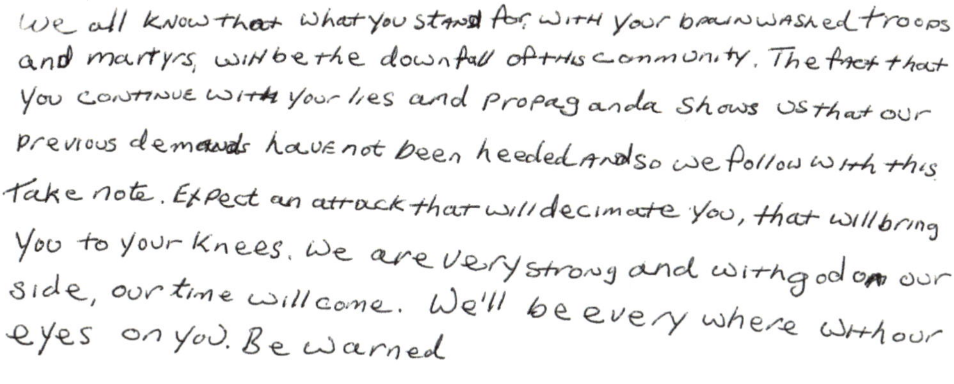

Figure 8.1 A naturally written handwriting sample displaying poor internal consistency. This kind of writing sample may be mistaken as one that has been created using a disguise behavior.

8.2.2 FDE Skill in Distinguishing between Disguise and Simulation

The ability to differentiate between disguised and simulated writing is a desired skill for an FDE. However, both types of writings are expected to display both similarities and dissimilarities when compared to natural writing, as well as exhibit poor line quality, fluency, and internal inconsistencies. In addition to the mixed signal of similarities and differences arising from the respective unnatural writing processes, writer skill can complicate the task of determining whether the writing is naturally prepared or not, as some people's natural writing may exhibit poor line quality or a wide degree of variation sometimes observed in unnatural writings, as illustrated in Figure 8.1.

Research illustrates that distinguishing between disguise and simulation behaviors can be a difficult task. Found and Rogers[15] analyzed 5 years of blind trials containing naturally written, disguised, and simulated writings, by both the specimen writer and different writers, where qualified FDEs attempted to answer questions regarding the potential writer of the questioned handwriting samples. A total of 30,100 opinions were expressed by examiners over the five trials, with the results summarized in Table 8.1. By far the greatest incorrect scores were associated with writings disguised by the known writer (12.07% incorrect) and simulated by a different writer (16.70% incorrect). Furthermore, these two writing types, along with writings disguised by someone other than the known writer, attracted the highest inconclusive scores. The incorrect writership opinions expressed on disguised writings by the known writer indicate that the

TABLE 8.1 MEAN PERCENTAGE INCONCLUSIVE AND INCORRECT SCORES FOR WRITERSHIP OPINIONS COMBINED OVER HANDWRITING TRIALS ADMINISTERED FROM THE YEARS 2000 TO 2004

	Natural by Known Writer	Natural Not by Known Writer	Disguised by Known Writer	Disguised Not by Known Writer	Simulated by Known Writer	Simulated Not by Known Writer
% inconclusive	1.42	21.77	41.28	44.60	28.49	43.90
% incorrect	0.12	0.96	12.07	0.41	1.73	16.70

Source: Adapted from Found and Rogers.[15]

TABLE 8.2 MEAN PERCENTAGE INCONCLUSIVE AND INCORRECT SCORES FOR WRITERSHIP OPINIONS COMBINED OVER SIGNATURE TRIALS ADMINISTERED FROM 2002 TO 2005

	Genuine	Disguised	Simulated
% inconclusive	14.2	63.3	50.5
% incorrect	2.3	21.3	2.9

Source: Adapted from Bird, Found, Ballantyne, and Rogers.[16]

differences in handwriting features observed between the questioned and known samples were taken to be indicative of a different writer. Conversely, the incorrect writership opinions relating to simulated samples written by a different writer are likely to be due to the simulation behavior not being detected.

The difficulty in distinguishing between disguise and simulation behaviors is not restricted to handwritten text. Research by Bird, Found, Ballantyne, and Rogers analyzed 4 years of blind trials containing naturally written and disguised signatures by the specimen writer and simulated signatures by a different writer. Qualified FDEs attempted to answer questions regarding the potential writer of the questioned signature samples, as well as the process of production (i.e. whether the signatures were naturally or unnaturally produced).[16] A total of 19,361 writership and process opinions were expressed by examiners over the 4 years of trials, with the mean percentage of inconclusive and error scores summarized in Table 8.2.

Like the handwriting trial results, disguised and simulated signatures attracted higher inconclusive scores than genuine questioned signatures, with the greatest error scores associated with disguised signatures. However, most disguised signatures with incorrect writership opinions had correct process opinion scores, indicating that many examiners detected the unnatural writing process but misinterpreted the observed feature dissimilarities as indicative of another writer rather than disguise. Meanwhile, the majority of simulated signatures with an incorrect writership opinion also had an incorrect process opinion. In these cases, the unnatural writing process was not detected and the examiner deemed the simulated signature to be genuine. It should be noted that this result was mostly due to one trial year, which included a particularly good simulator.

8.2.3 Disguise Behavior in Signatures

Several studies have investigated methods of disguise in signatures,[17–19] and one has focused on kinematic features of disguise behavior in signatures.[20] In addition, two studies have been published that focus on the consistency of disguise strategies used by writers over time. They found that the majority of writers (89% of 62 subjects[21] and 71% of 56 subjects[22]) use the same strategies when disguising their signature a second time, approximately a month later. The authors of the later study suggest that in cases where disguised writing is suspected, it is advisable to obtain deliberately disguised known writing material.[22]

Consensus on disguise behavior is that writers focus on altering the obvious and superficial features of their writing, while more subtle features remain unchanged. Disguised signatures may also display poorer fluency than genuine signatures due to the reduced speed of execution. The typically reported strategies of disguise in signatures include the following:

- Altered capital letters (see Figure 8.2)
- Change of slope

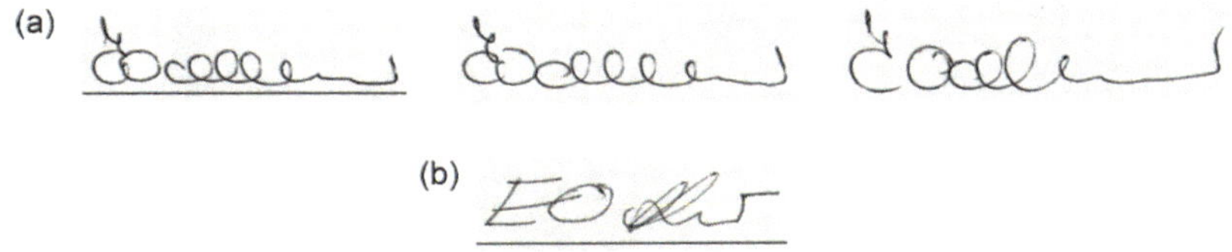

Figure 8.2 Three genuine signatures (a) and a disguised signature (b). The disguise employed includes an altered capital letter *E*, a change in slope, and a shortening of the signature.

- Altered letter construction/shape, including addition or deletion of initial lead-in strokes
- Omitted letters or misspelling
- Change in size or spacing
- Change in speed (faster or slower)
- Return to copybook or printing style (see Figure 8.3)
- Slow copying of genuine signature (auto-simulation, see Figure 8.4)

Michel observed that a large proportion of people are unable to successfully disguise their signature, creating signatures that predominately fall within the normal range of variation of their genuine signatures.[18] Wendt's study of disguised signatures written by 128 subjects observed only 2% of writers failing to introduce a disguise.[19] One to three different disguise strategies were most commonly employed (by 88% of writers), with the largest number of disguises utilized

Figure 8.3 A genuine signature (a) and a disguised signature (b). The disguise strategy could be described as a return to a copybook style.

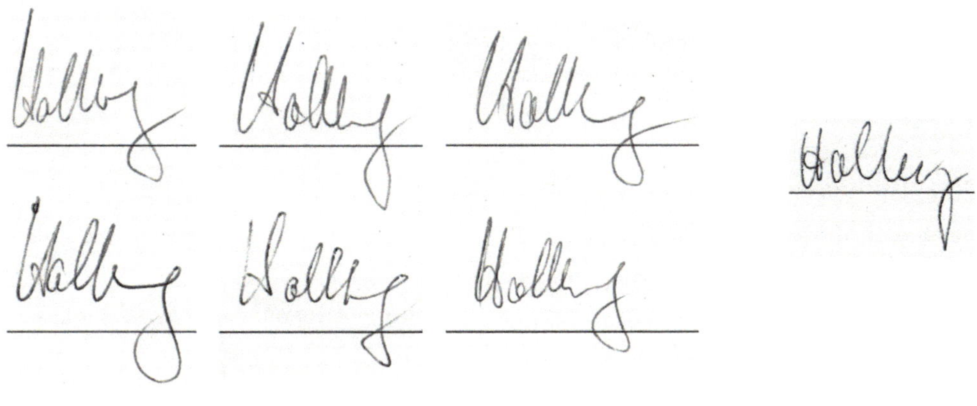

Figure 8.4 Six genuine signatures and a disguised signature on the right. The disguised signature has been more slowly written than the genuine signatures and exhibits an unusual pen lift just before the terminal descender. This disguise strategy can be described as auto-simulation.

Figure 8.5 Three genuine signatures (a) and a disguised signature (b). The disguised signature displays some dissimilarity in the initial section but similarities in the subtle features when compared to the known signature sample.

being five (observed in 2% of writers).[19] It should be noted that some of the disguise strategies observed, especially hesitations and retouches, may not be the result of an intention to adopt that strategy but an unavoidable by-product of introducing some other disguise.[23] Another example is an intentional dramatic change to slant resulting in a change of writing speed and the shape of letters and their connections.[24]

For freeform (i.e. non-traced) disguised signatures, indicators can be summarized as a combination of gross dissimilarities (for example, altered capital letters) and similarities in the fine or subtle features. These inconspicuous features, such as proportions of elements, shapes and sizes of enclosed spaces within characters, connecting and drag strokes, and pressure variations, have been described by Mohammed and Cunningham[25] and may be used to differentiate between writers (i.e. between disguise and simulation). In cases where the disguise attempt is so modest that any dissimilarities observed could be accounted for by variation within the normal range or an accidental feature (for example, Figure 8.5), the probability of the observed evidence, given the signature was written by a different writer, may be assessed by the FDE to be low. At the same time, the probability of observing the similarity in features, given the questioned signature was written by the same writer as the known sample, may be assessed by the examiner to be high. This would ultimately result in an opinion in support of writership by the known writer.

However, where the writer has opted to "draw" their signature, the resulting disguised signature may resemble a simulation attempt by a different writer (see Figure 8.4 above). Questioned signatures of this type are problematic for examiners who might consider the probability of observing the hallmarks of simulation to be low if the questioned signature was (unnaturally) written by the known writer and therefore conclude that the questioned disguised signature was simulated by a different writer.

8.2.4 Simulation Behavior in Signatures

As touched on above, the hallmark features of freehand simulation are generally believed to be:

- Poor line quality (tremor, abrupt changes in direction)
- Even pen pressure rather than variation in pressure between up and down strokes
- Blunt stroke beginnings/endings
- Pauses, unusual pen lifts, retouches
- Inconsistencies in pen direction, letter construction, proportions, or connectivity

Focused research has investigated some of the above listed features with results as summarized below.

Dewhurst, Ballantyne, and Found[26] examined and compared 2,280 simulated signatures against 285 genuine signatures of 19 different authors to determine the significance of pen lifts as predictors of simulation. Approximately two-thirds of the simulations had the same number and placement of pen lifts as the corresponding genuine signature, while 33% of the simulations had more or less pen lifts. Only 22% of simulations had more pen lifts than the corresponding genuine signature. The researchers suggest that pen lifts in isolation ought not to be relied upon to indicate signature simulation.

Earlier research by Black, Found, and Rogers[27] found that pen lifts within a word of the signed name occurred in 51.6% of the 620 simulated signatures (comprised of 20 simulations of the same signature by each of 31 writers) and in 18.1% of the genuine signatures. This result indicates that pen lifts are a part of natural variation in the genuine signature studied but they could be used in combination with other features (such as blunt endings and tremor) to contribute to discrimination between natural and simulated signatures. The authors noted that they could not assess the frequency of the studied features in disguised signatures as the genuine writer was unable to disguise her signature in a way that was comparable to the genuine and simulated signatures.

Two features that have been reported to be observed only in simulated signatures and not in genuine, naturally written signatures are touch-ups (observed in 19% of the 620 simulations) and splices (observed in 98.5% of the simulations).[27] Touch-ups, or retouching, can be defined as an extra line added to a portion of a signature to modify or improve its appearance, while a splice is a pen lift where the pen is replaced over the ink line to recommence the formation.

Research investigating the kinematics associated with the simulation of signatures[28,29] and signature-like handwriting (subjects were instructed to write "George Washington" as though it were their own signature)[30] has found that the average absolute velocity (or average and maximum horizontal and maximum vertical velocity) of simulations is decreased when compared to the genuine handwriting, with a corresponding increase in stroke or total duration of the simulation compared to genuine writing. These kinematic features may be detected in the static handwriting trace as poor line quality (including hesitations, pen lifts and tremor) and blunt beginning and ending strokes.

Although attempts at simulated signatures are generally believed to be able to capture one or the other of the spatial or line quality features of the genuine writing but very rarely both,[17] high-quality simulations of signatures have been reported.[31–35] An example of a reasonably fluently executed simulation of a complex signature is illustrated in Figure 8.6. In this example, an FDE made about 20 practice attempts prior to executing the questioned signature.

(a)

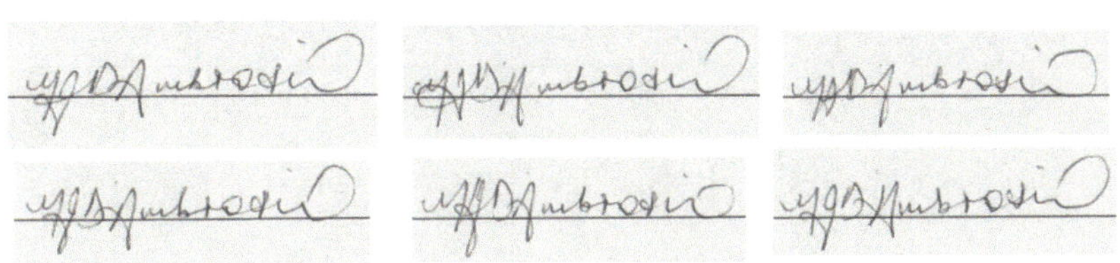

(b)

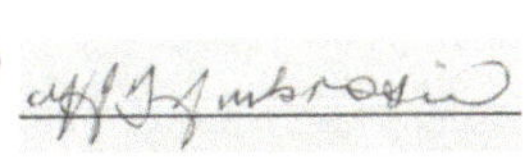

Figure 8.6 Six genuine signatures (a) and a simulation (b) that is both fluently executed and captures most of the spatial features of the genuine signature. This simulation was created by an FDE.

8.2.5 Disguise Behavior in Handwritten Text

Only a small number of studies have been carried out investigating the nature of disguise behavior in extended handwritten text.[36–38] Based on these studies, the common strategies of disguise in handwritten text are reported to be changes to the more eye-catching elements of the writing, including the following:

- Slope (see Figure 8.7)
- Size
- Writing speed/fluency
- Style
- Introduction of unusual letter forms (see Figure 8.8), with these often being capital letters, or via alteration of ascending, descending (see Figure 8.9), commencement, or terminal strokes.

Greater angularity of forms, pen stops, and pen lifts are also often observed, as is the use of the nonpreferred hand for executing the disguised writing sample.

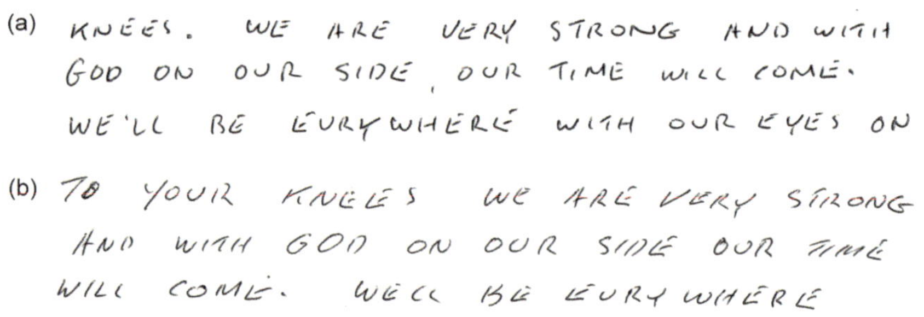

Figure 8.7 Naturally written handwriting (a) and a disguised sample (b) showing a change in slant. Note that construction of letters and more subtle features remain unchanged.

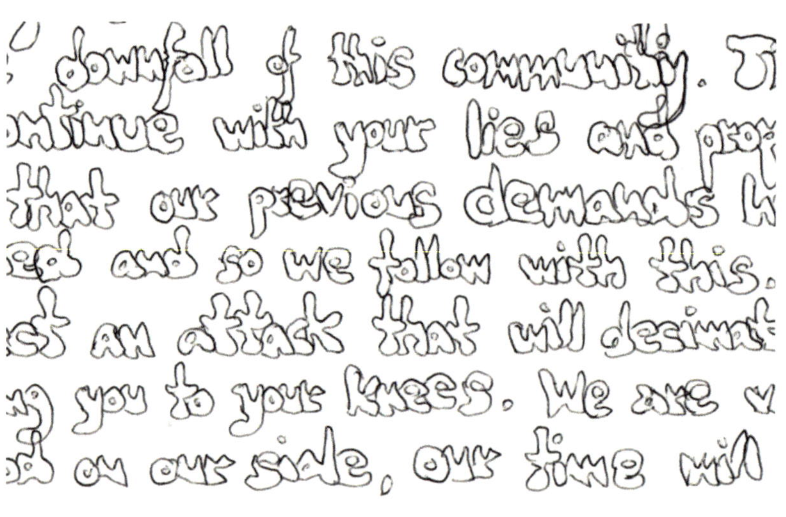

Figure 8.8 An obviously disguised sample where unusual letter forms have been used.

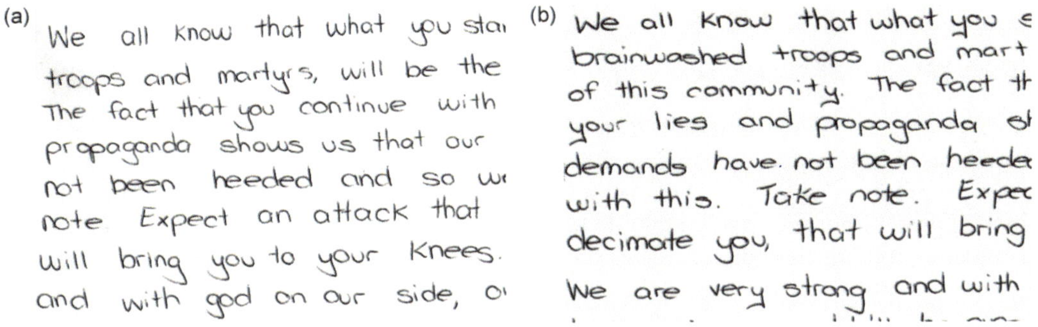

Figure 8.9 Naturally-written handwriting sample (a) and a disguised sample (b) with a minor disguise – the modification of descenders to the letter *y*.

Interestingly, as these features are somewhat subtle, studies have found that changes to the shape and placement of diacritics in Swedish writing[38] and the *i* dot or period in writings in English[36] occurs in more than 10% of disguised writings. Despite their somewhat inconspicuous nature, these features may have been chosen as they are relatively easy to modify.

Some studies report that writers typically do not alter the arrangement of their handwritten text on the page or in relation to printed baselines.[36,37] However, Hull's study investigating the relationship between the number and type of disguise methods used and a writer's years of education reported that 22% of subjects with less than 12 years of formal education altered margin or paragraph indent habits, which was a much higher rate than the other education categories of subjects.[39] This study also observed that disguised samples by individuals with 18 or more years of formal education employed a higher number and variety of disguise techniques than writing by individuals with less than 12 years of formal education.[39]

As noted for disguise in signatures, often a particular disguise method employed by a writer of extended text will result in other features of the writing being inadvertently affected. Regent investigated the handwriting characteristics that accompany a deliberate change to handwriting slant, and found that space used, apparent pen pressure, and formation of ascenders (of *t* and *d*) were affected, as well as the tendency to change capital letter style.[40] The nature of the change in these features was found to be largely dependent on the direction of the change in slant, i.e. a leftward or rightward change.

An early study investigating kinematic features of disguised handwriting found that this unnatural writing is larger and has longer duration and increased pen pressure than normal handwriting. However, unlike studies of disguise methods used in handwritten text, slant was not found to be significantly different in this study.[41]

Similar to the finding relating to disguise in signatures, research has found that some writers are unable to disguise their handwritten text (7% of writers in Konstantinidis' study of 98 Swedish adults).[38] The examples shown in Figures 8.7 and 8.9 would each be considered an unsuccessful disguise as so many of the writer's natural handwriting characteristics are present. Additionally, studies have found that any disguise is rarely consistent over more than a few lines,[36] resulting in internal inconsistency of the disguised writing sample. If this is the case and the naturally written portions of the writing can be extracted from the disguised portions of the sample, a meaningful examination between the naturally written questioned and known material can be undertaken.

8.2.6 Simulation Behavior in Handwritten Text

There have been very few published studies examining simulation behavior in handwritten text, although there are several papers covering prominent cases such as the Howard Hughes autobiography[42] and the diaries of Adolph Hitler[43] and Jack the Ripper.[44]

Leung and colleagues undertook qualitative and quantitative analyses of 20 simulated handwriting symbols or characters (as well as a signature) that contained certain target features which appear in normal handwriting.[45] The 189 simulators in their study were found to focus on the eye-catching spatial features of the writing rather than more inconspicuous structural or dynamic features such as tapered endings and pen direction. These general findings are supported by a later study of the graphomotor features of simulated handwriting, which had subjects write six repetitions of each of a six-word sentence and two isolated words, both in their normal handwriting and attempting to imitate the handwriting of two model writers.[46] Analysis was performed on the two words that were written in isolation and also present in the sentence; no significant difference was found between normal and simulation conditions in the spatial features measured (writing size and slope). Significant differences were observed, however, in the kinematic features of reaction time (time taken to commence the simulation after the subject was issued with an auditory signal), writing duration, and dysfluencies (based on reversals of the velocity signal lasting 10 ms or longer); all of these features were increased in the simulated condition compared to the natural writing. Movement velocity was slower in the simulations.

The reported success of simulators in imitating spatial features needs to be considered within the confines of these two studies, where the target writing was provided in the exact form to be reproduced and consisted of at most a six-word sentence. Additional complexities arise if imitating another person's writing where the desired text needs to be composed letter by letter or word by word. Figure 8.10 illustrates a simulation attempt where some of the gross features of the natural writing have been captured, but the more inconspicuous features of line spacing and line quality have not been reproduced. A lack of fluency in the line trace, a slow, drawn quality and interrupted movements are generally accepted to be key indicators of simulated writings.

However, a simulator may practice writing in the style to be imitated and if able to observe and reproduce some of the more subtle features, a reasonably fluent, graphically accurate simulation may result. An example of such a simulation attempt is given in Figure 8.11.

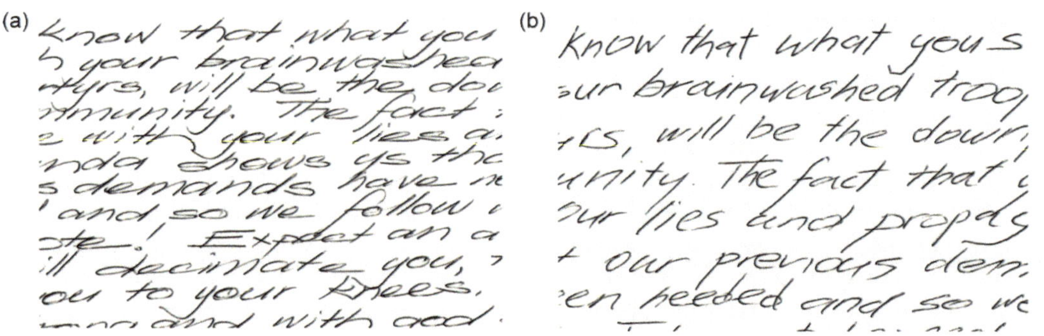

Figure 8.10 A naturally written sample (a) and a poor simulation (b). The imitation of gross features has been attempted (such as slant and letterforms), but subtle habits, including line spacing, have been ignored. The simulated sample also exhibits poor fluency.

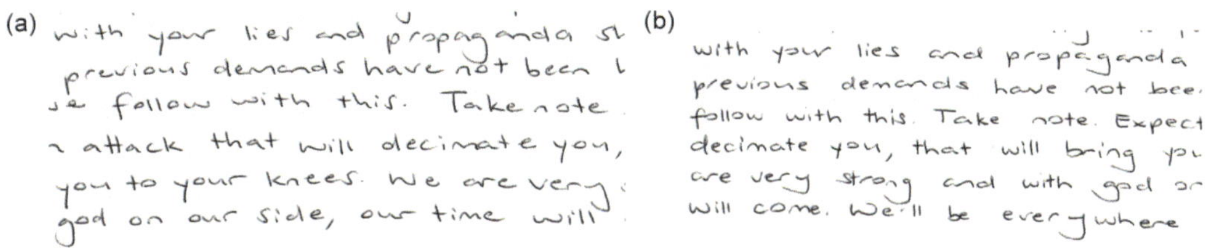

Figure 8.11 A naturally written sample (a) and a good simulation (b). The simulated writing shows reasonably good fluency and similarity to the natural writing in graphic features, although slightly smaller in size and with some subtle differences in forms such as the length of the "tail" of *e*, direction of tick on bottom of *T*, and proportions of *w*.

A comparison of predictor features of disguise and simulation in handwritten text has been reported.[47] The study investigated the relationship between FDEs' process opinions of questioned disguised and simulated samples and the features they recorded as indicative of the particular unnatural behavior. Results suggest that an altered slope in a questioned document when compared to a known writing sample may indicate disguise, while dissimilarities in features of construction and the presence of tremor in questioned writing may indicate simulation behavior.

Unpublished work by this author also investigated the kinematic differences between natural, disguised, and simulated handwritten text (11 sets of writing were examined) and found that disguised writing has decreased velocity and increased duration and normalized jerk (a measure of dysfluency) when compared to natural writing.[48] For simulated writings, the trends were the same but with amplified differences. These results were not constant across all individuals, but across the group, the differences in these features were significant. The findings in relation to simulated writings are also in agreement with the findings reported by van Gemmert and van Galen.[46] Translating these results to features that may be observed by an examiner in a static handwriting trace, decreased velocity and increased dysfluency may be inferred from features such as tremor, hesitations, and an absence of pen drag and tapering of lines. However, the overlap between values of the measures (velocity and jerk) for different writing types will make differentiation between simulation and disguise difficult in some cases.

8.2.7 Success of Simulation

It has been noted that there is a wide range of variation in the occurrence of features typically associated with simulation in the simulation attempts by different writers.[27] The extent to which the generally accepted hallmarks of simulation are observed in a simulation attempt of handwritten text or signatures depend on a range of factors affecting the success of simulation. These factors may include the following:

- Skill and ability of the simulator. This includes both writing skill and artistic ability, which are not necessarily related.[49] A writer may be sufficiently skilled to be able to simulate model writing relatively fluently or with a combination of skilled artistic drawing movement and fluent writing movement, without introducing an abundance of his or her own handwriting characteristics.
- Simulation method chosen (freehand, tracing). Herkt[17] suggests that freehand simulations are the most successful. Mechanically and digitally created simulations are not considered here.

- Complexity (including length and number of turning points, intersections, and pen lifts) and legibility of the target writing.
- Range of variation present in the target writer's normal writing. A larger range of variation allows for a less precise simulation.
- Similarity in style between the simulator's normal writing and the target writing.[28]
- Quality and range of samples available to the simulator.
- Amount of practice for the specific task that the simulator has undertaken.
- Writer skill or line quality of the target writing. Low skilled writing may be easier to simulate. However, if the target writing is tremulous, line quality has been found to be difficult to simulate.[30]

8.3 OTHER INTERNAL OR EXTERNAL FACTORS

The act of writing can be undertaken in a variety of environments, under a range of conditions that affect the writer or writing product either internally (for example, disease or excessive exercise) or externally (such as the writing implement or underlying writing surface). Any one or a combination of these circumstances may lead to distortion of spatial, structural, or line quality features in a handwriting sample. If the condition(s) occurred only in one of the two types of writing samples being compared (questioned or known), this is likely to result in observed dissimilarity when comparing the handwriting. A very brief summary of the effect of some of these internal or external factors on handwriting is provided below. However, it should be noted that for most of the mentioned conditions, research has found that the extent to which a person's writing is affected varies by individual.

- *Different writing posture* may affect the spatial or kinematic features of handwriting, although research suggests that writing under a variety of different postures (including kneeling on the floor,[50] lying down,[51] standing while either writing against a wall, on a handheld support, or with the document on a table[52,53]) does not significantly affect writing features. Increased variation in some features for some individuals may be observed.
- *Writing fatigue* has been reported to affect writers with lower speed and writing skill. Observed changes may include increases in size, length of ascenders and descenders, lateral spacing and speed, as well as a change in slope, departure from the baseline, and an increase in spelling mistakes.[54]
- *Sleep deprivation* may result in increased writing size and spacing, for both extended handwriting tasks and signatures.[55]
- There is an enormous range of *diseases/illnesses* and their effects on handwriting, which is condition- and usually individual-dependent. The handwriting of individuals with multiple sclerosis,[56] Alzheimer's,[57] Parkinson's,[58] and other neurological diseases[59] has been explored. Hilton notes that signatures of the elderly and seriously ill often have one or more false starts and display deterioration in both form and execution, including erratic changes in direction.[60]
- The effects of *alcohol* on handwriting has been extensively studied and found to include increases to size and lateral expansion as well as errors and omissions. Some summaries of studies report a decrease in speed, legibility, and regularity,[61,62] while another review notes increases in writing speed and acceleration, as well as in variation in dynamic features.[63]

- *Different writing implements* can affect the execution or appearance of handwriting. For example, writing with a spray can on a vertical surface may result in dissimilarities in connections, slant, spacing, size, and proportions when compared to conventionally written samples.[64] The writing implement used, such as fiber or felt tip pens, may affect the clarity of some of the finer features of writing, particularly elements of simulation.[65]
- *Restrictions to available writing space* unsurprisingly often result in smaller signatures displaying reduced spacing and speed, although relative spacing is usually retained. The type of constraint and the consequences of violating this (e.g. an official document where the signature will be rejected if it falls outside of the signing area) may be important.[66–69]
- *Unusual backing surfaces* on which writings are made can have varying effects on handwriting features.[70]
- *Poor ball-point pen function* can result in poorly defined stroke edges or voids in the written trace.[65]
- *Interaction between implement and substrate* may result in darker regions in the ink trace that are not the result of hesitations in writing movements but due to sharp deceleration/acceleration points.[71] An acute angle between substrate and pen, when writing on a soft underlying surface, may create "sister lines" parallel to the ink line.[72] Although these may appear similar to tracing guidelines, they can be differentiated since sister lines are always at a fixed distance, parallel to the inked line.[73]

The potential effects of some of these circumstances (for example, the available writing space or poor pen function) on both questioned and known documents may be observable or assessable during the examination. However, an observed feature could be the product of numerous different internal or external factors, so FDEs should take care to consider all possible causes.

8.4 COMPLEXITY OF WRITING

An examiner's assessment of the complexity of handwriting is a key step in the examination process, as the complexity of a sample of writing informs the examiner's expectations regarding the ease of simulation and likelihood of a chance match with writing by a different individual. Harris[74] inspected series of signatures in the same names from a Registrar of Voters and concluded that simple signatures that lack complexity may closely resemble other unrelated signatures by chance. Meanwhile, it is generally accepted that as the amount of writing to be simulated increases, so too does the difficulty of successful imitation.

Where writings display low complexity, such as low writer skill or poor fluency/rhythm, feature similarities between questioned and known material will be expected if the two samples were written by the same writer. However, similarities may also be expected to some extent if the questioned and known writings were written by different people. For writings of low complexity, this may be because the natural writing of someone else is similar by chance, and for writing that displays low skill or poor fluency this may be because someone else has copied the handwriting features of the known writer. The strength of the resulting opinion will potentially be reduced due to the low complexity factor, possibly even to an inconclusive opinion if the examiner determines that the observed features are approximately equally probable under the competing propositions of same and different writer.

The concept of complexity of handwriting is covered extensively in Chapter 10.

8.5 FOREIGN SCRIPTS AND LEGIBILITY OF WRITING

As the examination of writing relies on the comparison of like features, if an examiner is unfamiliar with the script of questioned handwritten text or the text is largely illegible (see Figure 8.12), locating the same character in questioned and known writing samples may be difficult. The examination may be able to proceed in these cases if a typed transliteration of the text is provided to the examiner and if they have access to appropriate known specimen material; for foreign scripts this should include writing samples written in the same script as the questioned document. However, the evaluation of evidence following the comparison of handwritten text in a foreign script may be limited due to the examiner's unfamiliarity with the features observed and their frequency in writings by people educated in the same geographic region. Therefore, it is beneficial for the examiner to have knowledge of writing systems taught and used in the relevant foreign country. This knowledge includes an awareness of the variations in character formation that can be expected to occur due to placement in a word, as well as intra- and inter-writer variation. Ellen describes the process of transliteration and study of specifically collected unrelated writings used to assist in the examination of a case in Urdu.[75]

Signatures written in a foreign script are typically believed to be less problematic for FDEs, especially if the questioned signature is stylized. FDEs, familiar with Arabic signatures or not, were asked to assess the quality of 100 freehand simulated Arabic signatures, based on line quality, form, and proportions.[76] No significant differences were found between the results of the two groups of examiners. Additionally, the ability of FDEs, familiar with Chinese script or not, to detect whether Chinese test signatures were genuine or simulated has been investigated, with no difference found between the two groups of examiners.[77] Proficiency tests have been developed

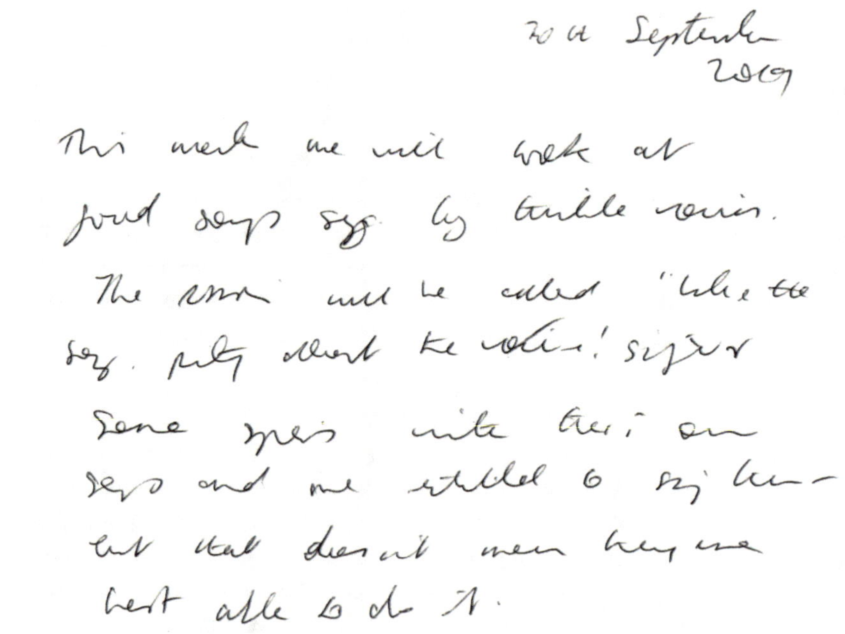

Figure 8.12 A writing sample showing poor legibility; this may affect the interpretation of evidence if distinct characters cannot be identified and compared.

and administered, testing the ability of Chinese-literate and Chinese-illiterate FDEs in examining Chinese signatures and handwriting.[78]

8.6 AMOUNT OF WRITING

An oft-quoted tenet of forensic document examination is that, given a sufficient quality, amount, and complexity of handwriting, the handwriting of different people can be differentiated. However, the determination of sufficiency is a subjective one, made by the examiner, as no explicit standard or guidelines currently exist for either the questioned or known writing required to undertake a meaningful examination. Textbooks suggest varying amounts of known writing as adequate. One suggests from one to two pages of extended writing of a skilled writer and more for other writers;[79] another recommends a working minimum of four to five pages of "carefully selected continuous natural writing."[80]

However, the quantity of questioned or known material can relate not only to the absolute amount of handwritten text present but also the number of repetitions of each character. If certain allographs/numerals are present in the known material once or only a few times, the examiner's ability to determine the known writer's range of variation can be limited. For this reason, Ellen suggests up to five to ten repetitions of the questioned passage should be sufficient as a known writing sample.[81] This range is supported by the results of a small study by Sciacca et al. which aimed to determine the number of samples theoretically necessary to account for within-writer variability.[50] Their research, based on 12 subjects each writing 32 repetitions of two different word-sets, found that around eight repetitions of the same word are required to account for approximately 80% of the within-subject variation when the writer was in a seated or kneeling writing position.

Any absent characters, particularly if present in the questioned writing but absent from the known material, limit the feature pool and may increase uncertainty in the writership conclusion.

The number of known specimen signatures required to undertake a meaningful examination has not been empirically investigated. Hilton asserts that in an ideal world, an examiner should aim to have 50–100 known signatures covering a range of dates, purposes, and probable writing conditions,[82] but in reality, this usually does not happen. There is consensus that 10–20 specimen signatures should form a satisfactory sample.[80,83] However, high complexity and consistency of a specimen signature set may mean that a smaller number of specimen signatures are sufficient. In cases where the writer has a large range of variation, a condition affecting health or motor control, or where simulation is suspected, a larger number of specimen signatures may be required, ideally drawn from course of business documents rather than request writing.

8.7 NON-ORIGINAL DOCUMENTS

Changes in business practices and technology mean that in an increasing number of cases, examiners are faced with non-original documents for examination, including photocopies, facsimiles, and electronic documents or digital images such as scans and photographs captured with a digital camera. Handwriting and signatures depicted on these documents will not contain the same level of detail as "wet-ink" writing on original documents. Line quality, particularly important in signature examinations, may not be able to be accurately assessed from non-original documents other than high resolution scans.

Copies produced on photocopy and facsimile machines are typically affected by both image degradation and distortion. Degradation is a failure to accurately and completely reproduce the original document; fine details such as connections, drag lines, and tapered endings are lost. Lines may become thickened or break up to form dots.[84] Degradation may also affect the legibility of the writing. Distortion, which may be either linear or nonlinear, is a variation to size or shape that may or may not affect legibility.[84] These issues are compounded with each additional generation of copy, by whatever process. However, Gervais reports that up to four generations of photocopies showed no significant distortion/degradation when created at a suitable density setting.[84]

Scanned documents have been typically found to accurately depict spatial features of writing, even at a relatively low resolution of 100 ppi, while black and white scans often result in degradation of subtle handwriting features often associated with line quality.[85] Grayscale scans provide better quality images than black and white scans at the same resolution, with color scans giving the best quality image. However, a first-generation photocopy results in a better-quality image than a low resolution black and white scan.[85]

The loss of feature detail and addition of extraneous features can make the examiner's task of identifying the actual features for comparison in non-original questioned or known material very difficult. This is likely to increase the uncertainty in the evaluation, resulting in a lower strength of opinion.

The ability of FDEs to perform handwriting comparisons on photocopied images of signatures has been investigated. Found, Rogers and Herkt compared FDEs' opinions on 260 photocopied questioned signatures and the same original signatures, in trials separated by 10 months. The questioned signatures were either genuine, disguised, or simulated. It was found that 97.6% (762 of 780) of opinions expressed on photocopied signatures were the same as the opinions expressed on the originals. No errors regarding writership were made for original or photocopied signatures. Discordant opinions were typically due to a reduced strength of writership opinions on the photocopied signatures compared to the original.[86] Further research by Found and Rogers involving 15 FDEs providing writership opinions on 80 questioned photocopied signatures (either genuine or simulated) found an overall error rate of 0.9% and an overall inconclusive rate of 22%.[87] Collectively, this research provides evidence that FDEs are capable of providing opinions regarding writership on photocopied signatures.

The above assumes that the non-original document examined is a true and accurate representation of the original document from which it was created. However, in some cases an original is not available. Handwriting from a legitimate source can be cut and pasted, either mechanically or electronically, onto a new fraudulent document. Close examination may reveal evidence of such manipulation, such as extraneous marks intersecting portions of the writing. In these cases, the examiner may reasonably opine that the document is not authentic, regardless of any opinion regarding the writing itself.

8.8 NATURE OF KNOWN WRITING

An additional consideration that relates to the known writing sample rather than the questioned writing is the extent to which the known writing sample fully and accurately represents the normal handwriting habits and ability of the individual in the relevant period. The known writing should reflect not only the writer's usual habits but also those that are occasional or rare. In other words, the known writing sample must represent the writer's range of variation.[82] Assessing observed feature similarity or dissimilarity between questioned and known writing samples becomes problematic if the known material is not representative of normal writing within the relevant period. This may mean a meaningful evaluation of the evidence cannot be undertaken, or that the strength of conclusion is lowered due to the increased uncertainty associated with the examination.

Already discussed is the issue of whether the known writing may have been created using a disguise. However, there are a few other circumstances that may need to be considered such as the known material not having been written within an appropriate timeframe of the questioned writing or the known writer having more than one natural writing style,[88,89] but the known material does not fully reflect them.

Writing habits may change over time, for example with age, illness, or a change of dominant hand.[90] The effects of aging and associated deterioration of health on writing have been studied,[60,91,92] with some other research summarized by Caligiuri and Mohammed.[59] Although aging tends to decrease writing speed and therefore fluency, the extent to which aging and health-related conditions affect writing varies greatly with the individual writer. The writing of children and adolescents has also been studied.[93–96]

A writer may have different forms of a signature or styles of handwriting for documents of varying importance or type. For example, shopping lists or working notes taken during a meeting may not be written with as much care as a greeting card or an application form. If the questioned and known samples are of different types, dissimilarity may be observed in some features, but similarities in subtle characteristics are expected. A more difficult circumstance arises for the document examiner if a writer has more than one natural (spontaneous or intentional) writing style of the same type. Whiting reports one such example where a suspect writer was able to maintain two different cursive writing styles that were dissimilar in both gross and subtle handwriting features.[89] Moszczynski provides three different samples of one writer's spontaneous handwriting, with demonstrated dissimilarity between the three in features, including interword and -line spacing, margin habits, slope, and letter construction.[88] These features were consistent within each of the three samples. In casework, this situation may be resolved with an extensive sample of known material aimed to be as heterogeneous as possible, particularly if the known sample includes writing with smooth transition from one writing style to another in the same sentence.[88] Although not studied extensively, it has been estimated that it is rare to encounter a person who uses two or more handwriting styles.[88]

For these reasons, handwriting examination opinions are likely to be strongest when the known material meets the following conditions:

- It has been sampled over an extended period of time,
- It brackets closely the time that the questioned writing being compared to it were allegedly produced,
- It contains material of a similar type/importance to the questioned documents (for example, legal documents, informal letters), and
- It is of a sufficient quantity.

If these conditions are not met, the examination may have increased uncertainty associated with it, sometimes to the extent that the examiner may not be able determine the probability of the observed features given one (or more) of the relevant propositions, i.e. the examiner may be unable to express an opinion regarding the potential writer of the questioned material.

REFERENCES

1. Evett, I., Towards a uniform framework for reporting opinions in forensic science casework, *Science & Justice*, 38, 198–202, 1998.
2. European Network of Forensic Science Institutes, *ENFSI Guideline for Evaluative Reporting in Forensic Science*, Approved version 3.0, ENFSI, 2015. Available at http://enfsi.eu/wp-content/uploads/2016/09/m1_guideline.pdf
3. Australia New Zealand Policing Advisory Agency National Institute of Forensic Science, *An Introductory Guide to Evaluative Reporting*, ANZPAA NIFS, 2017. Available at http://www.anzpaa.org.au/ArticleDocuments/220/An%20Introductory%20Guide%20to%20Evaluative%20Reporting.PDF.aspx
4. Matuszewski, S., Types of handwriting samples, *Problems of Forensic Sciences*, LXXXVII, 181–192, 2011.
5. Rile, H.C., Identification of Signatures, In: Kelly, J.S. and Lindblom, B.S., *Scientific Examination of Questioned Documents*. CRC Press, Boca Raton, FL, pp. 89, 2006.
6. Leung, S.C., Fung, H.T. Cheng, Y.S., and Poon, N.L., Forgery II – Tracing, *Journal of Forensic Sciences*, 38(2), 413–424, 1993.
7. Mohammed, L.A., *Forensic Examination of Signatures*, Academic Press, pp. 51, 2019.
8. Rile, H.C., Identification of Signatures, In: Kelly, J.S. and Lindblom, B.S., *Scientific Examination of Questioned Documents*. CRC Press, Boca Raton, FL, pp. 89–93, 2006.
9. Morris, R.N., *Forensic Handwriting Identification: Fundamental Concepts and Principles*, Academic Press, Boca Raton, FL, pp. 173, 2000.
10. Huber, R.A. and Headrick, A.M., *Handwriting Identification: Facts and Fundamentals*, CRC Press, Boca Raton, FL, pp. 279, 1999.
11. Osborn, A.S., *Questioned Documents*, Second Edition, Boyd Printing Co., Albany, NY, pp. 139–140, 1929.
12. Morris, R.N., *Forensic Handwriting Identification: Fundamental Concepts and Principles*, Academic Press, Boca Raton, FL, pp. 172, 2000.
13. Osborn, A.S., *Questioned Documents*, Second Edition, Boyd Printing Co., Albany, NY, pp. 407, 1929.
14. Huber, R.A. and Headrick, A.M., *Handwriting Identification: Facts and Fundamentals*, CRC Press, Boca Raton, FL, pp. 269, 1999.
15. Found B., and Rogers D., Problem types of questioned handwritten text for forensic document examiners, In: A. Marcelli & C. De Stefano (Eds.), *Proceedings of the 12th Conference of the International Graphonomics Society, June 26–29, Salerno, Italy*. Civitella, Italy: Editrice Zona, pp. 8–12, 2005.
16. Bird, C.L., Found, B., Ballantyne, K., and Rogers, D., Forensic handwriting examiners' opinions on the process of production of disguised and simulated signatures. *Forensic Science International*, 195, 103–107, 2010.
17. Herkt, A., Signatures disguise or signature forgery? *Journal of the Forensic Science Society*, 26, 257–266, 1986.
18. Michel, L., Disguised signatures. *Journal of the Forensic Science Society*, 18, 25–29, 1978.
19. Wendt, G.W., Statistical observations of disguised signatures. *Journal of the American Society of Questioned Document Examiners*, 3(1), 19–27, 2000.
20. Mohammed, L., Found, B., Caligiuri, M., and Rogers, D., The dynamic character of disguise behaviour for text-based, mixed, and stylised signatures. *Journal of Forensic Sciences*, 56, 136–141, 2011.
21. Durina, M.E., Disguised signatures: Random or repetitious? *Journal of the American Society of Questioned Document Examiners*, 8(1), 9–16, 2005.
22. Durina, M.E., Drexler, S.G., and Vargas, R., Do people always disguise their writing the same? The trilogy, *Journal of the American Society of Questioned Document Examiners*, 17(1), 25–31, 2014.
23. Herkt, A., Signatures disguise or signature forgery? *Journal of the Forensic Science Society*, 26, 257–266, 1986.
24. Morris, R.N., *Forensic Handwriting Identification: Fundamental Concepts and Principles*, Academic Press, Boca Raton, FL, pp. 169, 2000.

25. Mohammed, L.A. and Cunningham, L., Examination of genuine, disguised and simulated signatures, In: Mohammed, L.A., *Forensic Examination of Signatures*, Academic Press, pp. 65–67, 2019.
26. Dewhurst, T.N., Ballantyne, K.N. and Found, B., Exploring the significance of pen lifts as predictors of signatures simulation behavior, *Journal of the American Society of Questioned Document Examiners*, 18(2), 3–15, 2015.
27. Black, D., Found, B. and Rogers, D., The frequency of the occurrence of handwriting performance features used to predict whether questioned signatures are simulated, *Journal of Forensic Document Examination*, 15, 17–28, 2003.
28. Mohammed, L., Found, B., Caligiuri, M. and Rogers, D., Dynamic characteristics of signatures: effects of writer style on genuine and simulated signatures. *Journal of Forensic Sciences*, 60(1), 89–94, 2015.
29. Chatzisterkotis, T., *An examination of quantitative methods for forensic signature analysis and the admissibility of signature verification system as legal evidence*. Master of Science by Research (MScRes) thesis, University of Kent, 2015. Available at https://kar.kent.ac.uk/54048/
30. Harralson, H.H., Teulings, H. and Farley, B.G., Comparison of handwriting kinematics in movement disorders and forgery, *Journal of Forensic Document Examination*, 19, 41–52, 2008.
31. Buglio, J. and Gidion, H.M., Another adept penman, *Presented at the annual meeting of the American Society of Questioned Document Examiners*, San Francisco, California, 1997.
32. Dewhurst, T., Found, B. and Rogers, D., Are expert penmen better than lay people at producing simulations of a model signature? *Forensic Science International*, 180, 50–53, 2008.
33. Rile, H.C., Identification of Signatures, In: Kelly, J.S. and Lindblom, B.S., *Scientific Examination of Questioned Documents*. CRC Press, Boca Raton, FL, pp. 94–96, 2006.
34. Lee, F., An addition to the fraternity of adept penmen, *Presented at the annual meeting of the American Society of Questioned Document Examiners*, Indianapolis, Indiana, 1998.
35. Mohammed, L.A. and Cunningham, L., Examination of genuine, disguised and simulated signatures, In: Mohammed, L.A., *Forensic Examination of Signatures*, Academic Press, pp. 72, 2019.
36. Alford, E.F., Disguised handwriting, *Journal of Forensic Sciences*, 15, 476–488, 1970.
37. Keckler, J.A., Felonious disguise, *International Journal of Forensic Document Examination*, 3(2), 154–158, 1997.
38. Konstantinidis, S., Disguised handwriting, *Journal of the Forensic Science Society*, 27, 383–392, 1987.
39. Hull, M.J., The relationship between disguised handwriting and years of formal education: Final results, *Presented at the annual meeting of the American Society of Forensic Sciences Questioned Document Section*, Boston, Massachusetts, 1993.
40. Regent, J.A., Changing slant is it the only change, *Journal of Forensic Sciences*, 22(1), 216–221, 1977.
41. van Gemmert, A., van Galen, G., Hardy, H. and Thomassen, A., Dynamical features of disguised handwriting, *Presented at the fifth European conference for Police and Government handwriting experts*, The Hague, The Netherlands, 1996.
42. Cabanne, R.A., The Clifford Irving hoax of the Howard Hughes autobiography, *Journal of Forensic Sciences*, 20(5), 5–17, 1974.
43. Michel, L. and Baier, P.E., The diaries of Adolf Hitler. Implication for document examination, *Journal of the Forensic Science Society*, 25(3), 167–178, 1985.
44. Nickell, J., The "Jack the Ripper diary": History or hoax? *International Journal of Forensic Document Examiners*, 3, 59–63, 1997.
45. Leung, S.C., Cheng, Y.S., Fung, H.T. and Poon, N.L., Forgery I – Simulation, *Journal of Forensic Sciences*, 38(2), 402–412, 1993.
46. van Gemmert, G.P. and van Galen, A.W.A., Kinematic and dynamic features of forging another person's handwriting, *Journal of Forensic Document Examination*, 9, 1–25, 1996.
47. Bird, C., Found, B. and Rogers, D., Predictors of disguised and simulated handwritten text, *Journal of the American Society of Questioned Document Examiners*, 16(2), 13–18, 2013.
48. Bird, C.L., *Investigation of forensic handwriting examiners' skill in detecting unnatural handwriting processes*. PhD thesis, La Trobe University, 2012. Available at http://hdl.handle.net/1959.9/539881.
49. Mohammed, L.A. and Cunningham, L., Examination of genuine, disguised and simulated signatures, In: Mohammed, L.A., *Forensic Examination of Signatures*, Academic Press, pp. 70, 2019.

50. Sciacca, E., Langlois-Peter, M., Gilhodes, J., Margot, P. and Velay, J., The range of handwriting variability under different writing conditions, *Journal of Forensic Document Examination*, 19, 5–13, 2008.
51. Dziedzic, T., The influence of lying body position on handwriting, *Forensic Science International*, 61(S1), S177–S183, 2016.
52. Equey, C., Marquis, R., and Mazzella, W., Influence of writing posture on the dimensions of signatures, *Journal of the American Society of Questioned Document Examiners*, 10(2), 53–59, 2007.
53. Thiery, A., Marquis, R. and Montani, I., Statistical evaluation of the influence of writing postures on on-line signatures. Study of the impact of time, *Forensic Science International*, 230(1), 107–116, 2013.
54. Poulin, G., The influence of writing fatigue on handwriting characteristics in a selected population part one: General considerations, *International Journal of Forensic Document Examiners*, 5, 193–220, 1999.
55. Conduit, R., The effect of sleep deprivation on the spatial characteristics of handwriting, *Journal of Forensic Document Examination*, 19, 29–39, 2008.
56. Wellingham-Jones, P., Characteristics of handwriting of subjects with multiple sclerosis, *Perceptual and Motor Skills*, 73, 867–879, 1991.
57. Behrendt, J.E., Alzheimer's disease and its effect on handwriting, *Journal of Forensic Sciences*, 29, 87–91, 1984.
58. Walton, J., Handwriting changes due to aging and Parkinson's syndrome, *Forensic Science International*, 88, 197–214, 1997.
59. Caligiuri, M. and Mohammed, L., *The Neuroscience of Handwriting: Applications for Forensic Document Examination*, CRC Press, Boca Raton, FL, pp. 131–163, 2012.
60. Hilton, O., Influence of age and illness on handwriting: Identification problems, *Journal of Forensic Sciences*, 9, 161–172, 1977.
61. Huber, R.A. and Headrick, A.M., *Handwriting Identification: Facts and Fundamentals*, CRC Press, Boca Raton, FL, pp. 235, 1999.
62. Phillips, J.G., Ogeil, R.P. and Rogers, D., Alcohol consumption, dependence and the spatial characteristics of handwriting, *Journal of Forensic Document Examination*, 19, 15–27, 2008.
63. Linden, J., Marquis, R., Bozza, S. and Taroni, F., Dynamic signatures: A review of dynamic feature variation and forensic methodology, *Forensic Science International*, 291, 216–229, 2018.
64. Cadola, L., Cuany, S., Weyermann, C. and Marquis, R., Spray paint writing on walls: Is conventional reference material adequate for comparison? *Journal of the American Society of Questioned Document Examiners*, 21(2), 3–11, 2018.
65. Johari, C.K., Ball point pen and forgery, *International Journal of Forensic Document Examiners*, 3(2), 146–151, 1997.
66. Donato, I., Pirlo, G. and Rizzi, F., Characteristics of constrained handwritten signatures: An experimental investigation, In C. Rémi, L. Prévost & É. Anquetil (Eds.), *Proceedings of the 17th International Graphonomics Society Conference*, June 21–24, Pointe-la-Pitre, Guadeloupe, Martinique: Universite Des Antilles, pp. 165–168, 2015.
67. Fazio, K., The effects of constraint on a signature's static and dynamic features, *Journal of the American Society of Questioned Document Examiners*, 18(1), 41–55, 2015.
68. Morton, S., How does crowding affect signatures? *Journal of Forensic Sciences*, 25(1), 141–145, 1980.
69. Simsons, D., Spencer, R. and Auer, S., The effects of constraining signatures, *Journal of the American Society of Questioned Document Examiners*, 14(1), 39–50, 2011.
70. Masson, J.F., The effects of unusual writing position and/or surface on signatures, *Presented at the 44th annual meeting of the American Academy of Forensic Sciences*, New Orleans, 1992.
71. Frontini, S., Giordano, G., Dellavalle, F., Parziale, A. and Marcelli, A., Looking at the ink distribution for assessing writing modalities in forensic handwriting examination, In C. De Stefano & A. Marcelli (Eds.), *Proceedings of 18th International Graphonomics Society Conference, June 18–21, Gaeta, Italy*, Genova, Italy: Zona, pp. 37–40, 2017.
72. Vastrick, T.W., Illusions of tracing, *Journal of Forensic Sciences*, 27(1), 186–191, 1982.
73. Makris, J.D., Handwriting under acute inclination on soft writing substrate versus tracing drawn outlines, *Journal of the American Society of Questioned Document Examiners*, 19(2), 15–18, 2016.

74. Harris, J., How much do people write alike? A study of signatures, *Journal of Criminal Law, Criminology, and Police Science*, 48(6), 647–651, 1958.
75. Ellen, D., Handwriting examination of unfamiliar scripts, *International Journal of Forensic Document Examiners*, 5, 424–429, 1999.
76. Alkahtani, A., The ability of forensic handwriting examiners to judge the quality of signature simulations in an unfamiliar writing system, *Journal of the American Society of Forensic Document Examiners*, 13(2), 65–69, 2010.
77. Spencer, R., Investigating forensic document examiner opinions on signatures in a foreign script, *Journal of the American Society of Forensic Document Examiners*, 17(2), 13–38, 2014.
78. Li, C.K., Chan, L.P. and Wong, S.K., Organising a proficiency testing programme on Chinese handwriting and signature examination in accordance with ISO/IEC 17043 requirements, *Journal of the American Society of Forensic Document Examiners*, 18(2), 29–37, 2015.
79. Harralson, H.H. and Miller, L.S., *Huber and Headrick's Handwriting Identification: Facts and Fundamentals*, CRC Press, Boca Raton, FL, pp. 237, 2018.
80. Lindblom, B.S., Preparation and Collection of Signatures and Handwriting Standards, In: Kelly, J.S. and Lindblom, B.S., Scientific Examination of Questioned Documents. Second Edition, CRC Press, Boca Raton, FL, pp. 129, 2006.
81. Ellen, D., *Scientific Examination of Questioned Documents: Methods and Techniques*, CRC Press, Boca Raton, FL, pp. 83, 2006.
82. Hilton, O., Do we really have adequate signature standards? *Journal of the Forensic Science Society*, 11(3), 145–149, 1971.
83. Mohammed, L.A. and Cunningham, L., Examination of genuine, disguised and simulated signatures, In: Mohammed, L.A., *Forensic Examination of Signatures*, Academic Press, pp. 62, 2019.
84. Gervais, R., A study of photocopier distortion through interactive animations, *Journal of the American Society of Questioned Document Examiners*, 20(1), 23–31, 2017.
85. Masson, J.F., Scanned images: How well do they depict the subtle features in handwriting? *Journal of the American Society of Questioned Document Examiners*, 15(1), 41–47, 2012.
86. Found, B., Rogers, D. and Herkt, A., Comparison of document examiners' opinions on original and photocopied signatures, *Journal of Forensic Document Examination*, 14, 1–13, 2001.
87. Found, B. and Rogers, D.K., Investigating forensic document examiners' skill relating to opinions on photocopied signatures, *Science and Justice*, 45(4), 199–206, 2005.
88. Moszczynski, J., The multi-individuality of handwriting, *Forensic Science International*, 294: e4–e10, 2019.
89. Whiting, F., Alternate handwriting styles - One writer or two? *International Journal of Forensic Document Examiners*, 3(2), 167–175, 1997.
90. Lanners, B.N., A new-dominant hand: Training the non-dominant hand to perform the complex task of handwriting, *Journal of the American Society of Questioned Document Examiners*, 21(2), 13–28, 2018.
91. Kapoor T.S., Kapoor M. and Sharma, G.P., Study of the form and extent of natural variation in genuine writings with age, *Journal of the Forensic Science Society*, 25, 371–375, 1985.
92. Singer, K.A. and Cox, N.M., Study of signatures written over extended periods of time, *Journal of the American Society of Questioned Document Examiners*, 19(1), 5–10, 2016.
93. Masson, J.F., A study of the handwriting of adolescents, *Journal of Forensic Sciences*, 33(1), 167–175, 1988.
94. Cusack, C.T. and Hargett, J.W., A comparison study of the handwriting of adolescents, *Forensic Science International*, 42, 239–248, 1989.
95. Yang, C.Y., Lim, C.C. and Sim, Y.H.Y., A study on the handwriting of adolescents in Singapore, *Journal of the American Society of Questioned Document Examiners*, 19(2), 19–27, 2016.
96. Srihari, S.N., Meng, L., and Hanson, L., Development of individuality in children's handwriting, *Journal of Forensic Sciences*, 61(5), 1292–1300, 2016.

Chapter 9

Forensic Hand-Printing Examination

Linda L. Mitchell

CONTENTS

Hand-printing is the most basic form of written communication in society. Children first learn to read using a hand-printed alphabet of letterforms, which is the basis of almost all modern-day printed materials. The forensic document examiner (FDE) knows that just as with cursive writing, different writers produce different hand-printing, partly depending on where they learned to write and partly due to personal abilities and environment. When a person first learns to write, he or she must recall the letterforms and interpret the shapes, then have the manual dexterity to reproduce them. With practice and improved pen control, the writer begins to create a preferred hand-printing style. Often these preferences are related to social influences or visual appeal. After years of repetition, the mature writer develops habits that allow the FDE to differentiate one person's printing from someone else's, given a sufficient quantity and complexity of writing.

9.1 LEARNING TO HAND-PRINT

Children as young as 3 years old begin to learn to recognize the shapes of the alphabet, and as soon as kindergarten (about age 5), they are learning to imitate these shapes to form words and sentences. Models used for teaching hand-printing vary. Parents' hand-printed samples are likely the first source of letterforms a child sees, followed by the system chosen by each school district. In some school districts, students copy the teacher's hand-printed samples, or the school provides workbooks of a given writing style. These notebooks used to be referred to as *copybooks*. At that time, only a few styles of hand-printing were taught nationwide – the popular styles being Palmer, Zaner-Bloser, and D'Nealian.

Today, other hand-printing styles have been developed for beginning writers; both traditional styles and the new ones are available on the internet. School districts across the country and homeschoolers have adopted online systems into their curriculum, such as *Handwriting*

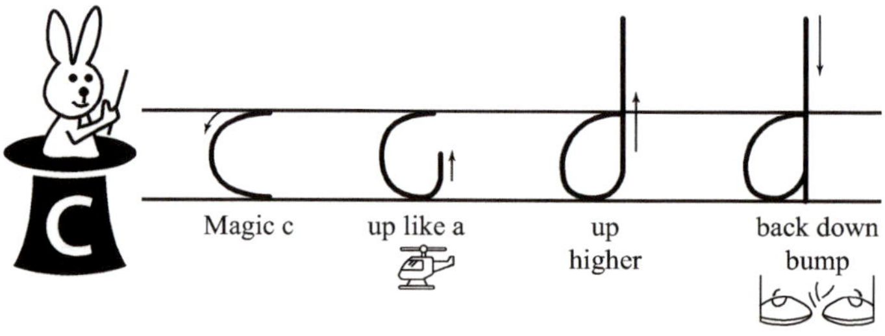

Figure 9.1 Excerpt from *Handwriting Without Tears* workbook describing how to write the letter *d*.

Without Tears.[1] This system includes workbooks, journals, and writing tools appropriate for little hands (see Figure 9.1).

With the development of these writing systems came the expectation of improving legibility or simplifying the writing process for the beginning writer. D'Nealian is a handwriting curriculum in which many letters have added ending strokes. The goal was to help children transition to cursive. However, research has shown that this curriculum had the unintentional effect of causing students to revert to simple printing.[2] Zaner-Bloser no longer uses their Ball-and-Stick method, where printed letters use variations of circles and straight lines to form letters. Zaner-Bloser's approach to lowercase letter formation is now similar to *Handwriting Without Tears* but with different teaching methods and materials.

In today's US classrooms, students begin learning to print the upper-case alphabet in kindergarten. Quite often, throughout the lower grades, hand-printing is incorporated into the reading module rather than setting aside time specifically for handwriting practice. Lower-case letters and spelling are soon added and refined in second grade. In the third grade, keyboarding is added, with varying degrees of cursive instruction. At a minimum, school districts require students to learn to sign their names and hand-print titles on projects or homework to encourage handwritten communication.

9.2 HAND-PRINTING EXAMINATION

Differentiation of hand-printing is essentially the same as differentiating cursive. Huber and Headrick describe 21 discriminating elements in a writing sample.[3] The elements of style include arrangement, class of letterforms, connection, construction, dimension, slant, and spacing. Among the elements of execution are abbreviations, alignment, starts and finishes, diacritics and punctuation, embellishments, legibility, line quality and continuity, pen control, and writing movement. Cumulatively, these characteristics and handwriting idiosyncrasies provide the basis for hand-printing differentiation. Figure 9.2 illustrates several hand-printing characteristics besides letterforms that help differentiate writers.

In essence, the only difference between cursive and hand-printing is the amount of connectedness of the strokes. Connectedness often appears in varying degrees in a writer's hand-printing as illustrated in Figure 9.3. The addition of connecting strokes in quickly-written hand-printing is sometimes referred to as *mixed text* and is considered one of many distinguishing features when the examiner takes into consideration which letters are connected and which are not. Furthermore, the lack of connecting strokes between letters gives rise to other features personal to the writer, especially the location and style of beginning and ending strokes for each letter.

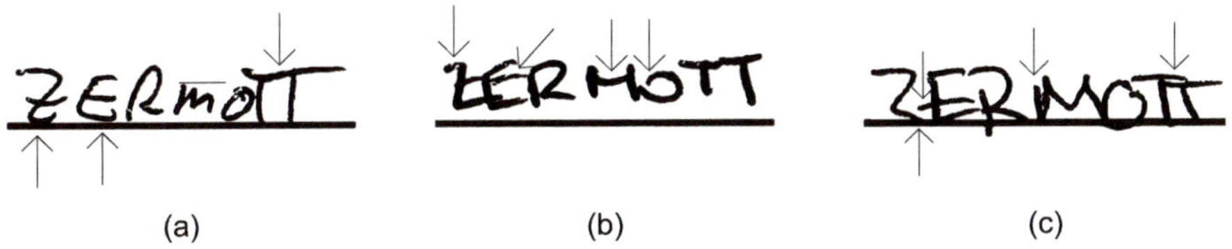

Figure 9.2 Samples of block printing from three different writers. Arrows point to distinguishing features in each: (a) short lower stroke *Z*, hooked lower stroke *E*, short *M*, one *T*-crossing for both *T*s; (b) short upper stroke *Z*, high *E* middle stroke, curved *M*, *O* begins and ends on the left; (c) downward slope of lower stroke *Z*, *E* middle stroke is low and crosses the staff, *M* initial downstroke not retraced, *T*-crossings at different levels.

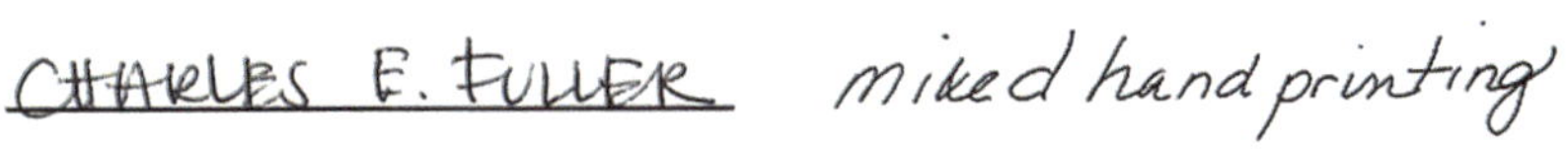

Figure 9.3 The block letters on the left were written quickly, indicated by pen drags that connect some of the letters. On the right is a sample of common connectedness in lower-case hand-printing.

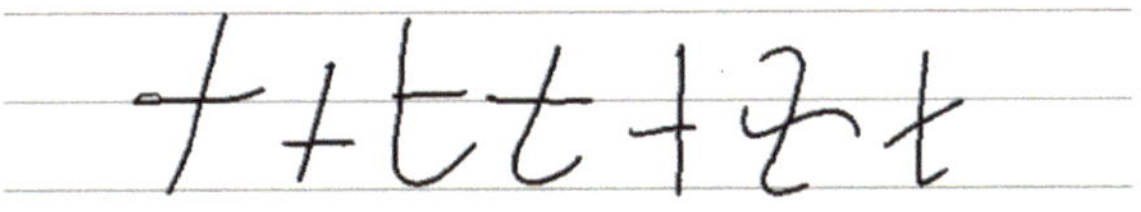

Figure 9.4 Some common examples of the variation in the hand-printed letter *t*.

Even individual letters can take several different forms as illustrated in Figure 9.4. For example, the staff of the letter *t* can be straight or curved, tall or short, slanted or vertical. The *t*-crossing can be high, low, or in the middle of the staff, and it can cross from left-to-right or right-to-left. The *t*-crossing can be longer on the left or right of the staff, or it can intersect in the middle, and it can be straight, slanted, or curved. There can be a difference in the formation of the *t*, depending on whether it appears at the beginning, middle, or end of a word. The letter can be taller, shorter, or the same height as surrounding letters.

Several variations of the same letter are often found in one person's writing. As is true with cursive writing, this range of variation can be one of the strongest features used for showing an association or disassociation between two hand-printing samples. The more variations of the same letter that exist in two samples of writing, the less likely they are to be written by two different people.

9.3 HISTORY OF HAND-PRINTING IDENTIFICATION

The identification of hand-printing has long been considered an integral part of the handwriting analysis process. Osborn dedicated an entire chapter to hand-printing in his 1929 seminal book.[4] He considered the analysis of hand-printing to be "like ordinary script, controlled by habit and often is the means of positively identifying the writer." Osborn defined the examination of hand printing as "the same without the connecting strokes." The same pattern recognition skills used to identify cursive (connected) writing has been applied to the comparison of hand-printing for over a century.

Conway proposed that hand-printing can be identified the same way as handwriting.[5] He stated that a hand-printing sample must include adequate individualities and characteristics in kind and number, and the FDE needs sufficient exemplars for comparison. Later publications authored by Ordway Hilton and Russell and Ralph Bradford echoed these sentiments.[6,7] In the past two decades, the community of FDEs have produced numerous studies and papers with the sole or separate focus on hand-printing.

9.4 RELIABILITY OF FDE EXAMINATIONS OF HAND-PRINTING

It is expected that an FDE with proper training and experience will provide accurate and impartial analysis in a hand-printing examination. Recent studies on hand-printing identification support the assertion that FDEs have the expertise to differentiate hand-printing.

This author tested the reliability of FDEs to identify block hand-printing, a writing style that is often erroneously considered to be lacking in distinguishing features.[8] This blind study offered participants 25 sets of sentence segments that were hand-printed in all-capital (block) letters. Each set was similar in appearance and style and contained one sample of questioned writing, along with known samples from three potential writers. Participants were asked to opine which, if any, of the three potential writers authored the questioned hand-printing. Each potential writer was either identified or eliminated to varying degrees of certainty. Participants answered 92% of the potential questions correctly, confirming that the FDE can reliably identify or eliminate the correct writer. Furthermore, only 2% of the opinions were incorrect. (The balance of the answers was either missing or inconclusive.)

Kam and Lin examined the topic of FDE hand-printing examination proficiency as part of a compendium of their research on FDE skills and reliability.[9] The hand-printed data was analyzed separately from the cursive data. The findings confirmed that FDE performance is significantly better than laypersons and that statistically, there is no difference in the accuracy results for hand-printing and cursive writing.

In another study, Caligiuri et al.[10] investigated whether the strength of the FDE's support for writership or non-writership opinions correlates to measurable kinematic writing features in hand-printing. Their hand-printing study found that examiner opinions of support for or against a common writing source vary according to handwriting features such as stroke height, slant, and straightness error (deviation of stroke trajectory from a straight line). Kinematic models of these features could be used to predict examiner responses for both printing and cursive writing, furthering the understanding of the FDE's ability to differentiate writings.

Current research supports the view that there is little difference in the process and accuracy of examinations of hand-printing and cursive writing.

REFERENCES

1. https://www.lwtears.com/hwt
2. Trap-Porter, J., Cooper, J.O., Hill, D.S. and Swisher, K. (1984) D'Nealian and Zaner-Bloser Manuscript Alphabets and Initial Transition to Manuscript Handwriting. *Journal of Educational Methods*, 77(6): 343–345.

3. Huber, Roy A. and Headrick, A.M. *Handwriting Identification: Facts and Fundamentals*, Tucson, Arizona: CRC Press, LLC, 1999 Chapter 3, 48.
4. Osborn, Albert S. *Questioned Documents*, Second Edition. Albany: Boyd Printing Company, 1929, 421–434.
5. Conway, James V.P. Handprinting and Numerals. In *Evidential Documents*. Springfield: Charles C. Thomas, 1959, 58–73.
6. Hilton, Ordway. Identification of Handlettering and Numerals. In *Scientific Examination of Questioned Documents*. New York: Elsevier Science Publishing Company Inc., 1982, 210–217.
7. Bradford, Russell R. and Bradford, Ralph B. *Introduction to Handwriting Examination and Identification*. Chicago: Nelson-Hall Publishers, 1992, 310–338.
8. Mitchell, Linda L and Merlino, Mara. (2016) A Blind Study on the Reliability of Hand-printing Identification by Forensic Document Examiners. *Journal of the American Society of Questioned Document Examiners, Inc.*, 19(1), 25–31.
9. Kam, Moshe and Lin, Erwei. (2003) Writer Identification Using Hand-Printed and Non-Hand-Printed Questioned Documents. *Journal of Forensic Science*, 48(6), 1391–1395.
10. Caligiuri, Michael, Ommen, Danica, Fuglsby, Cami, Saunders, Christopher, Bird, Carolyn, Mohammed, Linton, and Morris, Jonathan. "Kinematic Validation of FDE Determinations about Writership in Hand-Printing and Handwriting," *Presented at ASQDE Annual Session*, Cary, North Carolina, 2019.

Chapter 10

Handwriting Complexity

Miriam Angel

CONTENTS

Handwriting can be described as a complex neuro-muscular process that becomes an acquired skill. After years of repetition, an extensive combination of writing habits and patterns are executed without conscious thought and become relatively stable. Because the written trace is the result of a behavior, it can be changed, both intentionally and due to unusual writing conditions. This chapter explores the complexity of a handwritten trace in terms of how it is forensically assessed – by its degree of intricacy or, conversely, its simplicity. Simple, low complexity writing will have less features that serve to characterize the writer's habits and is thus more susceptible to effective simulation or coincidental likeness with the writing of another person. Studies have shown that forensic document examiners (FDEs) give more accurate writership opinions when a questioned writing exhibits higher complexity.[1,2] As such, accurate FDE assessment of complexity is important to the reliability of the opinion.

10.1 FOUNDATION FOR COMPLEXITY IN HANDWRITING EXAMINATION

Complexity of movement in general includes the number and duration of movement segments.[3] Although complexity was not explored in detail in early texts on questioned documents, leading authors stressed the need for a sufficient quantity of writing to decrease the possibility of accidental coincidence or undetectable simulation. In his seminal work, Osborn cautioned the examiner to "[a]void giving an opinion on a disputed writing too limited in extent."[4] Harrison mentioned complexity in context of the myriad features that comprise handwriting: "[I]n view of its complexity, the probability of any two persons having handwriting which are so similar that the presence of one or more consistent dissimilarities cannot be demonstrated, is extremely small."[5]

Early investigation into handwriting complexity originated in the exploration of algorithms for automatic signature verification (ASV) systems. In ASV, reference signatures are recorded so the system can "learn" what characterizes a genuine signature by that writer. A reliable ASV system is expected to accept new genuine signatures with a low false acceptance rate and reject non-genuine signatures with a low false rejection rate.

Brault and Plamondon[6] understood that ASV system performance can be improved if a signature can be characterized by how hard it would be to imitate by the average simulator. Signatures that are difficult to imitate could allow for more variation when accepting a new specimen as genuine. They derived an "imitation difficulty coefficient" from numerous writing characteristic criteria, many of which can be related to forensic document examination theory on simulation difficulty:

- *The number, quality, and progression of the strokes of a signature is related to its imitation difficulty.* This conclusion is drawn from the limitations in human memory capacity and the theory that the angles of a signature are the most important details. Examiner and layperson eye-tracking research supporting the latter demonstrated that the majority of visual attention was focused on the features in the middle zone, which has a more concentrated area of pen direction changes.[7] The more content the simulator must memorize and reproduce, the more difficult the task.
- *The more quickly a signature must be produced, the less accurate the pictorial reproduction will typically be.* This is a specific instance of the speed-accuracy tradeoff, a well-established phenomenon in motor control theory.[8] In forensic handwriting examination, accurate reproduction of spatial forms typically requires the simulator to slow down, resulting in a measured, drawn appearance that is detectable in the line quality. If the simulator tries to speed up, the accuracy of the forms is sacrificed.
- *The challenge of simulation is made more difficult by the simulator having to process more than one subtask at a time.* Brault and Plamondon derived this assertion from the theory that there is some degree of parallel processing involved in the brain's retrieval of the abstract motor program for the feature(s) currently being imitated and the message to the muscles required to carry out the action. They also recognized that the simulator is producing a signature based on perceived features and not those represented in his or her own well-learned motor program for handwriting. In other words, the simulator must suppress his or her own natural writing habits while at the same time adopting unfamiliar movements perceived in the signature to be imitated.
- *While executing a simulation, angular strokes in the model signature can be used to "plan" the next movement.* This follows due to the limits of human perception and memory. It is extremely difficult for the simulator to observe, memorize, and accurately reproduce an entire signature without having to pause during execution to plan a subsequent movement. Acute angles are more clearly perceived as stopping points than curved strokes. They provide an ideal resting place for the simulator to pause and assess the remainder of the imitation task because it is more difficult to detect a hesitation or pen lift at the turning point of an angular stroke than on a curve.

Other research in ASV systems has confirmed that the difficulty in software recognition of signatures is not the same for every writer. It is well established that highly variable and low complexity signatures degrade the performance of ASV systems.[9,10] As such, various researchers have adapted their algorithms according to the signature's complexity to significantly improve system accuracy. In one study, performance was three times more accurate for high over low complexity signatures.[11] ASV research has established that, in general, high complexity signatures tend to have more strokes, more legible characters, and a longer execution time; low complexity signatures are likely shorter, written in less time, and illegible.

Studies have also shown that there are few low complexity signatures.[12,13] This reflects the view that most signatures can be recognized as either genuine or simulated.

10.2 COMPLEXITY THEORY IN FORENSIC DOCUMENT EXAMINATION

Found and Rogers[14] recognized that the judgment of complexity is an integral part of the forensic handwriting examination process. Traditionally, it was thought that the examiner's expertise lay in the ability to assess the significance of similar and different individual handwriting features between two sets of writing. Questioning this assertion, they concluded that the notion that handwriting features could be reliably classified as being either class (common to a group of writers) or individualistic was no longer valid in this digital age where there is less concern for penmanship and students are not formally taught to write using a set copybook style. Indeed, Huber and Headrick reasoned that it is the combination of features in a writing that is individual, and the decline of class characteristics makes writings "more readily discriminated from one another than when copybook was the writing design that everyone struggled to emulate."[15]

Complexity theory, developed by Found and Rogers, introduces three relationships involving complexity that are thought to exist:

- *The more concatenated strokes there are, the higher the complexity of the writing.* The segmentation of strokes can be defined by the velocity minima or, in other words, when the writer has slowed down just before speeding up again. This typically happens when the pen changes direction.
- *The higher the complexity, the less likelihood of encountering a "chance match" of features with another writer.* The more strokes and features in a writing sample, the more likely a random sample with the same text by a different writer will diverge.
- *The higher the complexity, the more difficult it is to simulate the writing without evidence of the simulation process.* For example, it would clearly be more difficult to simulate a paragraph of writing than a straight line.

These relationships are supported using the same reasoning described in the preceding section on deriving an imitation difficulty coefficient for ASV systems.

Complexity assessment is significant in the reasoning process behind a handwriting comparison, Found and Rogers theorized. The examination involves two steps. First, the examiner compares the questioned and known writing samples to determine, if possible, whether they are generally similar or different. Each separate feature is not judged in terms of "uniqueness;" the examiner evaluates the similarity and difference of all features of the writing in combination. In the second step of the method, the examiner assesses a set of explanations that describes the overall similarity or difference while considering any limitations of the evidence, such as poor copy quality or lack of contemporaneousness of the writing. If the samples are generally similar, there are only three explanations: (1) the same writer wrote both samples, (2) one sample was written by a different person who simulated the other writing without revealing evidence of the simulation process, or (3) the samples are written by two different people who coincidentally have such a similar combination of writing habits and features present in those samples that they cannot be differentiated. It is the examiner's judgment of the complexity of the writing that is key to choosing which of the three explanations is best supported by the similarities. Alternatively, if the samples are different, the examiner needs to consider whether they were written by two different people or whether the same person wrote both samples, but one or both samples was written under unusual conditions. Evaluation of the evidence in terms of these propositions entails evaluation of the line quality or fluency and, again, the complexity of the writing.

10.3 COMPLEXITY MODELS

Found and Rogers endeavored to define the features that FDEs perceive make a writing sample complex. Beginning with static signatures (as opposed to those signed on a tablet with software recording stroke dynamics), they proposed the following as indicators of complexity: total line length, number of turning points, pen lifts, retraces/overwriting and line intersections, and tapered strokes. These features are similar to those identified by Huber and Headrick as relating to complexity.[16] Through statistical studies involving FDE judgment of complexity as low, medium, or high, they developed a model[17] which best explained FDE perception of complexity, where TP is the number of turning points and INTRT is the number of line intersections or retraces:

$$\text{High complexity}: \ (0.3407762 \times \text{TP}) + (0.2397084 \times \text{INTRT}) - 9.418039$$

$$\text{Medium complexity}: (0.1685134 \times \text{TP}) + (0.08713504 \times \text{INTRT}) - 2.915064$$

$$\text{Low complexity}: \ (0.09862483 \times \text{TP}) + (0.02637828 \times \text{INTRT}) - 1.508095$$

TP is calculated by counting the number of times the pen changes direction and excluding diacritics. INTRT is the number of times a stroke intersects or retraces over a previous stroke. The complexity of the signature will be the one indicated by the label corresponding to the equation giving the highest value (see Figure 10.1 for an example).

Alewijnse[18] also developed a complexity model, but she used different statistical tests and asked FDE participants to rate complexity and signature legibility on a continuous scale rather than the discrete levels of low, medium, and high. She also collected signatures on a digitizer tablet, which allowed the automatic calculation of most variables. The resulting complexity equation included the number of turning points and intersections but also additional features: line length, number of pen lifts, and legibility. Alewijnse also validated the Found and Rogers model by discretizing her subjects' complexity assessments. Her model requires calculations that cannot be made on static signatures, however. Nevertheless, her inclusion of legibility as a complexity factor has proved to be important. Recent research in signature complexity has demonstrated that FDEs perceive legible signatures as significantly more difficult to simulate than partially or fully illegible ones.[19] The rationale is that simulation of legible signatures requires the simulator to conceal his or her own long-established habits of writing the letters in the signature and assume unfamiliar movements at the same time. However, with the decline of cursive writing, this line of reasoning may grow to be outdated since cursive letters not used in one's signature may not become habituated. It should be noted that there is an opposing view, that at least some stylized signatures are more difficult to simulate due to the challenge of determining how they are constructed.

In an effort to further define what characteristics FDEs consider when assessing complexity, Angel and Caligiuri[19] studied kinematic features of signatures written on a digitizer tablet while running MovAlyzeR® software to record the measurements. FDEs rated the signatures' complexity, which was defined in terms of ease of simulation, and the average of the ratings across all

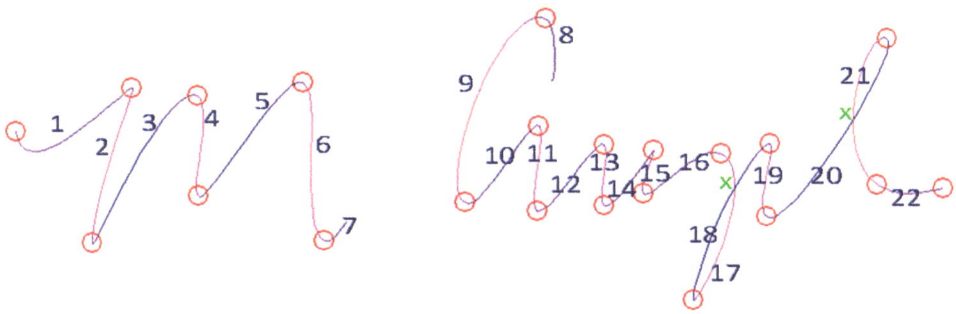

Figure 10.1 To calculate the complexity of a signature using Found and Rogers' model, substitute the number of turning points and the number of retraces/intersections (indicated by an "x" in the figure) into the equations.

$$\text{High complexity}: (0.3407762 \times 22) + (0.2397084 \times 2) - 9.418039 =\sim -1.44$$

$$\text{Medium complexity}: (0.1685134 \times 22) + (0.08713504 \times 2) - 2.915064 =\sim 0.97$$

$$\text{Low complexity}: (0.09862483 \times 22) + (0.02637828 \times 2) - 1.508095 =\sim 0.61$$

Since 0.97 is the highest number, this signature is classified as medium complexity (Image is based on an electronic signature recorded on a digitizer tablet using MovAlyzeR 6.1 software from Neuroscript.).

FDEs were calculated. Figure 10.2 shows examples of signatures rated low, medium, and high. Results indicate that the combination of features that best predict FDE complexity perception differs according to signature style: text-based (legible), mixed (partially legible), and stylized (illegible). These three models respectively accounted for 71%, 79%, and 76% of the variation in complexity judgment. Taking the average of feature measurements across all strokes of a signature, the following describes the combination of variables that explain FDEs perception of higher complexity, according to each signature style:

- Text-based: shorter duration of downstrokes, longer upstrokes, and a greater number of total strokes
- Stylized: shorter horizontal length of downstrokes, higher peak vertical velocity of upstrokes, lower average absolute velocity of upstrokes, and greater number of strokes
- Mixed: shorter upstrokes, steeper slant angle of up and downstrokes, greater deviation from a straight line for upstrokes, higher peak vertical velocity of downstrokes, lower peak vertical acceleration of downstrokes, higher average absolute velocity for upstrokes, and greater number of strokes

As the formulas require calculation of data that was captured dynamically, they cannot be used for static signatures in casework but could be implemented in software that collects electronic

(a) (b) (c)

Figure 10.2 Signatures rated as (a) low, (b) medium, and (c) high complexity.

signature images and data. The availability of an objectively determined complexity measure could be used to support an FDE opinion or compel the examiner to justify why it is inadequate for that specific set of circumstances. Though temporal features cannot be directly calculated on static writing, measurement qualities can be inferred by the FDE.[20]

10.4 COMPLEXITY AND EXTENDED HANDWRITING

To date, research on complexity has focused on signatures due to their being highly habituated and relatively compact in length. As signatures often have numerous connecting strokes, there is typically more information content (in terms of establishing writing habits) in a relatively small amount of writing. However, complexity theory applies to extended handwriting, both cursive and hand-printing. It was mentioned previously that a wide range of variation can lead to what is considered lower complexity in ASV systems. However, in forensic document examination, variation can also provide strong association with one writer if that variation is seen in both the known and questioned samples. Handwritten paragraphs, sentences, or form entries will often exhibit a sufficient range of variation to characterize the writer's habits (see Chapter 9 for more explanation).

10.5 FACTORS RELATED TO COMPLEXITY

It is important to understand that complexity is one of several interrelated features that can inform an FDE opinion on the ease of successful imitation of a signature. In ASV research, complexity is shown to have a strong correlation with variability among the reference signatures, where the higher the complexity, the lower the variance.[21] The rationale is similar in forensic document examination theory. Signatures are easier to simulate when there is inconsistency in the known signatures because the large range of variation gives the imitator room to err but still fit within that range.[22]

Huber and Headrick point out that complexity "must be appraised in conjunction with the presence or absence of fluency" when assessing simulation difficulty.[23] Thus, a writer's skill is also a factor related to complexity. Low skill writing exhibits less fluency than the average writer, allowing the imitator to more slowly and carefully reproduce the features.

Another factor that influences simulation difficulty is the presence of inconspicuous features. Simulators tend not to notice subtle details present in the writing; they focus on prominent features instead.[24]

10.6 CONCLUSION

Writing complexity has been shown to involve, or be closely related to, the following writing characteristics:

- Number of strokes
- Amount of retracing and overwriting
- Speed and fluency
- Writer skill

- Connectedness of strokes
- Curvature and length of strokes
- Variation present in the known writing
- Legibility
- Whether certain features are salient or inconspicuous.

Exploration of the nature of handwriting complexity increases FDE knowledge of what constitutes an adequate quality and quantity of writing to (1) establish a writer's distinctive habits and (2) provide defense against successful simulation by another person. Recognition of the possible limitations in a handwriting examination distinguishes the FDE from the nonexpert. Proficiency tests taken by both FDEs and laypeople demonstrate that FDEs possess superior skills in differentiating writing; laypeople tend to *over-associate* or assert that two samples by different writers are written by the same person (see Chapter 13). Indeed, there are some similarities between everyone's writing; otherwise we would not be able to read what each other writes. Thus, similarity between two writing samples is not sufficient to determine they were written by the same person. Complexity is key to the FDE's ability to accurately address writership questions.

REFERENCES

1. Jodi Sita, Bryan Found, and Douglas K. Rogers, "Forensic Handwriting Examiners' Expertise for Signature Comparison," *Journal of Forensic Sciences*, vol. 47 no. 5 (September 2002), 1117–1124.
2. Mara Merlino, "Validity, Reliability, Accuracy, and Bias in Forensic Signature Identification," accessed October 4, 2019, https://www.ncjrs.gov/pdffiles1/nij/grants/248565.pdf.
3. Richard A. Schmidt and Timothy D. Lee, *Motor Control and Learning: A Behavioral Emphasis*, (Champaign, IL: Human Kinetics, 5th edition, 2011), 196.
4. Albert S. Osborn, *Questioned Documents*, (Albany: Boyd Printing Co., 2nd Edition, 1910), 8.
5. Wilson R. Harrison, *Suspect Documents*, (London: Sweet & Maxwell Limited, 2nd Edition, 1958), 342.
6. Jean-Jules Brault and Réjean Plamondon, "Complexity Measure of Handwritten Curves: Modeling of Dynamic Signature Forgery," *IEEE Transactions on Systems, Man, and Cybernetics*, vol. 23 no. 2 (March/April 1993), 400–413.
7. Adrian G. Dyer, Bryan Found, and Doug Rogers, "Visual Attention and Expertise for Forensic Signature Analysis," *Journal of Forensic Sciences*, vol. 51 no. 6 (November 2006), 1397–1404.
8. Richard A. Schmidt and Timothy D. Lee, *Motor Control and Learning: A Behavioral Emphasis*, (Champaign, IL: Human Kinetics, 5th edition, 2011), 35.
9. F. Alonso-Fernandez, M.C. Fairhurst, J. Fierrez, and J. Ortega-Garcia, "Impact of Signature Legibility and Signature Type in Off-Line Signature Verification," *2007 Biometrics Symposium*, Baltimore, MD, 2007, 1–6.
10. Nesma Houmani, Sonia Garcia-Salicetti, and Bernadette Dorizzi, "Novel Personal Entropy Measure Confronted with Online Signature Verification Systems' Performance," *2008 IEEE Second International Conference on Biometrics: Theory, Applications and Systems*, Arlington, VA, 2008, 1–6.
11. Ruben Tolosana, Ruben Vera-Rodriguez, Richard Guest, Julian Fierrez, Javier Ortega-Garcia, "Complexity-Based Biometric Signature Verification," *2017 14th IAPR International Conference on Document Analysis and Recognition (ICDAR)*, Kyoto, 2017, 195–200.
12. Tahnee Dewhurst, Bryan Found, and Doug Rogers, "Relationship between Quantitatively Modelled Signature Complexity Levels and Forensic Document Examiners' Qualitative Opinions on Casework," *Journal of Forensic Document Examination*, vol. 18 (December 2006), 21–40.
13. Nesma Houmani and Sonia Garcia-Salicetti, "On Hunting Animals of the Biometric Menagerie for Online Signature," *PLoS ONE*, vol. 11 no. 4 (2016), e0151691. https://doi.org/10.1371/journal.pone.0151691

14. Bryan Found and Douglas Rogers, "Consideration of the Theoretical Basis of Forensic Handwriting Examination," *International Journal of Forensic Document Examiners*, vol. 4 no. 2 (April/June 1998), 109–118.
15. Roy A. Huber and A.M. Headrick, *Handwriting Identification: Facts and Fundamentals*, (Boca Raton, FL: CRC Press, 1999), 34.
16. Roy A. Huber and A.M. Headrick, *Handwriting Identification: Facts and Fundamentals*, (Boca Raton, FL: CRC Press, 1999), 36–37.
17. Bryan Found and Douglas Rogers, "Statistical Modelling of Experts' Perceptions of the Ease of Signature Simulation," *Journal of Forensic Document Examination*, vol. 11 (1998), 86.
18. Linda C. Alewijnse, C. Eliza van den Heuvel, Reinoud Stoel, and Katrin Franke, "Analysis of Signature Complexity," *Journal of Forensic Document Examiners*, vol. 21 (2011), 37–49.
19. Miriam Angel, Michael P. Caligiuri, and Melvin Cavanaugh, "Kinematic Models of Subjective Complexity in Handwritten Signatures," *Journal of the American Society of Questioned Document Examiners*, vol. 20 no. 2 (2017), 9.
20. R. Brent Ostrum and Tobin Tanaka, "Another Look at Handwriting Movement," *Journal of the American Society of Forensic Document Examiners*, vol. 9 no. 2 (December 2006), 57–67.
21. Christian Kahindo, Sonia Garcia-Salicetti, and Nesma Houmani, "Signature Complexity Measure to Select Reference Signatures for Online Signature Verification," *2015 International Conference of the Biometrics Special Interest Group (BIOSIG)*, Darmstadt, 2015, 1–8.
22. Liv Cadola, Pierre Margot, and Raymond Marquis, "Are Simple Signatures So Easy to Simulate?" *Journal of the American Society of Questioned Document Examiners*, vol. 16 no. 2 (December 2013), 3–11.
23. Roy A. Huber and A.M. Headrick, *Handwriting Identification: Facts and Fundamentals*, (Boca Raton, FL: CRC Press, 1999), 35.
24. S.C. Leung, Y.S. Cheng, H.T. Fung, and N.L. Poon, "Forgery I—Simulation," *Journal of Forensic Sciences*, vol. 38 no. 2 (March 1993), 402–412.

Chapter 11

Examination of Foreign-Influenced Handwriting

Elaine X. Wooton and Donna O. Eisenberg

CONTENTS

One of the ever-increasing challenges to forensic document examiners (FDEs) is the shift away from the teaching and strict adherence of handwriting from copybook systems, combined with the movement of people between countries and within diverse countries (like the United States). This chapter describes approaches and limitations for the FDE involved in the examination of handwriting from other countries, as well as from those who use different alphabets or writing systems.

In typical handwriting cases, FDEs assess not only the combination of handwriting habits and letterforms but also additional evidence within the document. The goal of this chapter is to describe a broader approach to foreign handwriting cases with the view toward assessment of the totality of the document, even when the examiner is unfamiliar with the particular copybook style, the language, or even the writing system.

11.1 FOREIGN-INFLUENCED HANDWRITING

The term "foreign-influenced handwriting" can include writings in alphabets or writing systems that are both familiar and unfamiliar to the FDE. The broad categories of writing systems used around the world include Latin alphabet-English, Latin alphabet-extended (to include additional allographs and accents), non-Latin alphabetic, and idiographic (see Figure 11.1).

The challenges vary when dealing with each category. Comparing handwriting in Latin-English to Latin-extended is often straightforward because the FDE is familiar with the basic letterforms of the alphabet and can determine which letters to compare. On the other hand, as

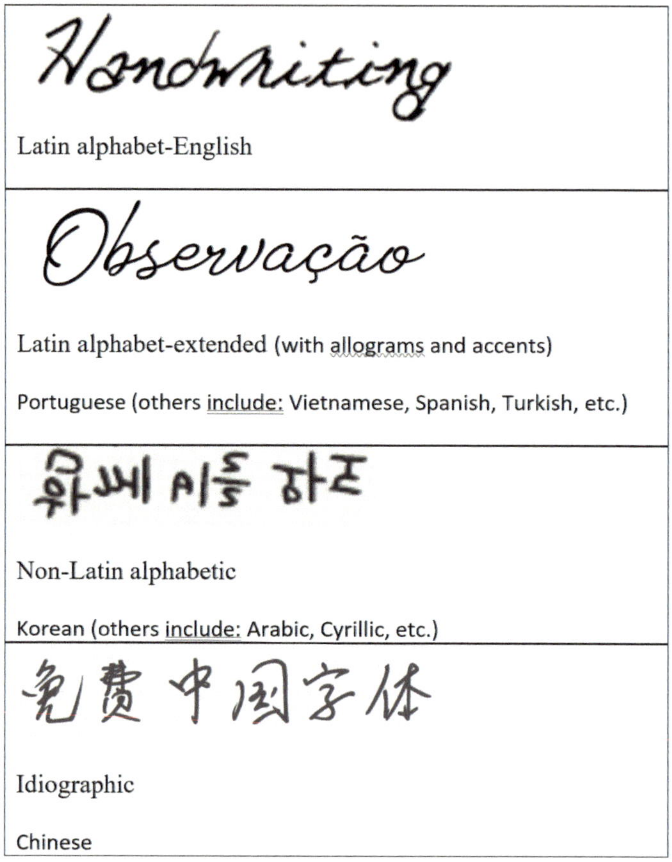

Figure 11.1 Examples of the four categories of writing systems.

illustrated in the two pairs of Latin and Cyrillic writing in Figures 11.2 and 11.3, Latin alphabet writings have limited comparable letterforms when compared to non-Latin alphabet writings.

The need to consider foreign influence in handwriting is certainly not a new issue, particularly in countries that have historically welcomed large numbers of immigrants. Ever increasing global travel and migration make encountering such writing more likely. The handwriting of immigrant populations can be influenced not only by handwriting characteristics reminiscent of their home country, but might also depend on the individual's participation in elementary

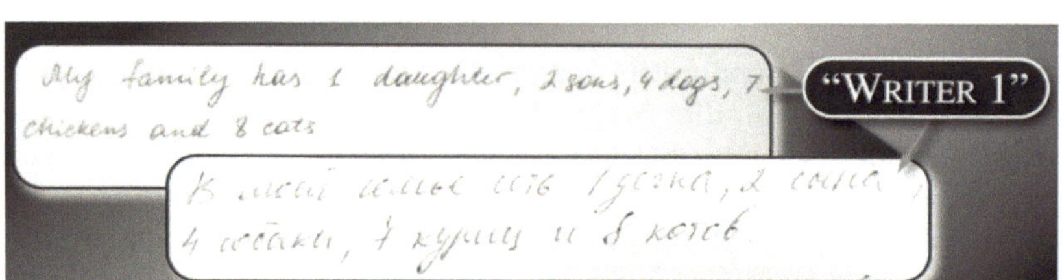

Figure 11.2 Writer 1 has limited comparable features between Cyrillic and English handwriting.

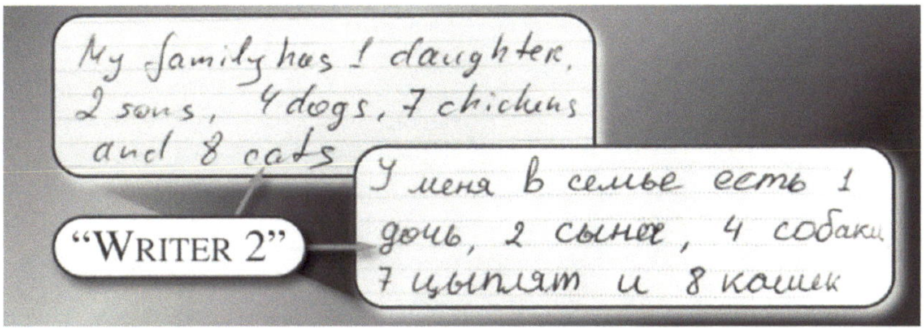

Figure 11.3 Writer 2, a different writer than in Figure 11.2, also exhibits limited comparable features between Cyrillic and English handwriting.

education or work environment, as well as the age and the amount of time since the immigrant's arrival. The resulting handwriting might include only a hint of an individual's prior handwriting; it could be entirely different from the handwriting typically encountered in their new home; or include a mix of features. In more linguistically homogenous countries with a single language/alphabet and only a limited number of copybook systems in the schools, the foreign influence in handwritten material will likely be more apparent.

Given diverse populations (in the US and many other countries), FDEs may erroneously evaluate features as uncommon when they are in reality caused by foreign influence. Foreign influence in a submitted handwriting sample can be detected by consulting laboratory reference collections, an examiner's personal collection, conference presentations and papers, online references and imagery, or reference books. In some instances, it may be necessary for a case submitter to obtain handwriting from additional individuals of the same national/regional origin, age, and educational background.

The examination of stylized foreign-influenced signatures is less problematic than foreign-influenced cursive handwriting or hand-printing. The FDE can conduct a signature comparison purely from a pattern evidence perspective. As the allographs of the signatures are not discernable or readily recognizable, they can be treated as stylized signatures. However, for text-based (legible) signatures, the FDE would benefit from knowing whether a particular formation in the signature is a copybook allograph or a stylized element. Figures 11.4 and 11.5 each depict the Portuguese-language signatures from a single writer. Each example shows the individual

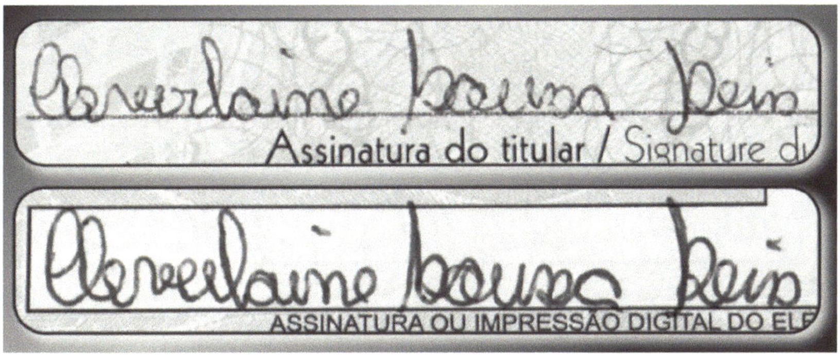

Figure 11.4 Portuguese (Brazilian) signatures.

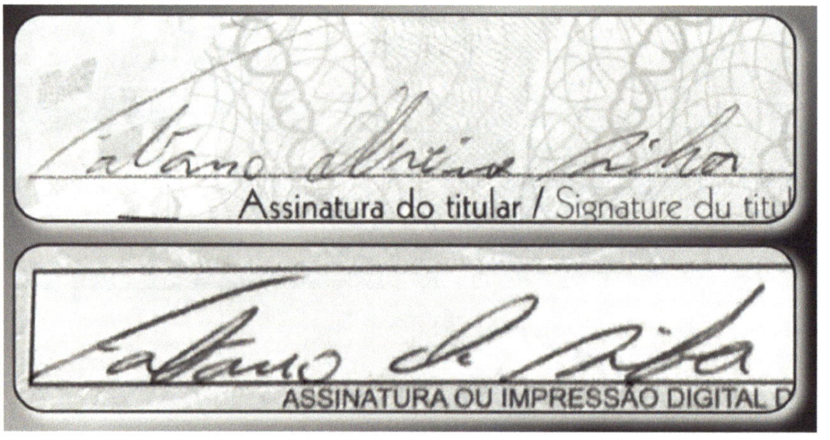

Figure 11.5 Portuguese (Brazilian) signatures of a different person than the writer of the signatures in Figure 11.4.

writer's tendency to use either copybook or stylized features. In Figure 11.6, the Cyrillic signatures demonstrate a very narrow range of variation, are nearly legible, and include cursive characters that are recognizable as letters of the Cyrillic alphabet.

It should be noted that a given individual can have multiple signature forms: a stylized signature, a formal signature (often with embellishments), and a written version of their name. These different forms are typically not comparable to each other.

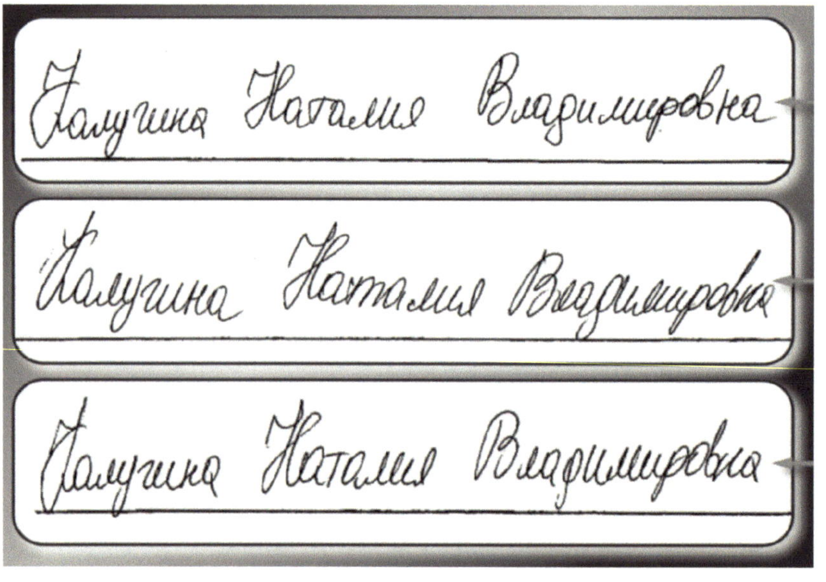

Figure 11.6 Signatures from the same writer, with legible letters of the Cyrillic alphabet.

11.2 SUPPORTING BASIS FOR FDEs TO EXAMINE FOREIGN HANDWRITING CASES

A forensic document examination involves the assessment of many handwriting features beyond letterforms such as:

- Arrangement (use of the paper's dimensions—margins, spacing, layout, format)
- Baseline adherence
- Pen pressure
- Relative letter heights
- Slant
- Spacing
- Speed
- Use and position of diacritics and punctuation

Consequently, regardless of familiarity with a writing system or copybook letterforms and elements, it is possible for FDEs to make determinations regarding writership by evaluating the features listed above. Two limited studies on the accuracy and reliability of FDE handwriting examinations on unfamiliar writing systems found that FDEs are often able to successfully assess writership, regardless of their familiarity with the writing system.[1,2] However, until additional research is completed, there remains uncertainty about the evaluation of signatures, handwriting and hand-printing in unfamiliar writing systems. In the interim, conservatism regarding opinions is warranted.

11.3 HANDLING FOREIGN HANDWRITING CASES

There are two stages in the submission of a handwriting case when the FDE should inquire about possible foreign influence in the handwriting to be examined. The first is at initial contact when the task-relevant submission information indicates that there is or might be foreign influence in the handwriting. The second is upon the initial assessment of the submitted handwriting if it contains an unfamiliar handwriting style or handwriting features that appear uncommon. At this point, the examiner should review existing reference materials from those sources described above to determine whether those features have been the subject of research in the past. In both scenarios, the inquiries must be rather detailed in order to ascertain the possible origin of the foreign influence and should include information concerning where the writer was born/educated, where the writer's parents and siblings were born/educated, and whether someone from another country/region helped teach them how to write (e.g., a grandmother or babysitter).

To examine foreign-influenced handwriting:

- For English and other Latin alphabet handwriting, ascertain which letter of the alphabet each letterform represents, and then compare like-to-like letterforms and features.
- For non-Latin alphabet handwriting, become familiar with the writing system, use an alphabet chart to determine letterforms, engage a translator to annotate a copy of the writing (dividing letters from each other and marking which letters correspond to those in the questioned material), and obtain writing samples which will enable the FDE to assess inter-writer variation. Local religious and community groups are excellent resources.

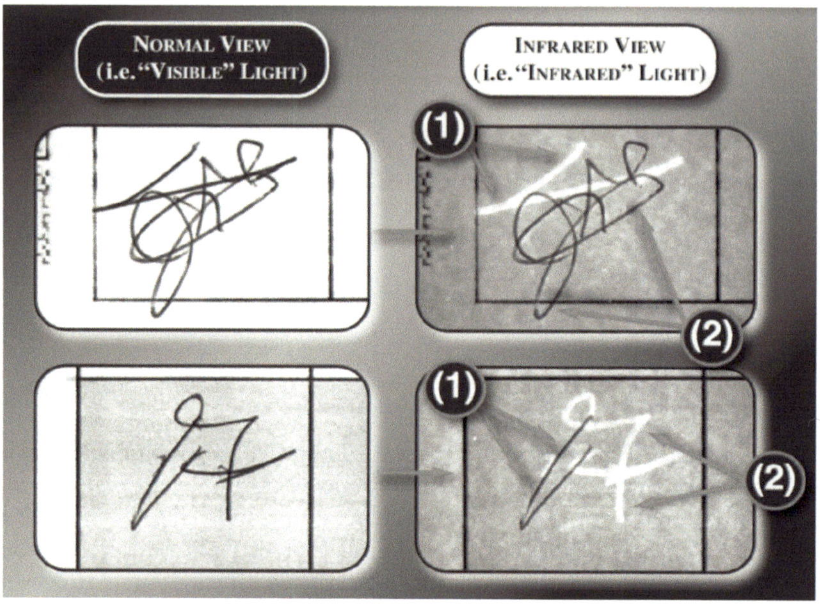

Figure 11.7 Visually similar inks were differentiated by instrumental examination.

While unfamiliarity with letterforms can be a challenge in foreign-influenced handwriting cases, many other features considered and assessed by document examiners are the same, regardless of the alphabet or writing system used. Likewise, the methods and evidence of simulations are the same regardless of language or script.

Although it is likely that an FDE's unfamiliarity with a writing system or alphabet will result in a qualified opinion regarding writership, or perhaps even an opinion of no-conclusion, such examinations and opinions are nonetheless valuable. That is, an examination, report, and/or testimony provided by an FDE could prevent investigators, judges, and juries from consciously or unconsciously conducting their own evaluation without proper knowledge of the limitations or an accurate basis for their conclusions.

In most instances, the FDE will evaluate handwriting cases as questioned document cases rather than focusing solely on the handwriting. Features within the documents that are pertinent to the handwriting examination can be enhanced or revealed using instrumentation, potentially revealing demonstrable physical evidence of manipulation or fabrication. For example, in Figure 11.7, visually similar inks within single signatures were differentiated by instrumental examination. The wide range of possible examinations is covered elsewhere in this text but includes evidence of tracing or simulation, over-writings, patching, indentations, insertions, misalignments, anachronistic dating, and alterations.

11.4 FOREIGN-INFLUENCED WRITING RESOURCES

As described above, FDEs can supplement their knowledge and experience with case-specific research. Such research should enable the FDE to learn how the letters are formed in the alphabets used by people from the influencing countries or regions. Depending on the age of the

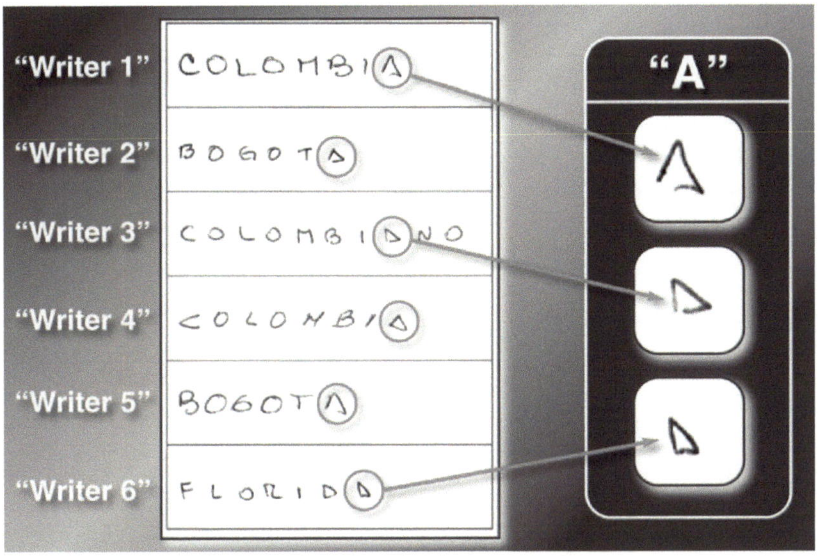

Figure 11.8 Class characteristics found in the writing of Columbian citizens traveling to the US. This Figure and all subsequent Figures were prepared from a collection of US immigration arrival cards maintained by the US Department of Homeland Security. To compile these images, the authors reviewed arrival cards from four countries, selected a small number of handwriting features within each country which appeared uncommon, and then reviewed the entire set of cards completed by individuals from that country to determine whether there were multiple instances of those seemingly uncommon letterforms. As shown, features that appeared "unusual" were in fact found to be class or relatively common characteristics.

document or the writer, reviews of copybooks from those areas may still be useful. For newer written materials, there may be computer applications (such as those that provide handwriting instruction on a mobile device) that allow an examiner to gain knowledge about an unfamiliar writing system. Reviewing reference materials regarding specific letters can provide an FDE with the basis for assessing letterforms in submitted case materials. For example, Figures 11.8–11.15 depict variations of some letters in foreign-influenced English handwriting.

By reviewing all available reference materials, as well as the handwriting samples collected specifically for a case, an examiner can more accurately evaluate whether features are common to a group, thereby avoiding the mistake of viewing them as distinctive and giving them undue weight in the evaluation. Therefore, it is critical that these resources be reviewed in cases that include handwriting features that are unfamiliar to the FDE.

11.5 CONCLUSION

It is recommended FDEs gather task-relevant information and examine all aspects of the questioned document before rejecting a case due to unfamiliarity with features in a writing sample. In some instances, FDEs can conduct foreign-influenced handwriting and signature examinations and report their findings regarding writership. When writership cannot be determined, FDEs can still conduct document examinations and provide results regarding the authenticity of documents, the presence of alterations, observations regarding the production method or

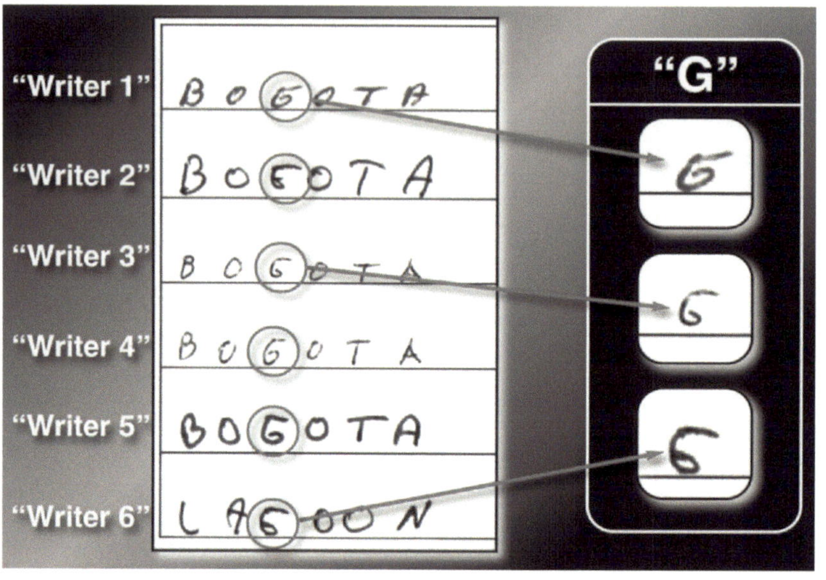

Figure 11.9 Additional class characteristics found in writers from Columbia.

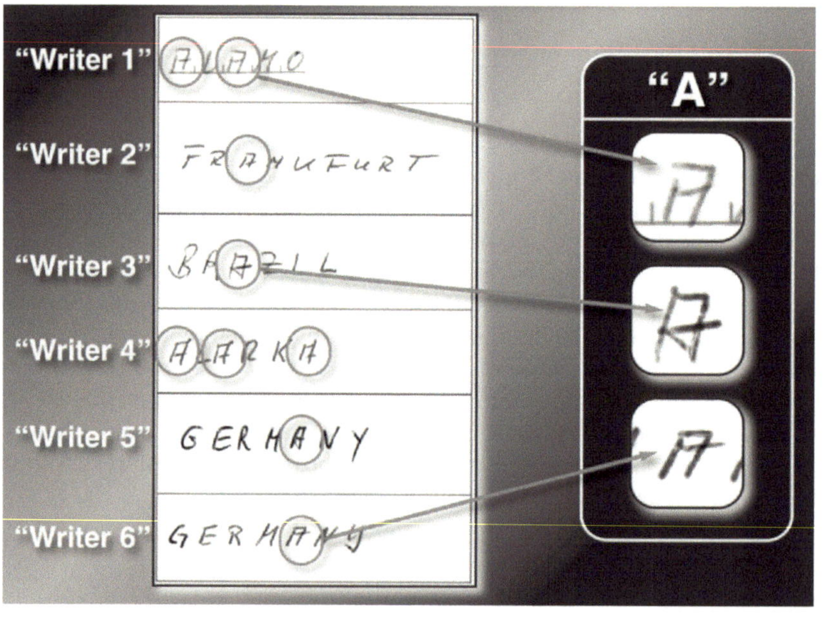

Figure 11.10 Class characteristics found in the writing of German citizens traveling to the US.

handling, or information regarding the preparation of the documents. Whether or not a finding is possible regarding writership, observations and study charts made during a forensic examination could provide investigators and the triers of fact with critically helpful and revealing information.

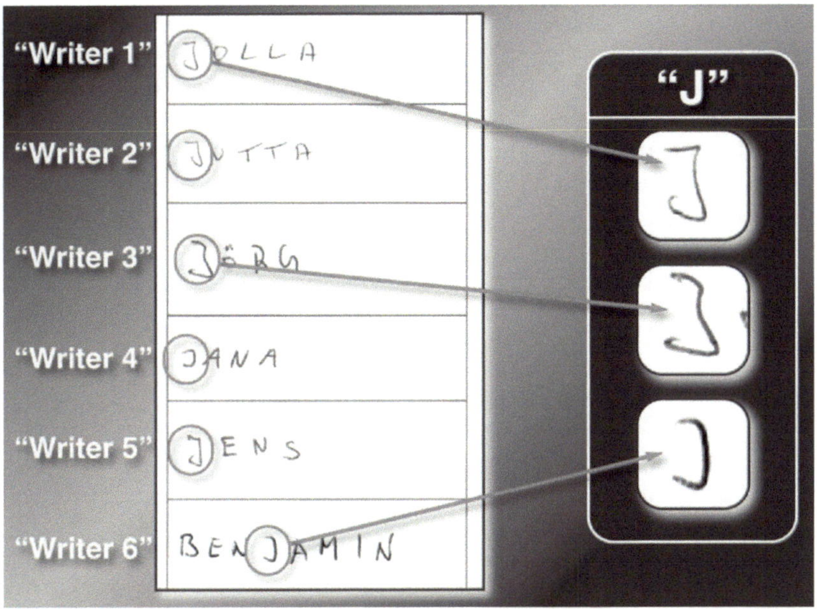

Figure 11.11 Additional class characteristics found in writers from Germany.

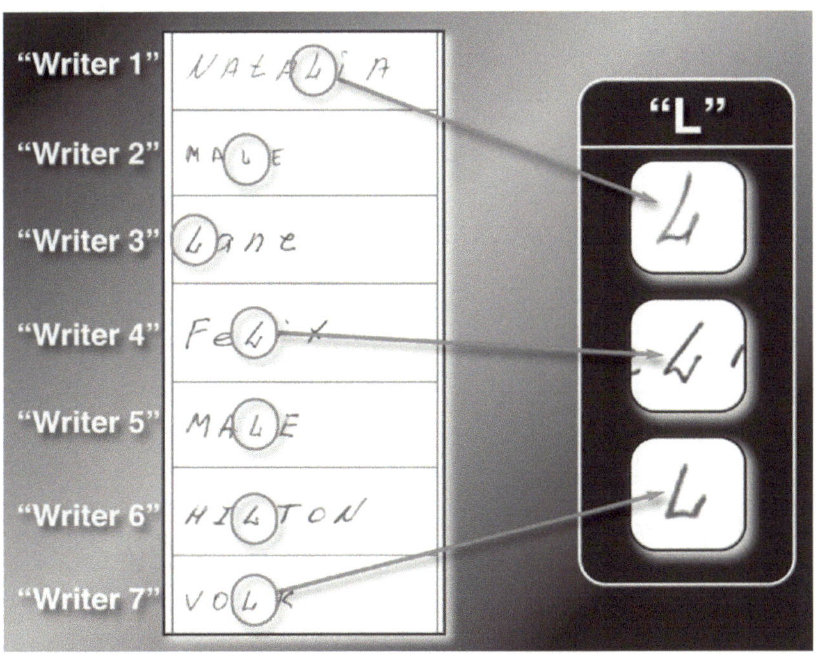

Figure 11.12 Class characteristics found in the writing of Russian citizens traveling to the US.

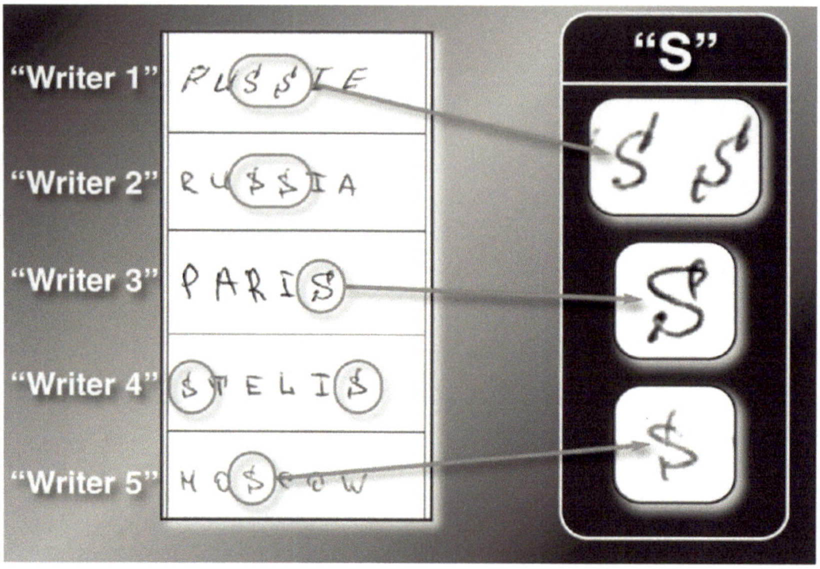

Figure 11.13 Additional class characteristics found in writers from Russia.

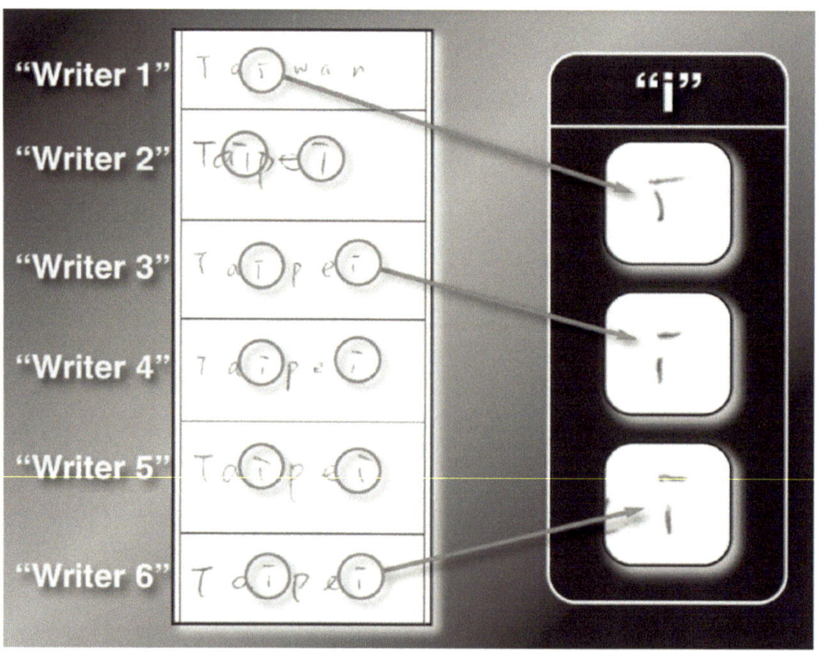

Figure 11.14 Class characteristics found in the writing of Taiwanese citizens traveling to the US.

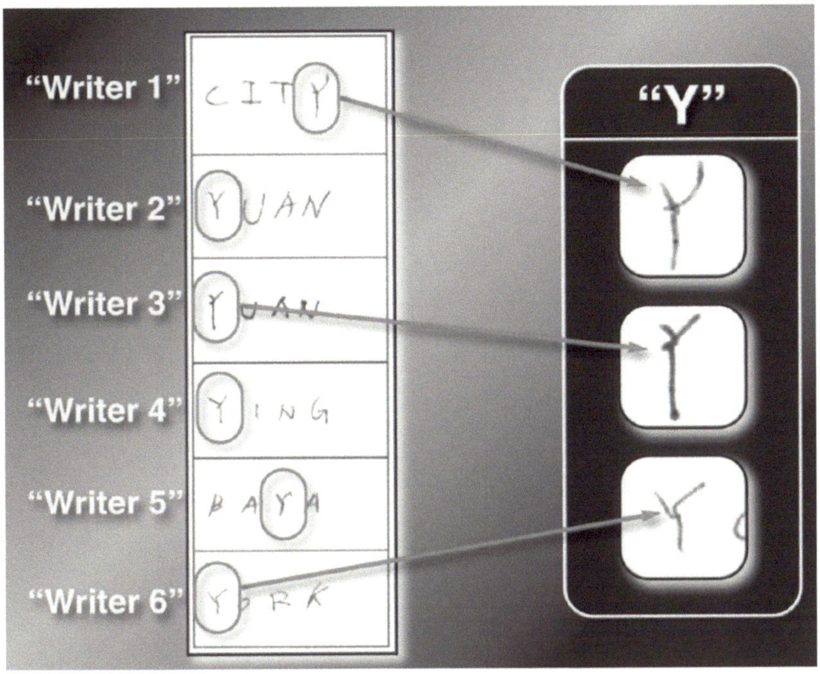

Figure 11.15 Additional class characteristics found in writers from Taiwan.

REFERENCES

1. A. Alkahtani, "The Ability of Forensic Handwriting Examiners to Judge the Quality of Signature Simulations in an Unfamiliar Writing System," *Journal of the American Society of Questioned Document Examiners*, vol. 13, no. 2 (2010), 65–69.
2. R. Spencer, "Investigating Forensic Document Examiner Opinions on Signatures in a Foreign Script," *Journal of the American Society of Questioned Document Examiners*, vol. 17, no. 2 (2014), 13–38.

Chapter 12

Frequency of Occurrence Proportions in Handwriting

Thomas W. Vastrick

CONTENTS

Forensic document examiners (FDEs) utilize many tools in conducting examinations and assessments. These tools include instruments such as microscopes and electrostatic latent handwriting detectors; measuring devices such as grids; and indexed data of materials such as watermark designs, computer printers, typewriters, and checkwriters. One such indexed data of materials, a database of frequency of occurrence in naturally written handwriting, hand printing, and numerals, may be useful in certain handwriting examinations. Huber and Headrick[1] note 21 discriminating elements that are considerations within a comprehensive examination process. Frequency of occurrence databases provide statistically based data for use in the evaluation of one of these discriminating elements and are one part of the comprehensive examination required to cumulate all of the data necessary for a reliable comparison.

12.1 WHAT IS FREQUENCY OCCURRENCE?

Frequency of occurrences, or more accurately, frequency of occurrence proportions, are relative measurements of the presence of a certain design feature in handwriting of a specified and represented population or individual. This calculation is properly deemed a *proportion* because it is a measurement of the percentage of writers within a population that utilize a specific feature within their writing repertoire. There are two forms in which frequency of occurrence proportions relate to handwriting comparisons. One form is the presence of a feature in individuals within a population sample - an inter-writer determination. For example, a review of handwriting specimens of 1,000 writers results in the determination that ten of the writers displayed the selected handwriting feature one or more times, making for a frequency of occurrence proportion for the number of writers in which the feature is present of 10/1,000 or 0.01 (1% of the sample population). The second form of frequency occurrence proportions is the frequency of occurrence of a selected feature with the number of times the character occurs in the sample of one writer – an intra-writer variation determination. Intra-writer frequency of occurrence is a qualitative analysis of variation. For example, Writer A may utilize a certain handwriting feature. However, in the provided handwriting sample, the character at issue is present 1,000 times but the writer only utilizes the form feature within the character 50 times. As such, the intra-writer frequency of occurrence proportion would be 50/1,000 or 0.05 (5% of the character sample from Writer A). Unless otherwise noted, this chapter will address the inter-writer form of frequency of occurrence proportions. Frequency occurrence proportions fall within a decimal range of 0.0 (no writers utilize a targeted feature) to 1.0 (all writers utilize a targeted feature) but can be expressed in decimal form, fraction form, or population percentage.

12.2 HISTORICAL APPLICATION

Some efforts at classification of handwriting[2–5] and frequency occurrence proportion establishment on various limited scales[6–14] have occurred. With the partial exception of Horton, these efforts were of a limited number of samples or features that fell short of providing comprehensive proportions that could be relied upon as representative of the US population. In 2010, a team of FDEs and statisticians undertook the beginnings of a comprehensive and ongoing statistical study of frequency occurrence proportions in handwriting and hand-printing within an appropriate population sampling of the United States.[15] This report was followed by a similar study of frequency occurrence proportions in handwritten numerals.[16]

FDEs are taught from the very beginning of training to observe and note characteristic similarities and differences between questioned and known writings with regard to any of a number of features such as design factors, spacing, letter height ratios, slant, etc. One of several reasons for an extensive training period in handwriting comparisons is to provide adequate time to develop an experience-based foundational understanding of how a combination of features may distinguish one writer from another. This ability is vital in properly evaluating weight of data as applied to a comprehensive examination and the ultimate conclusions.

Recent reports based on reviews of forensic science in general have recommended changes, and recent research efforts have provided assessment tools in keeping with those recommendations. Studies in 2009[17] and 2016[18] study groups have evaluated the work of forensic sciences. One common thread within recommendations from each study has been the need for better foundational research and of a more probabilistic approach to stating results. Academics and research scientists have indicated that predetermined frequency occurrence proportions would provide a more objective assessment of the heterogeneity or rarity of handwriting characteristics than the historically used experience-based method.[19] Experience-based assessment will never be fully replaced as it would be impossible to create a list containing all handwriting features, let alone a tested database of these features. However, a tandem approach allows for more objectivity in the analysis and evidence in support of the reliability of a comprehensive examination process.

12.3 DATABASE FEATURE SELECTION

It would not be possible to address all features of cursive handwriting, hand-printing, or handwritten numerals in a frequency of occurrence database. In selecting features for inclusion into the frequency of occurrence databases that currently exist, selection was based on objectivity in assessment of presence or absence of that feature in a writing sample. Objective features are those that reflect some reliable description that theoretically would be assessed and viewed in the same way by any FDE. Some examples of features that are not objective would include descriptions such as "long" strokes or "sharp" curves as these terms can be open to subjective determination that will vary from one examiner to another.

The reproducibility of results was tested through an Attribute Agreement Analysis (AAA). AAA is a quality control testing process used, in this instance, to determine whether an FDE would evaluate and assess a targeted feature in the same way at different times, and to determine whether multiple FDEs would evaluate and assess a targeted feature in the same way. By requiring 100% reproducibility of results through the AAA process, researchers were able to strengthen the integrity of the data. Johnson[15] noted that using non-original exhibits contributed to nonuniformity of results in AAA tests and concluded that frequency of occurrence measurements should be based on the use of original samples.

12.4 POPULATION SAMPLING

In order to properly create the databases to use in measuring frequency of occurrence proportions, Johnson started by identifying the population from which the sampling is to occur. In the United States, the logical sampling was one representative of the overall population. This would include citizens, foreign workers, visitors, tourists, etc. The population sampling was not restricted to just citizens as that sampling would be skewed.

Targeting is a quota method of collection in which sample sources are purposely sought out due to their quota parameters. Targeting will provide sampling more representative of the overall population but potentially at the expense of the insertion of biases in the selection process.

Johnson specifically addressed appropriate population sampling and developed a stratification process patterned after a multilevel sampling approach from the telecommunications field[20] and based on extrinsic and intrinsic factors that affect handwriting as noted by Huber and Headrick. Contemporaneous census figures were researched, and categories of selected factors were selected using 80% goal minimums, with 20% randomness in order to help with the potential of inclusion of factors not considered.

Johnson also conducted testing of the various factors that had been selected in order to quantify the effects of each. It was noted that age had the greatest impact on the results for both cursive and hand-printing, reinforcing the need for an accurate representation of the general population in age sampling. Conversely, it was noted that handedness had virtually no effect on the results. Interestingly, location of early elementary education had a major impact on cursive results and no significant impact on hand-printing results. This study provided strong statistical support of the need for proper selection of samples in any handwriting study.

12.5 FREQUENCY OF OCCURRENCE PROPORTIONS AND FORENSIC DOCUMENT EXAMINATION

Frequency of occurrence proportions can be used in naturally written, non-signature entries. The data provides the examiner with information as to the level of heterogeneity, or rarity, of certain handwriting features. However, that does not mean that an analysis of frequency of occurrence proportions will provide the ultimate answer of writership. The qualitative assessment process, whether experience-based, proportion-based, or a combination, is still only a portion of a complete examination. There are numerous aspects to an examination. While proficiency studies have demonstrated the effectiveness of proper training and use of standard methodologies, it is still imperative to strive to improve. The inclusion of proportion-based assessment data is a tool to improve the data used by the examiner in their overall assessment.

The frequency of occurrence proportions currently published in peer-reviewed scientific journals comprise only a small portion of the features of handwriting of which FDEs review. There are innumerable features that an FDE will observe and note in the course of examinations over time and it is impossible to note, record, and test each and every feature for a frequency of occurrence proportion. What this database of proportions can do is provide a foundational basis on which heterogeneity-based probabilities of handwriting can be assessed and demonstrated. In addition, this information can provide FDEs with objective, statistic-based proportions for use in their analyses when features that are recorded in the database are present in the writing at issue.

12.6 EXAMINATION LIMITATIONS

At least as important as understanding how this tool can be used is knowing how it cannot be used. There is no methodology that provides for an examiner to reach a conclusion of writership based solely on an analysis of frequency occurrence proportions, either by experience or by database proportions. Frequency of occurrence data is just that – data. The information is present to assist the FDE to navigate through a comprehensive examination. The mere presence or absence of certain features relative to frequency occurrence proportions is not the sole determining factor of writership, and any attempt to treat it as such will result in unreliable conclusions. For example, an analysis of the frequency occurrence proportions of a genuine signature will be precisely the same as that of a tracing of the same signature. However, a further examination of other pertinent data, such as line quality, pen pressure, blunt ending strokes, and pen lifts or hesitations, would provide ample evidence of the tracing process and the basis for the accurate conclusion of spuriousness of the traced entry. Conversely, disguise or any of a number of possible intrinsic or extrinsic factors that can affect handwriting could be the basis of a marked change in frequency of occurrence proportions for any given writing.

Character design, the principle factor behind frequency of occurrence features, is but one aspect of numerous factors that encompass a comprehensive forensic document examination. To limit an examination solely to the presence or absence of features, whether part of a frequency occurrence proportions database or not, is a roadmap to error.

Frequency of occurrence proportions are currently only valid for naturally written cursive writing, hand-printing, and handwritten numerals. This data cannot be effectively used in the evaluation of signatures, simulations, tracings, distorted handwriting, or disguised handwriting.

The database data is only valid for the population from which the samples were collected and for subgroupings therein. For example, the frequency of occurrence database for cursive writing in the United States would not be valid for use in France or Germany.

12.7 USE IN COURT

Using research in frequency occurrence proportions, an FDE can explain to a judge or jury that there is a basis for the claim that handwriting is distinguishable, backed by statistics. For example, in State of Florida v Michael Keetley (Thirteenth Judicial Circuit Court for Hillsborough County Florida Criminal Justice and Trial Division Case No. 10-CF-018429), testimony was presented in a hearing in front of Judge Laura E. Ward (Division 1) involving a motion in limine to exclude or limit the state's proposed handwriting expert testimony as it pertained to hand-printed entries at issue. In part, the defense, in their motion, argued that handwriting comparison "is not of a scientific, technical, or specialized knowledge nature [sic] pursuant to Florida Statute 90.702." The state called two witnesses. The first witness was the FDE who conducted the examination for the Florida Department of Law Enforcement Laboratory. The second, this author, testified to frequency of occurrence proportion research, explaining to the court how the study was developed, how the study was executed, and how the data provided sound statistical validation of processes utilized by FDEs. Further, this witness noted that the frequency of occurrence studies noted a high degree of independence in pairs testing and high overall heterogeneity of the tested features in hand-printing. Ultimately, the Keetly court ruled that the frequency of occurrence studies "supported this determination" that "handwriting analysis can reliably gauge the likelihood that the same individuals wrote two samples" (quoting U.S. v Prime, 431 F. 3d 1147 (9th Cir. 2005)).

12.8 FUTURE EXPANSION

As mentioned at the start of this chapter, a different form of frequency of occurrence proportions in handwriting consists of the frequency of which a certain feature occurs in all examples of the character in which the feature of study is defined. This intra-writer frequency of occurrence proportion for a tested writer would consist of the number of times a targeted feature exists in a particular letter as compared to the total number of times that the particular letter exists in the writing. This intra-writer frequency of occurrence would amount to a quantitative analysis of variation in handwriting. This aspect of frequency of occurrence proportions has yet to be explored but provides some interesting possibilities. Is intra-writer frequency of occurrence proportions of variations of letter designs constant, variable, or both, depending on the feature? Do the results change over time? Does the variability or stability of those ratios change based on population, written language, or other variables? If there is some level of constancy for these proportions, what quantity of specimens is necessary to reliably provide those results? We can but speculate as to uses of this information depending on the answers to the above questions, but possibilities abound. Could internal frequency of occurrence proportions of multiple features serve as its own method of association of writing to a writer? Are individual internal frequency of occurrence proportions sufficiently independent so that one could ultimately establish an overall probability of heterogeneity, based solely on this form of examination? This subject is worthy of further study.

REFERENCES

1. R. Huber and A. Headrick, *Handwriting Identification: Facts and Fundamentals* (Boca Raton, FL: CRC Press, 1998) 89–139.
2. C.D. Lee and R.A. Abbey, *Classification and Identification of Handwriting* (New York, NY: Appleton and Co., 1922).
3. A. Popkiss and J. Moore, "Handwriting classification," *Police Journal*, vol. 18 (1945): 39–55.
4. P. Nicolson, "A system for the classification of block capital letters," *International Journal of Forensic Document Examiners*, vol. 5 (Jan/Dec 1999): 138–145.
5. O. Livingston, "A handwriting and pen-printing classification system for identifying law violators," *Journal of Criminal Law and Criminal Police Science*, vol. 49 (1959): 487–506.
6. J.G. Wichman, K. Newman, J. Regent, and J. Wichmann, "A statistical examination of selected handwriting characteristics," *Journal of Forensic Sciences*, vol. 22, no. 1 (1977): 206–215.
7. B. Bishop, "Frequency of selected hand printing characteristics occurring within a national population," *Journal of the American Society of Questioned Document Examiners*, vol. 15, no. 2 (2012): 23–25.
8. M.A. Eldridge, I. Nimmo-Smith, A.M. Wing, and R.N. Totty, "The variability of selected features in cursive handwriting; categorical measures," *Journal of the Forensic Science Society*, vol. 24, no.3 (May 1984): 179–219.
9. R. Horton, "A study of the occurrence of certain handwriting characteristics in a random population," *International Journal of Forensic Document Examiners*, vol. 2, no. 2 (1996): 95–102.
10. J. Kelly, "Habits observed in naturally written numbers," *Journal of the American Society of Questioned Document Examiners*, vol. 2 (2002): 58–66.
11. O. Livingston, "Frequency of certain characteristics in handwriting, pen printing of two hundred people," *Journal of Forensic Sciences*, vol. 8 (1963): 250–259.
12. K. Savoie, "The frequency of occurrence of specific handwriting characteristics within a limited population," *Journal of the American Society of Questioned Document Examiners*, vol. 14, no. 2 (2011): 15–21.
13. N. Ahola, "Classification and frequency of occurrence of specific number styles," *Canadian Society of Forensic Science*, vol. 33, no. 1 (2000): 13–22.
14. C.-K. Li, N.L. Poon, W.K. Fung, and C.T. Yang, "Individuality of handwritten Arabic numerals in local population," *Journal of Forensic Sciences*, vol. 50, no. 1 (2005): 185–191.
15. Mark E. Johnson, Thomas W. Vastrick, Michèle Boulanger, and Ellen Schuetzner, "Measuring the frequency occurrence of handwriting and handprinting characteristics," *Journal of Forensic Sciences*, vol. 62, no. 1 (2017): 142–163.
16. Thomas V. Vastrick, Ellen Schuetzner, and Kelsey Osborn, "Measuring the frequency occurrence of handwritten numerals characteristics," *Journal of Forensic Sciences*, vol. 63, no. 4 (2018): 1215–1220.
17. National Research Council Committee on Identifying the Needs of the Forensic Sciences Community and Committee on Applied and Theoretical Statistics. *Strengthening forensic science in the United States: a path forward*, Washington, DC: National Academy of Sciences, 2009.
18. President's Council of Advisors on Science and Technology. *Report to the President – forensic science in criminal courts: ensuring scientific validity of feature-comparison methods*, Washington, DC: Executive Office of the President, 2016.
19. National Institute of Standards and Technology. *Forensic handwriting examination and human factors: the report of the expert working group for human factors in handwriting examination*, Washington, DC: National Institute of Standards and Technology Internal Report 8282:2020: 55.
20. M. Boulanger-Carey et al. (1984) "1982/83 end office connection study: analog voice and voiceband data transmission performance characterization of the public switched network," *AT&T Bell Laboratories Technical Journal*, vol. 63, no. 9 (November 1984): 2059–2119.

Chapter 13

Examination and Comparison of Handwriting by Forensic Document Examiners Compared to Laypersons

Marie E. Durina

CONTENTS

Forensic Document Examiners (FDEs) are commonly asked to determine whether or not a disputed body of writing or signature was written by a particular person. Beginning in the 1990s, several studies were undertaken in an attempt to determine whether FDEs possessed expertise at this task when compared to the ability of Laypersons.[1–8] Research on FDEs and Laypersons ability to determine writership continued in the ensuing two decades and included online methods of proficiency testing for signature comparisons,[9] participant eye-tracking during handwriting comparisons,[10] and examination of simulated and natural handwriting.[11] In addition, Lanners reported results of her study where separate groups of both FDEs and Laypersons examined specimens from writers using their nondominant hands.[12]

13.1 RESEARCH INTO THE ABILITY TO DIFFERENTIATE HOMOGENEOUS WRITING SAMPLES

An area of research that had not yet been addressed was how difficult it would be to differentiate writing by different people who wrote very similarly. Motivated by this question, a two-part research project was undertaken by Durina and Caligiuri.[13,14] The objective of the project was to ascertain how well or poorly humans would perform when examining and comparing writing samples prepared by persons who had been trained in the same school, by the same teachers, and using the same handwriting system they had learned in the same time period. All writers who submitted writing specimens had been taught to write using the *Palmer Method* of handwriting.

It was expected that these writing samples would therefore appear to be very similar to one another and, because of this, the error rate of FDEs comparing the samples might be affected. There were certain similar characteristics in the writing specimens collected for examination that were shared by the group of writers. These similarities (known as *class characteristics*) allowed the specimens to be defined as *homogeneous*.

This chapter will discuss the history of this two-part project, as well as several other studies assessing the abilities of both the group of FDEs and the Laypersons group, the performance results for each group, and the various factors that influence error rates.

13.1.1 The Palmer Method of Handwriting

In 1884, Austin N. Palmer developed an innovative system of handwriting that eventually came to be known as the *Palmer Method*. In 1894, Palmer began publishing lessons about this method of handwriting in his magazine *The Western Penman*. A group of Catholic nuns of the Order of the Immaculate Heart of Mary in Monroe County, Michigan, developed their skills in this writing method and convinced Palmer to incorporate it into a textbook that could be used in the Catholic schools. Palmer's book *The Palmer Method of Business Writing* was published in 1900. The goal of the book was to teach a writing system that would emphasize legible writing that could be quickly written. The Palmer Method of writing was quickly adopted for teaching handwriting at many Catholic schools throughout the United States.

Palmer's writing method used more shoulder and arm movements and necessitated the student to repeat numerous practice drills which emphasized rapid, easy, muscular movement. Palmer stressed the importance of strict adherence to instructions when practicing the writing method by stating "There is no value in any penmanship drill ever invented unless it is practiced with correct positions of the body, arms, fingers, penholders, paper, and with exactly the right movement, and at exactly the right rate of speed."[15]

Palmer's belief that writings resulting from the use of his method would not be executed with repeated machine-like precision is evident in his statement in the book: "Pupils practicing lessons acquire the general style ... but there is left to them the possibility of developing their own individuality."[15] Still, as Tamara Thornton remarked in her 1996 book *Handwriting in America*, at schools where the Palmer Method was taught, adherence to the copy book style was strictly enforced, and the introduction of individual characteristics was quite discouraged: "Certainly nothing in the Palmerian teaching methods - the calisthenics, the commands, the counting, the drills - encouraged students to assert their individuality through stylistic innovation."[16]

In 1904, the Superintendent of New York City schools attended an exhibition about the Palmer method in St. Louis, MO, and in 1905, decided to adopt the Palmer method in all NYC public schools. In the same year, Palmer opened the A. N. Palmer Company in New York City. By 1912, over one million copies of Palmer's textbook were sold. By the time of Palmer's death in 1927, over 25 million Americans had learned to write using the Palmer Method of Penmanship. This method continued to be taught, particularly throughout the United States, through the 1960s.

13.1.2 Writing Specimen Collection

The first phase of this research project involved the collection of handwriting specimens from 52 writers who had been taught cursive writing with the Palmer Method at OLPH Catholic elementary school in Brooklyn, NY by the same teachers between 1955 and 1961. Writing specimens were also obtained from some of the nuns who taught at the school during the 1960s and 1970s, and who had themselves learned the Palmer system earlier during the period of 1927–1941. Former students were contacted via e-mail through the school's website; through letter writing to the school's current principal and to the convent where retired Sisters of St. Joseph lived in Brentwood, Long Island, NY; and through contacts with this author's childhood friends who were former elementary school classmates. The youngest specimen writers were 48 years old at the time the writings were collected, and the oldest, a retired teacher and nun, was 88 years old. The median age of the writers was 52 years.

All recipients received the same information – a letter briefly describing the study and a questionnaire asking gender, handedness, and dates of attendance at the school. Two blank forms were also provided to recipients used to record their writing. One form contained ruled blank lines along with the printed text of the *London Letter*, a standard body of text containing 85 words and used by FDEs to obtain writing samples because it contains all letters of the alphabet, numerals, and abbreviations. The second form, a separate page, contained ruled blank lines with the text notation at the top "Memories you have of learning to write."

A total of 52 responses were returned from former students and teachers. Of the former students, 34 writers were females, and 6 writers were males. In addition to the 40 specimens obtained from former students, 12 were obtained from former teachers, all Catholic nuns who had taught at the school and who had themselves learned the Palmer Method of handwriting. Of all writers, only two were left-handed (both females), and one (a nun) was ambidextrous.

These writing specimens were subsequently separated into two groups. One group consisted of the *known specimens*, 52 samples of the London Letter, each written by one writer and randomly numbered as K1 through K52 (the Ks). The other group was the *questioned documents*, where 43 of the writers provided commentaries about their memories of learning to write in cursive Palmer penmanship. These *questioned documents* varied in length from 3 to 55 words and were randomly numbered Q1 through Q43 (the Qs).

13.1.3 Examination by the FDE Group

The next phase of the study involved distribution of the sets of writing specimens to 49 practicing FDEs in both government and private laboratories in the United States, Canada, Australia, the Netherlands, and Finland who had been notified about the study by email, and who had agreed to examine and compare the questioned and known writing specimens in an attempt to determine writership. The writing samples were photocopied on a black and white Canon photocopy machine, and the original documents were also scanned into PDF files at a resolution of 600 dpi. The photocopies and a compact disc of the digital images were then mailed to the participating examiners, along with instructions, a brief questionnaire requiring them to list years of experience and geographic location of practice, an answer sheet for recording their conclusions, and a question as to whether or not their recorded responses on the answer sheets were peer-reviewed by one or more additional FDEs. In the instructions, the FDEs were advised of the following:

- There are 52 known specimens, and 43 questioned documents.
- All writing is natural. There is no disguised writing.

- Each writer wrote only (1) known specimen.
- Not every writer wrote a questioned document. (There are nine more Ks than Qs.)
- Every questioned document will have a known specimen associated with it.

FDE participants were given up to 3 months to complete the examinations and comparisons of the specimens, and to return their completed answer sheets.

It is important to note that the answer sheets did not provide for rendering conclusions that were inconclusive or nondefinitive. This placed the FDEs in the position of having to render what are known as *forced call* opinions, where they would be required to make a selection of one of the writers of the known specimens as the author of one of the questioned documents. Participating FDEs were advised if they did not do so, their answer would be marked incorrect. In this regard, the study did not resemble real casework where examiners have the flexibility of rendering up to nine levels of conclusions, including opinions that are inconclusive and less than definitive (to account for various levels of uncertainty). In fact, many FDEs noted on their answer sheets that had certain specimens been encountered in real casework, they would have been far more conservative in their conclusions than those they were being forced to express for purposes of this study. More importantly, examiners who noted that their opinions would have been less than definitive or inconclusive had they been permitted to render such opinions, made these notations for many of the same specimens that resulted in the highest error rate. This group of specimens later came to be known as the problematic specimens.

The third phase of the study involved scoring of answer sheets submitted by FDEs and tabulating data from factors that would possibly affect error rates. Factors taken into consideration included years of experience of each of the participating FDEs (classified into two groups: those with 10 years of experience or less or those with more than 10 years of experience) and geographic location of practice (North America or non-North America). Additional factors taken into consideration were the number of words in each of the questioned documents and whether the FDE performing the examination engaged in peer review (i.e. examination of the examiner's results by another qualified FDE.)

13.1.3.1 Method of Scoring and Accuracy Scores for the FDE Group

A two-way analysis of variance (ANOVA) was used to evaluate the effects on response accuracy of the years of experience and of the geographic locations of the 49 examiners. In addition, a multiple regression analysis was employed to examine whether years of experience and whether the number of words in the questioned documents had a significant impact on the accuracy of the examiners' responses.

Test results were scored based on a perfect score valued at 100%. With a choice of 52 possible correct answers, 1.923 points were given for each correct answer, and 1.923 points were deducted for each incorrect response or answers left blank. Twenty-nine examiners scored 100%, 14 examiners scored 96%, 2 examiners scored 94%, 2 examiners scored 90%, 1 examiner scored 88%, and 1 examiner scored 85%. Overall accuracy for the group of FDEs tasked with determining writership correctly was approximately 98%. All of the 15 FDEs who engaged in peer review of their responses by at least one additional FDE had 100% accuracy scores. Although peer review was not required to achieve a perfect score, the results did support that peer review can be a valuable tool in real casework when it is available.

A factor that did not influence error rate was the number of years of experience the participating examiners had in examining handwriting. For example, 19 examiners with more than 10 years of experience achieved perfect scores, while 14 in this group did not. Of those FDEs with less than 10 years of experience, 10 achieved perfect scores, while 6 in this group did not.

The finding of no meaningful relationship between years of experience and correct associations are in line with results of a 2002 study conducted in Australia by Sita, Found, and others where "No relationship was found for experience and number of correct opinions made."[7]

A factor that did make a difference in accuracy scores was the geographic location of the FDEs performing the examinations. Those FDEs from countries outside North America made more errors, presumably because they were not familiar with the Palmer Method of handwriting. The Palmer Method had originated in, and was predominantly used in, North America. Therefore, it is possible that examiners practicing outside this geographic region may have given more weight to similarities in class characteristics than was warranted.

There was also a significant correlation between document length in words and examiner accuracy scores. Based on correlational analyses, questioned documents with fewer than 20 words were associated with greater error scores than questioned documents having more than 20 words. However, even in documents with more than 20 words, certain writing specimens were found to be more problematic than others for the FDEs. As all handwriting was executed using the same handwriting system, the specimens contained many similar class characteristics. Therefore, driving forces for writing variation were low, and abundant similar class characteristics throughout the writing specimens presented challenges to the determination of writership. These class characteristics caused many specimens to appear similar to one another, and this resulted in several repeated incorrect identifications of writers. It is noteworthy that the FDEs found many of the same writing specimens to be problematic. For example, questioned documents Q32 and Q28 and known documents K32, K9, and K48 caused the highest number of incorrect pairings by the group of FDEs (see Figure 13.1).

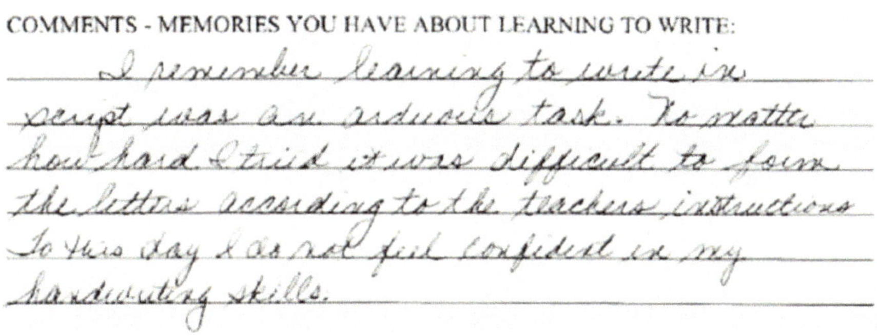
COMMENTS - MEMORIES YOU HAVE ABOUT LEARNING TO WRITE:
I remember learning to write in script was an arduous task. No matter how hard I tried it was difficult to form the letters according to the teachers instructions. To this day I do not feel confident in my handwriting skills.

Q28

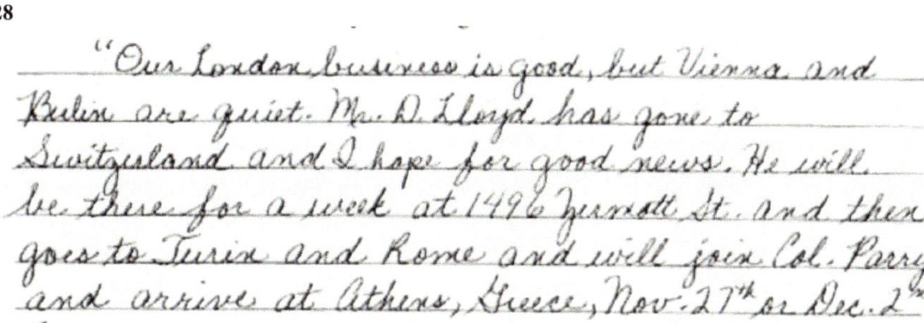
"Our London business is good, but Vienna and Berlin are quiet. Mr. D. Lloyd has gone to Switzerland and I hope for good news. He will be there for a week at 1496 Zermatt St. and then goes to Turin and Rome and will join Col. Parry and arrive at Athens, Greece, Nov. 27th or Dec. 2nd

K32

Figure 13.1 Image of document Q28, one of the problematic specimens erroneously paired on several occasions by FDEs, shown here with its correct partner, document K32.

13.1.4 Examination of Specimens by the Laypersons Group

The second part of this research project involved 46 college students from Grossmont College in El Cajon, CA (the Laypersons) in the examination of the same documents previously examined by the FDE group. These Laypersons had no prior forensic experience or training in comparison of handwriting.

The Laypersons were asked to attempt to correctly attribute writership of each of the specimens and were provided with the same documents and instructions previously provided to the FDE group. However, the Laypersons group was also offered an incentive for accuracy by their professor in the form of extra credit points for each correct answer rendered and a deduction of grade points for incorrect answers.

Layperson participants were given approximately 3 months to complete their examinations and comparisons of the same randomly numbered writing specimens, and they were permitted to engage in a loosely-structured peer review by having other Laypersons check their work, if they chose to do so.

Answer sheets were subsequently collected and scored in the same manner of scoring used previously for the FDE group. Accuracy rates and error rates were calculated. The 46 completed answer sheets with comments were collected and scored to determine the number of correct and incorrect responses. Additional information was also recorded, such as whether the respondent worked with another person when comparing the writings and how long each student took to complete the assignment. Of the 46 participants, only 4 stated that they were engaged in some form of peer review by another Layperson. Recorded amounts of time spent by each student in completing the answer sheet ranged from 5 to 42 hours, over periods of up to 5 separate days, with average time spent of approximately 9 hours.

As with the initial study that involved FDEs, scoring for the Laypersons was based on the total of 52 possible selections from the pool of known writers, which meant that each of the 52 possible answers had a value of 1.923 points. A perfect score of 100 points would require 100% correct pairings of the 52 known documents with the 43 questioned documents. For each incorrect response or answer left blank, 1.923 points were deducted.

13.1.5 Comparison of Scores by FDEs to Those of Laypersons

The Laypersons performed significantly more poorly than the FDEs. The overall accuracy score for the Laypersons group was only 76%—22 percentage points lower than the overall accuracy score of 98% for the FDE group.

Furthermore, the scores within the Laypersons group were lower in general than those attained in the FDE group. Approximately 65% of the Laypersons group scored at or below the single lowest score of 85% attained in the FDE group. Table 13.1 shows additional statistics.

A comparison was performed of the total number of incorrect associations made by the FDE group and those made by Laypersons group. These incorrect associations were tallied by counting the number of times each questioned (Q) and each known (K) document was erroneously paired. Results showed that the FDE group made a total of 67 incorrect associations, while the Laypersons group made a total of 861 incorrect associations (see Tables 13.2 and 13.3).

Given the fact that every participant had exposure to the same group of 52 K specimens when attempting to make associations to each of the 43 Q documents, there was a total of 2,236 possible pairings that could have been made (43×52=2,236). Therefore, a comparison of incorrect pairings made by both groups results in overall error rates of approximately 3% for the FDE

TABLE 13.1 DEPICTS COMPARISON OF HIGHEST, LOWEST, MOST FREQUENT, AND AVERAGE SCORES ATTAINED BY LAYPERSONS AND FDES WHO EXAMINED AND COMPARED THE SAME HOMOGENOUS WRITING SPECIMENS

Scores	FDEs	Laypersons
Highest	100% (29)	100% (1)
Lowest	85% (1)	33% (1)
Mode	100% (29)	90% (6)
Group average	98%	76%

TABLE 13.2 COMPARISON OF INCORRECT ASSOCIATIONS MADE OF Q DOCUMENTS BY FDES AND LAYPERSONS

Questioned Document Number	Number of Incorrect Associations by Laypersons	Number of Incorrect Associations by FDEs
Q1	6	
Q2	3	
Q3	2	
Q4	7	
Q5	5	
Q6	1	
Q7	13	1
Q8	2	
Q9	22	
Q10	14	1
Q11	2	
Q12	3	
Q13	17	
Q14	3	
Q15	12	
Q16	21	1
Q17	10	
Q18	15	1
Q19	18	
Q20	9	1
Q21	4	
Q22	12	
Q23	9	
Q24	2	

(Continued)

TABLE 13.2 (*Continued*) COMPARISON OF INCORRECT ASSOCIATIONS MADE OF Q DOCUMENTS BY FDES AND LAYPERSONS

Questioned Document Number	Number of Incorrect Associations by Laypersons	Number of Incorrect Associations by FDEs
Q25	23	5
Q26	1	
Q27	17	
Q28	17	8
Q29	6	
Q30	6	
Q31	19	2
Q32	24	11
Q33	2	
Q34	7	
Q35	10	1
Q36	12	
Q37	18	1
Q38	4	
Q39	34	6
Q40	9	
Q41	8	
Q42	13	
Q43	14	1
Total number of erroneous associations	456	40

Thirteen of the Qs were found to be problematic for the FDE group. All 43 Qs were found to be problematic for the Laypersons.

group (67/2,236 = 0.02996) and overall error rate of approximately 39% for the Laypersons group (861/2,236 = 0.03850).

Interestingly, there did not seem to be the same group of problematic samples for the Laypersons group as there were for the FDE group. Of the 43 questioned documents, a total of 13 Qs (or 30% of all Qs) were found to be problematic for FDEs and resulted in at least one incorrect association. Some of these incorrect associations occurred when the Q document contained fewer than 20 words. For the Laypersons group, all 43 of the questioned documents (100% of all Qs) proved problematic and were incorrectly associated one or more times.

In the group of 52 known documents, a total of 11 Ks (or 21% of all Ks) were found to be problematic for FDEs and resulted in at least one incorrect association. For the Laypersons group, 49 of the known documents (94% of all Ks) proved problematic and were incorrectly associated one or more times. Only three of the Ks were not incorrectly associated by the Laypersons group.

TABLE 13.3 COMPARISON OF INCORRECT ASSOCIATIONS OF K DOCUMENTS MADE BY FDES AND LAYPERSONS

Known Document Number	Number of Incorrect Associations by Laypersons	Number of Incorrect Associations by FDEs
K1	4	
K2	1	
K3	15	
K4	4	
K5	3	
K6		
K7	10	
K8	17	
K9	22	3
K10	13	
K11	1	
K12	4	
K13	5	
K14	5	
K15	3	
K16	15	1
K17	4	
K18	14	2
K19	7	
K20	14	
K21	7	
K22	5	
K23	12	
K24	5	1
K25	2	
K26	7	
K27	4	
K28	15	2
K29	2	
K30	4	
K31		
K32	33	11

(*Continued*)

TABLE 13.3 (*Continued*) COMPARISON OF INCORRECT ASSOCIATIONS OF K DOCUMENTS MADE BY FDES AND LAYPERSONS

Known Document Number	Number of Incorrect Associations by Laypersons	Number of Incorrect Associations by FDEs
K33	11	
K34	5	
K35	8	
K36	11	
K37		
K38	14	1
K39	15	1
K40	13	1
K41	1	
K42	6	
K43	3	
K44	5	
K45	2	
K46	3	
K47	15	
K48	10	3
K49	3	
K50	14	1
K51	6	
K52	3	
Total number of erroneous associations	405	27

Eleven of the Ks were found to be problematic for the FDE group. All but three Ks were found to be problematic for the Laypersons.

Although the Laypersons group were permitted to provide comments on their answer sheets about their participation in the study, only a few chose to do so. Most commented that they found the study interesting and wished to be advised of their scores. No comments were made about the constriction of not being permitted to render inconclusive or qualified opinions—a matter of great consternation to, and commentary by, many of the FDEs who previously participated in the study. The Laypersons group seemed readily willing to accept that answers left blank and incorrect associations would be scored as incorrect and result in deducted points.

Some in the Laypersons group commented about their strategy for completing the task of examination and comparison. For example, one Layperson referred to using "the process of elimination" by choosing to associate a writer with a particular specimen, then removing that writer from the pool of those remaining. Others did not seem to have a particular strategy. Many Laypersons chose to associate the same K writing specimen over and over again on the same answer sheet with several different Qs, perhaps in the hope that at least one selection would generate a correct answer. This strategy of associating multiple authors with the same Q document was never observed in the FDE group.

Some in the Laypersons group remarked that it took several sittings over many days to complete the task of associating the Q documents with the K specimens. Yet, many also remarked that they found the process somewhat "easy" to complete. For example, some of the comments in this vein included the following:

> Only the last 5 were hard to match.
>
> *(This Layperson scored 51%)*

> The samples were easily matched, but I had to look at the last few more closely.
>
> *(This Layperson scored 63%)*

> It seemed easy to pick them out. I want to know if it was as easy as I thought.
>
> *(This Layperson scored 73%)*

Much like results reported in a study conducted by Merlino, there appeared to be a higher degree of confidence among the Laypersons group in making the correct associations than their accuracy levels warranted.[10] The commentaries of this nature by the Laypersons are in stark contrast to those made by the FDEs, many of whom commented that they found the task of comparing the same group of homogeneous writings to be quite challenging. In fact, not a single FDE participant in the initial study implied in his or her comments that the assignment was performed with ease.

13.2 COMPARISON OF STUDY RESULTS

It is noteworthy that the results attained in the Homogeneous Handwriting research project are in line with results of research reported by others in the United States, Australia, and Canada. Figure 13.2 summarizes results from a number of studies where the FDE error rates are significantly lower than those of Laypersons.

13.3 CONCLUSION

The results of the study discussed in this chapter provide further support for the principle that handwriting is a relatively stable behavior in each individual writer but varies significantly between different writers. This is true even when driving forces for variation are low, such as when people learn to write using the same copybook system and are taught by the same teachers in the same schools. These results have also shown that FDEs have demonstrated the ability to source such writing with a significantly higher degree of accuracy than Laypersons.

There are now many published studies that address the abilities of FDEs to differentiate handwriting. It is hoped that this chapter will provide some information about the existence of empirical evidence to support that professional expertise in handwriting examination does exist. While results vary from study to study, as do the comparison tasks the participants have

Author(s)	Title	Publication	Type of Writing Samples	No. of FDEs	No. of Laypersons	Task	Error Rates of FDEs	Error Rates of Laypersons	Comments
Kam, M., Wetstein, J., and Conn. R.	**Proficiency of Professional Document Examiners**	JFS 1994	Extended Cursive and Hand Printing	7	10	86 documents prepared by 20 writers examined and compared, separate "pile" created for each writer.	.5714%	24.7%	Aka "Kam I": Small "pilot study"; no incentives provided. Study included "under-refinement errors" (bad IDs) and "over-refinement errors" (bad eliminations). Laypersons were about 56 times more likely to wrongly associate handwriting than FDEs. Kam also determined that Laypersons were about 36 times more likely to wrongly differentiate handwriting than FDEs. FDEs performed significantly better than the Laypersons Group, which consisted of college educated nonexperts. Kam concluded that the probability of FDEs and Laypersons having the same proficiency in performing writer identification was less than 0.001.
Kam, M. Fielding, G., and Conn, R.	**Writer Identification by Professional Document Examiners**	JFS 1997	Extended Cursive and Hand Printing	105	41	144 paired comparisons made between questioned and known samples	6.50%	38.30%	Aka "Kam II": Similar to 1994 study, but on a larger scale. FDEs incorrectly attributed authorship to writings at a rate of 6.5% of the time, compared to incorrect attributions of authorship at a rate of 38.5% by Laypersons who examined the same writings. In this study, Laypersons were nearly 6 times more likely than professional FDEs to incorrectly identify handwriting.
Kam, M., Fielding, G., and Conn, R.	**Effects of Monetary Incentives on Performance of Non-professionals in Document Examination Proficiency Tests**	JFS 1998	Extended Cursive and Hand Printing	105*	132	144 paired comparisons made between questioned and known samples	6.50%	22.7%	Aka "Kam III" re-tested 1997 results (*data compared to Kam II FDE group), this time providing monetary incentives to laypersons: $25 for correct responses, -$25 for incorrect responses, -$10 for failure to match. Slight improvement by laypersons in wrong association rate, but correct "hit" rate worsened. Even though these Laypersons were paid for every correct response they rendered, their accuracy scores showed no

Figure 13.2 Summary of studies conducted that assess performance of FDEs compared to Laypersons in the examination of handwriting.

(Continued)

									improvement over results reported from earlier studies that did not involve monetary incentives.
Kam. M., Gummadidala, K., Fielding, G., and Conn, R.	**Signature Authentication by Forensic Document Examiners**	JFS 2001	Signatures	69	50	12 signatures sets examined and compared; 6 sets of knowns vs. 6 sets of unknowns (including possible simulations)	Type 1: 0.49% Type II: 7.05%	Type 1: 6.47% Type II: 26.1%	Aka "Kam IV". Type 1 error=non-genuine signature declared genuine; Type II error = authentic signature declared non-genuine. Incentives given to laypersons of $8 for correct responses, -$8 for incorrect responses, -$4 for indecision., Laypersons were about 3 ½ times more likely than FDEs to call a "good" signature "bad". Laypersons were about 13 times more likely to call a "bad" signature "good" than FDEs were.
Kam, M., Lin E.	**Writer Identification using Hand Printed and Non-Hand printed Questioned Documents**	JFS 2003	Extended Hand Printing, Cursive and Mixed Samples	69	50	330 documents were examined and compared.	7.35% overall (see breakdown in Comments	39.2% overall (see breakdown in Comments)	Reanalysis of 1996-97 data (see Kam II) to show results for subsets of hand printing, cursive, and mixed writing styles. Hand Printed only: 7.3% error FDEs and 40.45% error Laypersons; Non-hand printing only: 5.5% error FDEs and 38.26% error Laypersons; Cursive only: 4.7% error FDEs, 42.56% error Laypersons; Non-cursive only: 8.97% error FDEs, 36.28% error Laypersons. Laypersons were about 4.35 times more likely to wrongly identify hand printing than FDEs. With regard to documents with a mixture of hand printing and cursive writing, Laypersons were about 7 7 times more likely to wrongly identify non-hand printing than the FDEs.
Kam, M., Abichandani, P. and Hewett, T.	**Simulation Detection in Handwritten Documents**	JFS 2015	Extended	19	26	FDEs: 200 packets of 2 Qs and 6 Ks each; Laypersons: 466 packets of 2 Qs and 6 Ks each.	ID error rate: 0%. Elim. error rate:9.97%	ID error rate: 17%. Elim. error rate:17.6%	Results take into account "inconclusive" responses not counted as errors. Mock jury laypersons were chosen by professional consultants. The error rates of the FDEs were smaller than those of the laypersons when detecting simulations in the questioned documents. FDEs never labeled a questioned document that was written by the same person who wrote the known documents as "simulation." There was a significant statistical difference between the responses of the FDEs and layperson for documents without simulations.

Figure 13.2 (CONTINUED) Summary of studies conducted that assess performance of FDEs compared to Laypersons in the examination of handwriting.

(*Continued*)

Sita, J., Found, B., and Rogers, D.	**Forensic Handwriting Examiners' Expertise for Signature Comparison**	JFS 2002	Signatures	17	13	150 Signatures were examined and compared.	3.40%	19.30%	This study permitted both the rendering of "inconclusive" opinions (uncalled) and definitive opinions (called.) When inconclusive (uncalled) opinions were permitted, FDEs were correct at a rate of 54.8%, inconclusive at a rate of 41.8%, and incorrect at a rate 3.4%. Laypersons were correct at a rate of 57.4%, but inconclusive at a rate of 23.6% of the time, and incorrect at a rate of 19.3% These error rates for the FDE group of 3.4% (when uncalled), are significantly lower than those of the Layperson group 19.3% (when uncalled.) When only definitive (called) opinions were permitted, the gap between the two groups was even more evident: error rates for the FDE group was 5.8% compared to 25.3% for the Laypersons Group. In this study, Laypersons were about 5.6 times more likely to make a mistake in attributing authorship than were the FDEs.
Dyer A.G., Found B., Rogers D.	**Visual Attention and Expertise for Forensic Signature Analysis**	JFS 2006	Signatures	9	12	32 questioned Signatures were compared with 4 known Signatures	77.8% Accuracy	45.3% Accuracy	Eye-tracking study recording eye movements, response times, and opinions. Laypersons made approximately 7 times as many errors compared to the FDE group. Both laypersons and FDE subjects looked at signature features in a very similar way, but FDEs were significantly more accurate than laypersons. Even though both groups spent approximately the same amount of time viewing the signatures, the difference in the accuracy of their opinions can be accounted for by different cognitive processing of the visual information that they extract from the images.
Holmes, L., Ostrum, B., Barton, A.	**Online Proficiency Testing for Signature Comparison by Forensic Document Examiners and Non-Examiners**	JASQDE 2011	Signatures	32	32	14 Known specimen Signatures were compared to 50 questioned signatures	1.88%	16.29%	1600 opinions rendered by each group of FDEs and laypersons; the study allowed for inconclusive opinions. There was no significant difference between the number of inconclusive opinions by FDEs vs. Laypersons, but there was a significant difference in number of misleading "calls", with the FDE group

Figure 13.2 (CONTINUED) Summary of studies conducted that assess performance of FDEs compared to Laypersons in the examination of handwriting.

(Continued)

									being more accurate than the laypersons.
Durina, M., and Caligiuri, M. P.	**The Determination of Authorship from a Homogenous Group of Writers**	JASQDE 2009	Extended Cursive Writing	49	46	52 known samples compared to 43 questioned documents. All writers taught Palmer system of writing at same school by the same teachers.	2.996%	See below for Laypersons' rates	Part 1 of 2-part study (see below for Part 2 notes.) Involved FDEs only, and permitted only "forced call" conclusions. FDEs attained 98% accuracy. Sources of error included number of words in Questioned documents, geographic location of FDE. Peer review found to increase accuracy for FDEs. Years of experience were not a significant factor. The same small group of samples were consistently problematic for those FDEs who made errors.
Durina, M. and Caligiuri, M. P.	**Laypersons' Performance in the Determination of Authorship from a Homogenous Group of Writers**	JASQDE 2016	Extended Cursive Writing	49	46	Same as above.	See above for FDEs rates	38.50%	Part 2 of 2-part study (see above for Part 1 notes) involved Laypersons only, who examined same samples previously examined by FDEs, and permitted only "forced call" conclusions. Incentives given to Laypersons (all college students) were extra-credit points for correct responses, and deduction of points from grade for incorrect responses. Peer review by other laypersons did not improve accuracy. Strategies used by laypersons in performing examinations differed from those used by FDEs. All samples proved problematic for laypersons.
Merlino, M.	**Validity, Reliability, Accuracy, and Bias in Forensic Signature Identification**	NCJRS Doc. #248565 In 2015	Signatures	49	43	30 signature specimens analyzed and compared using eye-tracking software.	31.9%	44.2%	Eye-tracking study found FDEs were significantly more accurate, demonstrated greater reliability and would make more qualified (i.e. more conservative) calls than Laypersons. FDEs were significantly more accurate overall than were Lay participants" and "FDEs outperformed Lay participants in 24 of the 30 signature examinations. For 20 of 30 signature specimens, FDEs were "significantly more accurate than were Lay participants in 17 of these 20 cases". Eye-tracking software used yielded data showing differences between the eye movements of FDEs when compared to those of Laypersons that "clearly demonstrate expertise-based differences between the FDE and Lay participant groups on the signature comparison

Figure 13.2 (CONTINUED) Summary of studies conducted that assess performance of FDEs compared to Laypersons in the examination of handwriting.

(*Continued*)

									task. Out of the 16 hypotheses in the study that predicted performance of FDEs when compared to Lay participants, only two were not supported by the results of the study. These were one hypothesis that predicted that training education, and experience would relate to the type and number of features given weight by FDEs; and another hypothesis that the years of education, training and experience would reliably predict the extent to which FDEs would outperform Lay participants on signature examination tasks.
Lanners, B.	**A New-Dominant Hand: Can Forensic Document Examiners Correctly Associate the Dominant-Hand Writing to the Non-Dominant-Hand Writing of the Same Person?**	JASQDE 2018	Extended Cursive and hand printed writing	15	9	Compare 32 pairs of cursive and 32 pairs of hand printed writing samples from writers using both dominant and non-dominant hand to prepare samples and attempt to determine authorship.	6.25% for cursive 12.78% for hand printed	18.98% for cursive, 25.93% for hand printed	This study provided empirical evidence to support that FDEs can identify the non-dominant-hand writing of a person given only that person's dominant-hand writing, and that they do so with greater accuracy than laypersons. Because writing with the non-dominant hand is often a strategy used to deliberately disguise one's writing, this study was significant in that it assessed the abilities of FDEs to examine and compare a form of disguised writing.

Figure 13.2 (CONTINUED) Summary of studies conducted that assess performance of FDEs compared to Laypersons in the examination of handwriting.

been asked to perform, the performance of FDEs has been found to be consistently superior to that of Laypersons performing the same tasks. The absence of expert opinion testimony can lead to incorrect conclusions by Laypersons, and professional FDEs can offer valuable assistance to the courts and the triers-of-fact with regard to the examination and comparison of handwriting evidence.

REFERENCES

1. M. Kam et al., "Proficiency of Professional Document Examiners in Writer Identification," *Journal of Forensic Sciences*, vol. 39, no. 1 (January 1994): 5–14.
2. M. Kam et al., "Writer Identification by Professional Document Examiners," *Journal of Forensic Sciences*, vol. 42, no. 5 (September 1997): 778–786.
3. M. Kam et al., "Effects of Monetary Incentives on Performance of Non-Professionals in Document Examination Proficiency Tests," *Journal of Forensic Sciences*, vol. 43, no. 5 (September 1998): 1000–1004.
4. M. Kam et al., "Signature Authentication by Forensic Document Examiners," *Journal of Forensic Sciences*, vol. 46, no. 4 (July 2001): 884–888.
5. M. Kam et al., "Writer Identification using Hand-Printed and Non-Hand-Printed Questioned Documents," *Journal of Forensic Sciences*, vol. 48, no. 6 (November 2003): 1391–1395.
6. B. Found et al., "The Development of a Program for Characterizing Forensic Handwriting Examiners' Expertise: Signature Examination Pilot Study," *Journal of Forensic Document Examination*, vol. 12 (January 1999): 69–80.
7. J. Sita et al., "Forensic Handwriting Examiners' Expertise for Signature Comparison," *Journal of Forensic Sciences*, vol. 47, no. 5 (September 2002): 1117–1124.
8. A.G. Dyer et al., "Visual Attention and Expertise for Forensic Signature Analysis," *Journal of Forensic Sciences*, vol. 51, no. 6 (November 2006): 1397–1404.
9. L. Holmes, et al., "Online Proficiency Testing for Signature Comparison by Forensic Document Examiners and Non-Examiners," *Journal of the American Society of Questioned Document Examiners*, vol. 14, no. 1 (June 2011): 19–35.
10. M. Merlino, "Validity, Reliability, Accuracy, and Bias in Forensic Signature Identification," Doc. No. 248565, PDF available electronically from NCJRS at http://www.NCJRS.gov/app/publication/abstract/aspx?ID#270668 (January 2015): 1–1470.
11. M. Kam et al., "Simulation Detection in Handwritten Documents by Forensic Document Examiners," *Journal of Forensic Sciences*, vol. 60, no. 4 (July 2015): 936–941.
12. B.N. Lanners, "A New-Dominant Hand: Can Forensic Document Examiners Correctly Associate the Dominant-Hand Writing to the Non-Dominant-Hand Writing of the Same Person?" *Journal of the American Society of Questioned Document Examiners*, vol. 21, no. 2 (December 2018): 29–43.
13. M.E. Durina et al., "The Determination of Authorship from a Homogenous Group of Writers," *Journal of the American Society of Questioned Document Examiners*, vol. 12, no. 2 (December 2009): 77–90.
14. M.E. Durina et al., "Laypersons' Performance in the Determination of Authorship from a Homogenous Group of Writers," *Journal of the American Society of Questioned Document Examiners*, vol. 19, no. 2 (December 2016): 5–14.
15. A.N. Palmer, *The Palmer Method of Business Writing*, 1935 Edition, (The A.N. Palmer Company, New York, 1935).
16. T.P. Thornton, *Handwriting in America, A Cultural History* (Yale University Press, New Haven, CN, 1996), 166.

Section III

Applications of Technology in Forensic Document Examination

Chapter 14

Forensic Analysis of Handwritten Electronic Signatures

Kathleen Annunziata Nicolaides and Khody R. Detwiler

CONTENTS

14.1 WHERE ARE ELECTRONIC SIGNATURES FOUND AND WHY IS IT IMPORTANT TO BE ABLE TO AUTHENTICATE THEM?

Just as many forensic document examiners (FDEs) experienced a decline in the number of typewriter cases being submitted as the "computer age" was emerging in the late 1980s, technological advancements taking place today are certain to change the landscape of the field once again. With the innovations in modern technology and the appeal of a paperless workflow, the use of e-signatures as a means of conducting day-to-day business is quickly becoming second nature in most industries. This is especially true with insurance companies, banking institutions, hospitals, and virtually every point of sale merchant. While it may seem like a much more efficient way to conduct business, this process undoubtedly raises a host of authentication concerns, creating the need for FDEs to be able to authenticate and verify electronic signatures just as they do with traditional "wet-ink" signatures.

Although there are several additional steps when conducting an analysis of an electronically-captured handwritten signature as compared to a traditional wet-ink signature, the methodology and principles established in the field over a century ago still apply. Specifically, in both analyses, the FDE relies upon a variety of factors, including writing speed, fluidity, directionality, pictorial agreement, skill, and overall writing quality, when forming his or her ultimate opinion of authenticity. In a traditional signature analysis, these characteristics are often interpreted in a subjective manner by the examiner, based upon his or her training, experience, and knowledge. However, when using the information contained in the raw signature data file associated with an electronically-captured handwritten signature, many of these features can be quantified. The international FDE community has conducted research developing and validating the techniques used in handwritten electronic signature examinations for more than two decades. This research and methodology will be extensively discussed in this chapter.

14.2 HISTORY OF ELECTRONIC SIGNATURE LAWS

As with many technological expansions, the overall effectiveness of a product or system is often decided by its efficiency and use by the general public. Considering the potential power and wealth that is often associated with the execution of a signature, it is imperative that electronic signatures have the capability of being authenticated and verified. Although the concept of electronic signature analysis may seem like a relatively new area of forensic document examination, federal and state e-signature laws have been in effect for the past two decades.

In 1999, the National Conference of Commissioners on Uniform State Laws (NCCUSL) adopted the Uniform Electronic Transactions Act (UETA). In short, UETA provides that a record or signature may not be denied legal validity or enforceability solely because it is in an electronic format.[1] It should be noted that UETA is not intended to encompass all transactions, only business, commercial, and governmental matters. Since its inception, 47 states, as well as the District of Columbia, Puerto Rico, and the US Virgin Islands, have adopted UETA. Although Illinois, New York, and Washington have yet to do so, all three states have similar counterparts addressing the legality of electronic records and signatures.

Like UETA, on June 30, 2000 the federal government passed the United States Electronic Signatures in Global and National Commerce Act (ESIGN Act), which addresses the validity of electronic records and signatures used in transactions influencing interstate or foreign commerce.[2] In consideration of both UETA and ESIGN, an electronic signature may be deemed legally valid when meeting or exceeding the following requirements:

1. *Intent to sign* – As the heading suggests, for an electronic signature to be considered valid, there must be a recognized intention from all involved parties to sign electronically.
2. *Consent to do business electronically* – All parties must give consent to conduct business electronically, which is often verified by the circumstances surrounding the transaction. (Please note that special considerations to this requirement may apply under ESIGN and UETA.)
3. *Association of signature with the record* – Every transaction executed with an electronic signature must include a record that specifies how the electronic signature was created.
4. *Record retention* – Lastly, all electronic signature records must be stored and archived in a manner so that they can also be accurately reproduced in the event that any party to the transaction wishes to do so.

14.3 DYNAMIC SIGNATURE RESEARCH

There are many types of electronic signatures. Some do not include the physical act of signing your name, instead employing cryptographic techniques (or *digital signatures*) to authenticate a document. Entering a PIN number at an ATM machine is an example of a digital signature being used in lieu of a signed checking withdrawal.

Handwritten electronic signatures include signatures collected on digitizing devices that have been (a) captured as images only or (b) captured as temporal and movement data. The first subgroup is often referred to as *static signatures* and the latter subgroup as *dynamic signatures*.[3] Of the two subgroups, questioned dynamic signatures tend to be more identifiable since they contain a graphical representation of the signature as well as timing and movement data that aids greatly in signature verification.

Signature dynamics have been researched for decades for both authentication or biometric applications. Tytell describes an on-line signature verification system developed and tested in the 1970s by Veripen, Inc. using their SIGNAC system. Research conducted found "that a dynamic pressure pattern in the signature writing of an individual is consistent over time, varies significantly between individuals, and is almost impossible for another person to imitate."[4] A decade later, the IBM Thomas J. Watson Research Center developed and tested an automatic signature verification system which used analysis of pressure and acceleration data to determine if the signer was intoxicated; the last trial of this system resulted in a success rate of over 99%.

When casework first started in the area of handwritten electronic signatures, methodology had to be developed that would work in analyzing the dynamic data collected using various devices and software. This was important since the FDE might not have access to the proprietary software used to collect the dynamic data, nor be able to explain to a jury how that software works.

Flynn, who in the late 1990s had worked with Topaz© in developing forensic software for analysis of signatures captured with Topaz tablets,[5] was one of the first North American FDEs to research and codify methodology for the forensic examination of dynamic data and electronically-captured biometric signatures. Using a Topaz tablet where both a wet-ink and dynamic signature were captured simultaneously, he conducted a study to determine if signatures plotted in Excel using dynamic data were an accurate representation of the corresponding wet-ink signatures. Flynn found that the plotted signatures overlaid the wet-ink signatures, thus establishing the accuracy of the dynamic data in recreating the graphical representation of the original, wet-ink signature.[6] He did note that there was one writer who wrote portions of his signature with such light pen pressure, the tablet did not register the movements; these portions of the dynamic signature were therefore not congruent with the wet-ink signature. Flynn further found that, using basic data captured in a dynamic signature, it was possible to plot the acceleration or deceleration of the pen during the signing event.

Annunziata Nicolaides studied the acceleration/deceleration plots of 119 signatures from 25 writers.[7] She found that acceleration/deceleration plots were consistent in signatures of one individual, that these plots differed between writers, and that acceleration/deceleration plots of genuine signatures differed from those of simulated, traced, or spurious signatures. She also found that these plots would greatly aid FDEs in determining authenticity of dynamic signatures because they quantified rhythm, an individualizing feature of a writer's signature habit and a feature that is extremely difficult – if not impossible – for another writer to simulate. Osborn defined rhythm as "a harmonious recurrence of stress or impulse or motion." He considered rhythm to be very important to the determination of writership or genuineness, and he asserted "There is nothing in handwriting so difficult to successfully imitate as the exact quality of this muscular rhythm, and a violation of it is the most common symptom of forgery..."[8]

The usefulness of acceleration/deceleration plots (or velocity plots) in writer identification was proven in another study conducted by Annunziata Nicolaides where she compared signatures executed with a pen stylus to signatures written with a finger.[9] Signatures from the same writer were compared to determine how greatly the method of signing affected the signature habit.

In this study, subjects were asked to sign with their finger on a device which allowed them to support their elbow (see Figure 14.1). She noted that finger signatures varied from stylus signatures in connections, movements involving change of direction, and strokes naturally written with great speed. However, velocity plots of signatures written with a finger were consistent with plots of signatures written with a pen stylus. She also found that finger signatures were written more slowly than signatures written with a pen stylus. FDEs routinely consider writing conditions in traditional signature examinations; they must do the same in dynamic signature examinations.

In 2015, Annunziata Nicolaides and Flynn compiled the quantifiable data of 344 dynamic signatures collected by their laboratory to ascertain whether forensic analysis supported or refuted tenets of forensic signature identification such as: (1) no two individuals write alike; (2) no one signs their name the exact same way twice; and (3) unnaturally executed (simulated or traced) signatures are typically written more slowly than naturally executed signatures.[10] The dynamic signatures were from multiple writers and included samples of genuine, simulated, traced, and spurious signatures. Thirteen samples of disguised signatures were also obtained, but the sample size was determined by the authors to be too small.

They evaluated signature execution times, average segment (stroke) length, average "speed" of the signatures, and the standard deviation of the calculated velocity. Data were sorted by time of execution to determine: (1) if two writers shared the exact same data; (2) if the data of one writer was identical in more than one signature; and (3) the average speed of genuine, simulated, traced, and spurious signatures. They found that even in instances where the time of execution was the same, signatures were differentiated by the other quantitative data (see Figures 14.2 and 14.3). They also found that nongenuine signatures were written more slowly than genuine ones, as illustrated in Figure 14.4. Based on their analysis, they found that: (1) there are quantifiable differences between signatures written naturally and unnaturally (simulated or traced); (2) there are quantifiable differences in signatures executed by different writers; and (3) there are quantifiable variations in naturally executed signatures of one writer. They concluded that the principles of forensic signature identification are corroborated by analysis of dynamic signature data.

Figure 14.1 Subject is signing the screen using his finger. His elbow is supported on the desk.

Sig #	Sig Type	Name	Total # Data Pairs	# Data Pairs in Stroke		Time = Data Pairs / 1/188 seconds	AVG Distance	AVG stroke length (data pairs)	Standard Deviation - velocity/ distance
K-51-1	gen	CMK genuine collected 9/11/14	328	205	stroke 1	1.744680851	8.159092127	109.3333	5.532716908
K-51-1	gen	CMK genuine collected 9/11/14	328	17	stroke 2				
K-51-1	gen	CMK genuine collected 9/11/14	328	106	stroke 3				
K-53-3	gen	CMK genuine collected 9/17/14	328	216	stroke 1	1.744680851	7.16175231	65.6	4.536515678
K-53-3	gen	CMK genuine collected 9/17/14	328	17	stroke 2				
K-53-3	gen	CMK genuine collected 9/17/14	328	82	stroke 3				
K-53-3	gen	CMK genuine collected 9/17/14	328	5	stroke 4				
K-53-3	gen	CMK genuine collected 9/17/14	328	8	stroke 5				

Figure 14.2 Although two signatures of signer CMK were executed in the same amount of time, other dynamic data differentiates the two.

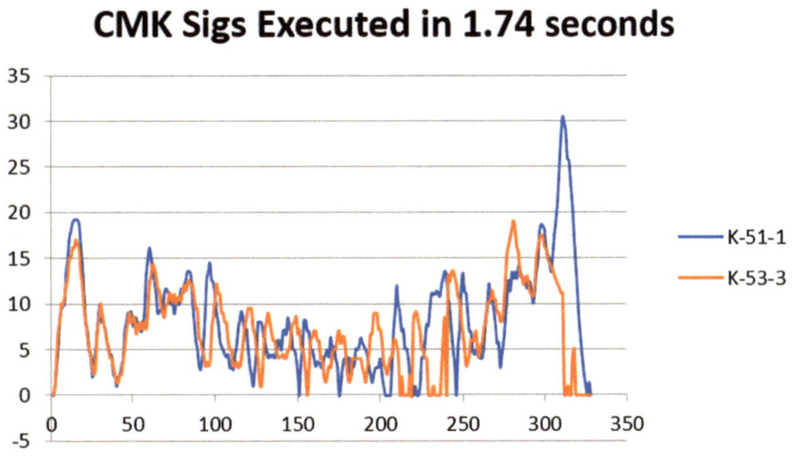

Figure 14.3 By overlaying the velocity plots of the two CMK signatures executed in the same amount of time, the differences in the dynamic data are visualized. While the rhythm of the two signatures is very similar, it is not exactly the same.

A study of the relationship between vertical stroke duration and absolute amplitude of genuine signatures and forged signatures by Caligiuri, Mohammed, Found, and Rogers also corroborated the principle that forged signatures are written more slowly. In their study of signatures from 60 writers, Caligiuri et al. found that forged signatures are produced with less efficiency of movement than genuine signatures. They found that "pen strokes forming forged signatures had significantly greater duration-amplitude slope coefficients than genuine signatures."[11]

In Australia, Strach also began researching electronic signatures in the late 1990s. He worked with Florentis, which later became Wacom. Strach, Novotny, and Devlin conducted an extensive research project on signatures collected using the Wacom STU-430 Signature Pad and examined using Wacom SignatureScope® software. The purpose of the research was to ascertain if the genuineness of dynamic signatures collected on the Wacom STU-430 Signature Pad and examined using Wacom SignatureScope software could be forensically determined, and, if so, how did the examination of dynamic signatures compare to examinations of wet-ink signatures. Strach et al. concluded that examinations of dynamic signatures "were found to have an advantage

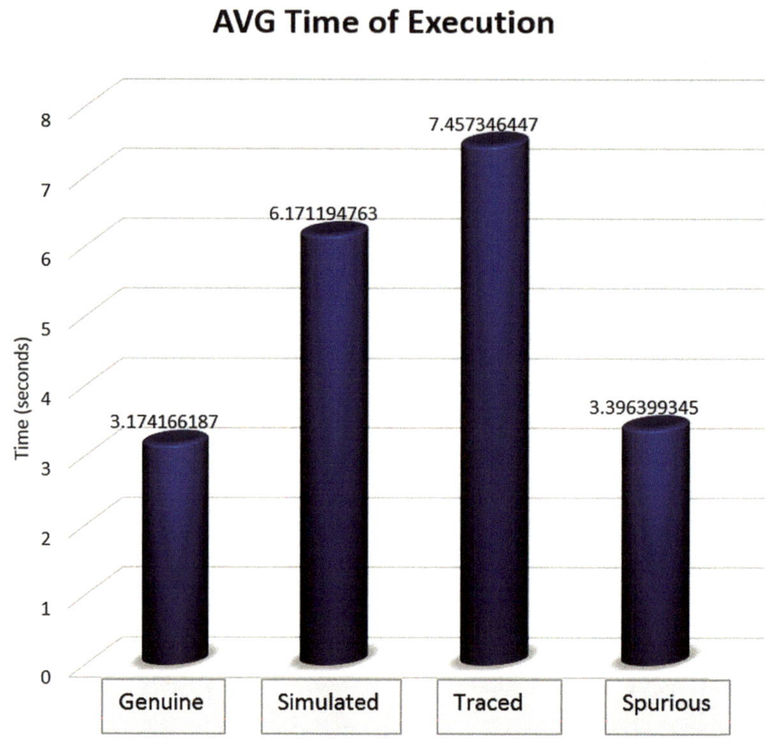

Figure 14.4 The average time of execution for the genuine, simulated, traced, and spurious signatures studied. As seen on the chart, genuine and spurious signatures are made the most quickly (because they both employ natural handwriting habits) and traced and simulated signatures (which employ unnatural handwriting habits) are made significantly more slowly.

or were equivalent to examinations of ink on paper signatures." For dynamic signature examinations using SignatureScope, they found the ability to "play-back" the signature in real-time or reduced speeds, to analyze the correlating timing information for signature segments, to determine stroke direction of complex signatures, and to analyze "pen up" data (tracking movements of the pen/stylus above the pad) all extremely useful. They found the "pen up" data significantly enhanced the signature examination, writing that, in some cases, the "pen up pattern in the specimen signatures of one person were quite characteristic of that person's (three spatial dimension) signature."[12]

During the course of the study, Strach, Novotny, Devlin, Graydon and Westwood developed a draft methodology for the examination of dynamic signatures using SignatureScope software.[13] This methodology includes the data analysis of speed, pressure, pen stops (unusually long pauses of the pen), pen lifts, stroke beginnings and endings, sequence and direction of stroke, line smoothness, pen position, baseline alignment, and overall size. The methodology is designed to assist examiners in comparison of dynamic signatures as well as comparisons of dynamic and wet-ink signatures. It lists a definition of each recommended signature characteristic and the location of the data in the SignatureScope software. This methodology is expected to be updated following results of continuing research. The researchers also are exploring the possibility of using SignatureScope software to analyze data collected on other manufacturers' tablets.

In a study by German researchers Heckeroth and Boywitt, electronic signatures were found to be as suitable for determination of authenticity as wet-ink signatures.[14] Electronic signatures were collected on a Galaxy Note 4 smartphone using signotec® software. FDEs in this study did not have access to velocity data for their examination, but they were provided with video of the signing in real-time, which they found beneficial. They were also supplied with plotted signatures containing data points.

Some tablet manufacturers have developed signature analysis software for use in forensic signature examinations. Videos showing the signing of a signature (as recreated from the data collected during the signing event) can be part of this software. Observing the execution of the signature in real-time can reveal direction of stroke, speed, and pressure differences (depending on the software) – characteristics of a signature which a full, dynamic data file would provide.

Research of nonvisible signature dynamics has received attention in recent years. The aim of this research is to identify the kinematic parameters that would indicate nongenuineness. Someone trying to imitate another's genuine signature often uses the static trace of a signature as a model. Therefore, the unseen habits of air movements within pen lifts or how a pen is held while signing could provide valuable discriminating evidence in determinations of genuine or nongenuine signatures.

In a study of the nonvisible, intra-signature dynamics, Dewhurst, Kaye, and Found analyzed the kinematic data collected during pen lifts of both genuine and simulated signatures. They found that nonvisible movements during a signing act (such as pen lifts between first and last names, *i*-dots, or *t*-crossings) tended to be as habitual as the visible portions of a writer's genuine signature. They also found that by comparing kinematic parameters of the nonvisible, intra-signature movements in genuine and simulated signatures, discrimination between the two sets of signatures could be made. None of the simulation attempts "were able to replicate the jerk, nor duration measurements as recorded within the nonvisible segments of the known model formations." Duration was defined as "the movement time in seconds between two points," and jerk was defined as "a disfluency measure, the rate of change of acceleration for stroke size and duration."[15]

Hecker conducted a preliminary study collecting 50 of his own signatures on an Apple iPad Pro using an Apple Pencil and an app he developed, Forensic Signalyzer.[16] Consistency in speed, pressure, altitude, and azimuth were visualized in plots. Future efforts will further explore altitude and azimuth, which quantify the vertical and horizontal angles of how a pen is held during signing.

Mohammed describes kinematic studies in handwriting and signatures, including studies of the dynamics of genuine and disguised signatures, with the aim to aid FDEs in casework involving static signatures.[17] The kinematic studies allow the quantitative collection of dynamic features that FDEs typically rely upon when forming conclusions of authenticity. By examining patterns prevalent in the quantitative data in these studies, FDEs can apply this knowledge in their own casework.

There has been a tremendous amount of research in dynamic signatures – too much to include in this chapter. This research has been conducted by the FDE community as well as those in fields such as pattern recognition, electrical engineering, computer science, biometrics, and neuroscience.

14.4 TABLETS AND CAPTURE DEVICES

As modern technology continues to expand and grow, more and more companies are designing, redesigning, and manufacturing a wide variety of electronic signature capture devices. In today's market, there are numerous manufacturers that offer electronic signature capture devices or e-signature tablets, including Topaz®, Fujitsu®, Wacom®, VeriFone®, Huion®, ePadlink®, signotec®, Ambir®, StepOver®, and Scriptel® (see Figures 14.5 and 14.6 for examples). Depending upon the cost concerns and the specific needs of the consumer, many of the manufacturers offer a variety of models and price ranges within their individual product lines. In addition, there are countless computer software companies developing applications for use with each of the different capture devices being manufactured.

When conducting dynamic signature analysis, knowing the exact make and model of the specific capture device can be invaluable for several reasons. Some capture devices display the signature in real time (LCD display) while others do not. When the signer is using a blank tablet surface versus an LCD screen, they may experience lag time issues (i.e. when he or she cannot see their signature in real time as it is being executed). This may result in the presence of unintended characteristics or features appearing in the signature when viewed after execution. Specifically, portions of a signature appear "cut off" as a result of the writer extending outside of the actual image area, such as is depicted in Figure 14.7, or misplacing strokes such as *i*-dots and *t*-crossings. This is due to the writer not receiving any visual feedback as a point of reference. Knowing the make and model of the capture device allows the examiner to appropriately consider and fully account for these and other potential anomalies that may appear in the rendered electronic signature. Other influential factors may include the type of stylus being used (or lack of a stylus if the tablet accepts finger-made signatures), differences in tablet sizes and types, writing position of the tablet (i.e. vertical vs. horizontal), writing position of the signer, and the writing surface.

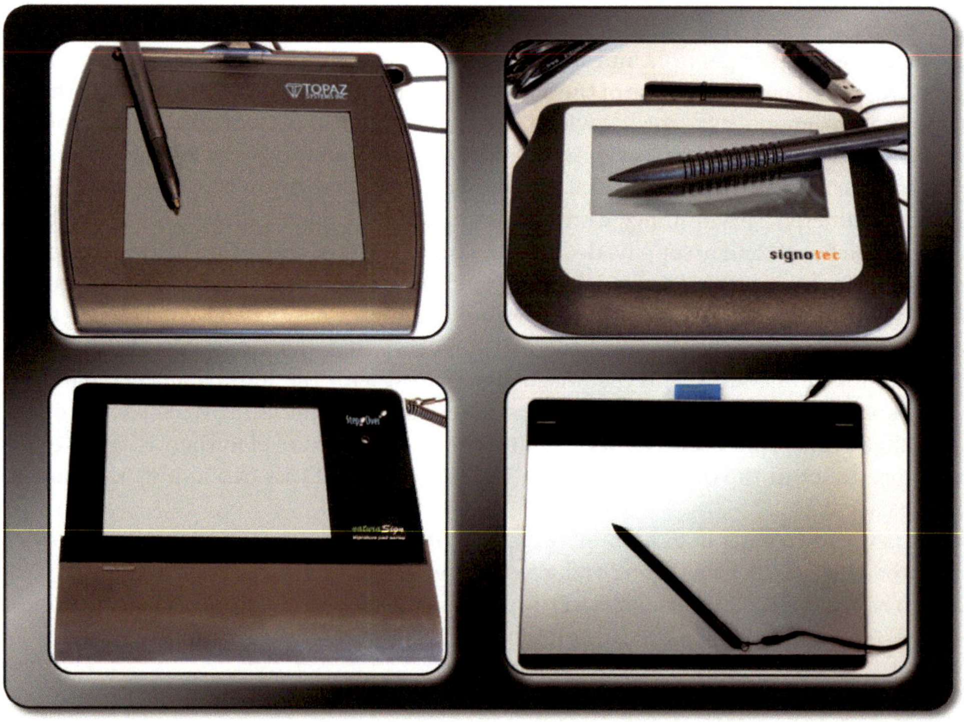

Figure 14.5 Depending upon consumer needs addressed by the manufacturer, electronic signature capture devices can come in many shapes and sizes. Additionally, some capture devices contain an LCD display screen while others only contain a blank writing surface.

Figure 14.6 A variety of electronic signature capture devices, such as the one depicted here, also have the capability of simultaneously recording the raw signature data as the signer is executing the signature in original ink.

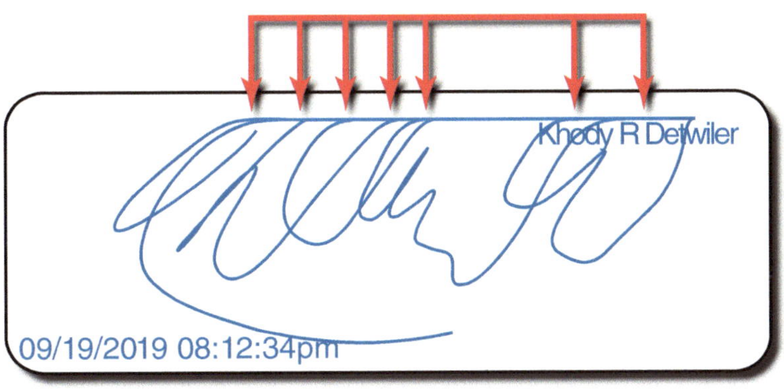

Figure 14.7 The straight lines appearing in the top potion of the signature were formed when the stylus exited the top edge of the device's signing window. These horizontal lines can be key indications of a handwritten electronic signature.

Although there are many factors to consider when conducting an analysis of a dynamic signature, perhaps the most important may be the capture rate of the specific tablet or device being employed. The capture rate is the number of (x, y) cartesian coordinates, or data pairs, the device records as the writer moves the stylus (or writing instrument) across the surface during the execution of the signature. The resolution of the signature will be directly dependent upon the capture rate of the specific tablet model being used; however, most devices currently available typically fall somewhere between 100 samples per second and 500 samples per second.

According to ISO/IEC 19794-7, the minimum accepted capture rate for an electronic signature is 50 samples per second, which is easily surpassed by many capture devices on the market today.

Even at the lowest ISO/IEC accepted sample rate of 50 samples per second, the information contained in the raw signature data will allow an examiner to not only determine the precise execution time for each individual stroke of the signature (and the signature as a whole), but also the acceleration and deceleration of each stroke as the signature was being executed. Depending upon the make and model of the device used, an examiner may also be able to evaluate the pressure patterns of the writer through additional *z*-axis data.

Lastly, depending upon the manufacturer, raw signature data can also include formatting information such as pen (or line) color and pen (or line) width.

14.5 WHAT IS GAINED AND WHAT IS LOST IN THE ANALYSIS OF A DYNAMIC SIGNATURE?

In many cases, the ultimate goal, regardless of whether the examiner is conducting a traditional wet-ink signature analysis or a dynamic signature analysis, is to determine the authenticity of a questioned signature. As discussed above, although these two examination processes are quite similar in many respects, they are certainly not the same. As a result, not only is it necessary for an examiner to understand how these two processes differ but also to understand exactly what is gained and what is lost as a result of each.

As mentioned, when conducting a traditional wet-ink signature analysis, many handwriting features and characteristics are often evaluated and interpreted by the examiner in a subjective manner. This includes the execution rhythm of the writing, the exact stroke sequence, and the overall speed and fluidity of the writing or signature itself. In traditional handwriting comparisons, these characteristics and features are often described with the phrases "smooth and natural," "executed with a high degree of speed and fluidity," and "naturally and spontaneously written," yet no precise language can be used as these features cannot be numerically quantified. On the contrary, when conducting a dynamic signature analysis and using the raw signature data, these features can be quantified and expressed with precision.

Although there is a great deal of forensically significant data that can be obtained from the raw electronic signature file, from a forensic document examination standpoint, the three most relevant items contained within a dynamic signature data file are as follows:

1. The precise stroke timing information, which is ultimately governed by the sample rate of the specific electronic signature capture device being used.
2. The precise acceleration and deceleration exhibited by the writer during the execution of the signature.
3. The precise stroke sequence of the signature, including the placement of *i*-dots, *t*-crossing, and periods in relation to the overall construction. In addition, the stroke sequencing information allows an examiner to determine the direction and exact formation of complex and retraced writing movements.

Specifically, through dynamic signature analysis, the acceleration/deceleration characteristics exhibited by the writer during execution can be tabulated and graphically illustrated to assist the trier of fact (see Figure 14.8). Furthermore, the exact stroke sequence of highly complex or overlapping writing movements can be graphically demonstrated with ease. The speed of not

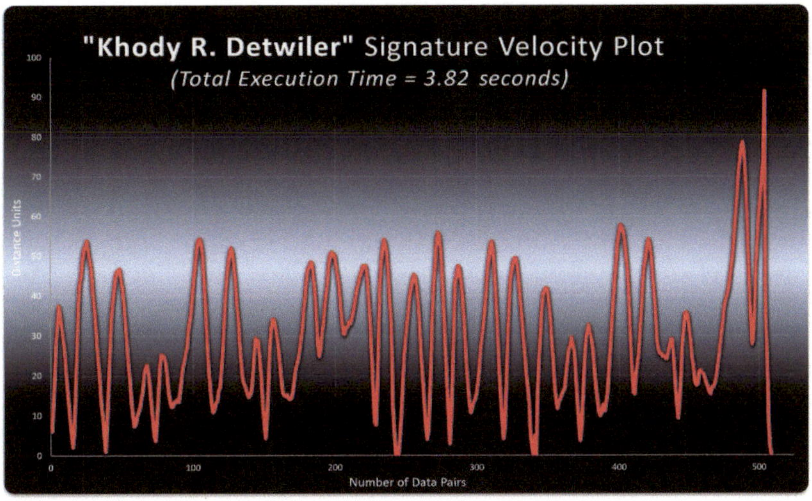

Figure 14.8 The acceleration/deceleration data (i.e. velocity plot) is essentially a graphical representation of the writer's overall spontaneity and execution rhythm exhibited during the act of writing itself.

only the signature as a whole, but also the individual strokes comprising the signature, can be expressed with exact numerical values. Figure 14.9 shows an example.

Although much information is gained through the analysis of a dynamic signature, there are some aspects that may be affected. Most notably, the potential loss of resolution since the quality of a dynamic electronic signature will only be as good as the capture rate of the device being

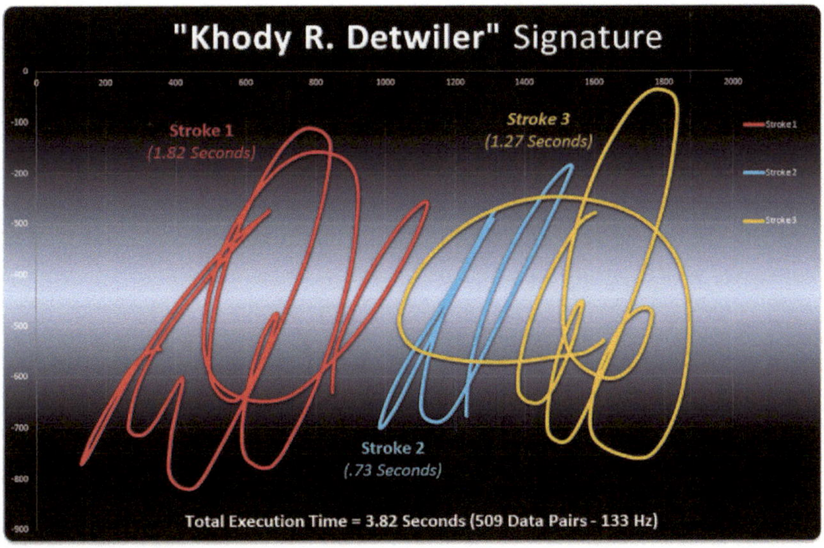

Figure 14.9 Unlike a traditional wet-ink signature examination, when conducting a dynamic signature analysis, the exact speed (i.e. timing) of the signature or strokes comprising the signature can be quantified and expressed with precision.

used. Nevertheless, as technology advances and electronic signature capture devices become more sophisticated, this specific limitation will likely be minimized, if not entirely eliminated in the future.

Another aspect of the overall forensic document examination process that may be affected as a result of signatures being captured electronically is the different types of supplemental examinations that are routinely conducted in typical casework. For example, if the signature is captured electronically, evaluating a multipage contract for the presence of latent handwriting impressions through Electrostatic Detection testing may no longer produce relevant results. Furthermore, conducting different types of filtered light examinations will have very little if any probative value as the signatures or writings being examined are obviously not produced with original writing ink.

Despite the potential for several limiting factors imposed as a result of a signature being captured electronically, the information that is gained far outweighs any potential loss or limitation. Based upon the invaluable data that is gained, electronic signature analysis is arguably just as reliable, if not more, as a traditional wet-ink signature examination.

14.6 ELECTRONIC SIGNATURE ANALYSIS IN CASEWORK

Modern FDEs are increasingly likely to encounter handwritten electronic signatures in casework. They may be questioned signatures or included in samples of known signatures.

There are some characteristics of handwritten electronic signatures that can make them easy to spot. Signatures where portions of loops at the top of ascenders or bottom of descenders have been replaced with a straight, horizontal line can be products of signatures where the signer has crossed beyond the data capture area of the signature pad or the stylus itself has hit the edge of the signing window and caused a horizontal movement, much as writing with a ruler (see Figure 14.10). Another common characteristic of handwritten electronic signatures is a date stamp or data string near the signature. As this is a product of the signature device, the text font and size may be different than the rest of the document. An example is depicted in Figure 14.11. Finally, straight, mechanical lines observed within the signature itself, particularly where pen lifts would be expected (such as between names, *t*-crossings, or *i*-dots), could be indications of a handwritten electronic signature. Such lines represent "air movements" within a signature, specifically, the point where the stylus went off the surface of the tablet and the point where the stylus went back on the surface. These two points are connected with a straight line when a signature is reconstructed using the dynamic data. Most manufacturers will not include these lines

Figure 14.10 The straight line at the bottom of the "y" descender was formed when the stylus hit the bottom edge of the device's signing window. These horizontal lines at the tops of ascenders or bottom of descenders can be indications of an e-signature.

Figure 14.11 An example of an electronically captured signature stamped with the date and time it was completed.

in the signature display, but signatures may be encountered where these lines are included in the printed signature (see Figure 14.12).

One of the first tasks when facing a forensic examination of a handwritten electronic signature is to determine if the signature on the document was saved as an image only, or if the dynamic data was collected during the signing event and saved (oftentimes hashed into the stored document file). This is an important determination for both the attorney submitting the case and the FDE working the case. Let us look at each scenario:

1. *Signature stored as an image only.* With sufficient evidence for comparison, an FDE may be able to determine writership of the questioned handwritten electronic signature. However, the examiner will not be able to definitively opine whether that signature was placed on the document by the author. In other words, if a handwritten electronic signature is captured and saved as a .jpeg file, this .jpeg image can be transferred onto any document. This type of forgery has been employed for years and is known as a *cut and paste* forgery. With these types of questioned handwritten electronic signatures, attorneys should inquire as to how these signatures were collected and stored (or not)

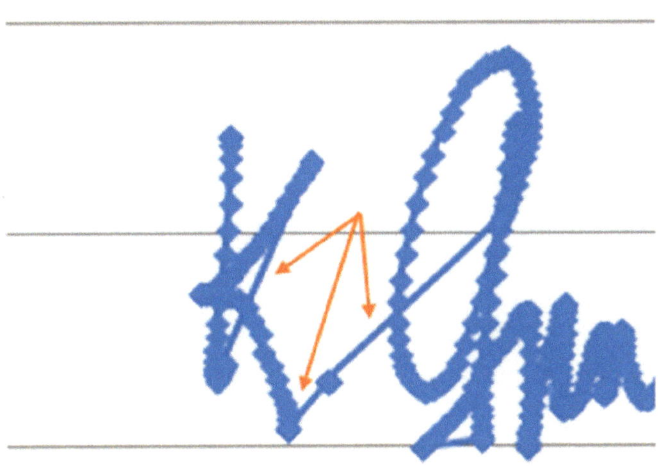

Figure 14.12 The straight lines within the signature represent "air movements" or places where the stylus was off the surface of the tablet. These most frequently coincide with the natural pen lifts within a signature.

and who would have the means and opportunity to place the signature image on a document without the signer's consent.

2. *Signature stored as dynamic data.* If the raw data file has been saved along with the graphical representation of the signature, an FDE trained in these types of examinations will be able to give a writership opinion when there is sufficient evidence for comparison. Comparison evidence could be other unquestioned dynamic signatures within the same document or traditional wet-ink signatures. The best evidence, of course, would be a mixture of both. Comparisons of questioned signature dynamic data to unquestioned signature dynamic data provides the strongest possible evidence.

Determining whether dynamic data was collected during signing often involves some detective work on the part of the attorney, but the rewards are well worth the effort. If the dynamic data has been collected, then oftentimes it is those persons responsible for implementing the technology associated with the form or storing the data collected from the forms that are the most helpful. These data technicians could be employees of the company asking that the form be completed, or they could be employees of a third-party vendor. Once the raw data file associated with the questioned signature has been located, the file should be decrypted before submitting it to the document examiner. Again, this must be done by the persons responsible for the data storage and collection. Finally, the data technician should be asked if the raw data signature file was downsampled, and if so, what was the effective capture rate. For instance, an insurance agent may use a signature pad with a capture rate of 133 Hz to acquire client signatures. However, due to storage size limitations and transmission time considerations, the insurance company's home office decides to downsample the dynamic signature raw data files to 100 Hz. Therefore, although the dynamic signatures were collected at a rate of 133 Hz, their effective capture rate is 100 Hz.

The raw data file should be submitted along with the following:

1. A body of known signatures, of which some should be contemporaneous to the questioned signature and, ideally, include unquestioned dynamic signature raw data files;
2. The make and model of the signature capture device;
3. The data capture rate of the signature device or the effective capture rate of the raw data file;
4. A copy of the document containing the questioned signature;
5. Information regarding how the signature was collected, such as
   a. Was a stylus used?
   b. Was the signature made in a setting where both the signature device and arm were supported?
   c. Was the signer sitting, standing, or lying down?

Given the raw data file, an FDE can plot a graphical representation of the signature, determine how long it took to execute the signature, scrutinize direction of strokes and sequence of strokes within a signature, and plot the writer's rhythm. Speed, rhythm, and direction of stroke are all vital aspects of determination of signature writership. With the raw data, these aspects are quantifiable.

14.7 ELECTRONIC SIGNATURE ANALYSIS IN COURT

As with any advancement in forensic science, a new method should not only be validated by the scientific community but also withstand challenges in court. Although research and work pertaining to electronic signature analysis began over a decade ago, only a limited number of cases have been submitted and examined to completion, and an even smaller number of those cases have found their way into a courtroom. Consequently, it comes as no surprise that when one of these cases finally went to court, the merits of the entire process would be subject to a legal challenge.

On November 3, 2011, in the case of *American General Life Assurance Company of Columbus v. Glenda Biles, et al.*, Federal Judge Tom S. Lee of the US District Court, Southern District of Mississippi denied a defense motion to exclude the expert testimony of FDE William J. Flynn. It was further cited that the forensic analysis of electronically captured signatures satisfies the Daubert requirements for admissibility. Specifically:

> ...AFLAC's expert William Flynn based his analysis on a comparison of the signatures created based on the raw captured signature data and the known exemplars of Biles' signature. Based on that comparison, he identified the signatures on the AFLAC documents as the signatures of David Biles. It is manifest from Mr. Flynn's testimony that defendants' challenge to the reliability of Mr. Flynn's opinion is without reasonable basis; and therefore, the motion to strike/exclude will be denied.[18]

On April 30, 2013, the Fifth Circuit Court of Appeals upheld the admission of electronic signature analysis testimony in this matter.[19] Without question, this ruling is a landmark victory in the field of forensic document examination, paving the way for future testimony pertaining to electronic signature analysis in courts throughout the United States. To date, no state or federal courts have denied the admissibility of expert testimony pertaining to the analysis of electronically captured handwritten signatures.

14.8 LOOKING FORWARD

As with many advancements in forensic testing methods, although much work has been completed, there will always be much work left to do. It goes without saying that handwritten electronic signature analysis has been well-established and rooted on solid ground; however, as handwritten electronic signature technology advances and paperless workflows increase, so too will the need for additional research and development. Many studies are currently underway throughout the United States and abroad in an effort to advance the capabilities of electronic signature analysis in a variety of different areas. In particular, several collaborative studies are being conducted with hardware and software manufacturers, focusing on the analysis of handwritten electronic signatures written by finger, rather than a stylus. These types of signature collection methods are becoming increasingly more common, and the need for verification is inevitable. Other studies are being conducted focusing on the implications of pressure data (z-axis) in a dynamic signature examination; more specifically, the impact that pressure data may have on determining the authenticity of a questioned signature.

Along with the evolution of these new examination techniques and methods, there will come the need for redesigned proficiency tests, as well as the development of verification guidelines and standard operating procedures specific to the analysis of handwritten electronic signatures. Many of these needs are actively being addressed and will continue to be researched for years to come. Nonetheless, the research conducted to date is more than promising, and clearly demonstrates that handwritten electronic signature analysis can yield accurate and reproducible results.

REFERENCES

1. http://euro.ecom.cmu.edu/program/law/08-732/Transactions/ueta.pdf
2. https://www.fdic.gov/regulations/compliance/manual/10/x-3.1.pdf

3. Linden, J., Marquis, R., Bozza, S., and Taroni, F., "Dynamic signatures: A review of dynamic feature variation and forensic methodology," *Forensic Science International*, vol. 291 (2018): 216–229.
4. Tytell, P., "Pen pressure as an identifying characteristic of signatures: Verification from the computer," *Journal of the American Society of Questioned Document Examiners*, vol. 1 (1998): 21–31.
5. Flynn, W., *Electronic Signature Forensics*, 1999 white paper prepared for Topaz: https://docplayer.net/8881723-Article-electronic-signature-forensics-copyright-topaz-systems-inc-all-rights-reserved.html
6. Flynn, W. J., "Conducting a forensic examination of electronically captured signatures," *Journal of the American Society of Questioned Document Examiners*, vol. 15, no. 1 (2012): 3–10.
7. Annunziata Nicolaides, K., "Using acceleration/deceleration plots in the forensic analysis of electronically captured signatures," *Journal of the American Society of Questioned Document Examiners*, vol. 15, no. 2 (December 2012): 29–43.
8. Osborn, A. S., *Questioned Documents*, Second Edition, (Montclair, NJ: Patterson Smith, 1973) 98–99.
9. Annunziata Nicolaides, K., "Biometric Electronic Signatures: Pen Stylus v. Finger," *paper presented at American Society of Questioned Document Examiners Annual Meeting*, August 23, 2016.
10. Flynn, W. J., and Annunziata Nicolaides, K., "An Analysis of Digitally Captured Signatures: Are Principles of Forensic Signature Identification Corroborated by Analysis of Quantifiable Data?" *presented at the American Academy of Forensic Sciences Annual Scientific Meeting*, February 19, 2015.
11. Caligiuri, M., Mohammed, L., Found, B., and Rogers, D., "Nonadherence to the isochrony principle in forged signatures," *Forensic Science International*, vol. 223, nos. 1–3 (2012): 228–32, http://dx.doi.org/10.1016/j.forsciint.2012.09.008
12. Strach, S., Novotny, M., and Devlin, A., "Evaluation of WACOM'S Electronic Handwritten Signature Technology," *white paper* (February 2018): 8–9.
13. Strach, S., Novotny, M., Devlin, A., Graydon, C., and Westwood, P., "Development of a Draft Methodology for Electronic Signature Examination using Wacom SignatureScope," *paper presented at the American Society of Questioned Document Examiners Annual Meeting*, Pensacola, FL, August 20–25, 2016.
14. Heckeroth, J., and Boywitt, C.D., "Examining authenticity: An initial exploration of the suitability of handwritten electronic signatures," *Forensic Science International*, vol. 275 (2017): 144–154.
15. Dewhurst, T., Ballantyne, K., and Found, B., "Empirical investigation of biometric, non-visible, intra-signature features in known and simulated signatures," *Australian Journal of Forensic Sciences*, vol. 48, no. 6 (January 2016): 4–7. DOI:10.1080/00450618.2015.1126637.
16. Hecker, T., "Forensic Signalyzer: Collecting and Analyzing Data of Dynamic Features of Handwriting," *paper presented at the American Society of Questioned Document Examiners Annual General Meeting*, San Diego, CA, August 28, 2017.
17. Caligiuri, M., and Mohammed, L., *The Neuroscience of Handwriting*, (Boca Raton, FL: CRC Press, 2012) 95–126.
18. American Family Life Assurance Company of Columbus v. Glenda C. Biles, et al. (2011). *US district court Southern district of Mississippi, Jackson division, civil action No. 3:10cv667tsl-Fkb.* Memorandum Opinion and Order dated November 3, 2011.
19. American Family Life Assurance Company of Columbus v. Glenda C. Biles, et al. (2013). *US court of appeals fifth circuit.* Case No. 12–60235. Filed April 30.

Chapter 15

Indentation Development and Visualization

Tobin Tanaka

CONTENTS

15.1 SOURCES OF INDENTATION

The act of writing upon pages that are stacked together may leave indented writing or impressions on the lower sheets. The depth of any impression will depend on the applied pressure, the writing instrument, the nature of the paper, and the writing surface support. Impressions or disturbances to the paper may range from clearly visible to latent. When impressions are made, they do not necessarily have to be from an organized bundle of paper such as a notepad. Overlapping papers that are scattered on a surface may get impressions or disturbances.

Mechanical handling of documents may also cause impressions. Paper transport and separating hardware may impart subtle or visible markings on paper. Such handling of the documents could occur prior to document creation (such as during paper manufacture), during document creation (such as a document being printed by an inkjet printer), or after document creation (such as sending it through the postal system).

Indented impressions may disclose information on how, when, and where a document was produced. While the focus of this chapter will be on the indentations that are seen on paper, it is important to keep in mind that there are other types of materials that may get indentations. These materials include plastic substrates such as bags, wooden surfaces such as countertops, or any other sufficiently deformable material. The severity and persistence of any mechanical handling markings will depend on the interaction and physical properties of the object(s) causing them and the substrate receiving them.

Although indentations may be easily seen, the decipherment of them is not necessarily a straightforward matter. There may be complications due to the variety of materials and circumstances that led to the indentations, as well as the handling of the item after indentations were made. For these reasons, it is sometimes necessary to use a variety of techniques to optimize the visualization of the decipherment. Some techniques harken back to the earliest ones used in the profession, whereas others are recent and better suited for specific types of materials.

15.2 HISTORY OF DEVELOPMENT METHODS

Over the past 100 years, forensic document examiners (FDEs) have used a variety of means to visualize and record indented writings on paper and other substrates. Many techniques that have been proposed are not generally used today as they are destructive to the document or render the development by other means impossible. A summary of development methods by Brown in 1998 provided a comprehensive listing of these types of techniques.[1] Many of these methods cannot realistically be used due to health and safety reasons in the modern laboratory.

One method of development that should never be used is that of pencil or graphite rubbing onto the surface. Wilson Harrison summed it up well[2]:

> Many a valuable document has been defaced and ruined for further investigation by the stupid practice of dusting the surface with a black powder such as graphite or the graphite mixture used for developing fingerprints. This dusting is carried out in the pious hope that the powder will obligingly collect in the depressions, which will then be rendered decipherable by direct lighting.

Most techniques discussed in this chapter will focus on development and visualization methods that are nondestructive and do not have significant health and safety issues when applied properly.

15.3 OBLIQUE (RAKING) ILLUMINATION

Even without directional illumination, it is often possible to see indentations on a page when conditions permit. Sometimes simply having the document on a table with daylight from a window may permit viewing of indentations.

Controlled lighting that is directional and adaptable is well suited to the visualization of indented impressions. Oblique illumination, grazing illumination, and side lighting are just some of the terms used to describe the condition where a thin plane of light is brought parallel to the surface of the page. In the conservation and archaeology community, the term *raking light* is often used to describe the illumination in the same plane as the object. Raking light reveals the surface details and texture of paintings and other objects, including paper.[3] The casting of shadows that are dependent on the direction of illumination may occur, revealing indentations. Over the years, there have been a variety of illumination sources that may project light in such a manner. The more successful ones have greater control over the intensity, thickness of the illumination plane, and directionality that may be offered. Early attempts by Duxbury and Warren (1956) described the making of an "Indented Writing Box", where adjustable wooden doors were moved to create better conditions to see indentations.[4,5] Harrison suggested using light that could be easily moved to various locations to create the shadows that allow for indentation decipherment and a cylindrical lens to create a flat beam of light.

In recent times, a large range of illumination sources have been produced, such as those in spectral comparators or LED illumination strips that have a multipurpose use for crime scene officers or laboratory work. However, the use of a handheld flashlight may sometimes be sufficient for recording of indented writings by photography. This may be especially valuable when there are many documents to examine quickly, as may be seen in "triage" types of examinations, where an initial screening for indentations is desired.

With improvements in illumination technologies, including light emitting diode (LED) systems, several advantages are realized. First, energy efficiency is improved, permitting extended use of such sources even when operating with batteries. Second, their compactness permits them to be taken nearly anywhere, such as those examinations that must take place in the field. Third, many of these sources are highly luminous, with output in the range of 5,000 lumens (lm).[6] Compare this to a conventional tungsten light bulb of 100W which only outputs 1,750 lm.[7] Fourth, some LED systems are cool to the touch, although those that are exceptionally intense can potentially degrade papers that are more sensitive to heat or light, such as thermal papers. Fifth, some LED systems are available with different color temperatures, permitting the possibility of color balance and channel separation if needed. The latter may not be as critical in the modern context of digital photography, where the camera may make white balance adjustments during photography.

Fiber optic illumination systems that are used with some microscopes may be fitted with attachments that provide raking illumination, as shown in Figure 15.1.

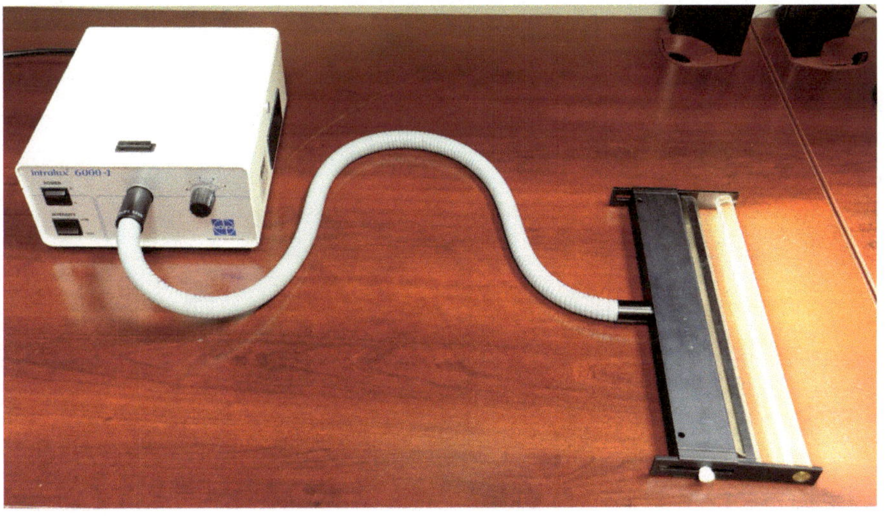

Figure 15.1 An adjustable cylindrical lens that projects a plane of light.

There are potential advantages to photographing with raking illumination from different directions or using combinations of directions. This may especially be important when the impressions are very deep.

In the author's laboratory, the use of a vacuum bed with a mild air pump provides a most useful apparatus for indentation visualization, as shown in Figure 15.2. Raking illumination has been achieved using a combination of fiber optic attachments similar to that shown in Figure 15.1. Further optimization has been achieved by using an optical bench which permits the rapid placement of all document and illumination elements. Optical benches also allow subtle adjustments to be made along the horizontal, vertical, and height axes.

Even without a vacuum bed, the recording of images of indented writing using a number of raking illumination directions may provide a legible decipherment, as shown in Figure 15.3. The advantages of photographic techniques are their nondestructive nature and relative simplicity to use.

If needed, subsequent image processing may provide better decipherment. Image processing may be achieved by a variety of means. Some equipment with built-in raking light systems may have image processing routines in place that allow for the processing of two or more images, as shown in Figures 15.4 and 15.5. If multiple images are recorded where the only change is the direction of illumination, the size and scale of the image will be unchanged. This permits basic arithmetic operations to be easily performed from the equipment software and may result in an improved image for decipherment. Outside of the equipment software, programs such as Adobe® Photoshop® or ImageJ are well suited to perform operations such as imaging or averaging of multiple images. For example, these programs can take two images and output an average of the recorded pixel values, providing highlights of the indented regions.

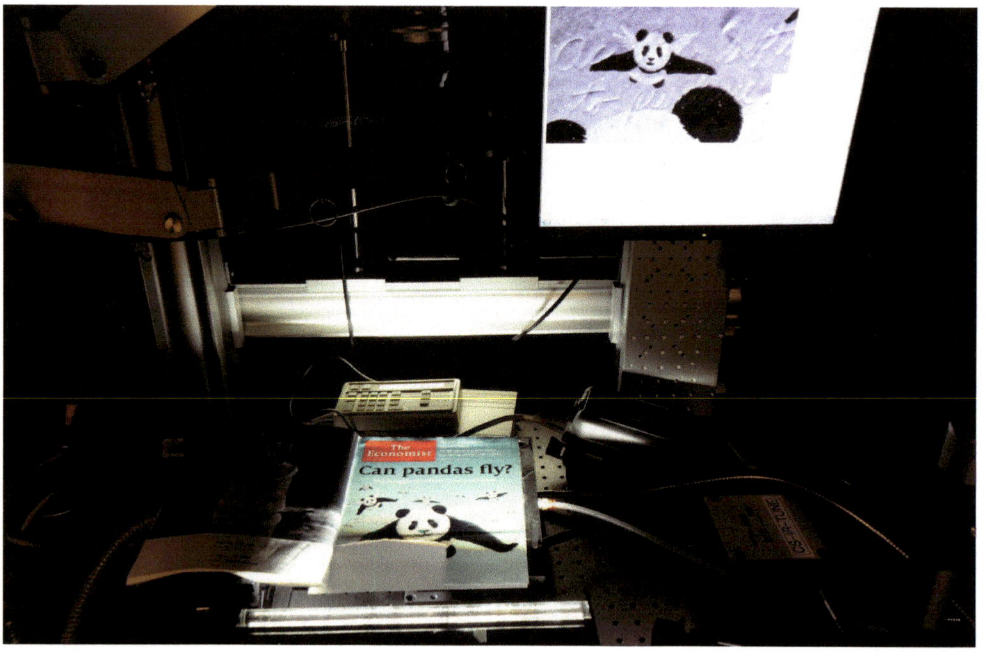

Figure 15.2 Optical bench setup.

(a) (b)

Figure 15.3 Raking illumination from (a) the left side and (b) the right side.

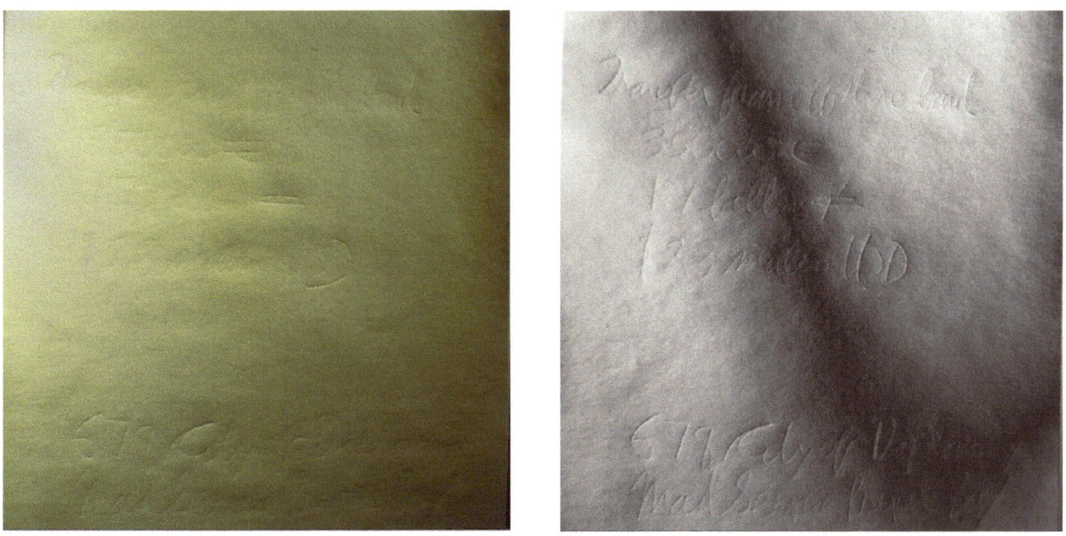

(a) (b)

Figure 15.4 (a) Average and (b) difference of pixel values from left and right raking illumination images.

More complex filters that may reduce effects of background noise and interfering portions can also be used.[8] It should be noted that excessive post-processing of images is no substitute for quality images recorded with a variety of raking illumination positions. For most situations, the use of image post-processing will not result in a substantial improvement in the legibility of the indented writings.

(a) (b)

Figure 15.5 (a) Maximum and (b) minimum of pixel levels from left and right raking illumination images.

Depending on the nature of the substrate and the indentations, there is ample opportunity to test different illumination and imaging configurations to determine what configuration provides optimum visualization. Given the desire for nondestructive laboratory work, it is often worthwhile to see if such optical methods result in visible indented impressions.

15.4 ELECTROSTATIC DETECTION DEVICE (EDD)

The public premiere of electrostatic detection of indented writing at the International Association of Forensic Sciences (IAFS) meeting in 1978 brought a new sensitive method to the document examiner's toolkit.[9] Developed in conjunction with the London School of Printing, the Electrostatic Detection Apparatus (ESDA®) was first tested at the Metropolitan Police Forensic Science Laboratory in London. It was used to detect indented writing on a bank robbery note, although the original intent was to develop fingerprints on fabric materials, which was not successful.[10]

ESDA® is a tradename under Foster + Freeman®. Other similar instruments have been invented over the years, such as the Docustat DS-220®, a tradename of Projectina®/Ultra Electronics Forensic Technology®. The Scientific Working Group for Forensic Document Examination (SWGDOC) standard for the development of indented impressions uses the generic term Electrostatic Detection Device (EDD) to describe such instruments.[11]

The EDD operates similarly to the electrophotographic process in regards to charging and application of toner via cascade and aerosol development.[12–14] The primary difference is that there is no photoreceptor (imaging drum) but a layer of plastic film, document, and vacuum bed.

The basic steps to develop indentations are as follows:

1. The document to be developed is humidified if the ambient conditions are dry.
2. The document is placed on top of an electrically grounded vacuum bed (having an electrical connection to the earth via the electrical plug).

3. The pump is energized, drawing the document down toward the vacuum bed.
4. Plastic imaging film is drawn across the document.
5. A high voltage corona wire is moved over the surface.
6. Toner is applied over the film that covers the document.
7. An adhesive sheet is used to "fix" the result.

The resulting adhesive sheet, toner, and plastic film combination recording the indentations is referred to as an EDD lift or simply "lift". These steps are described in detail in the next sections.

15.4.1 Pre-Handling of Documents

A variety of experiments and tests have found conditions that tend to provide better developments. As EDDs will tend to develop fingerprints, it is good practice to use gloves when handling documents before and during the development phase. The type of glove used, document storage, document handling, and solvent exposure can affect indentation development results. Wiping the surface of the paper with latex or cotton gloves may degrade the development significantly on the side of the page that has been subjected to the wiping. However, the reverse side of the same pages could still result in detectable impressions. Likewise, solvents will either degrade development or totally destroy the possibility of development via EDD. Some reports have found that certain types of gloves may degrade the development if handling is not carefully conducted. Excess handling by paper to paper friction may also degrade impressions.[15]

Documents should be handled as little as possible, even with gloves, and document to document contact should be minimized as much as possible. This is important due to the potential of *secondary impressions* which may result from direct paper to paper contact or from folded documents within envelopes.[16–18]

For environments which are particularly dry, the exposure to increased humidity levels before development usually results in superior results.[19–21] Generally, the humidity in the air is measured as relative humidity (RH), which refers to the percentage of water vapor to the maximum (saturation) that is possible for a given temperature. Warmer air can hold more water vapor, so the same RH value for air at different temperatures does not mean that the humidity levels are the same. For example, an RH value of 60% means air at a temperature of 18°C has much less humidity than air at 30°C.[22]

Practically speaking, if one is operating an EDD in a tropical climate, it may not be necessary to subject the document to elevated humidity for better results. This will of course depend on the area where the EDD is used. If it is in a room with powerful air conditioning, the air may be significantly dried out to require humidification of the document.

When working in colder environments in the winter months, the air tends to be extremely dry, especially when heating systems are at work. Humidification is typically achieved by placing the documents onto shelves within a cabinet, with a shallow pan of water at the base. This boosts the humidity of the interior of the cabinet and any documents within. For humidity cabinets, it is advisable not to let condensed water drip onto the paper or supporting shelf as this may damage the document.

There is no universal agreement in the forensic community on how long to humidify the document. Experience has found that very thick papers require longer times than thin ones, but this will depend on the type of paper. Beal found that document conditioning in an environmental chamber with a water temperature of 55°F (12.8°C) for 10 minutes produced superior developments in contrast to using hot water for a few minutes as suggested by the

(a) (b)

Figure 15.6 (a) Photo of humidity cabinet with shelves and (b) with the temperature/humidity controls.

EDD manufacturer.[23] This study was performed in Colorado, which was described as a "dry, high altitude climate."

Some laboratories have humidity cabinets, such as those shown in Figure 15.6, or even entire rooms where temperature and humidity (RH) can be controlled. This type of environment has the advantage of no water droplet condensation, and it permits many documents to be subjected to elevated humidity simultaneously.

When ready for development, the document is placed on the vacuum bed, the pump powered on, and the plastic film drawn across the document. There has not been published research into the use of alternative types of plastic films. The possibility that other plastic films could offer an improved development is an enticing area of research that could be fruitful.

15.4.2 Charging

The charging of the plastic film has its origins in the electrophotography process. The high voltage wire used for charging causes a phenomenon known as corona, which is the electrostatic breakdown of the gaseous molecules in the air to create charged ions. The corona creates a negative ion current that is about 90% CO_3^- ions. A detailed account of the physics of how the corona does this may be found in Williams and Moore.[24,25] Most EDDs operate using negative voltage coronas. One drawback to negative coronas is that they tend to be less uniform along the length of the wire compared to positive coronas. Another drawback is that there is about ten times more ozone created with negative corona compared to positive corona. Accordingly, protective measures should be taken to mitigate exposure to ozone. Fortunately, ozone does not naturally persist for long time periods at lower altitudes. Specific tests of ozone measurement found that prolonged operation of the corona for long periods with no ventilation may result in levels of ozone that exceed occupational health and safety standards. Short duration operation of less than one minute with no room ventilation did not cause levels to exceed the regulatory limits of the US Occupational Safety and Health Administration Personal Exposure Limits (PEL) or the Short-Term Exposure Limit (STEL), which is a California Code of Regulations limit.[26]

By varying the movements of the corona across the surface of the film, it is possible to significantly reduce the variations that exist along the corona. If the motion is kept in a straight, uniform movement, "streaks" may result. Charging of the film for approximately 10–30 seconds is sufficient for suitable development. This has been confirmed from measurements of the extent of charging and from manufacturer's technical notes.[27,28]

15.4.3 Toner Application

The application of toner to the charged plastic film should ideally result in a preferential deposition of toner into areas with indented writings. As described in Section 15.4.9, the voltages of indented areas are not as negative compared to voltages of non-indented regions. The preferential deposition of toner on indented regions does not imply that no toner will be deposited on non-indented regions; a proportion of toner will still adhere to non-indented regions but much less than the indented regions. If a number of pages have impressions in a paper stack, then the pages that are closer to the one being written upon will usually result in a greater deposition of toner, as shown in Figure 15.7. In other words, the development will be darker than pages that are lower in the stack.

The toner itself is electrostatically charged. This charging is usually achieved by contact or frictional means, which is commonly called static electrification. Static electrification is familiar to everyone, and its effects are easily seen and felt. For example, rub a cloth over a balloon, and the balloon may cling to the wall. Walk over carpet and touch a doorknob, and the resulting shock is certainly felt. Whilst it is a familiar physical phenomenon, the reasons why electrification take place at an atomic level are complex, as described by the classic works of Loeb and Harper.[29,30]

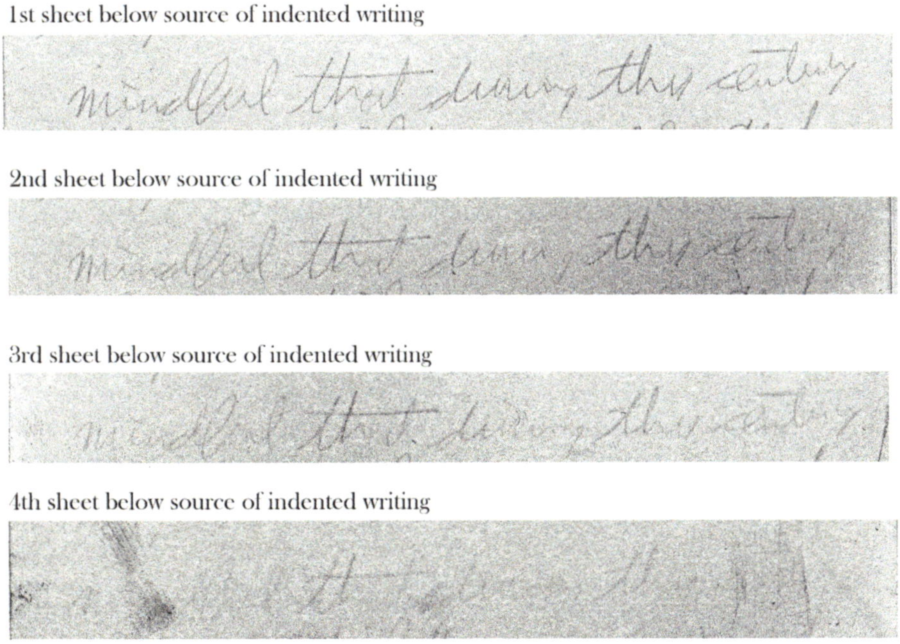

Figure 15.7 Images of indented writing showing lower contrast and less clarity with progressively deeper sheets in a paper stack.

15.4.4 Cascade Development

In the application of toner by cascade development, the toner is charged from contact and friction interaction with the glass beads that are used as a carrier. As the surface of the vacuum bed is angled to permit the flow of the glass beads over the surface, the toner tends to be deposited at sites of indented writing.

Prior to deposition, the toner is electrostatically attracted to the glass beads. The charging relies on triboelectrification, which is caused by friction between two dissimilar insulating materials (toner and glass). Variation in the degree of charging will be present due to chemical composition of materials, area of surface contact, and other factors. The manner in which particles, including toner, become charged via contact electrification is complicated and difficult to control. Some indication of the factors that are involved can be found in research from the materials handling and processing fields.[31,32]

Practical tests have found that the properties of the glass beads used for cascade development may influence the quality of the ensuing development. Field tests have also disclosed that overuse of the cascade glass beads results in poor development. Accordingly, the glass beads should be replaced after a period of use that can be determined by visual examination of the glass beads under magnification of 10–30×. Unsuitable glass beads will be observed to have pitting where the toner becomes "welded" within the pitted areas.[33–35]

Lewis found that the application of moisture to the cascade developer via a plant mist sprayer resulted in improved clarity for 35 out of 50 documents that were developed. These documents were limited to one type of multiple-use paper in one laboratory.[34]

Cascade development is preferred by some FDEs due to the localized nature of the application. In other words, more toner can be deposited to regions where indented writing begins to appear, allowing for improved legibility. A drawback to cascade development can be the persistence of the glass beads on the vacuum bed and imaging film. Without removal, these beads may leave small markings on subsequent documents that are developed.

15.4.5 Brush or Applicator Development

Some FDEs prefer to apply toner by employing brushes or applicators. This technique takes practice and skill but allows more precise toner application to desired areas. In a manner similar to cascade development, the materials that are used have to be electrostatically compatible, allowing for the deposition of toner where indentations are located.

15.4.6 Aerosol or Cloud Development

With this technique, toner is applied by aerosol spray or precipitation particulate. Application by this means may result in a more homogeneous application of toner on the plastic film than cascade development, where the first point of contact for the carrier beads tends to have a heavier toner deposition.

15.4.7 Recording Results

At this stage, the toner on the imaging film is held in place by electrostatic forces, and some permanent record must be made to preserve the result. Photographing the image of the indented writings in proximity to the visible writings is an advantage when there is the need to consider the sequencing of indentations and visible writing intersections. This will be described in a later section. There are also advantages as the toner will not be disturbed.

For ease of preservation, a transparent fixing sheet is carefully applied to stick to the toner and imaging film. In the application process, there should be an attempt to minimize disturbance to the resultant image. This can be achieved with a sufficiently stiff adhesive sheet that can be shaped into a "U", with the trough of the "U" being placed at the central portion and then unrolling the left and right sides of the sheet until uniformly flat. While it may not necessarily be required to retain negative lifts, those where no indentations are developed, it is not always obvious that there are no impressions. As a result, it may be advantageous to record all indentation developments for detailed inspection.

15.4.8 Indentation Test Sheets or Strips

To ensure proper operation of an EDD, many examiners will use test sheets or strips before or during developments. Some examiners will make a page with indentations and develop it before processing any questioned documents. Others will make a thin strip of paper with indented writing that can be developed at the same time as the questioned documents.

A device that would produce test indentations in a gradient (heavy to light in depth) was described by Purdy.[36] This was a rectangular metal slab with a slotted center and attachment for a ballpoint pen. It was made to permit the pen to make heavy to light impressions as it was moved along the slot. His tests found that the resultant EDD development did show differences in the heavy to light impressions that generally corresponded to the depth of the impressions, thus verifying its operation.

15.4.9 Why Does It Work?

Foster and Morantz attempted to explain the reason for the EDD success in indentation development as being due to a difference in electrical capacitance in areas where such indentations were present.[37] Wanxiang and Xiaoling published a paper in 1988 that attempted to account for how the EDD process worked.[38] In this work, the authors advanced the theory that the result was due to the variation in the paper texture rather than the variation in paper thickness. In this model, the paper, imaging film, and electrically grounded plate were considered to be an electrical capacitor circuit. This model does not account for some observed features, such as when visible writing will develop as dark lines rather than transparent lines.

A model of greater complexity was advanced by Seward.[39] Seward found that it was the paper-to-paper friction that was detectable by EDD development rather than indentations alone. The experiments conducted included one where indentations were made onto a stack in the order that follows:

- top paper sheet (called P_0)
- Mylar film
- middle paper sheet (called P_1)
- bottom paper sheet (called P_2)
- aluminum plate

A stainless-steel rod was used to make an impression onto P_0, the top item in the stack. It was found that EDD development was visible for the front side of P_2 and the reverse side of P_1, but no development was seen for the front side of P_1, which was directly in contact with the Mylar film. This is, at least in part, similar to findings made by FDEs, where the development for impressions with an EDD does not generally work for the page surface that was in direct contact with the plastic film. However, this may depend on the type of plastic film that was present.[40,41]

Part of the difficulty in getting a completely satisfactory theory is the difficulty in achieving significant control over variables. In certain instances, contradictory results are obtained.[42] When attempts are made to only change one variable for an experiment, such as the type of carrier beads for example, it is difficult to fully control other factors like variations in room humidity and degree of charging the imaging film. This does not mean that experiments to improve the development should not be attempted, but it should be realized that such efforts may require many repetitions and an equal amount of patience.

Practically speaking, it has been determined that regions where indented impressions develop have a difference in the electrical potential (voltage). Those sections have a voltage which is different from the areas that do not have impressions. Yaraskavitch et al. found that indented portions had an electrical potential that was approximately 30–50V less negative than regions without impressions.[43]

15.5 INDENTATION DEVELOPMENT FOR PRINTER/ PAPER HANDLING MARKS

The production and handling of documents may involve interaction with printing or handling devices that impart roller marks or other mechanical impressions to the paper. Certain office machines will tend to leave roller marks that can be developed by EDDs. Such marks may be made from different areas of the machine: from the paper source tray; to the feed mechanisms in the printing area; to finishing steps involving stapling, folding, or hole punching; to the output tray.

An earlier preliminary study by LaPorte found that inkjet-printed documents had roller marks that could be made from the mechanical parts of the printer.[44] Such examinations may be of value when access to a suspect device is available. He described how it may be possible to detect individualizing markings on paper due to wear on rollers that had similar class characteristics. Several caveats were described that may explain differences in the roller marks and how they appear, including variation within the same printer and the potential of paper being fed through another printer without print occurring. Other differences may occur from the paper production and manufacturing processes leaving marks on the page even before printing takes place.

Olson described another source of mechanical markings that may arise from automatic document feeders in copiers.[45] This study describes how photocopiers could produce indentations from the document feeder. Examination disclosed evidence indicating that the document feeding mechanisms were the cause of specific roller marks on the documents. As a result of this study, Olson suggested that access to a copier be made available when conducting a copier association examination, along with appropriate service records with schematic diagrams of the paper transport mechanism when needed. The significant finding was that to avoid interfering markings, evidential documents should be hand-placed on the platen, not copied by an automatic document feeder. This information should be conveyed to investigators as well.

15.6 OVERLAYS OF EDD LIFTS AND IMAGE ENHANCEMENT

FDEs sometimes use an EDD to develop impressions on the same document more than once. This is done to improve development in a specific area or due to the tendency to get undesirable heavy toner deposit on one side of the document after cascade development. Multiple EDD lifts can be physically superimposed, sometimes resulting in greater legibility of faint indentations. Generally, such superposition results in a localized alignment of developed indentations. In other words, the developed indentations will not be precisely superimposable over a large area but rather over a smaller portion. This is due to the slight shifts of the toner when fixing sheets are placed over the film.

Overlapping of EDD lift images digitally may be used to create a similar effect as the physical overlay. Giles and Giles describe the use of imaging software that is capable of stacking many short-exposure astronomical images to improve the signal to noise ratio. When applied to EDD lifts, a significant improvement in the legibility was achieved. The reason is that the signal (indentation line) does not change significantly from lift to lift, whereas the noise tends to not be amplified as much when images are stacked.[46] Other image processing software such as Photoshop® or ImageJ may assist in making low contrast or low legibility developments clearer. If such software is used, it should be set to retain a record of what types of processing were performed so that it is repeatable and demonstrative.[47]

15.7 FRACTURE MATCH COMPARISONS

Barton[48] describes how fracture comparisons of torn pages may be enhanced by EDD development. When torn pages are delaminated, i.e. there is a sheering action, the resulting edges will tend to reveal darker development when the inner layers are "face up" during development. When the corresponding portion is developed after it is flipped over, the delaminated areas may be clearly outlined, making the matching of edges to be achieved with greater ease. The success of this technique will depend on the paper type and the extent of document wear, handling, and exposure to external agents such as liquids.

15.8 SEQUENCING OF DEVELOPED EDD IMPRESSIONS AND VISIBLE WRITING

EDD development may assist in determining the sequence of events when visible writing intersects with indented impressions. Visible writing refers to the inked writing on the document itself. It generally appears as clear lines on an EDD lift. Indented writing is the impression from writing on a different document that generally develops as dark lines on an EDD lift[49,50] (see Figure 15.8).

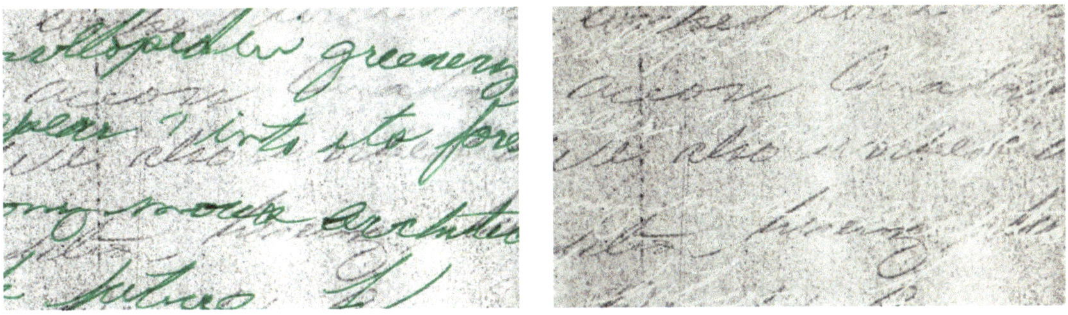

(a) (b)

Figure 15.8 (a) An EDD lift superimposed on the document developed for indented writing. The visible writing is in green ink, and the indented writing appears as dark lines. (b) Depicts an EDD lift against a white background, where the visible writing from the document appears as clear lines, and the indented writing appears as dark lines.

If dark lines (indentations) appear to be continuous when they intersect with clear lines (visible writing), there is strong evidence that the indentations were made after the visible writing. If dark lines appear to have breaks in them from clear lines, this suggests that the visible writing was made after the indentation. However, as will be described below, some careful examination and interpretation is needed. The sequencing determination must be considered with the source of indentations document in hand.

A comprehensive step-by-step explanation of when this technique may be used, the interpretation of the crossings, and other important factors can be found in the paper by Radley and Lindblom.[51] As the authors describe, these following factors must be considered:

1. Writing instrument type-aqueous (water-based) ink, gel, or ballpoint. Water-based inks tend to affect straightforward interpretation as long as the writing instrument is functioning properly. Ballpoint or gel pen writing instruments may be misinterpreted if care is not taken to account for the possibility of pen skipping or the presence of pen striations.
2. Paper surface roughness. Rough papers may cause deep valleys where the pen may "jump" over the line as illustrated in Figures 15.9 and 15.10. The illustrations provide a schematic of how such discontinuities in the EDD line may occur. Therefore, multiple points of intersection should always be examined to ensure consistency in the appearance at intersections.
3. Irregular, hard, or smooth surfaces on which the document was written. For reasons similar to that of paper surface roughness, the pen may jump over writing tracks or indentations.
4. Applied pressure when writing. Writing or indentations made with greater pressure usually have a higher contrast between clear lines (visible writing) and dark lines

Figure 15.9 This illustration shows how deep valleys in an underlying page may result in noncontact between the top page being written upon the underlying page. (Graphics by Robert Gervais, from the Journal of the American Society of Questioned Document Examiners, volume 14, number 2, used with permission.)

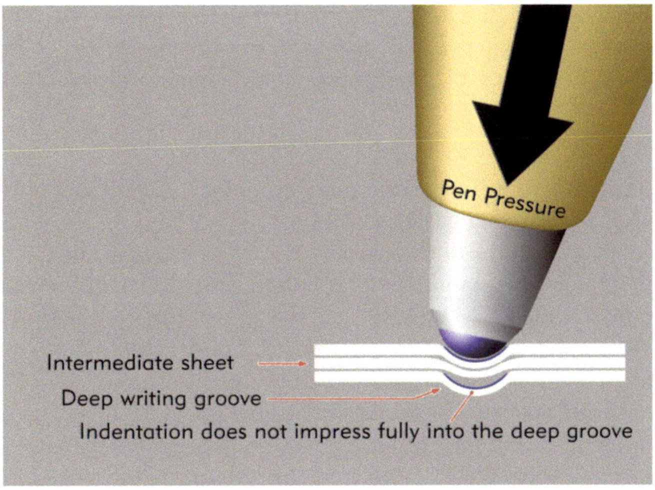

Figure 15.10 A similar illustration as for Figure 15.9 but with an intermediate page between the page being written upon and the bottom page developed by EDD. (Graphics by Robert Gervais, from the Journal of the American Society of Questioned Document Examiners, volume 14, number 2, used with permission.)

(indentations). Stated another way, the dark lines will usually appear darker when greater pressure was applied.

5. Impressions that are made on top of "wet" ink. The interpretation of sequencing is not reliably done when indentations are made over ink that was written recently, typically less than 30 minutes.

15.8.1 Non-Ballpoint Pens and EDD Impressions

Non-ballpoint inks such as fiber tip, roller ball, and fountain pen nib will typically disrupt an EDD impression line. The dark indentation development line will be discontinuous when the non-ballpoint ink is written after the impression occurs (refer to Figures 15.11 and 15.12).

Figure 15.11 Magnification of the EDD lift overlaid on the document developed for impressions; the visible writing appears in blue liquid ink.

Figure 15.12 The same EDD lift in Figure 15.11 overlaid against a white background shows the visible writing as clear lines and the indented writing as dark lines. In this instance, the clear lines "break" the dark lines, making them discontinuous. This is strong evidence that the visible writing was made after the indented writing.

On the other hand, when the indentation is made *after* the visible writing, the EDD impression line will be continuous and the indented dark line will not have "breaks". Generally, the interpretation for non-ballpoint pen writings and intersections is not as vulnerable to misinterpretation.

15.8.2 Ballpoint Pens and EDD Impressions

Radley and Lindblom stress that intersections of ballpoint pen writings with indentations must be carefully evaluated in sequencing determination. The EDD line from ballpoint pen impressions may have some thinning, the darkness may not be as intense, and a "slight encroachment" into the clear line (visible writing) may be seen. When the ink line of the visible writing has discontinuities caused by striations or skips of the writing instrument, the toner from the intersecting indentation may be deposited at these sites instead of developing as a clear line. Radley and Lindblom suggest paying particular attention to dark indentation lines that are nearly parallel to and overlap the clear visible writing lines, as shown in Figures 15.13 and 15.14.

To assist in the interpretation of intersections, it may be of assistance to partially interleave a sheet of white paper between the EDD lift and the document bearing the visible ink writings. Movement of the interleaved sheet from a position of blocking the underlying sheet (showing the EDD lift over a white background) to not blocking the underlying sheet (showing the EDD lift over the visible writing) assists in the visualization of the intersections. Care must be taken to ensure that the EDD lift remains superimposed on the corresponding visible ink lines (see Figure 15.15).

Additional consideration may be needed when there are deep writing grooves in the paper that impede contact between the top sheet writing that is the source of indentations on lower sheets. The deep grooves may lead to discontinuities in the clear writing line that may be misinterpreted as the dark lines (indentations) being over the clear lines (visible writing).

Not all EDD lifts are suitable for sequencing of indented and visible writings. Radley and Lindblom write that sequencing should not be attempted under the following conditions:

- Visible ink lines where there are many skips, striations, or malfunctions in the operation of the pen.
- When the visible writing develops as dark lines, such as often happens with pencil writing.
- Indentation lines that do not develop as fairly sharp lines.

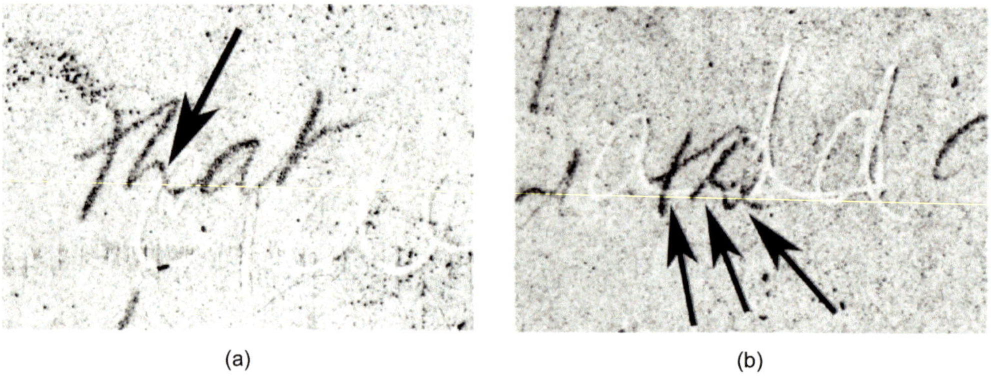

(a) (b)

Figure 15.13 (a and b) Two examples illustrate the intersections where the dark lines (indentations) are continuous at the intersections with the clear lines (visible writing), demonstrating that the indentations occurred after the visible writing.

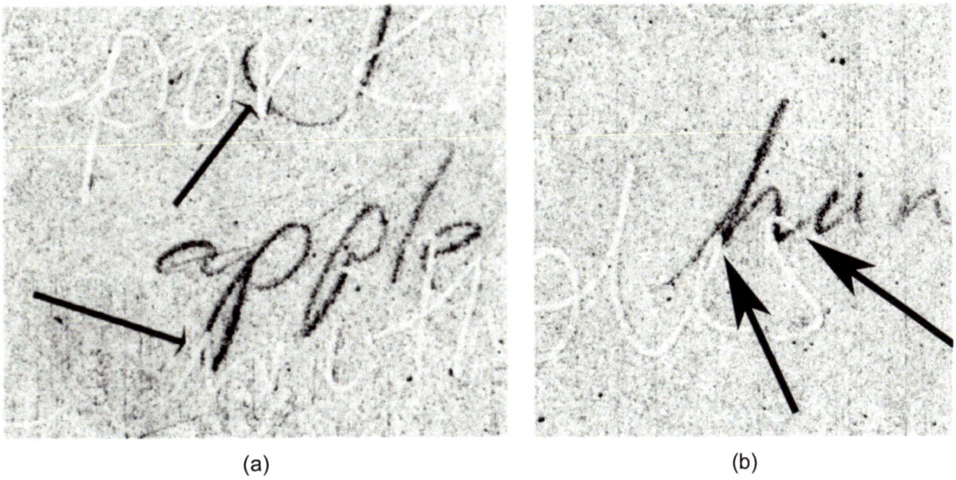

Figure 15.14 (a and b) Two examples illustrate where the dark lines (indentations) are interrupted at the intersections with the clear lines (visible writing), meaning the indentations occurred before the visible writing.

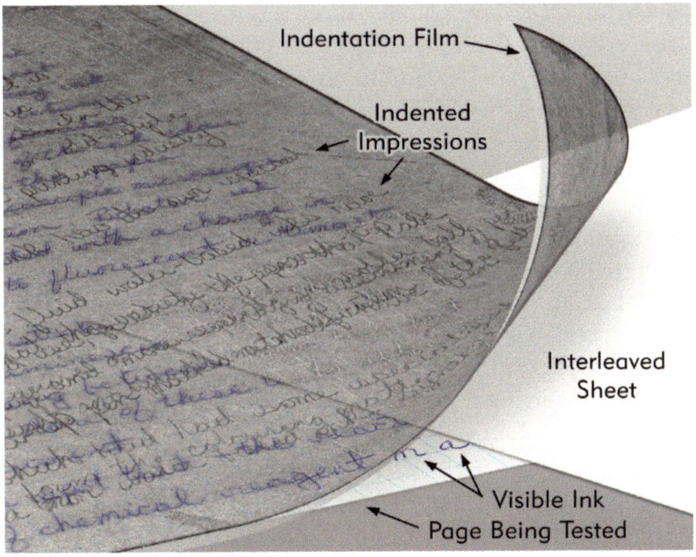

Figure 15.15 An illustration of how an interleaving sheet may be used to assist in the interpretation of the intersections of indentations and visible writing. (Graphics by Robert Gervais, from the *Journal of the American Society of Questioned Document Examiners,* Volume 14, Number 2, used with permission.)

- Intersections of toner from electrophotography (toner-based) printing and indented writings.
- Low quality development of the indented writing, including low contrast impressions.
- "Wet" ink, where there is a short time span, approximately less than 30 minutes, between visible writing followed by indentations.

The papers from Radley[50] and Radley and Lindblom[51] are contrary to the findings of Daéid et al.[52], where a statistical evaluation was conducted of intersections without accounting for the condition of the written line intersection with the indentation. Radley and Lindblom devote several paragraphs to account for the contrary findings. The Daéid et al. study did not account for the lack of variation in writing pressure and did not address the situations where there are jumps across the boundaries when deep indentations are present in the page. Extensive testing by practicing FDEs has confirmed the validity of sequencing as described by Radley and Lindblom when interpretations of the intersections is conducted properly.

15.9 OTHER TECHNIQUES FOR INDENTATION DEVELOPMENT

As a quasi-destructive technique, gelatine lifters have the potential to give superior results compared with EDDs as reported by de Koeijer et al.[53] This is especially the case with glossy surfaces or thin and commercially-printed papers. Their testing found that some caution must be taken as the adhesion of the gelatine on the paper surface may disrupt it, causing damage.

It was revealed that when EDD and gelatine lifts were both performed, no degradation of the EDD impression development was seen when the EDD processing step was conducted before gelatine lifting. In certain instances, there was actually a better result, which was thought to be a result of the removal of fine paper dust that caused background noise on the EDD lift. However, if gelatine lifting was performed before EDD development, there was a degradation in the EDD development.

De Koeijer et al. describe that the methodology for photography is key to getting a clear, legible image of the indented impressions. Manufacturers of gelatin lifters suggest that the illumination source be as close to the axis of the camera lens as possible.

15.10 THERMAL PAPER

Thermal papers are commonly used for applications where rapid, quiet printing is desired, such as at point-of-sale terminals. This printing process relies on the paper being heated by elements in a matrix formation that darken the paper via a chemical reaction to create the desired printing or graphics. The temperature at which this transition takes place is called the transition temperature. It varies between 60°C and 150°C.[54,55]

Recent research discusses using a careful application of heat to thermal paper to visualize indented writing.[56] The authors found that greater legibility may be achieved when the thermal paper was sandwiched between glass and a hot plate with controlled application of heat between 49°C and 51°C. This improvement in legibility was observed when there were two or more sheets between the source writing and the indented thermal paper. The authors hypothesize that the indented regions of the thermal paper have a greater concentration of the chemicals responsible for the thermally induced color change. It is thought that the higher concentration of heat reactive chemistry results in a lower transition temperature of the indented regions. Note that this is an irreversible technique and, as such, should be conducted with great caution.

15.11 CONCLUSION

Indentation development and visualization constitute significant physical evidence in many document examination cases. Information about how and sometimes when a document was produced may be disclosed upon the proper interpretation of the evidence.

REFERENCES

1. J. Brown, "A summary of development methods," *Journal of the American Society of Questioned Document Examiners*, vol. 1, no. 2, pp. 107–112, December 1998.
2. W. R. Harrison, *Suspect Documents Their Scientific Examination*, Chicago, IL: Nelson-Hall Publishers, 1981 (reprint of 1958 edition), pp. 37–38.
3. C. Bigras, M. Choquette and J. Powell, *Lighting Methods for Photographing Museum Objects*, Canadian Conservation Institute, 2010.
4. N. W. Duxbury and J. W. Warren, "Deciphering and Photo-Recording of Indented Writings," in *Proceedings of RCMP Crime Detection Laboratories Seminar No 4*, 1956, pp. 27–38.
5. W. R. Harrison, *Suspect Documents Their Scientific Examination*, Chicago, IL: Nelson-Hall Publishers, 1981 (reprint of 1958 edition), pp. 33–34.
6. Foster + Freeman, "Crime-lite 82L brochure," 23 March 2019. [Online]. Available: http://ffsupport.co.uk/Brochures/Crime-lite_82L.pdf. [Accessed March 2019].
7. L. Stroebel, J. Compton, I. Current and R. Zakia, *Basic Photographic Materials and Processes*, London: Focal Press, 1990, p. 28.
8. C. Forno, "A new method for displaying indented and other markings on documents," *Science & Justice*, vol. 35, no. 1, pp. 45–51, 1995.
9. D. J. Morantz, D. J. Foster and D. M. Ellen, "An Electrostatic Method for Identifying Indented Impressions," in *8th Meeting of the International Association of Forensic Sciences*, Wichita KS, 1978.
10. Foster + Freeman, "Foster + Freeman ESDA History," [Online]. Available: http://www.fosterfreeman.com/product/qde-products/678-esda-history.html. [Accessed March 2019].
11. Scientific Working Group on Document Examination (SWGDOC), "SWGDOC Standard for Indentation Examination," 2013. [Online]. Available: https://www.swgdoc.org/documents/SWGDOC%20Standard%20for%20Indentation%20Examinations.pdf. [Accessed March 2019].
12. R. G. Vyverberg, "Charging Photoconductive Surfaces," in *Xerography and Related Processes*, edited by J. H. Dessauer and H. E. Clark, London: The Focal Press, 1965, pp. 201–216.
13. R. W. Gundlach, "Development of Electrostatic Images," in *Xerography and Related Processes*, edited by J. H. Dessauer and H. E. Clark, London: The Focal Press, 1965.
14. J. T. Bickmore, "Aerosol Development," in *Xerography and Related Processes*, edited by J. H. Dessauer and H. E. Clark, London: The Focal Press, 1965.
15. G. Licht and E. Murano, "ESDA effects in light of current discussions," *Journal of the American Society of Questioned Document Examiners*, vol. 7, no. 1, pp. 7–21, June 2004.
16. K. J. Barr, M. L. Pearse and J. R. Welch, "Secondary impressions of writing and ESDA-detectable paper-paper friction," *Science & Justice*, vol. 36, pp. 97–100, 1996.
17. S. J. Strach, G. M. McCormack and P. D. Westwood, "Secondary Indented Writings: Indented Writing Impressions Caused by Contact, Not by the Act of Writing," in *13th Meeting of the International Association of Forensic Sciences*, Dusseldorf, 1993.
18. A. J. Barton and J. D. S. Walker, "Secondary impressions," *Journal of the American Society of Questioned Document Examiners*, vol. 4, no. 1, pp. 3–11, June 2001.
19. I. J. Riebeling and H. J. Kobus, "Some parameters affecting the quality of ESDA results," *Journal of Forensic Sciences*, vol. 39, no. 1, pp. 15–20, 1994.
20. M. G. Noblett and E. L. James, "Optimum conditions for examination of documents using an electrostatic detection apparatus (ESDA) device to visualize indented writings," *Journal of Forensic Sciences*, vol. 28, no. 3, pp. 697–712, July 1983.
21. P. E. Baier, "Application of experimental variables to the use of the electrostatic detection apparatus," *Journal of Forensic Sciences*, vol. 28, no. 4, pp. 901–910, October 1983.
22. M. L. Pearse and J. S. Brennan, "Importance of absolute humidity in the operation of the electrostatic detection apparatus," *Forensic Science International*, vol. 83, pp. 121–131, 1996.
23. B. L. Beal, "Effects of water temperature vs. time in humidifying documents for electrostatic detection apparatus examination," *Journal of the American Society of Questioned Document Examiners*, vol. 5, no. 2, pp. 78–87, December 2002.

24. E. M. Williams, *The Physics and Technology of Xerographic Processes*, Verlag: Krieger Publishing Company (reprint of original 1984 version by John Wiley & Sons Inc.), 1993, pp. 49–52.
25. A. D. Moore, *A.D. Moore's Electrostatics* (2nd edition), Morgan Hill, CA: Laplacian Press, 1997, pp. 65–72.
26. M. Cameron, "Evaluation of ozone exposure from use of the electrostatic detection apparatus," *Journal of the American Society of Questioned Document Examiners*, vol. 4, no. 1, pp. 20–23, June 2001.
27. T. A. Tanaka, "Voltage and indentation development," *Journal of the American Society of Questioned Document Examiners*, vol. 10, no. 1, pp. 9–18, June 2007.
28. P. Forder, "ESDA Process Technical Note," Foster & Freeman, 2005.
29. L. B. Loeb, *Static Electrification*, Berlin: Springer-Verlag Heidelberg, 1958.
30. W. R. Harper, *Contact and Frictional Electrification*, Morgan Hill, CA: Laplacian Press (original publication Oxford University Press), 1998, p. 4.
31. P. M. Ireland, "Triboelectrification of particulate flows on surfaces: Part I - Experiments," *Powder Technology*, vol. 198, pp. 189–198, 2010.
32. P. M. Ireland, "Triboelectrification of particulate flows on surfaces: Part II - Mechanisms and models," *Powder Technology*, vol. 198, pp. 199–210, 2010.
33. B. L. Beal, "Choosing cascading beads for the electrostatic detection apparatus," *Journal of the American Society of Questioned Document Examiners*, vol. 3, no. 2, pp. 85–90, December 2000.
34. J. A. Lewis, "Indentation examination enhancement," *Journal of the American Society of Questioned Document Examiners*, vol. 8, no. 2, pp. 65–69, December 2005.
35. M. H. Cavanaugh Jr, B. L. Torres and W. P. Grose, "ESDA cascade developer awareness," *Journal of the American Society of Questioned Document Examiners*, vol. 2, no. 2, pp. 102–103, December 1999.
36. D. Purdy, "A method for determining the condition of an ESDA or IMEDD," *Journal of the American Society of Questioned Document Examiners*, vol. 2, no. 2, pp. 97–101, 1999.
37. D. J. Foster and D. J. Morantz, "An electrostatic imaging technique for the detection of indented impressions in documents," *Forensic Science International*, vol. 13, pp. 51–54, 1979.
38. L. Wanxiang and C. Xiaoling, "A study of the principle of the electrostatic imaging technique," *Journal of the Forensic Science Society*, vol. 28, pp. 237–242, 1988.
39. G. H. Seward, "Model for electrostatic imaging of forensic evidence via discharge through Mylar-paper path," *Journal of Applied Physics*, pp. 1450–1456, 1998.
40. G. H. Seward, "Practical implications of charge transport model for electrostatic detection apparatus (ESDA)," *Journal of Forensic Sciences*, pp. 832–836, July 1999.
41. J. Welch, "Electrostatic Detection, or Not, of Indented Writing Made Through Plastic," in *American Society of Questioned Document Examiners/Southwestern Association of Forensic Document Examiners*, Park City UT, 2018.
42. W. R. Harper, *Contact and Frictional Electrification*, Morgan Hill, CA: Laplacian Press (original publication Oxford University Press), 1998.
43. L. Yaraskavitch, M. Graydon, T. Tanaka and L.-K. Ng, "Controlled electrostatic methodology for imaging indentations in documents," *Forensic Science International*, vol. 177, pp. 97–104, 2008.
44. G. M. LaPorte, "The use of an electrostatic detection device to identify individual and class characteristics on documents produced by printers and copiers - A preliminary study," *Journal of Forensic Sciences*, vol. 49, no. 3, pp. 307–317, May 2004.
45. L. A. Olson, "Indentations produced by the document feeder mechanisms of two black and white photocopiers," *Journal of the American Society of Questioned Document Examiners*, vol. 12, no. 1, pp. 1–18, June 2009.
46. A. B. Giles and A. Giles, "Electrostatic detection apparatus enhancement using astronomical image stacking and processing software," *Journal of the American Society of Questioned Document Examiners*, vol. 12, no. 1, pp. 19–25, June 2009.
47. G. R. Sperry and D. K. Tolliver, "Applying specific digital enhancement techniques to ESDA-developed impressions," *Journal of the American Society of Questioned Document Examiners*, vol. 4, no. 1, pp. 12–19, June 2001.
48. B. C. Barton, "The use of an electrostatic detection apparatus to demonstrate the matching of torn paper edges," *Journal of the Forensic Science Society*, vol. 29, no. 1, pp. 35–38, 1989.

49. R. W. Radley, "Determination of sequence of writing impressions and ball pen inkstrokes using the ESDA technique," *Journal of the Forensic Science Society*, vol. 33, no. 2, pp. 69–72, 1993.
50. R. W. Radley, "Determination of sequence of Intersecting ESDA impressions and porous tip, fibre tip and rollberball pen inks," *Science & Justice*, vol. 35, no. 4, pp. 267–272, 1995.
51. R. W. Radley and B. S. Lindblom, "Impressions/ink intersection sequencing - A comprehensive overview," *Journal of the American Society of Questioned Document Examiners*, vol. 14, no. 2, pp. 3–13, December 2011.
52. N. N. Daéid, L. Whitehead and M. Allen, "Examining the effects of paper type, pen type, writing pressure and angle of intersection on white and dark dominance in ESDA impressions of sequenced strokes - An application of the likelihood ratio," *Forensic Science International*, vol. 181, pp. 32–35, 2008.
53. J. A. de Koeijer, C. E. H. Berger, W. Glas and H. T. Tadhuizen, "Gelatine lifting, a novel technique for the examination of indented writing," *Journal of Forensic Sciences*, vol. 51, no. 4, pp. 908–914, July 2006.
54. M. C. Jürgens, *The Digital Print: The Complete Guide to Processes, Identification and Preservation*, London: Thames & Hudson, 2009, p. 137.
55. H. Sato, J. Ohwaki and K. Murase, "New method for evaluating the thermo-sensitivity of thermal recording papers," *Journal of Imaging Technology*, vol. 10, no. 5, pp. 186–189, 1984.
56. M. Johnson and J. W. Bond, "Visualizing indented writing on thermal paper by the controlled application of heat," *Journal of Forensic Sciences*, vol. 62, no. 5, pp. 1366–1371, September 2017.

Chapter 16

Examination of Cut, Torn, Shredded, and Perforated Documents

Larry A. Olson

CONTENTS

16.1 INTRODUCTION

Disassembled documents are those which have been separated into pieces by cutting, shredding, or tearing. This disassembly may be done to hide a crime, for security purposes, or may have even occurred accidentally. The entire document may have been disassembled, or only certain portions removed. There are also certain types of documents designed to be separated into parts (e.g., postage stamps, bank checks, notebook pages, etc.).

Forensic document examiners (FDEs) are occasionally called upon to examine and reconstruct disassembled documents. Several standard texts and professional papers have addressed these types of exams over the years.[1–10] The project may be as small as a few pieces of paper found in a wastebasket or as large as a bag of document shred.

Fortunately, while this task may represent a challenge, it is not necessarily impossible to achieve.

The ultimate questions to be answered are: (1) Did portions of a document once belong to the same sheet? and (2) What were the contents of the original document?

16.2 REASSEMBLY METHODS

It is possible to successfully reassemble documents manually, as well as with the help of computers and software. Many of the same methods used to reassemble documents will apply no matter how the document has been altered. These methods will be discussed in general first, before dealing with the specific type of alteration. Computer-assisted reconstruction will be discussed at the end.

The following are the major tasks to be done in a manual reassembly:

- Preliminary examination and assessment of the problem
- Sorting the pieces
- Associating like pieces
- Assembling the pieces
- Finishing the project (validating/documenting/imaging/preserving)

16.2.1 Preliminary Assessment

The problem begins with asking several questions:

What is the nature of the problem?

That documents were disassembled and the manner in which it was done may be obvious. Or part of a document may have been subtly trimmed off, which may only become apparent later.

What is the goal of the submitter? Is the problem determining whether the documents are from the same source, determining their original contents, or both?

What specifically is the submitter hoping to find (i.e., certain names, numbers, or other items of text)?

Knowing this can guide the examiner's efforts so that precious time is not being wasted on an unimportant document.

How many documents appear to be present? Is there at least more than one?

There are a couple of ways of estimating the number of documents present, and although this is not a vital step, it may give an idea of the extent of the problem at hand, especially when dealing with shredded documents.

16.2.2 Sorting

This step, to group document fragments by their class characteristics, is by far the most time-consuming. Fortunately, it is a task that can also be performed by someone other than the examiner assigned, with minimal training or instruction to save time.

Fragments can first be sorted with the naked eye for any visible features including the following:

- Paper type/color/any ruling present
- Presence of any kind of markings:
  - Text and/or images
  - Handwriting
  - Color of printing/writing/highlighter ink used

The intent is to reduce the overall mass to groups of the lowest common denominator.[11]

An examination of the fragments with long-wave ultraviolet illumination is often helpful to distinguish fluorescent differences in the paper stock (due to the presence or absence of brighteners).

The fragments being sorted can be placed in piles by subgroup on sheets of cardboard or glass, or in trays or shallow boxes. Something that is easily portable might be helpful, to be able to take them to another workspace. Thought should also be given to keeping them protected from air currents, air conditioning, or passing workers by covering them with box tops, large sheets of cardboard, poster board, or paper. Handling the fragments with gloves or forceps is recommended if the assembled document is likely to be further subjected to an examination for fingerprints.

It may not be necessary to sort all the material prior to moving on to the next step, depending upon the urgency of the exam.

16.2.3 Associating the Pieces

Once the document fragments have been grouped, one of the subgroups can be selected for association and assembly. The group chosen could be the one with the least number of pieces or the one whose contents may be of greatest importance to the case.

The pieces should be laid out in an orderly manner so they can be located during association and assembly. They can be laid out in boxes or trays, on cardboard, or under glass sheets. Using some type of low-tack adhesive board/material works well to keep the pieces together. A clear medium (plastic or glass) is ideal if pieces are double-sided, since both sides can be seen.

Fragments are first, usually, visually associated by the following:

- Matching printing, writing, or ruling on the document,
- Matching some surface effect (stains, folds, creases), or
- Matching a gross fracture pattern (the cut or torn edges) by their shapes. Figure 16.1 shows a fracture match between two documents.

16.2.4 Positive Fracture Matching

Eventually, the goal is to demonstrate a match between fracture edges by "a sufficient (unspecified) number of individual characteristics."[12] This may be accomplished through one of the methods above. If not, it can usually be achieved by comparing individual paper fibers across the cut or tear using low-power microscopy.

Typically, in order to conclusively demonstrate the existence of a physical match, one needs to find not one, but *several* matches along the length of a cut/tear because false matches are very likely to occur over a short span. A match of several paper fibers is illustrated in Figure 16.2.

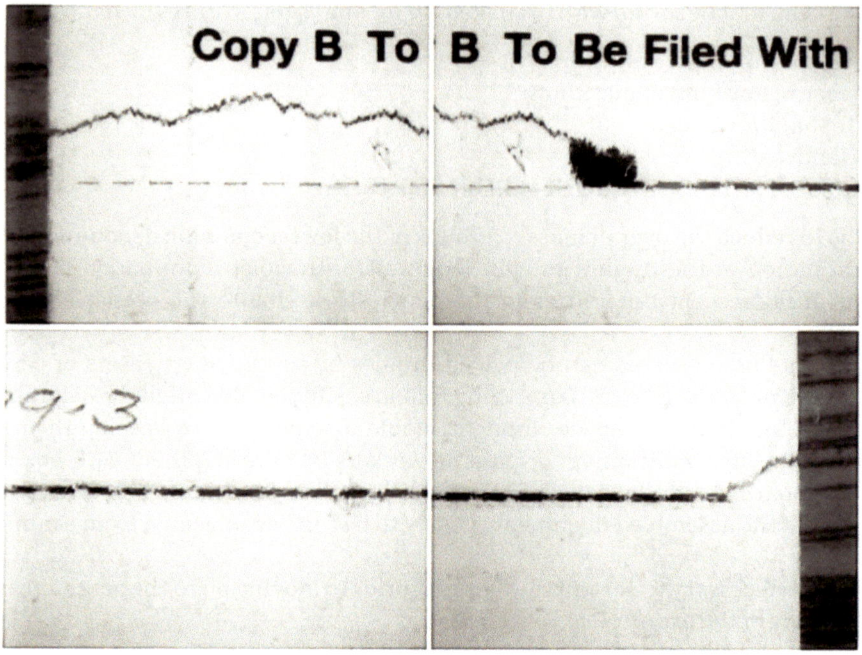

Figure 16.1 Comparison of two perforated W-2 forms in four locations by a gross match of the paper tears.

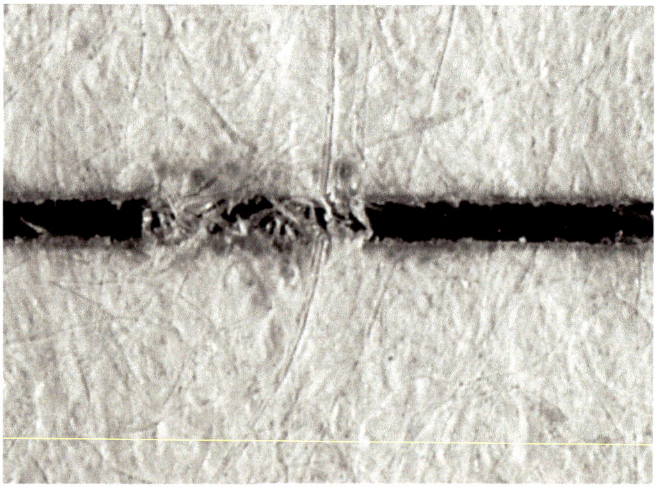

Figure 16.2 A microscopic comparison between two perforated paper edges showing a positive fracture match between several individual paper fibers.

Individual characteristics have also been detected in the literature through the use of the following:

- Oblique lighting (from one side only)
- Transmitted light

- Laser or ultraviolet (UV) illumination
- An electrostatic detection device

Ultraviolet illumination is frequently helpful at this stage. If the paper stock contains fluorescent features like randomly distributed fluorescent fibers, this might greatly facilitate the comparison of edges as illustrated in Figure 16.3.

16.2.5 Assembling the Pieces

This task involves piecing together parts of a document from various fragments into a semipermanent state. As a substrate for assembly, material with a low-tack adhesive works very well. It should be of a size larger than the anticipated size of the original document.

Clear plastic (a document protector with roll-on adhesive or clear plastic laminating sheets with low-tack adhesive) is ideal for the following reasons:

- One can see both sides of the document while assembling,
- Notes can be made with permanent or removable markers, and
- The assembly can be sealed for protection and/or preservation.

Whatever adhesive is used, it should be removable or low-tack because changes may need to be made.

16.2.6 Finishing

Once the assembly is completed, several final steps (discussed at the end of the chapter) should be performed such as:

- Assembly verification
- Imaging of the results
- Assembly preservation

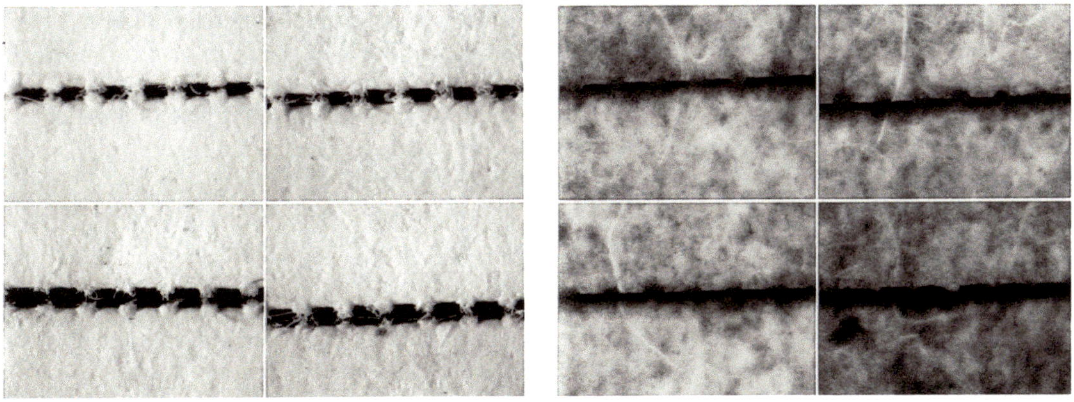

(a) (b)

Figure 16.3 (a) A difficult comparison due to very small perforations with no distinctive fracture pattern (shown at four places along the edges of two documents being compared) whereas (b) UV illumination of the same papers results in a positive fracture match of fluorescing individual paper fibers.

16.3 SPECIFIC TYPES OF DOCUMENT DISASSEMBLY

This section deals with the various ways in which documents can be altered and their appropriate handling. Documents that are cut, torn by hand, or shredded by machine each have different characteristics and may have their own optimal means of reassembly. Another category of documents to be considered here are *perforated documents*, which are designed to be disassembled (like postage stamps or checks in a checkbook).

16.3.1 Cut Documents

There are several types of paper cutting instruments, designed for different purposes:

- Scissors – a set of pivoting paired blades operated by hand, usually used to cut single sheets of paper,
- Paper cutter – a longer blade that operates on a pivot to cut one or more sheets of paper against a metal edge,
- Paper knife/letter opener – a single blade of variable sharpness that operates against a folded paper edge to cut or tear the paper,
- Rolling blade – a wheel with a sharpened edge that cuts one or more sheets as it moves past the paper, or vice versa, and
- Guillotine blade – a blade that operates vertically with the entire cutting surface striking the paper simultaneously, designed to cut large quantities of paper, like a ream.

Unless the paper was handmade, virtually every sheet of paper an examiner encounters has already been cut from a much larger roll during the paper conversion process. It will have four machine-cut edges, usually made with rolling and/or guillotine-type blades.

One should examine all the edges of a document suspected of being cut or trimmed. There is likely to be a difference in appearance between machine-cut edges and those cut by scissors or other cutting instruments. Unless the cutting blades are very sharp, the blade may both compress the fibers as well as cut or tear them. Cutting blades may, through damage or use, develop individual "marks, nicks, burrs, or chips" that may help identify or associate the instrument.[13,14]

One should also consider the size and shape of a document suspected of being altered by cutting. Paper may have been trimmed from its original size if it does not conform to one of the standard paper sizes in use, e.g., 8.5 by 11 inches in North America or A4 size (210 × 297 mm, or 8.3 × 11.7 inches) internationally.[15] A scissor cut may not be very straight with reference to a paper edge. Paper cut with a scissor or even a desktop paper cutter may not have corners cut at 90-degree angles.

16.3.1.1 Matching

As stated above, in order to determine if cut edges truly match, a microscopic examination is necessary. The edges should match in the gross areas (the shape of the line, where the blade has stopped), as well as the fine detail (that is, sufficient individual fibers should match across the width of the cut). Ultraviolet or laser illumination may also detect correspondence in luminescent features across the cut.

Large quantities of paper cut together that are still in their original stacked order (as in a ream of paper, or a stack of currency or index cards) may exhibit toolmarks ("striations") from the cutting blade. It may be possible that, with proper exemplars from the same blade, the striations may be matched to the same cutter.[16]

16.3.2 Torn Documents

Documents that are torn may have been forcibly separated by hand, or the tear may have been guided along a hard surface. Tearing generally creates a ragged, nonuniform edge, which may be much easier to match than a cut document. Torn paper may also “delaminate” or separate into layers creating a “feathered” edge.[17] It may then not be easy to see the correspondence of the fracture edges.

16.3.2.1 Associating/Assembling

Associating and assembling is much the same as with cut documents. In addition to a microscopic examination of the paper fibers, the following may be useful:

- Oblique light from one side only may show more detail in the tear.[18]
- The use of transmitted light (as illustrated in Figure 16.4) or even processing with an electrostatic detection device[19] may reveal where feathering has occurred and where layers of different thicknesses overlap.

Regarding multiple papers torn at the same time, recent research suggests that if two papers are torn longitudinally at the same time, each will exhibit unique edges.[20,21]

16.3.3 Perforated Documents

These documents are designed to be disassembled. Several common examples include the following:

- Postage stamps in a roll or on a sheet[22]
- Checks in a checkbook
- Perforated leaves in a notebook
- Receipts in a booklet
- Standard forms in a booklet or attached in a continuous form

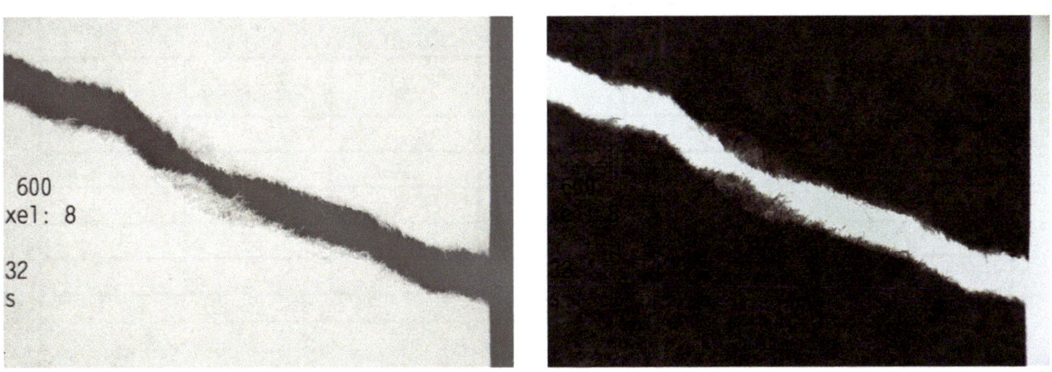

(a) (b)

Figure 16.4 (a) The match between the torn edges is not obvious due to feathering along the tear, but (b) using transmitted light, the correspondence of the two feathered areas becomes clear.

The ways in which documents might be perforated are many and varied, and a discussion of the manner of perforation is beyond the scope of this article. In general, the space between individual items is usually punched with small cuts and/or holes, and then the separation of the items is effected using a slight amount of force to tear them apart. One item may have been attached to another item, or to a stub that remains behind in bound form. The FDE's tasks are those of matching the pieces, document to document or document to stub, to determine if they were, at one time, attached to each other along any of the edges. Associating, assembling, and matching the pieces are still accomplished as above. An edge to be compared is likely to have both cuts and tears. Any or all of the following might aid in demonstrating a match: microscopy, the use of laser or UV illumination, and transmitted or oblique light.

If a perforated form has been printed on a coated paper (like carbonless copy paper), the comparison and matching of individual paper fibers will likely be more difficult because the coating may hide the individual fibers.

When comparing several like items with perforations on more than one edge (top/bottom or left/right sides), creating a matrix on paper or a computer spreadsheet may help in annotating the results of the comparisons, as illustrated in Figure 16.5.

16.3.3.1 Paper Safety Matches

This is a special category of "document" which, like perforated documents, are both cut and torn.

Paper safety matches are sheets of chemically treated cardboard that have been partially cut into individual paper sticks that are torn from a stub in the booklet. The paper used is typically cheap quality cardboard with many inclusions among the paper fibers (bits of dirt or other foreign material).

These inclusions are highly individual. They may be both visible with the naked eye and have luminescent qualities that can be seen using a laser or UV illumination. Their presence may enable an individual stick to be matched to neighboring sticks; the torn edges on the match and stub might be visualized using microscopy with or without oblique light.

This type of examination may be performed by trace evidence examiners as well as FDEs. The topic rarely appears in current document examination literature because the methods for examination are rather well established. Several pertinent papers are referenced at the end of this chapter.[23–28]

Comparison of questioned perforated W-2 forms					
bottom edge (across) vs top edge (down)	Q5-2	Q6-2	Q11-6	Q14-4	Q16-2
Q5-2	X	---	---	---	M
Q6-2	---	X	---	---	---
Q11-6	M	---	X	---	---
Q14-4	---	---	---	X	---
Q16-2	---	---	---	---	X
(X) - cannot be compared					
(---) - no association					
(M) - positive fracture match					

Figure 16.5 A comparison table of similar forms perforated on the top and the bottom edges. In this case, an original sequence of three forms can be demonstrated - The bottom edge of Q16-2 matches the top edge of Q5-2, and the bottom edge of Q5-2 matches the top edge of Q11-6.

16.3.4 Shredded Documents

Shredded documents may be difficult to reassemble but not impossible. Several papers have dealt with the manual reassembly of shredded documents.[29–33] The task is very time-intensive, and the amount of time expended may not be worth the result. It must be approached with a mindset of what is most time- and cost-effective.

It is usually, however, not necessary to reassemble any shredded document in its entirety, merely the portions with writing or printing. Once a portion of a document is reassembled, the text revealed may help determine whether that assembly is worth continuing.

A shredder works simply by moving paper(s) between sharpened rotating blades. There are several different types of shredders, including:

- Strip cut – uses multiple sharpened rotating wheels around an axle that cut a document into strips the length of the sheet
- Crosscut – uses two oppositely-rotating cylinders with cutting surfaces that cut a document into fragments of a desired size and shape (a sort of parallelogram/rectangle or even diamond shape)
- Confetti (high security) cut – shredder with two oppositely-rotating cylinders that cut a document into very tiny fragments. These fragments are all but impossible to reconstruct.

Different types of shredded material are pictured in Figure 16.6.

16.3.4.1 Shred direction

One helpful characteristic of some crosscut shredders is to cut fragments in a way that indicates the direction in which the document was shredded (shred direction). The cutting surfaces on crosscut cylinders may be diagonal or *v*-shaped. (*V*-shaped blades are pictured in Figure 16.7a.) The *v*-shaped blades cut fragments into an arrow shape, as illustrated in Figure 16.7b. The direction in which the arrow is pointing is the direction in which the document entered the shredder.[34] Knowing the shred direction may be useful in sorting and laying out shred for assembly.

16.3.4.2 Types of Shredded Documents (Paper vs. Plastic)

The examiner's task most often consists of dealing with shredded paper fragments. However, someone committing a financial or identity fraud may destroy plastic cards (e.g., credit, debit, or identification cards) used in the commission of the crime. Nowadays, many shredders are capable of shredding plastic (as in plastic cards and CDs) as well as paper (an example is shown in Figure 16.6). Fortunately, as a rule, credit or debit cards are easier to reassemble than most paper documents – there are far fewer pieces to deal with, and only certain portions of the card need to be reassembled (e.g., the issuing institution's name, the card number and card holder's name and/or signature on a credit/debit card). A reassembled card is pictured in Figure 16.8.

16.3.4.3 Reassembly

Shredded documents may be reassembled manually or with the aid of a computer. As stated before, the manual reassembly is not impossible to do, but it may take several months or more to accomplish. Methodologies have been outlined in several papers. Listed are the major steps:

1. Estimating the number of documents present – this could be *very* useful at the beginning to determine how large the project is likely to be.

Figure 16.6 Types of shredded material: front, from left: strip cut, crosscut, and confetti paper shred; and rear, a crosscut card/CD shredder and drawer of plastic shred.

Estimating by weight – If there is a large number of pieces or fragments of the same media, they could be weighed to estimate the number of items present (Mokrzycki, G., Federal Bureau of Investigation, personal communications, 2015–2016). The fragments are weighed both with and without the container. Then, a representative sample of the same type of document present (e.g., an 8.5 × 11-inch sheet of #20 paper or a 3 × 4-inch plastic credit card) is weighed, and the estimated number of documents is calculated.

Estimating by counting like parts – If the documents appear to be of the same type or format or have a similar content, at some point it may be possible to count the number of like elements found (images, letterheads, footers, logos, or document corners) to estimate the number present.

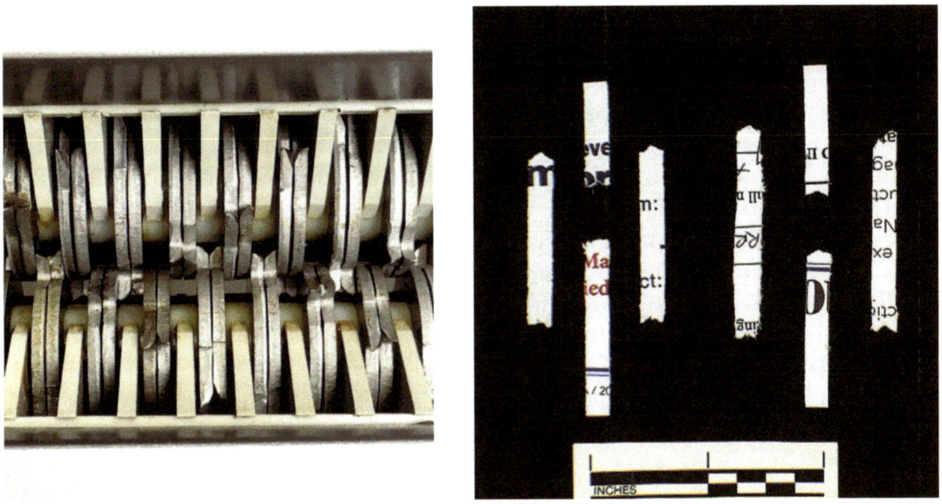

(a) (b)

Figure 16.7 (a) Shredder equipped with v-shaped cutting blades and (b) arrow-shaped fragments created by ν-shaped cutting blades. The documents these fragments came from were fed into the shredder with the top edge first, in the direction the shred is pointing.

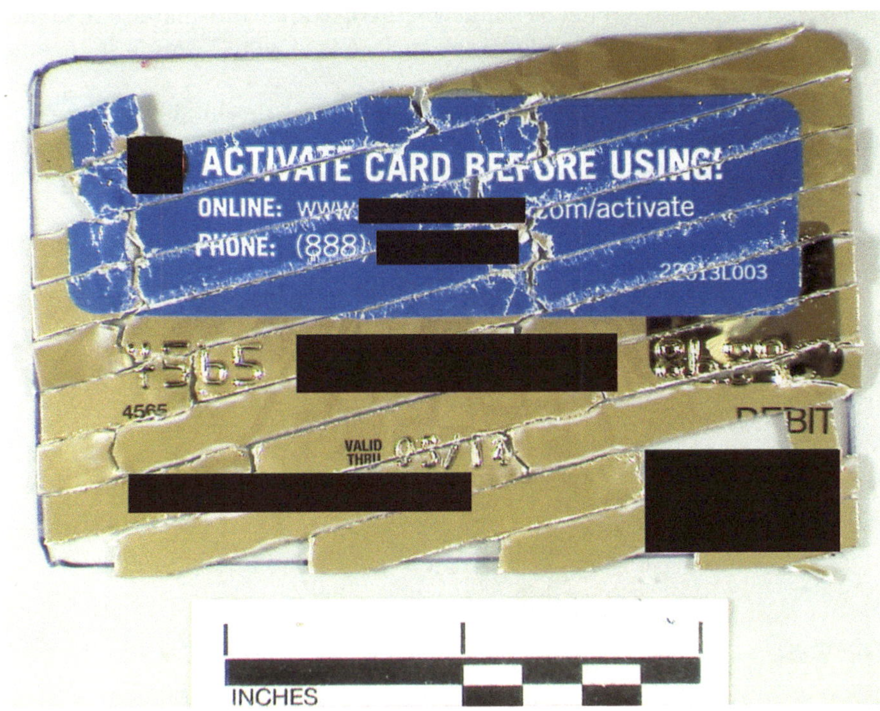

Figure 16.8 An almost completely reassembled debit card of 28 pieces with a complete (but masked) account number.

2. Sorting – this is the most time-consuming part of the task. As mentioned before, fragments are sorted by their physical characteristics, e.g., media, color, printing, and size (as shown in Figure 16.9). Regarding fragment size, it should be noted that crosscut shredders typically produce fragments of either one or two uniform lengths,[35] but document edge fragments may be a multitude of lengths and widths.

   Shredded paper documents have a special category of fragment called *packets* (Hartnett, D. and Romanovich, V., Fellowes Incorporated, personal communication, 2012) or *stacks* (Parkinson, J., German, G., Dempsey, P., Wildey, P., and Bear, T., Martin Yale Industries, personal communication, 2012), which may be worth setting aside and handling separately. Packets are multilayer clumps of fragments resulting from either the shredding of multiple documents at the same time or the shredding of folded documents, as depicted in Figure 16.10. Each layer in the packet is from a different document or different folded portion. If kept in their original order and dealt with in a methodical manner, it may be possible to assemble the documents from the different layers at the same time.[36]
3. Laying out – After sorting, a subgroup is selected to begin with. It may be the smallest group or the group that appears to have the most relevant text or images. Fragments should be laid out on a suitable surface (cardboard trays, sheets of glass, clear plastic, or low-tack adhesive, as mentioned above). Fragments should also be laid out in the shred direction, if that can be determined. If fragments are double-sided, a transparent medium is best so that both sides of the fragment can easily be seen. One side may be scanned and a print made so that both sides can be seen at the same time.
4. Associating – Fragments should be found where edges appear to match due to the printing, writing, or image present. A low-tack surface is ideal to keep these together and available for assembly.
5. Assembling – The examiner should start an assembly on a suitable medium of a size larger than the anticipated document – usually larger than 8.5 × 11 (clear, low-tack adhesive works best). If single-sided, any surface may do. If double-sided, a transparent medium is best so the image can be seen from either side.

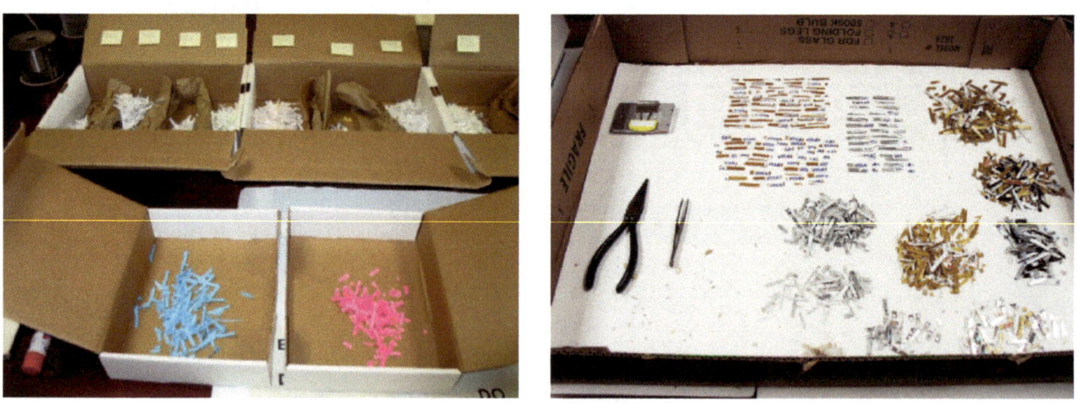

(a) (b)

Figure 16.9 (a) Sorting paper fragments by class characteristics and (b) sorting and laying out of plastic card fragments.

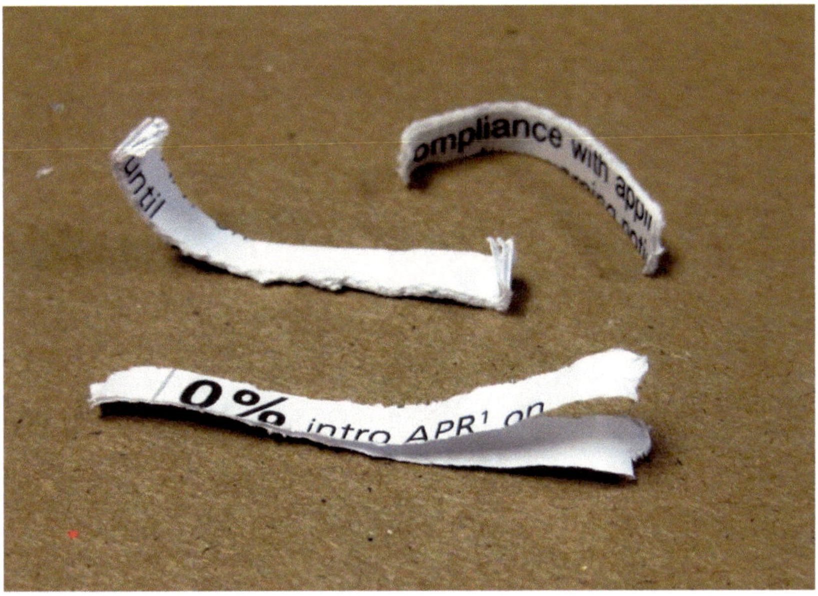

Figure 16.10 Multilayer packets of shred.

Predicting the shred pattern (if desired) – once at least four adjacent rows of fragments are assembled, it should be possible to determine the shred pattern.[37] Having this pattern allows the examiner to predict the position of other fragments.

Alternatively, the assembly can be flipped over for marking on the clear plastic backing. The corresponding cut ends in every other row should be marked as well. A direction of those cuts will be indicated, and the places where other cuts occur in every other row can be extrapolated in both directions. A lined grid underneath the assembly (ruled at the width of the fragments) helps determine where the ends of the missing fragments should occur. On the adjacent rows the cut ends should then be marked, preferably in a different color, and the cuts can be extrapolated in all directions as before. The shred pattern will be visualized, as in Figure 16.11.

Once the pattern has been mapped, voids in the assembly can be filled by selecting possible matches from the remaining fragments that have been laid out.

A positive match is usually accomplished by matching text, lines, or images, or matching the size and shape of the fragment with the surrounding pieces. A microscopic paper fiber match would be too difficult to do for all the cuts concerned.

The assembly can continue until the examiner and/or submitter are satisfied with the results.

16.3.4.4 Computer-Aided Assembly

At its simplest, shredded fragments can be mounted on a transparent medium and then scanned into a computer. Using a suitable image-enhancement program (e.g., Adobe PhotoShop™) allows the background to be removed so that fragments may be manipulated individually. A few examiners have reported employing this method in casework.[38,39] One commercial product called Unshredder,[40] which has been available for several years and is billed as the "first commercial document reconstruction tool in the world," works in this way.

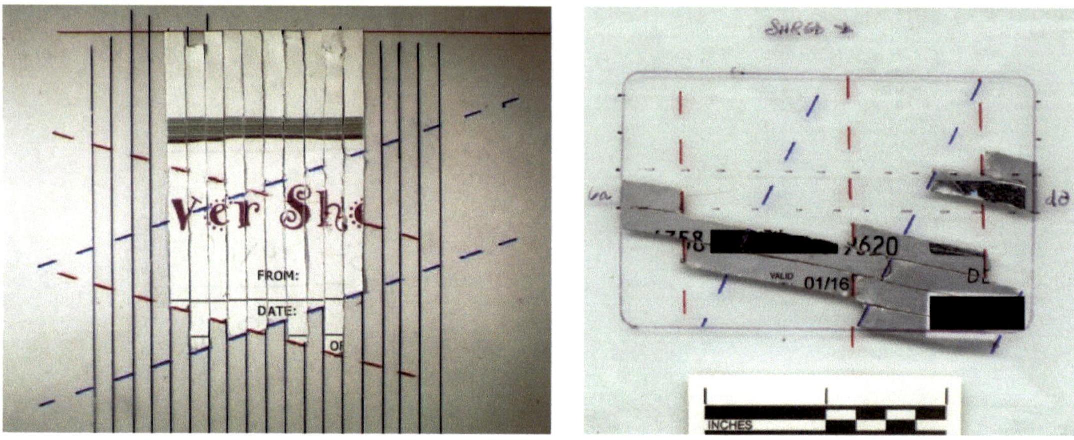

(a) (b)

Figure 16.11 (a) Shred pattern diagram plotted over paper fragment assembly and (b) plotted over credit card assembly allowing the estimated placement of fragments not attached to the main assembly (upper right corner).

More advanced software is the FBI's MatchMaker program[41] that makes use of OCR technology to suggest possible matches between fragments based on matching lines of text or individual letters. In addition, over the past two decades, many researchers have employed various experimental methods to attempt to digitally solve the shredded document problem.[42–47]

16.3.4.5 Finishing the Project

At some point, the document reassembly will be considered complete to the examiner's (and/or the submitter's) satisfaction. No matter how the assemblies were done, several final steps need to be performed which are as follows:

- Verification of the results
- Imaging of the results
- Preservation of the results

The completed assembly (physical or virtual) should be verified by (at least) a second person to determine that the assembly is correct. Care should be taken to avoid false paper fiber matches, which occur frequently at the microscopic level. Several small fragments may appear to fit the same void in a shredded document.

The results should be imaged in an image type file at a reasonably high resolution (300–600 dpi). Tiff or pdf is recommended. The images can be included in the report. As a document reconstruction may take many months to accomplish, especially with shredded documents, it is recommended that partial, preliminary results be reported to the submitter on a regular basis, either verbally, with images, or both (Mokrzycki, G., Federal Bureau of Investigation, personal communications, 2015–2016). The submitter may then determine whether more work needs to be done on any particular assembly.

Finally, each completed assembly should be sealed to keep pieces from moving or becoming unattached. This also protects the assembly for shipping, handling, and possible introduction into evidence in court. It is recommended that this sealing not be permanent, in case additional work needs to be done at some future date.

16.4 CONCLUSION

Examiners will likely encounter cut, torn, shredded, or perforated documents at some time during their careers. Determining a common source of the separated parts or reconstruction of their original configuration is not necessarily an insurmountable task. The methods outlined above and the comprehensive collection of references below should help with the process.

REFERENCES

1. Osborn, A.S., *Questioned Documents*, 2nd Ed., Nelson Hall, Chicago, IL, reprint of the 1929 edition.
2. Harrison, W.R., *Suspect Documents, Their Scientific Examination*, Praeger, New York, NY, reprint of the 1958 edition.
3. Hilton, O., *Scientific Examination of Questioned Documents*, Revised Edition, Elsevier, New York, NY, 1982.
4. Peace, L.L., "The Examination of Torn and Perforated Documents," *Canadian Society of Forensic Science Journal*, 15, 3–4, 1982.
5. Gencavage, J. S., "The Examination of Torn or Cut Paper," *paper presented at the American Society of Questioned Document Examiners (ASQDE) Annual Meeting*, Savannah, Georgia, September 21–25, 1986.
6. Ellen, D., *The Scientific Examination of Documents: Methods and Techniques*, Taylor & Francis, Bristol, PA, 1997.
7. Levinson, J., *Questioned Documents: A Lawyer's Handbook*, Academic Press, San Diego, CA, 2001.
8. Vastrick, T.W., *Forensic Document Examination Techniques*, IIA Research Foundation, Altamonte Springs, FL, 2004.
9. Kelly, J.S., and Lindblom, B.S, *Scientific Examination of Questioned Documents*, 2nd Ed., Taylor & Francis, Boca Raton, FL, 2006.
10. SWGDOC Standard for Physical Match of Paper Cuts, Tears, and Perforations in Forensic Document Examinations, 2013, Available at www.SWGDOC.com.
11. Vail, C.L., "Reconstructing Shredded Documents," (unpublished) Antioch School of Law, 1978, 9.
12. Luber, J.H., "Physical Match of Torn Paper," unpublished, 1.
13. Purtell, D., "The Identification of Paper Cutting Knives and Paper Cutters," *Journal of Criminal Law, Criminology, and Police Science*, 44, 2, 263, 1953.
14. Chavigny, P., "Identification of Scissors by Traces Left on Paper," *Journal of Criminal Law and Criminology*, 26, 6, 1936, 920–924.
15. *Pocket Pal: A Graphic Arts Production Handbook*, 20th Ed., International Paper Company, Memphis, TN, 2007.
16. Purtell, D., "The Identification of Paper Cutting Knives and Paper Cutters," *Journal of Criminal Law, Criminology, and Police Science*, 44, 2, 265–266, 1953.
17. O'Neill, E., "Matching of a Torn One Dollar Note in a Robbery Case," *Journal of Criminal Law and Criminology*, 30, 1940, 941–942.
18. Luber, J.H., "Physical Match of Torn Paper," unpublished, 2.
19. Barton, B.C., "The Use of an Electrostatic Detection Apparatus to Demonstrate the Matching of Torn Paper Edges," *Journal of the Forensic Science Society*, 29, 1989, 35–38.
20. Welch, T.W., Bacon, M.K., Bacon, C.R., and Bohn, S.A., "Fracture Match: A Validation Study of Paper Tears, Part 1," *Journal of the American Society of Questioned Document Examiners*, 13, 1, 2010.
21. Bacon, M.K., Bacon, C.R., Welch, T.W., and Bohn, S.A., "Fracture Match: A Validation Study of Paper Tears, Part II," *paper presented at the Northwestern Association of Forensic Scientists (MAFS) Annual Meeting*, Kansas City, MO, April 29–30, 2010.
22. Owens, M.C., "The Comparison of Round Hole Perforations of Postage Stamps," *Journal of Forensic Sciences*, 30, 4, 1985.
23. Funk, H.J., "Comparison of Paper Matches," *Journal of Forensic Sciences*, 13, 1, 1968.

24. Dixon, K.C., "Positive Identification of Torn Burned Matches with Emphasis on Crosscut and Torn Fiber Comparisons," *Journal of Forensic Sciences*, 28, 2, 1983.
25. Von Bremen, U.G., "Laser Excited Luminescence of Inclusions and Fibers in Paper Matches," *Journal of Forensic Sciences*, 31, 2, 1986.
26. Gerhart, F.J., and Ward, D.C., "Paper Match Comparisons by Submersion," *Journal of Forensic Sciences*, 31, 4, 1986.
27. Johnson, R.C., "A Systematic Examination and Comparison of Paper Safety Matches," *Journal of Forensic Identification*, 42, 2, 1992.
28. Horton, R.A., "Systematic Non-Destructive Examinations of Paper Matches," unpublished.
29. Vail, C.L., "Reconstructing Shredded Documents," (unpublished) Antioch School of Law, 1978, 7–11.
30. Schuetzner, E.M., and Commella, K., "The Shredded Paper Puzzle: the reconstruction of shredded documents," *paper presented at the American Academy of Forensic Sciences (AAFS) Annual Meeting*, New York, NY, February 17–22, 1997.
31. Nobles, K., and White, K., "Shredded Paper: A Sticky Situation," *paper presented at the SAFDE Annual Meeting*, Atlanta, GA, April 18, 2008.
32. Moryan, D., "Shredded Document Reconstruction," *Journal of the American Society of Questioned Document Examiners*, 16, 2, 2013.
33. Olson, L.A., "An 'Ideal' Methodology for Manually Assembling Crosscut Shredded Documents," *Journal of the American Society of Questioned Document Examiners*, 16, 1, 2013.
34. McDonald, M., and Olson, L.A., "A Comparison of Class Characteristics Among Several Crosscut Shredders," *Journal of the American Society of Questioned Document Examiners*, 16, 1, 2013.
35. Olson, L.A., "An 'Ideal' Methodology for Manually Assembling Crosscut Shredded Documents," *Journal of the American Society of Questioned Document Examiners*, 16, 22, 2013.
36. Olson, L.A., "An 'Ideal' Methodology for Manually Assembling Crosscut Shredded Documents," *Journal of the American Society of Questioned Document Examiners*, 16, 21–22, 2013.
37. Olson, L.A., "An 'Ideal' Methodology for Manually Assembling Crosscut Shredded Documents," *Journal of the American Society of Questioned Document Examiners*, 16, 24–26, 2013.
38. Hammond, D., "Paper Reconstruction: A Methodology," *paper presented at the Southeastern Association of Forensic Document Examiners (SAFDE) Annual Meeting*, Atlanta, GA, April 29–30, 1994.
39. Herbertson, G., *Document Examination on the Computer: A Guide for Forensic Document Examiners*, WideLine Publishing, Berkeley, CA, 2002 (citing Gibson, R. E., Computer-Assisted Reconstruction of 'Cross-Cut' Shredded Documents, paper presented at the SWAFDE Spring Meeting, San Diego, California, April 27, 2002).
40. Unshredder, available at: https://www.unshredder.com/.
41. Federal Bureau of Investigation, MatchMaker software, from FBI Annual Laboratory Report, 2007.
42. Ukovich, A., Ramponi, G, Doulaverakis, H., Kompatsiaris, Y, and Strintzis, M.G., "Shredded document reconstruction using MPEG-7 standard descriptors," 2004. Available at: http://www.iti.gr/SCHEMA/files/document/18-10-2004/isspit04_cameraready.pdf
43. Justino, E., Oliveira, L.S., and Freitas, C., "Reconstructing Shredded Documents through Feature Matching." *Forensic Science International*, 160, 2006, 140–147.
44. Skeoch, A., "An Investigation into Automated Shredded Document Reconstruction using Heuristic Search Algorithms," University of Bath dissertation, 2006.
45. DeSmet, P., "Reconstruction of Ripped-Up Documents Using Fragment Stack Analysis Procedures," *Forensic Science International*, 176, 2008, 124–136.
46. Prandstatter, M. and Raidl, G.R., "Combining Forces to Reconstruct Strip Shredded Text Documents," *Hybrid Metaheuristics: Lecture Notes in Computer Science*, Volume 5296, Springer-Verlag, Berlin, 2008.
47. Daniels, Z. and Idrees, H., "Semi-Automatic Reconstruction of Cross-Cut Shredded Documents," 2013. Available at: https://www.crcv.ucf.edu/REU/2013/zachary_daniels/report.pdf.

Chapter 17

Electrophotography

Tobin Tanaka

CONTENTS

17.1 INTRODUCTION

The ubiquitous presence of electrophotographic (toner-based) office machines in the modern workplace and home may lead one to believe that it has been this way for many decades. It bears remembering that this was not always so. The introduction of the Hewlett Packard Laserjet "Classic" in May 1984 was listed at a price of $3,495.[1] Although high priced, this was considered a breakthrough given that the nearest competitor was on the order of $30,000. The cost of color photocopiers (strictly photocopiers, not printers) in the early 1990s started at just below $10,000.[2] Color printers and multifunction devices did not dip below $1,000 until the year 2000. Due to the flexibility, lower cost, and small size, the document examiner can be expected to encounter more toner-based documents than ever before.

Electrophotography is the term used to describe document printing or copying via toner and a photoconductive imaging drum. Its invention in 1938 is credited to Chester Carlson. It took many years for Carlson to find a willing partner to make a practical version of a copier that did not require extensive manual steps. The Battelle Memorial Institute eventually agreed to perform the extensive research and development that ultimately lead to the Xerox 914 photocopier in 1959. Electrophotography may also be referred to as xerography, although the latter term is often synonymous with Xerox.

Early photocopiers were analog in function and relied upon optical components of mirrors and lenses to project the document to be copied. Later versions started to use digital processes, where light-sensitive electronics converted the illumination into a signal that permitted a laser to create the image to be copied. The integration of the laser in this manner permitted the development of laser printers and later the multifunction devices that are commonplace now.

While the focus of this chapter will be on modern electrophotographic devices and their output, some review of the earlier processes will be mentioned. Questioned documents created many decades ago do arise in casework, and some knowledge of the technological capabilities of the devices of that time is essential. Several landmark publications describe the early invention of electrophotography and the technological and commercial developments in the period between the late 1980s to mid-1990s.[3–9]

17.2 STEPS OF THE ELECTROPHOTOGRAPHIC PROCESS

Although paper types and the specific materials and configuration of components within the devices have changed over the years, the basic steps of the process are the same. The interaction of materials with electrostatics is the key to how and why such document production is possible. There are a significant number of variables in the electrophotographic process, and these have a significant impact on the quality of the output. While the processes and materials have been refined to the point of high-quality images and text, it has not always been so.

Figure 17.1 illustrates the electrophotographic process. Most references for electrophotographic systems describe six steps as follows:

1. Charge – A photoconductive material (photoconductor) is electrostatically charged in the dark. The photoconductor (or photoreceptor) is the heart of the device. It is the material that bears the electrostatic pattern of the image or text to be copied or printed. Electrostatic charging can be been done by frictional means, high voltage wires, high voltage wire grids, and charged rollers that come into contact with the photoreceptor. Modern devices use a charge roller, which is a metal core at a high voltage surrounded

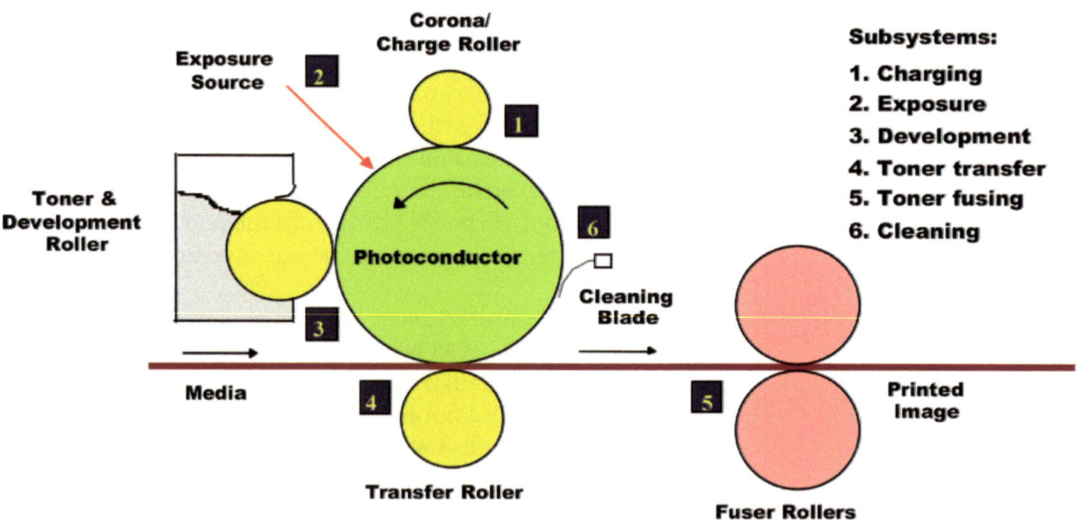

Figure 17.1 Six steps of the electrophotographic process. (Diagram Courtesy of Dr. Ming-Kai Tse, Quality Engineering Associates (QEA), Billerica, MA, USA.)

by an insulative material that charges the photoreceptor as it turns. Ideally, the areas of the photoreceptor that have been charged are charged uniformly. Depending on the condition of the photoreceptor, this may not be the case.
2. Expose – A latent electrostatic image is made onto the photoreceptor by optical means. In a modern device, the charged areas are discharged by a laser, using a pattern that corresponds to the image to be printed/copied. Analog copiers relied upon the optical pattern of reflected light from the document to be copied to discharge the drum in a corresponding pattern. At this stage, whether it is a modern device or analog, the photoreceptor has differences in voltage that correspond to what is to be eventually printed.
3. Develop – Toner is applied to the photoreceptor and remains on the portions with the latent electrostatic image. There are several techniques for applying toner. Some techniques are no longer used due to their inefficiency or poor image characteristics.
4. Transfer/Development – The toner on the photoreceptor is transferred to the substrate, which is usually paper. Electrostatic transfer plays an important role, and the selection of the toner properties must be suitable for the application. Depending on the device, transfer may involve mono-component development (the toner is transferred directly) or dual-component development, where the toner is electrostatically attracted to carrier beads.
5. Fuse – The toner on the substrate is fused by a variety of means. Modern machines almost exclusively use heated fusing rollers with application of pressure. Fusing is achieved by consideration of a combination of heat, pressure, dwell time, and toner thickness.
6. Clean – The photoreceptor is cleaned of any residual toner that did not get transferred. This may be achieved by a combination of blades or transfer belts. Toner cleaning may not be complete, which may degrade future prints or copies. The photoreceptor is also "erased" at this stage by exposure to illumination which is meant to discharge it before the cycle repeats itself. This erasure is referred to as the seventh step in some publications.

As the device is used, there is the potential for defects to be introduced onto the output as a result of one or more of these steps. Some features may be persistent, while others may be transient if there are serviceable parts or consumables. For example, many desktop laser printers have a user-changeable cartridge which contains many of the parts utilized in the six-step process. When the cartridge is changed, many of the defects that have potential forensic value are no longer present. A sample cartridge is depicted in Figure 17.2.

Early devices did not produce high resolution copies by the standards of today. Such early devices were also not able to reproduce larger areas of solid black or dark color due to the manner of toner deposition. These limitations may be important to the document examiner if documents of earlier time periods are presented as being photocopies made by these older devices.

17.3 COMMON QUESTIONS FOR ELECTROPHOTOGRAPHY OUTPUT

The presence or absence of defects and materials as described in the next sections may be used to determine the following:

1. If a questioned document was printed by a specific printer.
2. If a group of questioned documents was printed at the same time from the same device. (Differences in defect marks may be evidence to the contrary.)
3. If documents from a particular time period are from a suspect electrophotographic device.

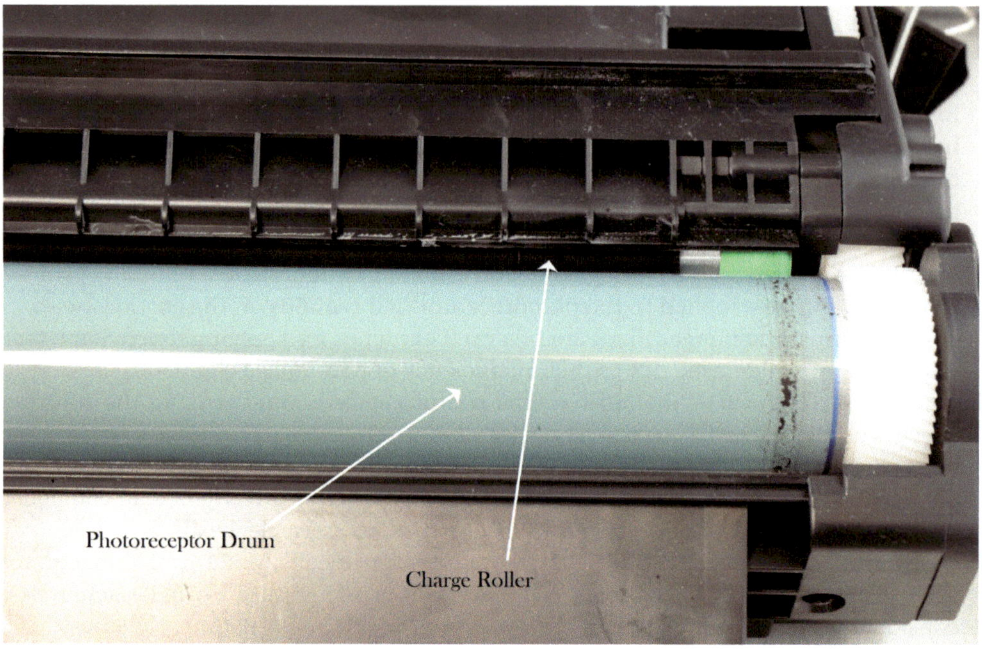

Figure 17.2 Cartridge shown with photoconductor/photoreceptor and charge roller.

Modern electrophotographic devices have improved overall output quality, usually leaving the document examiner with fewer "obvious" features to address questions about documents. Advances in instrumentation and interdisciplinary research have provided some additional techniques that may assist in examinations. Some of these will be outlined in this chapter.

17.4 COPY PLATEN AND OPTICAL SYSTEM DEFECTS

From the earliest copiers to the modern period, the copy process involves the placement of a document onto a glass platen surface where light and optics are used to create an image for copying. The optical system used may have contamination from debris or scratches which lead to printed defects on the copies. These defects are often referred to as *trash marks*,[10] and they may be in the same position from copy to copy. Such copying defects may be thought of as spatially-static defects as they are in the same approximate location from copy to copy. If there are many defects, they form a pattern that can be used to associate copies made on a particular device at a given time.

Similarities in the pattern of spatially-static defects between questioned documents and those from the electrophotographic device's copy platen provide strong evidence of a common source. A common source does not necessarily mean that the questioned document in hand was a direct copy made of the original. There is the potential for intermediate (multiple-generation) copies with a similar pattern plus other defects due to intermediate copies. Another complication is that documents could be scanned on a particular device and then printed on another. Accordingly, when spatially-static defects are being examined, it should be kept in mind that it is the condition of the optical system that is being compared. If a document is copied multiple times by making a *copy of a copy*, then additional spatially-static defects may be introduced to any subsequent copies. A *copy of a copy* is produced when the original document is copied, and that copy is then placed upon a copier platen to make secondary or second-generation copies.

Spatially-static defects are subject to change as the device is used further. Additional dust or scratches can manifest themselves on copies. There is the potential that some of these defects are transient, i.e. they will not persist or could change. This will depend on the cause of the defects. For example, loose dust on the optical system may move to a different position. Other defects from deep markings on the platen glass will not be transient; only replacement of the platen glass will remove them. If the platen glass is not replaced, the defects may eventually change as additional wear occurs from continued use.

Spatially-static defects will be visible on copies in an arrangement that depends on how documents are placed on the platen. In Figures 17.3 and 17.4, a portion of two pages copied on the same device is shown with some of the corresponding defects.

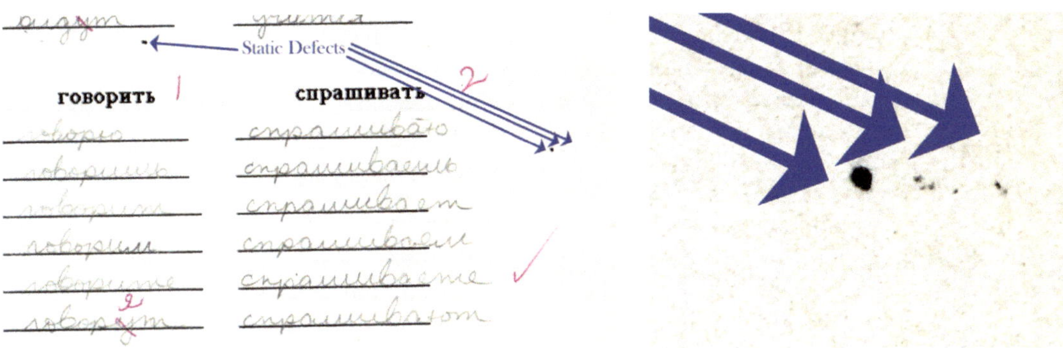

(a) (b)

Figure 17.3 (a) First page of a two-page document with some spatially-static defects noted and (b) an enlargement of spatially-static defects on the right side.

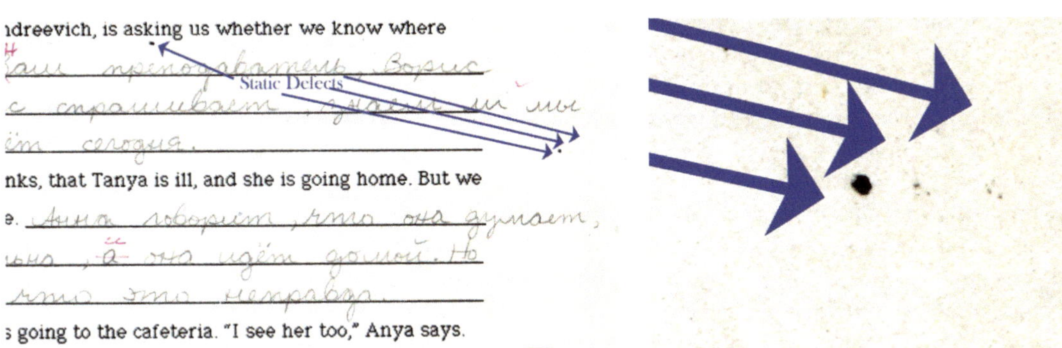

(a) (b)

Figure 17.4 (a) Second page of the same two-page document in Figure 17.3, with some spatially-static defects noted and (b) enlargement of spatially-static defects on the right side.

Spatially-static defects may be large enough to require no magnification to be seen, or they may vary to sub millimeters in size. Comparing the static defects between copies can be conducted by visual inspection between pages, with or without the use of aids such as transparent overlay sheets to record the position of defects. Overlays or superposition by digital means may be used in conjunction with visual inspection.

A congruence of a significant number of spatially-static defects is strong evidence that the imaging or scanning was from a common device. Depending on how much the copy platen is used, the condition may persist for a long time period, or it may be fleeting.

Certain spatially-static defects are not transient as they are from physical damage that will only get progressively worse until the device is repaired.

17.5 SPATIALLY-PERIODIC DEFECTS

In contrast to spatially-static defects, spatially-periodic defects are those that are repeated at specific intervals and dependent on the circumference of the drums or rollers within the electrophotographic device. One of the most common spatially-periodic defects that can be observed on the output is due to damage to the photoreceptor. Early generations of photocopiers used selenium photoreceptor drums which tended to be durable. However, when the drums did develop defects, they would often be tolerated as replacement of the drum was expensive. Replacement was only performed by trained service personnel.

Most modern photoreceptors are organic materials that are thinly coated onto metal drums.[11,12] For smaller printers where the drum is self-contained in a toner cartridge, the coating of the photoreceptive material need only last as long as the toner supply. Although efforts are made to ensure that the coating will provide satisfactory output, damage can occur where portions of the drum are worn right down to the metal. The result is that the drum will leave a marking on the output page similar in shape to the wear.

Damage to the photoreceptor may include scratches or holes in the photoreceptive material. If deep enough, the result will be a defect of that scratch or hole shape on all output. The defect will repeat at a distance on the output that corresponds to the circumference of the photoreceptor drum. At the locations where there is damage down to the underlying metal, the charge cannot be retained. As a result, toner will always be attracted to this location on the photoreceptor and will be transferred onto the page. The damage to the photoreceptor may be visible on the printed page under certain illumination conditions as shown in Figure 17.5. This may permit correlation of the printed defect to defects on the drum.

As seen in Figure 17.6, a deep scratch to the photoreceptor is clearly visible. The shape and position of this scratch can be shown to correspond to output from test prints made with the printer that had this photoreceptor. If the paper length along which printing is made is longer than the circumference of the photoreceptor, then the spatially-periodic defect will be repeated on the page at an interval of 95.5 mm (which corresponds to the circumference of the photoreceptor in this example).[13,14]

Subtle defects may not be readily apparent as they may be of the order of 1 mm or from slight physical wear rather than a deep scratch or obvious erosion to the metal. Specialized laboratory equipment can be used to test the condition of the photoreceptor. This type of equipment mimics the conditions under which the photoreceptor is subjected during the six steps of the electrophotographic process. The difference is that printing of pages does not occur during these tests.

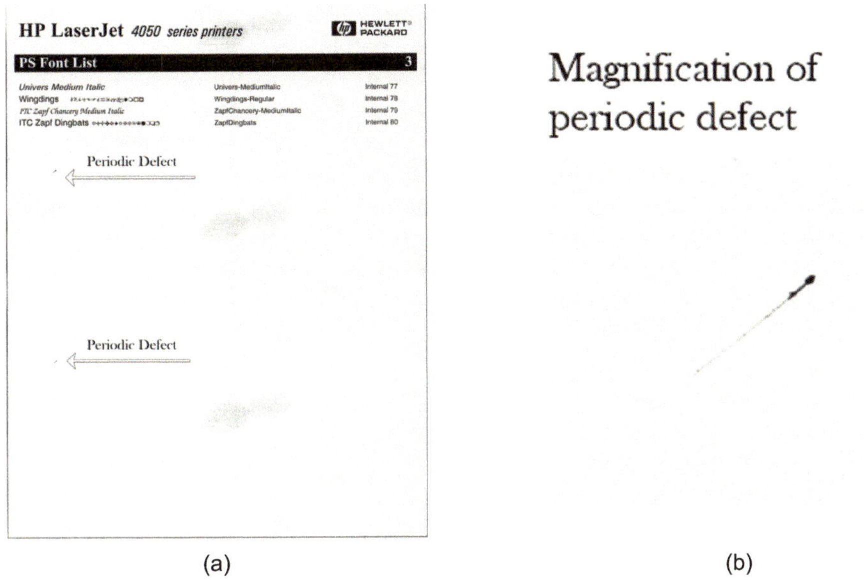

Figure 17.5 (a) Spatially-periodic defect on page (95.5 mm between defects) and (b) magnified image of the defect.

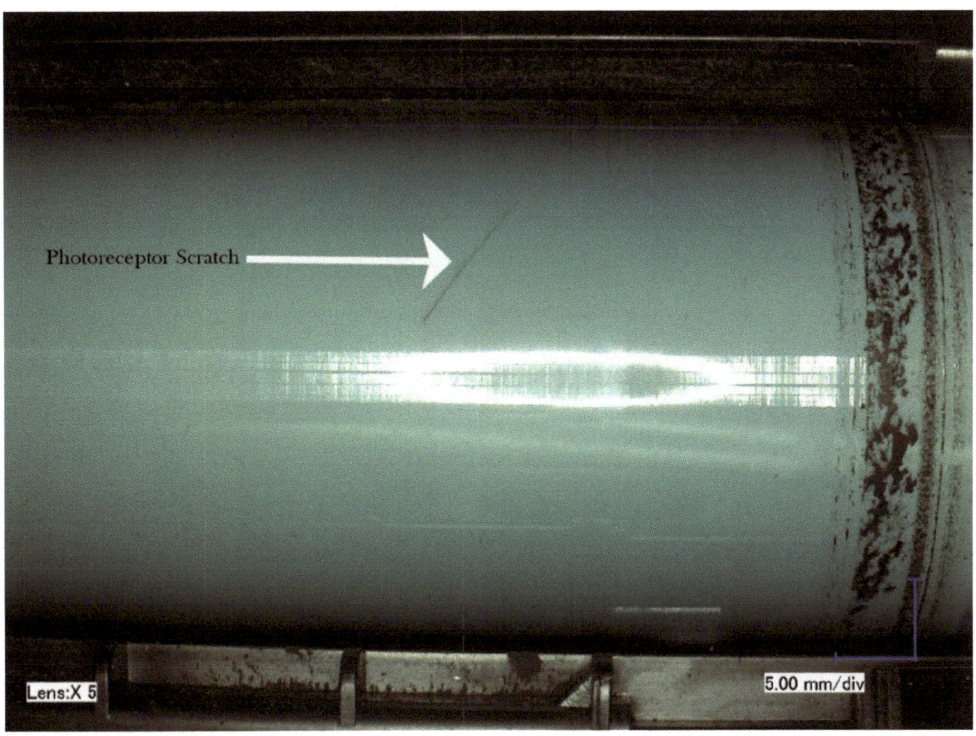

Figure 17.6 The scratch on the photoreceptor that produced the defect in Figure 17.5.

The procedure requires the disassembly of the printer cartridge and the careful mounting of the photoreceptor into an electromechanical mount, as shown in Figure 17.7.

As the photoreceptor is subjected to repeated cycles, its electrical properties may change. In the electrophotography industry, the term *photoreceptor fatigue* is used to describe how the photoreceptor does not properly charge and discharge as required. The result is an output that is less than ideal and can result in lower contrast and no sharp edge detail.

Equipment to test the electrical properties of the photoreceptor can show how the surface is non uniform, as shown in Figure 17.8. Ideally, the surface of the photoreceptor would have uniform characteristics over the entire surface, i.e. similar voltage corresponding to a similar color in the plotted data. In the Figure 17.8 example, there are two larger areas shown in black. These regions will produce spatially-periodic defects on the page at intervals that correspond to the circumference of the drum.

While this type of testing is only possible when the photoreceptor from a suspect device is available, it does open the potential for the comparison between the electrical properties of the photoreceptor and questioned documents when the defects are more subtle in nature.

A damaged photoreceptor is not necessarily the only drum or roller within the device that can lead to periodic defects. Another cause that can be visualized is that of the fusing roller. The fusing roller is designed to fix the toner in place by a combination of heat and pressure. It should not displace the toner appreciably from where it was deposited during the transfer step in the electrophotographic process. Through wear or heating malfunction, the fused toner may become partially "de-tacked" onto the fusing roller, resulting in a repeated partial printed pattern onto ensuing output. This is akin to an automobile tire that crossed wet paint and, as a result, keeps leaving markings onto the pavement as it travels.

Another source of defects can be attributed to scratches in the fusing roller that leave similar scratches within the toner on the output.[15] Some of these scratches can be subtle; others may be more evident. To fully realize the presence or extent of subtle scratches, specialized instrumentation, such as application of confocal scanning microscopy may be required.[16]

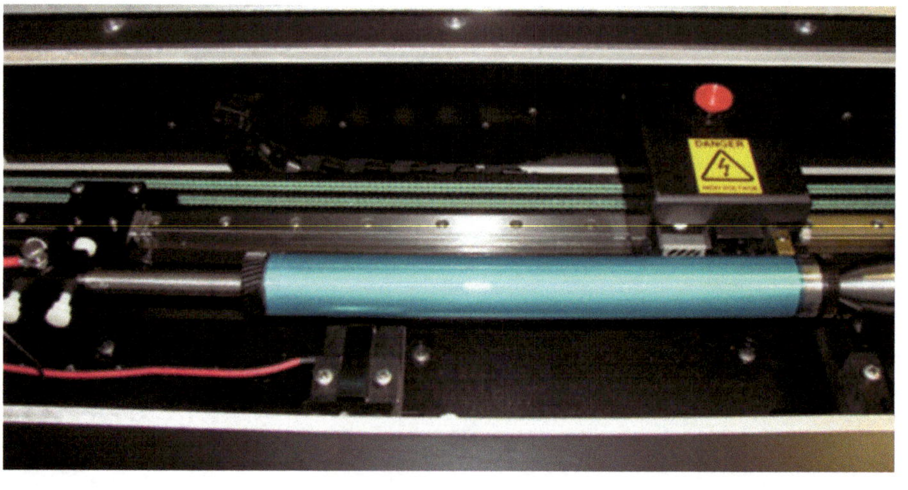

Figure 17.7 Photoreceptor loaded into drum testing equipment.

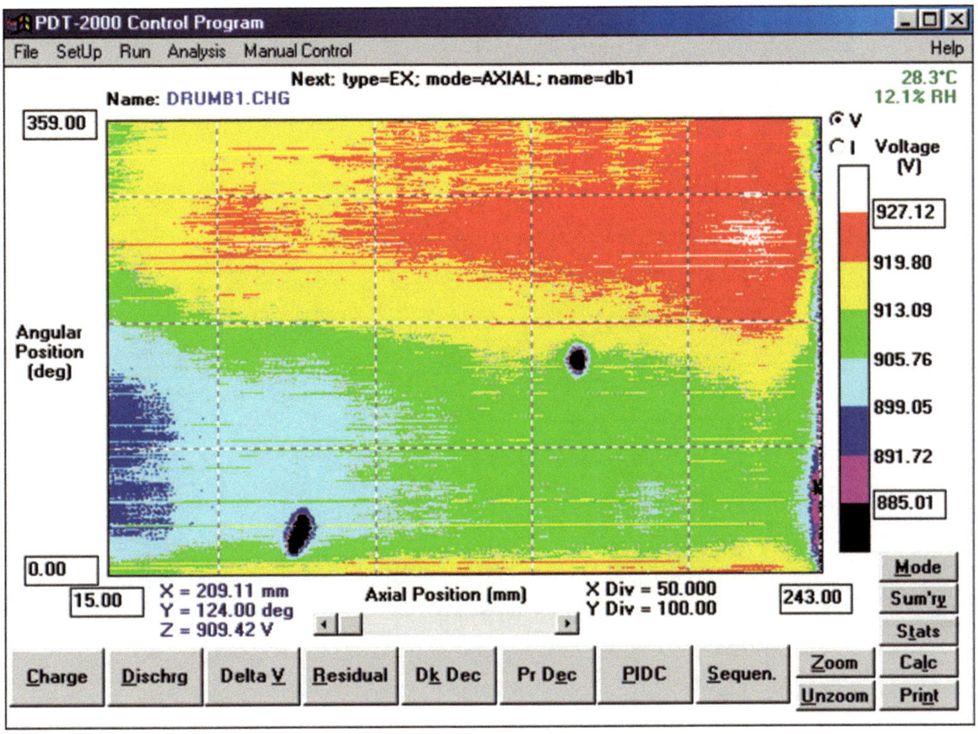

Figure 17.8 Example of a voltage profile for a tested drum – areas that are black are worn down to the base metal and will leave spatially-periodic defects.

17.6 OBTAINING SPECIMEN OUTPUT FROM ELECTROPHOTOGRAPHIC DEVICES

When a suspect electrophotographic device is available, several considerations should be made when taking specimens. Many modern devices have internal memory in the form of hard disks or similar computer storage. As a result, consultation with appropriate specialists in digital forensics may be needed to ensure that the integrity of any such evidence is maintained. This should be done before any specimen output is obtained.

Assuming that the potential for digital evidence is accounted for, the procedure to obtain specimens from suspect devices for document examination must consider spatially-static defects and spatially-periodic defects, as outlined in the preceding section.

Copy platens in many modern devices actually have at least two imaging areas: the main copy platen for hand placement of documents and a slit glass used by the automatic document feeder, as shown in Figure 17.9.

The slit glass region is a far smaller surface compared to the main copy platen. Some devices have another scanning platen located in the mechanism of the automatic document feeder to permit simultaneous two-sided scanning of documents sent through the automatic document feeder.

For each copy platen, efforts should be made to obtain specimens at darkest, lightest, and medium contrast settings. Copies made from the automatic document feeder should also be done at these settings, using both single-sided and double-sided mode. Additionally, copies made

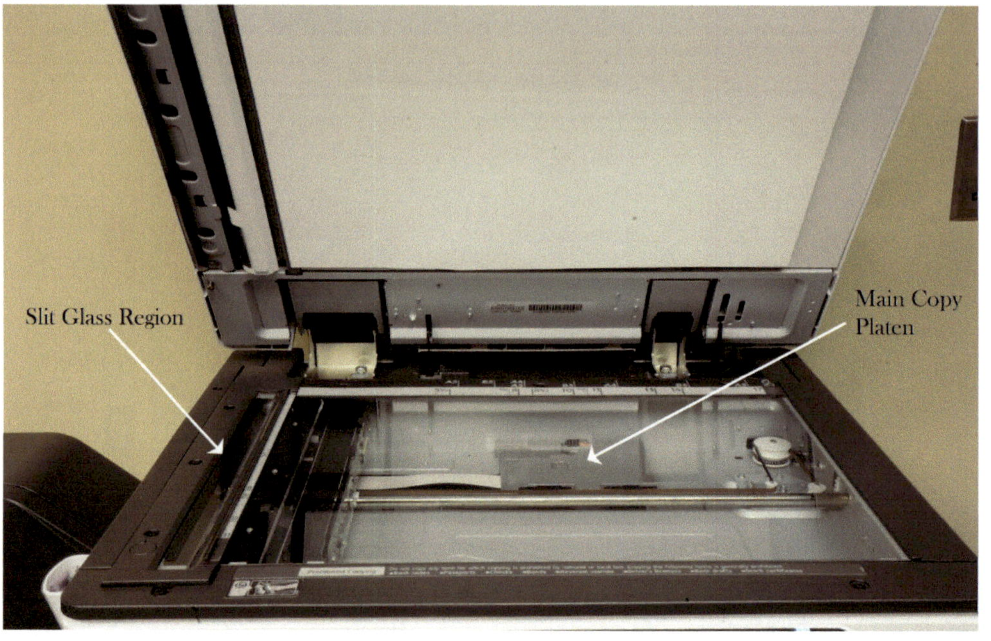

Figure 17.9 Photograph showing the slit glass portion and main copy platen on a device equipped with an automatic document feeder.

from the main copy platen should be done using the above settings with the copy cover down and with no paper, as well as with a sheet of white paper. To assist in the assessment of spatially-periodic defects, the direction of paper processing can be recorded as the pages are output. The direction of paper processing will indicate which way the paper was printed and the distance between the defects.

Consultation with an operator's and service manual may provide additional insight into the scanning areas and settings available for a device.

17.7 TONER COMPOSITION

Toner is a complex material made with organic and inorganic materials that are prepared to provide a clean, crisp output on the page at a low cost. Toner must have particular electrostatic properties that enable devices to rapidly place toner accurately on the output without clogging device components.

As electrophotographic devices were developed with increased printing speed, there was a need to also increase developer speed. This led to the use of magnetic brush development. Essentially, the properties of magnetism are used to attract toner where it is desired in the development step. The toner itself may be magnetic (contain magnetic compounds) or nonmagnetic. Therefore, questioned printed documents can be tested to determine whether there is a difference in magnetic properties.

Magnetic "visualization" or detection equipment like the one seen in Figure 17.10 can be used for qualitative evaluation of the magnetic properties of toner. The sensitivity of different

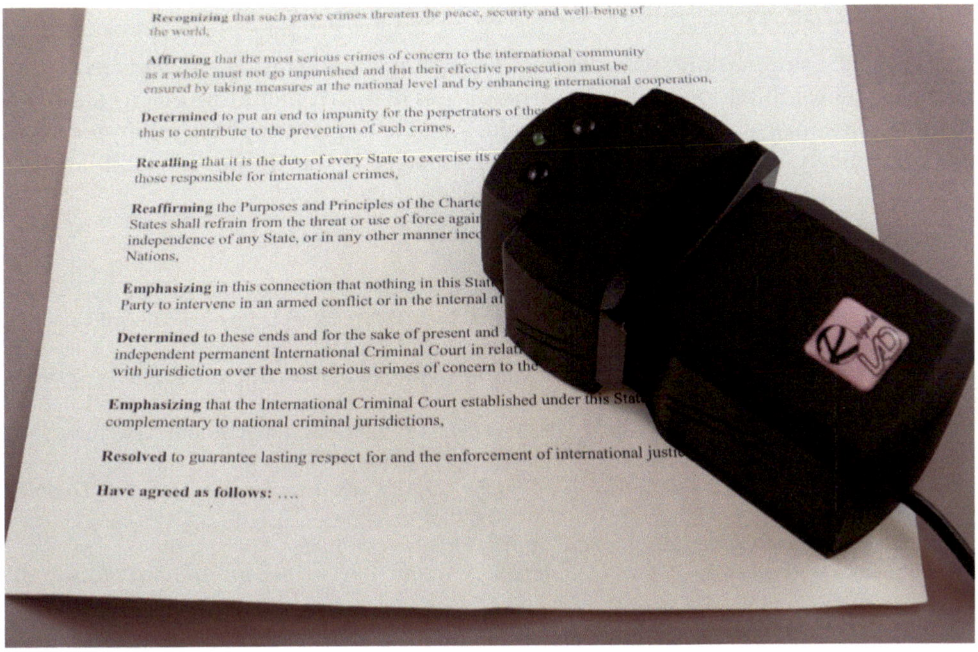

Figure 17.10 Magnetic toner/ink instrument device. (Regula® MagMouse.)

instruments will vary. In the past, some were designed primarily for the detection of Magnetic Ink Character Recognition Printing (MICR).[17]

Qualitative examination of toner for the simple presence or absence of magnetic compounds is relatively straightforward as long as the printed areas are similar in size. Additional differentiation between magnetic toners may be possible by quantifying the magnetic flux. Several efforts to do this have been undertaken by various research groups.[18–20]

In spite of significant progress, there are complications in measuring magnetic flux due in part to: the surface areas of toner being measured, nonlinear response of the magnetic measurement instrumentation, and reproducibility of measurements between instruments.

17.8 BANDING IN ELECTROPHOTOGRAPHY

Banding is a feature that may be clearly visible on output that is about 33% gray (high toner coverage but not completely black output). As there are many rollers, gears, and belts within a device, the mechanical vibrations and interactions of the components may produce banding, where there is a striped appearance rather than a nonuniform deposition of toner on the output. Kawamoto wrote extensively about this problem from a print quality perspective.[21,22]

Other research teams devoted significant effort to see if the banding feature could be exploited for forensic use.[23–26] These research efforts have not led to method implementation in forensic applications partly because of the subtle nature of banding on most documents where toner coverage is not high and the technical nature of detection and explanation.

17.9 CONCLUSION

Many document examinations will not require cutting-edge equipment and interpretation. Conversely, other examinations will require new types of instrumentation and a careful evaluation of the significance of any findings. The widespread use of electrophotography for numerous applications is likely to keep the 21st century FDE engaged in these types of examinations.

REFERENCES

1. E. Webster, *Print Unchained A Saga of Invention and Enterprise*, West Dover, VT: DRA of Vermont, Inc., 2000, p. 72.
2. E. Webster, *Print Unchained A Saga of Invention and Enterprise*, West Dover, VT: DRA of Vermont, Inc, 2000, p. 48.
3. J. H. Dessauer and H. E. Clark, *Xerography and Related Processes*, London and New York: The Focal Press, 1965.
4. J. H. Dessauer, *My Years with Xerox The Billions Nobody Wanted*, Garden City, NY: Doubleday & Company Inc., 1971.
5. R. M. Schaffert, *Electrophotography*, London: The Focal Press, 1965.
6. L. B. Schein, *Electrophotography and Development Physics* (Revised Second Edition), Morgan Hill, CA: Laplacian Press, 1996.
7. E. M. Williams, *The Physics and Technology of Xerographic Processes*, Malabar, FL: Krieger Publishing Company, 1993.
8. I. Batterham, *The Office Copying Revolution*, Canberra, ACT: National Archives of Australia, 2008.
9. F. Romano and M. Mitrano, *History of Desktop Publishing*, New Castle, DE: Oak Knoll Press, 2019.
10. R. N. Totty and D. Baxendale, "Defect marks and the identification of photocopying machines," *Journal of the Forensic Science Society*, vol. 21, pp. 23–30, 1981.
11. P. M. Borsenberger and D. S. Weiss, *Organic Photoreceptors for Xerography*, New York, NY: Marcel Dekker Inc., 1998.
12. P. M. Borsenberger and D. S. Weiss, *Organic Photoreceptors for Imaging Systems*, New York, NY: Marcel Dekker Inc., 1993.
13. M.-K. Tse, D. J. Forrest and F. Y. Wong, "Advances in Instrumented Defect Mapping Technology for Photoreceptors," in *NIP International Conference on Digital Printing Technologies*, Springfield, 1998.
14. M.-K. Tse, "Quality Control Test Equipment for Photoreceptors, Charge Rollers and Magnetic Rollers," in *NIP Advances in Non-Impact Printing Technologies*, Springfield, 1994.
15. F. James Gerhart, "Identification of Photocopiers from Fusing Roller Defects," in *American Society of Questioned Document Examiners (ASQDE)*, San Jose, 1990.
16. M. Gaudreau and D. Purdy, "Applications of Confocal Laser Scanning Microscopy to Forensic Document Examination," in *American Society of Questioned Document Examiners (ASQDE)*, Milwaukee, 1992.
17. Plastiform® Brand Magnetic Viewer B-1022, St Paul: Industrial Electrical Products Division/3M.
18. A. Biedermann, S. Bozza, F. Taroni, M. Fürbach, B. Li and W. D. Mazzella, "Analysis and evaluation of magnetism of black toners on documents printed by electrophotographic systems," *Forensic Science International*, vol. 267, pp. 157–165, 2016.
19. C. Polston, W. Mazzella, M. Furbach and P. Buzzini, "Assessing the repeatability of magnetic flux measurements and their potential to discriminate toner printed documents," *Journal of the American Society of Questioned Document Examiners*, vol. 21, no. 2, pp. 45–56, December 2018.
20. K. Herlaar, M. Mieremet and M. Fakkel, "Measuring magnetic properties to discriminate between different laser printers," *Journal of the American Society of Questioned Document Examiners*, vol. 18, no. 2, pp. 51–66, December 2015.
21. H. Kawamoto, "Vibration induced in driving mechanism of photoconductor drum in color laser printer," *Journal of Imaging Science and Technology*, vol. 48, no. 4, pp. 306–311, July 2004.

22. H. Kawamoto, "Self-excited vibration induced in paper-feed-roller in electrophotography copy machine," *Journal of Imaging Science and Technology*, vol. 43, no. 4, pp. 398–402, July 1999.
23. P.-J. Chiang, G. T.-C. Chin, E. J. Delp and J. P. Allebach, "Optimized Embedding and Decoding of Extrinsic Signatures for Electrophotographic Halftone Images," in *NIP & Digital Fabrication Conference*, Springfield, 2008.
24. P.-J. Chiang, T.-C. Chiu, A. K. Mikkiliheni, O. Arslan, R. Moshe, G. Kumontoy, E. Delp and J. P. Allebach, "Extrinsic Signature Embedding in Text Document Using Exposure Modulation for Information Hiding and Secure Printing in Electrophotography," in *NIP & Digital Fabrication Conference*, Springfield, 2005.
25. P.-J. Chiang, G. N. Ali, A. K. Mikkilineni, E. J. Delp, J. P. Allebach and G. T.-C. Chiu, "Extrinsic Signatures Embedding Using Exposure Modulation for Information Hiding and Secure Printing in Electrophotography," in *NIP & Digital Fabrication Conference*, Springfield, 2004.
26. N. Liu, L. Zhang and C. Chen, "A preliminary study on sources of banding artifacts for the identification of monochromatic laser printers," *Journal of Forensic Sciences*, vol. 62, no. 6, pp. 1542–1553, November 2017.

Chapter 18

Typography

Zain M. Bhaloo, Tobin Tanaka, and Peter Tytell

CONTENTS

18.1 INTRODUCTION

Typography is the appearance, arrangement, design, study, technique, and art of organizing and arranging type, typefaces, text, letter forms, and printing, in order to make it readable, enjoyable, relatable, captivating, attractive, and welcoming. Typography is relevant to document examination for a number of reasons, ranging from the comparison of typefaces on different documents, to dating issues, to alteration examinations. One example would be examination of packaging of suspected counterfeit pharmaceuticals where the graphics and typefaces used do not correspond to that used for the genuine product.

While it will not be possible to list every situation where questions involving typography may arise, there are some common situations. It must be emphasized that any correlation between different typefaces is conditional; an inability to differentiate type is the result if no differences are found from a comparison. This may be complicated by factors such as but not limited to: a document's copy quality, variation of printing, size of printing, the substrate printed upon, and the quantity of typeface for comparison.

While the issues surrounding typography have been in the Forensic Document Examiner's (FDE's) purview since the origin of the profession, the widespread use of computers in the 1980s and subsequent deployment of software for word processing and graphics in the 1990s has resulted in an ever-increasing creation of documents. These documents could be made with complex graphics and typefaces, many of which were previously only available from commercial print shops.

In the early days of document examination, questions about typewriting were the primary typography issue addressed.[1] Typewritten specimens were classified and categorized by FDEs for a variety of examinations involving typewriters and typewritten documents. While the use of typewriters has diminished, the need to address questions pertaining to historic documents that bear original or copied typewriting will continue.

Typography is widely used in many documents, and it is used in all manner of impact printing (e.g., typewriters and dot-matrix printers), nonimpact printing (e.g., laser-printers and ink-jet printers), and graphic arts in the printing industry (e.g., offset lithography, letterpress, and gravure).

While many documents will be on regular office paper for items such as forms, handouts, school assignments, contracts, and similar output, documents also include packaging, signage, and similar applications. Even further, documents can be made from materials such as plastic or composites, such as bags, currency, passports, identification cards, and credit cards.

The term *font* has become widely used to refer to a style of typeface such as Courier or Arial, but it had traditionally referred to all the letters and symbols that comprise a typeface. Within this chapter, typeface will be used to refer to a type style or design, and font will be used as traditionally described above.

18.2 HISTORY OF TYPEFACES

The influence of handwriting on typeface development may not be readily apparent.

> ...we can have no knowledge of the types of to-day and their history without knowing the history of types back to the invention of printing, and that we can have no knowledge of the first types or their relative place in the scheme of things unless we know how earlier calligraphers formed the letters of their manuscript book-hands.[2]

During the period of printing press development in Europe, the typefaces used were meant to mimic handwriting. From the 10th to 14th centuries, handwritten letter forms underwent national and regional influence with German handwritten manuscripts adopting a Blackletter form. These Blackletter forms were used in metal type for early printing done by Johannes Gutenberg. An early example is the 42-line Bible from the period of 1450. Later typefaces were influenced by the development of Humanistic writing, which was influenced by the Renaissance. Humanistic writing was calligraphy with a broad nib pen held at the same angle with respect to the baseline, the result being a variable stroke width. Typefaces that were inspired by these developments were classified into categories that speak to their origin. More will follow on this topic later in the chapter.[3–6]

18.3 TYPOGRAPHIC TERMINOLOGY

There are many different terms used for many features on many different characters, and this can lead to confusion and uncertainty. Figures 18.1–18.4 include some basic definitions of pertinent typographic features and concepts compiled into an illustrated lexicon. The 64-term glossary was adapted from www.fontsmith.com,[7] with reference made to other typography works.[8–11] Several of these terms will be addressed in greater detail below due to their importance in examining documents.

18.4 TYPEWRITERS

The patents granted to Henry Mill by Queen Anne in 1714 comprise what is considered to be the earliest conceptual description of a typewriter. An American typewriter was first made by William Burth, with patents granted in July 1829. As for a commercially made and distributed typewriter, credit is due to Christopher Latham Sholes.[12]

The classic document examination literature describes the comparison of typewriter typefaces and the many examinations related to typewriter-produced documents.[13–15] Early FDEs realized the need to obtain specimen typewriting from the ever-increasing range of machines introduced to market. In doing so, typewriting was classified according to letter designs in a manner that differed from that used for metal typefaces used in commercial printing.

Typewriting also differed in that the size was generally not classified by points but by the escapement, or letter spacing between characters. For example, in North America, common escapements were 10 characters per inch (pica spacing) and 12 characters per inch (elite spacing). Most typewriters marketed outside of North America commonly had escapements of 2.10, 2.50, or 2.60 mm per character.[16] Other escapements have been used as well, and some typewriters were capable of dual or even triple escapement.

Most typewriters were mechanically designed to operate using monospaced typefaces, where each character occupies the same width independent of the width of the character. In that way, the narrower characters such as *i*, *j*, and punctuation occupy the same width as wider characters such as *W* or *M*.[17] Proportional spaced typewriting, where narrow characters occupy less width, did exist, although it was far less common due to the significantly greater mechanical complexity.

Some typewriting classification systems, most notably that of Interpol, relied heavily upon escapement measurement as a starting point. Subsequent typewriting differentiation relied upon certain design features of characters, specifically the *f*, *t*, *M*, *2*, *3*, *4*, *5*, *6*, and *9*. Classification systems of these kinds did not require the typewriting typeface style to be classified into a specific style such as Courier or Prestige.

The Haas Typewriter Atlas is a comprehensive compilation of typewriter typefaces that was assembled by Josef and Bernhard Haas. The Pica Monotone Atlas was organized to permit locating a specific monotone typeface by means of punched cards and letter descriptions.[18] A later version with Non-Pica typefaces was grouped by typestyle: Elite, Special, Courier, Sans Serif, Cubic, Gothic, Shaded, Medium (Roman), Cursive, Mini, Script, and Proportional.[19]

In the late 1980s, Dr. Phillip Bouffard developed a computer database search program to facilitate the use of the Haas Atlases. Bouffard designed the database search criteria in a manner first prescribed by de la Durantaye and Crown.[20,21] Using this program, the typestyle was the primary starting point to conduct searches.[22–29] In about 2010, adaptation of Bouffard's work for a modern Windows®-based computer system resulted in the WinType database that operates with the Microsoft® Access® program.[30,31]

APERTURE
The opening between the interior and the exterior of a character. The size can vary from open to closed depending on the typeface.

APEX
The topmost point of a character where two strokes meet to form a junction of less that 90°.

ARC
The curved part of a letter leading from a straight stem but that does not form a complete bowl.

ARM
A horizontal or diagonal stroke that extends from a vertical stroke.

ASCENDER
The portion of a lower case character that ascends above the x-height of the other lower case characters.

ASCENDER LINE
The invisible line at which the ascenders of all lower case characters with ascending vertical strokes stop.

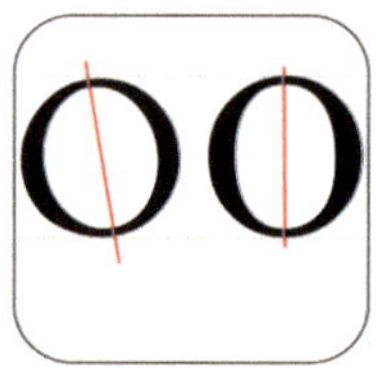

AXIS / STRESS
The vertical, horizontal, or diagonal emphasis of a character's stroke, or lack thereof.

BALL TERMINAL
A rounded termination on the arm of a lower case character.

BASELINE
The visible or invisible line on which the main body of the character rests.

BODY SIZE
The absolute vertical height from the highest point of the ascender or diacritic to the lowest point of the descender (if applicable).

BOLDFACE
a.k.a Weight contrast, is used to create emphasis and draw attention by increasing the weight of the strokes (the relative darkness or thickness).

BOWL
A curved stroke that creates the rounded portion of a character. The bowl can be open or closed.

BRACKET
The connection point and transition between the main stem of a stroke and the serif. Not all serifs are bracketed and brackets can be curved or angular.

CAP HEIGHT
The height of an upper case character from the baseline to the cap line at the top of the character. Cap height can vary between type faces.

CONDENSED
a.k.a. Narrow face, the narrower version of a typeface specifically designed with narrow line widths, narrow spaces between letters and sometimes taller glyphs.

COUNTER
The open spaced formed in the interior of a character that are partially or fully enclosed by the strokes.

Figure 18.1 Typography terminology visual glossary, Plate 1.

CROSS STROKE

The horizontal stroke that crosses the stem in the lower case "t" and "f".

CROSS BAR

The horizontal stroke that connects the two strokes in the upper case "A" and "H".

CROTCH

The space formed by the angle where two strokes connect. The angles can be acute (<90°) or obtuse (>90°).

DESCENDER

The portion of a lower case character that descends below the baseline of the other characters.

DESCENDER LINE

The invisible line at which the descenders of all lower case characters with descending vertical strokes stop.

DIACRITIC

The symbols placed above and/or below a character to modify its pronunciation, e.g. acute, diaresis, cedilla.

DIAGONAL STROKE

The diagonal or angled portion of a character.

EAR

The small stroke that extends from the bowl of the lower case "g" in some typefaces.

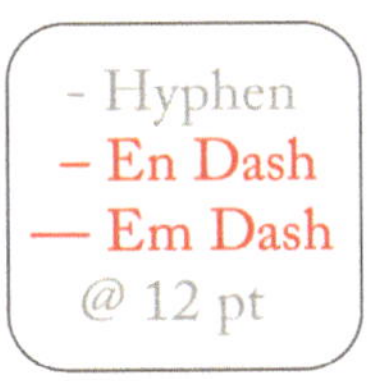

EM/EN DASH

Em: A dash of equivalent size to the type size in use.
En: a dash ½ the size of an Em dash.
E.g. 1 Em dash is 12 pt in a 12 pt typeface, 1 En is 6 pt.
Word spacing is generally ¼ of an Em unit.

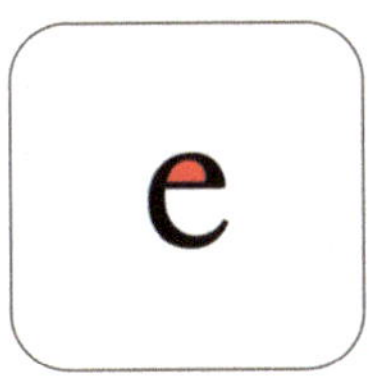

EYE

The enclosed interior space formed by the strokes of the lower case "e".

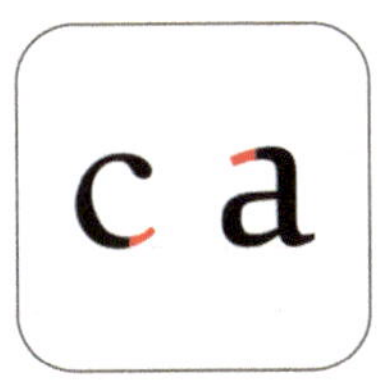

FINIAL

The tapered terminal point of a stroke on characters such as "c" or at the top of a two storey "a" in some typefaces.

FLAG

The horizontal stroke at the top of the numeral "5".

FOOT

The portion of the stem of a characters that sits on the baseline.

GLYPH

The graphical representation of one character, numeral, symbol, or punctuation mark in one particular typeface. The same character in another typeface/font = another glyph.

HOOK

The curved portion of the stroke in a lower case "f".

INK TRAP

The area of a counter or crotch that is removed in specific type faces to allow ink to flow, designed for printing on newsprint.

Figure 18.2 Typography terminology visual glossary, Plate 2.

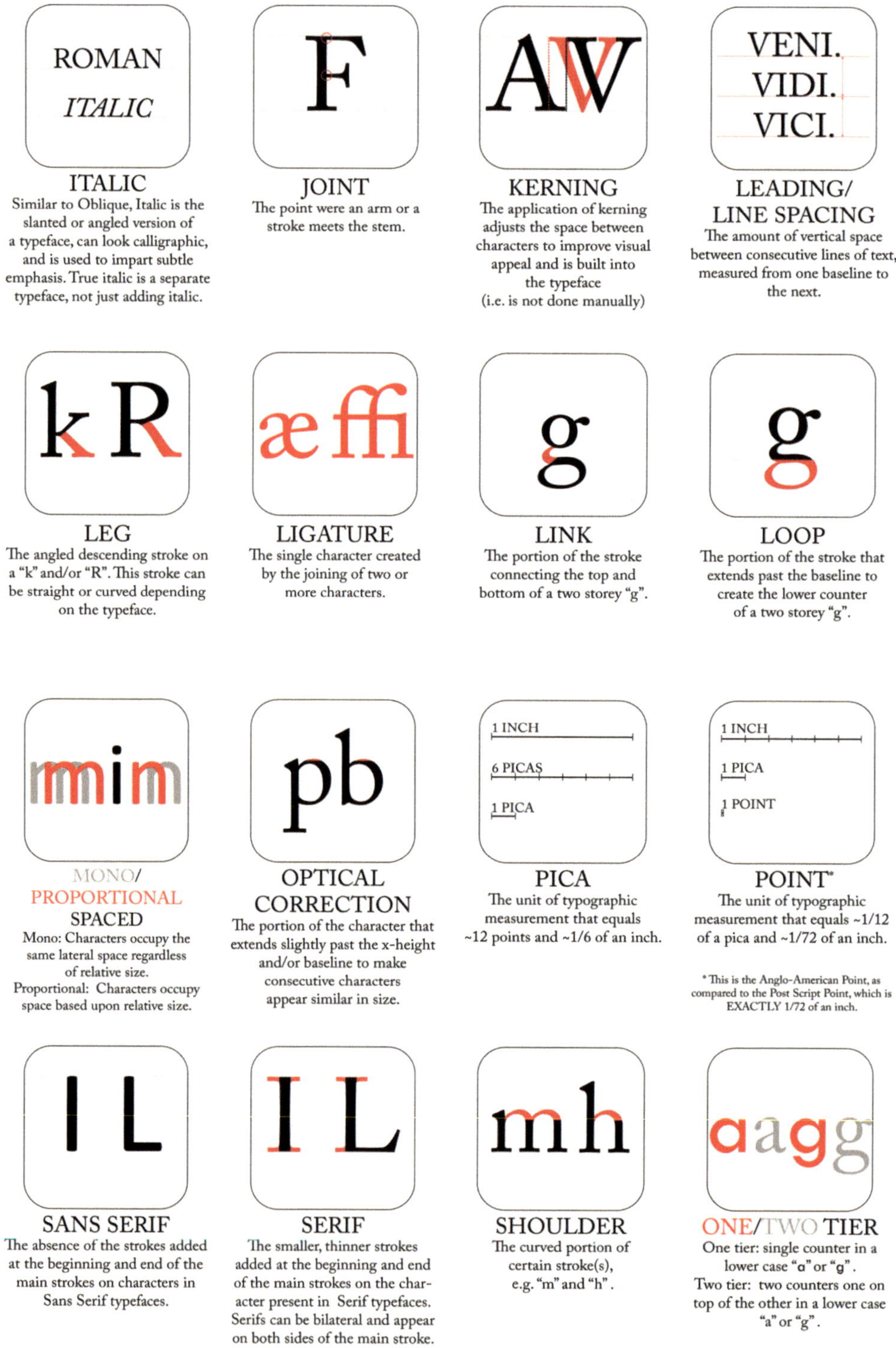

Figure 18.3 Typography terminology visual glossary, Plate 3.

Figure 18.4 Typography terminology visual glossary, Plate 4.

18.5 TYPEFACE CLASSIFICATION

While the FDE may not have the same specific need for typeface classification as a typographer, some basic knowledge of type classification is desirable to assist in finding similar typefaces when conducting comparisons and examinations.

Typographers have classification systems that rely upon the general characteristics of the letters in their appearance. Examples are sans-serif (without serifs), slab-serif (with thick broad serifs), or scripts (which are meant to be similar to handwritten letters). These categories may be further subdivided into smaller groups.[32]

Classifications can be ambiguous, so a typeface may not be categorized the same way by all typographers. As a result, some typefaces may be placed in multiple categories. To ensure a potentially similar typeface is not overlooked during a search, one should consider other categories.

Perhaps the most widely adopted classification system for Latin scripts is based on the work of Maximilien Vox. It was introduced with six categories in 1954 and later expanded to ten categories in 1962. In 1962, the *Association Typographique Internationale* adapted this classification system for typefaces.[33] Nearly all typefaces in use at that time were metal type; the later technology of phototypesetting was just beginning to be used in the printing industry. Printers in that era ordered typefaces from foundries that cast metal type, or in the case of phototypesetters, made photographic images of the characters in compatible equipment. To enable finding a particular typeface, the foundries supplied catalogs of typefaces that were grouped according to classification systems. Even today with digital typefaces, the continuing use of classification systems for typefaces is relevant for the FDE when attempting to identify a typeface of a document. This will apply even when the document is very old, in which case review of older trade catalogs or books may be needed.

Classification is also the basis of many "font finding" software programs. Some programs such as *What the Font*[34] permit uploading of an image with an unknown typeface for making queries. Some resources such as identifont.com[35] have multiple query options, including a series of questions with graphic images to assist with searches.

These programs provide assistance in the determination of probable typefaces for printed matter, but there are several reasons why FDEs should not exclusively rely on them to determine the probable typeface:

1. For websites that allow for uploading an image of the text, the passage of text to be "shared" must be one that is not subject to data privacy or confidentiality protections. It may be possible to upload a portion of the text which is not subject to such issues. Alternatively, resources that do not require input of the image avoid any potential privacy issues.
2. When the text is poor copy quality, the manner of printing has not resulted in a clean image, or there is poor contrast due to paper background or overlapping graphics/text, then the software may not perform so well. This is especially the case with the emergence of "grunge fonts" that attempt to mimic imperfections of dirty or damaged typefaces. The resulting candidate list of possible matches may be totally different from the actual typeface used. Verification will still require a manual comparison.
3. A candidate list of typefaces must be carefully reviewed. This includes all aspects of the type design, including the weight and subtle features. This type of examination requires a methodical review of the typeface features that cannot be solely accomplished by software algorithms.

Notwithstanding these limitations, testing of the mobile version of the *What the Font* application with 50 different typefaces by Shiver found that the claimed success rate of searches being in excess of 90% was indeed correct.[36] Even greater success was achieved with typefaces from the Monotype® database, which is not surprising as *What the Font* is available from Monotype®.

Welch outlined an examination procedure for digital type including several web-based resources. She also provided a case study of documents that were purportedly prepared decades earlier than when the typeface in question became available.[37]

It must be emphasized that any identification of a typeface must be done with caution due to one or more limitations from copy quality, multiple releases of a typeface from different foundries, and the variety of glyphs available for comparison. As a result, categorical conclusions about a questioned typeface classification may not be possible.

18.6 WORD PROCESSORS, COMPUTERS, AND DESKTOP PUBLISHING

General widespread use of typography emerged with the implementation of personal computers and the advent of desktop publishing. A detailed history of desktop publishing can be found in the book by Romano and Mitrano.[38]

Certain typefaces are used for different applications. The use of particular typefaces may be due to the default settings of many software packages or computer operating systems. Common software will often use the installed typefaces controlled by the computer operating system. For example, Microsoft® Excel® will be capable of using any of the installed typefaces as long as they are compatible. On the other hand, specialized software such as AutoCAD® can have typefaces that are only recognized by AutoCAD®.

In the digital typeface realm, a similar typeface may be released by several type foundries with subtle differences. Such typefaces can be very difficult to differentiate given their closeness in design. The careful study of certain letters (glyphs) may allow for differentiation between similar typeface designs offered by multiple foundries. However, this is conditional on the printed copy being of adequate copy quality and size.

18.7 TYPOGRAPHY APPLIED TO DOCUMENT EXAMINATION

For documents produced by computerized systems, there are several steps that can be taken for examination of typefaces. Depending on the type of question to be answered, the examination may not involve all steps.

As a starting point, the entirety of all pages in question should be examined at a macroscopic level, including the general quality of the printing and the printing process used, such as inkjet or electrophotography.

Many typography questions in forensic document examination relate to substitutions or additions on a page in whole or in part. When alterations are made to documents, the alteration or substitution may not be done with the same typeface as the surrounding text. As a result, the combination of a different typeface with misalignments that cannot be accounted for as a result of the printing process is strong evidence of alteration. In modern digital printing, the use of a different point size in a line does not necessarily mean that an alteration took place as the size of type can be changed part way through the line.

18.8 SOFTWARE TO DESIGN/CHANGE TYPEFACE

When metal type and, later, phototypesetters were the only option for printing typefaces, the skill level to design and modify a typeface was in the domain of the professional trained in such matters. Since the 1990s, the widespread availability of computers and software allows users with some technical knowledge to make subtle changes to typefaces. Fontlab® and Fontographer® are examples of software that can be used for this purpose. Subtle changes may be very difficult to detect. As a result, the degree of specificity with regards to the exact name and foundry of a typeface will often have to be more generalized. Although it is relatively easy to make slight changes to typefaces, most general users do not have much need nor desire to do so. Use of typeface software does not by itself constitute typography expertise; however, it has allowed for the emergence of self-taught typeface designers in the digital realm who have not necessarily been formally trained in typography.[39]

There is some potential for software to be used to reproduce older typefaces to create a backdated document. For example, a document that appears to have been typewritten could be made by recreating a typewriter font. However, such a typeface would not have the variation in appearance that would be present with actual typewritten documents, at least those done by a typebar machine. In other instances, typefaces could be copied from a specific document and then used to produce false documents that appear to be from that time period.

18.9 SOURCES OF TYPEFACES

Many typefaces can be found online, but those originally created from metal type or by phototypesetting may not be. For documents commercially set by printers or with older dates, reference books that include such typefaces will need to be consulted.[40–42]

Common digital typefaces are supplied with computer operating systems. Additional digital typefaces are directly available from a variety of web-based type foundries. Some digital typefaces are available for free while others require payment. Several modern typefaces have been inspired from past designs or are updates to classic typefaces.[43] The reason that past designs still resonate in modern times is that certain typefaces are well suited for specific applications. For example, for extended reading in books, typefaces with serifs tend to be used rather than sans-serif styles.

18.10 POINT SIZES AND DEFINITION

The use of points to define typeface size leads to confusion due to the different measurement systems that have been used. Type sizes originate from metal type and are measured by the body of the physical type, not the face of the type.[44] Type size in the modern era is defined by the bounding box of the letter.[45] The height for a specified bounding box is the same; the width will usually vary unless the typeface is monospaced.

At different time periods, the definition of point as a type size varied by geographic region. The American System was commonly used in the United States and the United Kingdom. The Didot point was commonly used in Continental Europe into the 1980s.[46] Accordingly, in the event that documents of that era are encountered, the Didot point system should be considered as the point measurement.

Modern documents use the PostScript Point, sometimes referred to as Digital Typographic Point. A summary table of the point systems that are known to have been used is provided in Table 18.1.

TABLE 18.1 POINT SIZE DEFINITION SUMMARY

Point Size System (1 Point)	Imperial (inch)	Metric (mm)
PostScript Point (circa 1982)[47]	1/72 (exactly)	0.3527777
American System (circa 1872)[48]	0.0138 (about 1/72 inch)	0.35052
Didot (France circa 1784)[48]	0.0148	0.37592
Fournier (France circa 1742)[48]	0.0136	0.34544

18.11 TYPOGRAPHY RULERS

Typography rulers and measuring devices are useful for a variety of examinations. Many are economical and adaptable to a variety of substrates as they are often printed onto flexible material. This flexibility permits them to be curved to fit the surface of a document. Although most documents are flat, if there is a need to measure packaging or a page that is bound in a book, a flexible ruler permits better accuracy.

The same glyph in two different typefaces of the same point size will not necessarily be the same height.[49] This does not preclude the use of typographic rulers, especially when comparisons are made for the homogeneity or inhomogeneity of the size of typefaces. If the document has been made using modern word processing, then the typographic ruler to use should be the Digital Type Point (DTP) kind, where 1 point = 1/72 inch. For most type gauges, only the letters *E* and *x* are provided. For the lower-case height, the *x*-height is used because it illustrates the height of lower-case letters without inclusion of descenders or ascenders. For text in English, *x* occurs infrequently in most written passages. As a result, one may be forced to use other lower-case letters with minimal ascender or descender height as an approximation for the x-height.[50] *E* is used for capital height as it has well-defined parallel lines that enable accurate measurement. In English, *E* also benefits from a high frequency of occurrence.

Caution should be used with typographic rulers because there is no set relation between these measurements of the characters and what is referred to as the nominal point size. This becomes evident in modern word processing software if the same word is repeated across a line in the same selected point size but different typefaces; not all the characters are the same height as shown in Figure 18.5.

As noted earlier, it is the bounding box that defines the point size for digital typefaces. There is no set ratio for *x*-height to capital height or capital height to bounding box size. Generally, the capital height is about 70% of the bounding box size. The *x*-height is about 50%–66% of capital height.[51] The bounding box size and what was referred to as body size for metal type refers to the vertical height measured from the highest descender to the lowest descender for a particular typeface. However, there is usually slightly greater space allocated so that ascenders and descenders do not overlap on adjacent lines.[52]

Even with these limitations, the comparisons of typographic size can be achieved by the overlay of a type gauge to printed text (Figure 18.6). Type gauges are usually provided with serif and sans-serif letters. An example is provided below (typography ruler images used with permission of Galaxy Gauge™):

Macroscopic examination may disclose misalignments for some entries that are easily seen. Shorter entries or those that have a very subtle misalignment may require microscopic examination. The FDE has a range of tools available to detect misalignments. As modern word processing enables spacing between lines to be fractions of a point, the creation of a variety of grids will assist in the detection of interlineations and misalignments. Flynn describes how word processing programs such as Microsoft® Word® can be used to make grids with line spacing increments of 0.05 DTPs.[53] Any printed transparency grid should be verified with rulers of

Handgloves x-ray (Garamond 12 pt) Handgloves x-ray (Times New Roman 12 Pt)

Figure 18.5 Example showing the same point size with different typefaces.

(a)

(b)

Figure 18.6 (a) Portion of typography ruler (16 pt. serif) and (b) overlay of ruler on text that is 16 pt. serif (slightly offset).

known accuracy before use. To make grids that are suitable using Microsoft® Word®, the following steps are given:

1. Create a table that is one column wide and several rows long to cover the entire page.
2. Set all rows to the exact height desired, based on estimate of the type size, preferably by measurement with a typographic ruler.
3. Overlay transparencies to see if misalignments are visible.

18.12 SPACING OF TYPE

The spacing between lines of text became far more flexible in the era of desktop publishing. When type was mechanically assembled in metal, the spacing between lines was generally limited to the available spacers. These leads were 1 point, 1 1/2 point, 2 point, and 3 point.[54] Fractional point spacing was not common, and there was generally not much demand for it. Even though this kind of spacing is not currently common in books and typeset materials, technology easily permits it.

Business documents that are simply typed in default settings in word processing may have fractional point spacing. This is in addition to the potential for fractional point type sizes. Depending on the type of document and the questions to be addressed, the nature of line spacing may be important to address insertions or alterations to documents.

The differences in appearance for different line spacing can be seen in the examples below. The heading at the start of each paragraph is the size followed by the spacing in points. For example, 12/15 pt. means that the type is 12-point with 15-point spacing between lines, as seen in Figure 18.7. In Figure 18.8, the 12-point type has 18-point spacing between the lines. Figure 18.9 shows 12/12 pt., which may also be called *set solid*. This was as close as lines could be made when they were done with metal type. As the type size is defined by the physical size of the slug upon which the glyph was made, it could not be made less than the size of the slug.

12/15 pt.
"Lorem ipsum dolor sit amet, consectetur adipiscing elit, sed do eiusmod tempor incididunt ut labore et dolore magna aliqua. Ut enim ad minim veniam, quis nostrud exercitation ullamco laboris nisi ut aliquip ex ea commodo consequat. Duis aute irure dolor in reprehenderit in voluptate velit esse cillum dolore eu fugiat nulla pariatur. Excepteur sint occaecat cupidatat non proident, sunt in culpa qui officia deserunt mollit anim id est laborum."

Figure 18.7 12 pt. typeface with 15 pt. spacing.

12/18 pt.
"Lorem ipsum dolor sit amet, consectetur adipiscing elit, sed do eiusmod tempor incididunt ut labore et dolore magna aliqua. Ut enim ad minim veniam, quis nostrud exercitation ullamco laboris nisi ut aliquip ex ea commodo consequat. Duis aute irure dolor in reprehenderit in voluptate velit esse cillum dolore eu fugiat nulla pariatur. Excepteur sint occaecat cupidatat non proident, sunt in culpa qui officia deserunt mollit anim id est laborum."

Figure 18.8 12 pt. typeface with 18 pt. spacing.

12/12 pt. (set solid)
"Lorem ipsum dolor sit amet, consectetur adipiscing elit, sed do eiusmod tempor incididunt ut labore et dolore magna aliqua. Ut enim ad minim veniam, quis nostrud exercitation ullamco laboris nisi ut aliquip ex ea commodo consequat. Duis aute irure dolor in reprehenderit in voluptate velit esse cillum dolore eu fugiat nulla pariatur. Excepteur sint occaecat cupidatat non proident, sunt in culpa qui officia deserunt mollit anim id est laborum."

Figure 18.9 12 pt. typeface with 12 pt. spacing.

18.13 WEIGHT OF TYPEFACE

Weight of a typeface describes the boldness of the type; when bolder, there is less white space within the glyphs. Generally, the width of the glyphs becomes wider for heavier weights, and the height becomes taller.[55]

18.14 TYPOGRAPHY IN CASEWORK: AN EXAMPLE

Typography examinations arise in many questioned document problems, some allegedly produced in the distant past. For example, if the typeface on the document was not available at the purported date the document was created, this would demonstrate the document is spurious.

The case of the former Pakistan president Nawaz Sharif and the "Panama papers" garnered the attention of officials investigating corruption. The Panama papers attributed some offshore corporations controlled by the Sharif family to ownership of real estate in London. Certain documents bearing a date of February of 2006 were produced listing Maryam Sharif as a trustee of the properties. When the documents were examined, they were observed to be made with Calibri typeface, which was not commercially released until 31 January 2007. However, Calibri was available for beta testing in 2005. This is an example where the conclusions from typography examination are conditional and caution is warranted.[56,57]

18.15 SUMMARY

A variety of questions about documents may be related to typography. While this chapter does not provide all examples of where typography examinations can be conducted, it does provide insight into how this field intersects with the required knowledge of the modern FDE.

REFERENCES

1. A. S. Osborn, *Questioned Documents* (Second Edition), New York: Boyd Printing Co, 1929, pp. 573, 579.
2. D. B. Updike, *Printing Types, Their History, Forms & Use*, Boston, MA: The Merrymount Press, 1922, p. 39.
3. J. Pohlen, *Letter Fountain* (Fourth Edition), Köln: Taschen GmbH, 2015, pp. 18–25.
4. D. B. Updike, *Printing Types, Their History, Forms & Use*, Boston, MA: The Merrymount Press, 1922, pp. 38–57.
5. A. Bartram, *Typeforms a History*, New Castle, DE: Oak Knoll Press, 2007.
6. R. Dodd, *From Gutenberg to Open Type*, Vancouver, BC: Hartley & Marks Publishers, 2006.
7. Fontsmith Limited, 2019. [Online]. Available: www.fontsmith.com [Accessed October 2019].
8. S. Coles, *The Anatomy of Type*, New York, NY: Harper Design, 2012.
9. T. Seddon, *The Evolution of Type: A Graphic Guide to 100 Landmark Typefaces*, Richmond Hill, ON: Firefly Books Ltd, 2015.
10. J. Pohlen, *Letter Fountain* (Fourth Edition), Köln: Taschen GmbH, 2015.
11. "Glossary of Typographic Terms," 2019. [Online]. Available: https://www.adobe.com/ca/products/type/adobe-type-references-tips/glossary.html [Accessed 17 September 2019].
12. B. Bliven Jr, *The Wonderful Writing Machine*, New York, NY: Random House, 1954, pp. 24–57.
13. A. S. Osborn, *Questioned Documents*, Rochester, NY: The Lawyer's Co-operative Publishing Co, 1910, pp. 437–465.
14. J. V. P. Conway, *Evidential Documents*, Springfield, IL: Charles C Thomas, 1959, pp. 109–138.
15. W. R. Harrison, *Suspect Documents, Their Scientific Examination*, New York, NY: Praeger, 1958, pp. 242–287.
16. O. Hilton, *Scientific Examination of Questioned Documents* (Revised Edition), New York, NY: Elsevier, 1982, p. 47.
17. O. Hilton, *Scientific Examination of Questioned Documents* (Revised Edition), New York, NY: Elsevier, 1982, pp. 48–49.
18. J. Haas and B. Haas, *Atlas der Schreibmaschineschrift PICA*, 1972.
19. J. Haas and B. Haas, *Atlas der Schreibmaschineschrift*, 1985/86.
20. G. de la Durantaye, "A classification system for typewriting specimens," *Canadian Society of Forensic Science Journal*, vol. 1, no. 4, pp. 61–64, 1968.
21. D. A. Crown, "The differentiation of pica monotone typewriting," *Journal of Police Science and Administration*, vol. 4, no. 2, pp. 134–178, 1976.
22. P. D. Bouffard, "An Index To Typestyles in the Haas Non-Pica Atlas," in *American Society of Questioned Document Examiners (ASQDE) / Southwestern Association of Forensic Document Examiners (SWAFDE)*, Aurora, 1988.
23. P. D. Bouffard, "A PC-based memo-pad system for locating typewriter standards," *in American Society of Questioned Document Examiners (ASQDE)*, Arlington, 1989.

24. P. D. Bouffard, "A PC Based Typewriter Typestyle Classification System for Prestige Typestyle Specimens," in *American Society of Questioned Document Examiners (ASQDE)*, Ottawa, 1993.
25. P. D. Bouffard, "A PC Based Typewriter Typestyle Classification System for Elite Sans Serif Typestyle Specimens," in *American Society of Questioned Document Examiners (ASQDE)*, Long Beach, 1994.
26. P. D. Bouffard, "A PC Based Typewriter Typestyle Classification System for Pica Monotone Typestyle Specimens," in *American Academy of Forensic Sciences (AAFS)*, Nashville, 1996.
27. P. D. Bouffard, "A PC Based Typewriter Typestyle Classification System for Cubic Typestyle Specimens," in *American Society of Questioned Document Examiners (ASQDE)*, Washington, 1996.
28. P. D. Bouffard, "A PC Based Typewriter Typestyle Classification System for Script Typestyle Specimens," in *American Academy of Forensic Sciences (AAFS)*, New York, 1997.
29. P. D. Bouffard, "A PC Based Typewriter Typestyle Classification System for Courier Typestyle Specimens (updated)," in *Southwestern Association of Forensic Document Examiners (SWAFDE)*, Las Vegas, 1999.
30. K. J. Nobles, "An update of the typestyle classification program [TYPE] into Windows® based format [WinType]," *Journal of the American Society of Questioned Document Examiners*, vol. 13, no. 2, pp. 37–42, December 2010.
31. K. J. Nobles, "WinType an Update of the Typestyle Classification Program (TYPE) into a Windows® Based Format," in *American Society of Questioned Document Examiners Meeting*, Indianapolis, 2013.
32. J. Pohlen, *Letter Fountain* (Fourth Edition), Köln: Taschen GmbH, 2015, pp. 56–57.
33. G. A. Glaister, *Encyclopedia of the Book* (Second Edition), New Castle, DE: Oak Knoll Press, 2001, pp. 503–504.
34. "MyFonts by Monotype," MyFonts Inc. [Online]. Available: https://www.myfonts.com/WhatTheFont/ [Accessed 13 November 2019].
35. "Identifont," [Online]. Available: http://www.identifont.com/index.html [Accessed 13 November 2019].
36. F. Shiver, "An Evaluation of the New "WhatTheFont" Mobile App," in *American Society of Questioned Document Examiners (ASQDE)/Southwestern Association of Forensic Document Examiners (SWAFDE)*, Park City, 2018.
37. K. Welch, "A Methodology Utilzing Digital Type Fonts the Determination of the Age of a Document," in *American Society of Questioned Document Examiners Annual Meeting*, 2019.
38. F. Romano and M. Mitrano, *History of Desktop Publishing*, New Castle, DE: Oak Knoll Press, 2019.
39. A. Julien, *Digital Fonts The Complete Guide to Creating Marketing and Selling*, London: Thames & Hudson, 2012.
40. M. McGrew, *American Metal Typefaces of the Twentieth Century* (Second, Revised Edition), New Castle, DE: Oak Knoll Books, 1993.
41. F. Merriman, *A.T.A. Type Comparison Book*, New York: Advertising Typographers Association of America Inc, 1965.
42. V & M Typographical Inc, *The Type Specimen Book*, New York, NY: John Wiley & Sons Inc, 1974.
43. P. Shaw, *Revival Type Digital Typefaces Inspired by the Past*, New Haven, CT: Yale University Press, 2017.
44. T. Rosendorf, *The Typographic Desk Reference* (Second Edition), New Castle, DE: Oak Knoll Press, 2016, p. 160.
45. J. Pohlen, *Letter Fountain* (Fourth Edition), Köln: Taschen GmbH, 2015, p. 132.
46. J. Pohlen, *Letter Fountain* (Fourth Edition), Köln: Taschen GmbH, 2015, p. 52.
47. T. Rosendorf, *The Typographic Desk Reference* (Second Edition), New Castle, DE: Oak Knoll Press, 2016, p. 201.
48. G. A. Glaister, *Encyclopedia of the Book* (Second Edition), New Castle, DE: Oak Knoll Press, 2001, p. 386.
49. J. Pohlen, *Letter Fountain* (Fourth Edition), Köln: Taschen GmbH, 2015, pp. 54–55.
50. J. Pohlen, *Letter Fountain* (Fourth Edition), Köln: Taschen GmbH, 2015, p. 630.
51. K. Cheng, *Designing Type*, New Haven, CT: Yale University Press, 2005, p. 11.
52. J. Pohlen, *Letter Fountain* (Fourth Edition), Köln: Taschen GmbH, 2015, p. 594.
53. W. J. Flynn, Typography. *Scientific Examination of Questioned Documents*, J. S. Kelly and B. S. Lindblom, Eds., Boca Raton, FL: Taylor & Francis Group, 2006, pp. 166–168.

54. G. A. Glaister, *Encyclopedia of the Book* (Second Edition), New Castle, DE: Oak Knoll Press, 2001, p. 276.
55. E. Spiekermann and E. M. Ginger, *Stop Stealing Sheep & Find Out How Type Works* (Second Edition), Berkeley, CA: Adobe Press, 2003, pp. 111, 113.
56. "GAN Business Anti-Corruption Portal," [Online]. Available: https://www.ganintegrity.com/portal/news/font-could-be-the-key-to-corruption-probe-of-pakistans-prime-minister/ [Accessed 31 October 2019].
57. R. Radley, "The Availability of the Calibri Type Font Prior to Its Commerical Release," in *American Society of Questioned Document Examiners (ASQDE)/Southwestern Association of Forensic Document Examiners (SWAFDE)*, Park City, 2018.

Chapter 19

Computer Generated Documents

Timothy A. Campbell

CONTENTS

It should be stressed here first that this is not an in-depth study of computer files at a forensic level, but an overview to the degree with which a forensic document examiner (FDE) should be familiar. A proper forensic examination of digital files should be conducted by a properly trained Digital Forensic Investigator, and the FDE should contact such an analyst when it is required.

However, due to the increasing crossover of physical and digital domains when regarding documents, it does the FDE well to understand the complex machinery that produces a modern document, much like the typewriters and Gutenberg press of yesteryear.

19.1 COMPUTER FILES

A computer file is a collection of information organized into a particularly logical format, such that a computer can make use of it in a meaningful way. All computer files are, at their most essential, collections of binary digits 1 and 0, meaning *on* and *off*. They are digital switches, which when concatenated, give an instruction to the computer. At a higher level, those 1s and 0s are combined in groups of 8 bits, called a byte. The basic byte is what is being described when the file size is described in kilobytes or megabytes, or a storage disk is quantified in gigabytes or terabytes.

Before the computer can read the data in a computer file, it needs to know something about what the data in that file looks like so that it can be interpreted correctly. Data that describes more data is called metadata and is stored at the beginning of the file called the header. This allows the computer to distinguish an image file from an audio file, for instance. It also allows variants of image files to be distinguished by their color depth, data arrangement, compression, etc. A Photoshop PSD file contains different and more complex data than a simple JPG image file. The actual image data will follow the header data within the file and be stored as a list of values.

The simplest file format is the text file, often seen with the file extension.txt following the filename, but may also have different extensions like .bat, .html, or.docx. Text files make sense to the computer but are also readable by a human using a simple text editor.

When a file has been deleted, the data will physically remain on the storage medium, but the record of it will have been removed, allowing that data to be overwritten. If, however, it is not overwritten, that information can often be recovered using forensic software tools. A Digital Forensic Investigator should be consulted for such analysis as it is out of the scope of forensic document examination.

Files that might concern an FDE can be roughly split into two groups, control files and data files. Control files are those that are required to complete an operation, such as run the computer, operate a software application, or print a document. Data files are those that are the actual content that the user wishes to interact with, be it editing, viewing, or printing, such as digital photographs of evidence or the written case report.

19.1.1 Software and Printer Drivers

A *printer driver* allows a software program to print without requiring the computer's operating system to know the technical detail of a particular printer. Instead, the driver translates a file to be printed from the computer into the printer's language. There may be more than one driver for a high-end printer.

Advanced drivers are specific to the printer model and will have additional features such as faux watermarking or secure PIN printing capabilities. At the other end, a *universal printer driver* is often available for an entire line of printers from a single manufacturer and includes basic printing capabilities that are more compatible with a broad range of devices.

Multifunction printers (MFPs) can have both a printer and a fax driver, allowing them to be controlled across a network, but a scanner driver is present less frequently since a scanner requires physical user interaction, and that function occurs within the machine. An MFP can act in isolation by way of accessing a memory card, or it can scan and print a copy without the need for any computer connection.

A *Raster Image Processor (RIP)* takes the image pixel data and processes it into information on how ink should specifically be deposited onto the substrate by first converting the source file to a bitmap (raster image) that is then printed. Modern printers have a built-in RIP, but professional users tend to use a third-party RIP to bypass the built-in version. Such a third-party RIP may be hardware-based, like the OS-independent EFI™ Fiery® printer server, or software-based to be installed separately on a computer. This gives full control to the user, including spooling, formatting, fonts, and color management, functions beyond which a printer driver may be capable. Given that a third-party RIP intentionally bypasses the built-in RIP of a printer, it is possible that a Counterfeit Protection System (CPS) code would not be printed when it would otherwise be expected.

19.1.2 Computer Font Files

The font used for a given piece of text was historically determined by the printer itself. A dot matrix printer could be directed to print in normal or italics at the push of a button. Early laser printers such as the HP LaserJet III (introduced in 1990) had fonts installed in their onboard memory. They could be selected by the user through the computer software and were upgradable. Eventually, the general trend was, and is, to store the fonts on the computer system, and the printer merely outputs what is directed by the software, though the printer may retain other operational controls. This evolution coincided with the rise of WYSIWYG (what you see is what you get) word processing programs that displayed fonts on-screen instead of unformatted text encased in control codes.

PostScript Fonts, also known as *Type 1* fonts, are stored in the Adobe PostScript file format and were introduced in 1984. When it was released in 1985, the Apple LaserWriter became the first PostScript capable printer. The initial PS fonts were outline/vector-based and resided only in the printer itself, while the coordinated bitmap/raster font of lower resolution was used for screen display.

TrueType is an outline/vector font type that was released in 1991 by Apple and licensed to Microsoft. Being vector-based, such fonts are mathematical lines and curves and therefore infinitely scalable, allowing for pixel-level control over the appearance for each point size. Previously, all computer fonts available were bitmaps, which did not scale well and produced an aliased image. *OpenType* is an extension of TrueType released by Microsoft in 1996 with support from Adobe.[1]

19.1.3 Image Files

It is important for the 21st century FDE to understand how digital image files work because so much casework involves the use of a scanner or digital camera to acquire an image during the examination and to process it for use and display. Notably, digital imaging is an even more important consideration in the production of a document that becomes an examined casework item because of the myriad ways that a document may be digitally manipulated prior to output.

Digital images can be thought of as spreadsheets that record 1 of 256 values for each of red, green, and blue per pixel, depending on the intensity of each color contacting a pixel on the sensor.[2] The 256 possible values are based on an 8-digit binary number ($2^8 = 256$). In this way, an RGB image is called 24-bit (3 channels × 8 bits/channel = 24 bits or 16.7 million colors). Each group of 3 channels is combined into a single pixel, and it is this combination that provides the color that we can see for that pixel. By combining the pixels *en masse*, a full image can be constructed. Since a computer starts counting at 0, not 1, the actual range is 0 to 255 states. If a pixel has the values of 255 for red, 255 for blue, and 255 for green, then it has the full intensity for each color, and since they are additive colors, they combine to give the final color white for that pixel.[3]

A grayscale image has only one channel (8 bits) with no color information, so it has 256 shades of gray.

19.1.4 Compression

The size of most files can be reduced by way of compression, whereby data that is not necessary to store the file can be removed and restored when the file is accessed again. If a file is uncompressed for storage, it is at its maximum size; every bit of information is retained. When a file is compressed, space savings can be small or great, depending on the file type and compression algorithm used. There are two main types of compression: *Lossless*, in which no information is lost upon restoration and *lossy*, in which there may be some slight degradation due to the loss of some information.

19.1.4.1 Uncompressed Image Files

BMP (Bitmap) was created by Microsoft and supports from two to millions of colors, transparency and can be compressed by Run Length Encoding (RLE) compression.

RAW is a classification of files rather than a particular file format. As such, it is also called a digital negative since it is a direct record of the values of incident light on the sensor pixels rather than an interpretation. A RAW file is not an image itself but contains the information to create one.[4] A special decoder is required in the computer editor to read a RAW file, but a high-end program like Adobe Photoshop is generally able to read most formats. It affords the photographer the ability to use many more editing options afterward, including brightness, color, white balance, and overexposure correction. It frequently allows 12- or 14-bit files. The result can then be saved in the "digital positive" format the user prefers. Examples of RAW formats are Nikon (NEF, NRW), Canon (CRW, CR2, CR3), and Adobe (DNG), among many others. A RAW file can be uncompressed or use lossless or lossy compression.

19.1.4.2 Lossless Compressed Image Files

GIF (Graphics Interchange Format from CompuServe) is a raster image file format limited to 256 colors and appears grainy when used for complex images but may display multiple images in rapid succession as a short clip. It is suitable for straight-edged graphics, vacant of artifacts. It uses LZW compression.

PNG (Portable Network Graphics) arose after GIFs and produces reduced file sizes but is larger than JPG. PNG is good for graphics-heavy images with compression artifacts, and it supports transparency.

TIFF or *TIF* (Tagged Image File Format) is a container file format popular among photographers. It can use compression, including LZW, but can also be uncompressed. The maximum file size of a TIFF is 4 GB, and it supports a bit depth of 8, 16, and 32 bits per channel in many different color spaces.

19.1.4.3 Lossy Compressed Image Files

JPEG or *JPG* (Joint Picture Experts Group) reduces image size by about ten-fold compared to the same image saved as a GIF, but it introduces compression artifacts, especially around edges found in nonphotographic images. It is best suited to a general photo, whereas a GIF is better for graphical use. The amount of compression can be selected.

SVG (Scalable Vector Graphics) is not a raster image format but is vector-based, meaning that instead of individual pixels having color values, an image is drawn by mathematical formulae and thus can be infinitely scaled with no loss in image quality. The file size is therefore quite small since independent pixel values are not stored but calculated each time the image is displayed.

Adobe Photoshop's native file format is the *PSD* file (for Photoshop Document) and supports a maximum image size of 30,000 pixels square, or about 2 GB. It is a container format and includes layer information for text, masks, transparency, channels, etc. If a larger size is required, the *PSB* (Photoshop Big) format is needed since it supports 300,000 pixels square, or about 4 exabytes. The ability to save a PSB file must be enabled in Photoshop Preferences.

Adobe Acrobat's native file format is the *PDF* (for Portable Document File) and has become a standard, OS-independent file for viewing documentation.[5] A font can be embedded, either fully or partially, within a PDF file if the font manufacturer allows for it in the font's settings. Partial embedding includes only the character set used in the PDF at creation and is named uniquely within to ensure that the application renders the desired font and not another. It is possible that a font may be substituted in a PDF when the file is viewed on a different computer from the one it was created on. This happens when a font is used on the source computer but does not exist on the end computer. If there is a font close enough in appearance to the original, it may be used instead. If no such font exists, the PDF will create 1 of 2 fonts on-the-fly, one serif and one sans serif. These fonts are named AdobeSerifMM (for Multiple Master) and AdobeSansMM, and they are based on Minion Pro and Myriad Pro respectively. Moreover, these are ephemeral fonts, so it's not possible for the user to edit them.[6]

19.2 COLOR MODELS, SPACES, AND DEPTH

The FDE interacts with color on a regular basis. Indeed, fine discrimination of color is tested for, prior to acceptance as a trainee. A basic understanding of color, as humans perceive it, is beneficial here because it not only concerns physical documents but also their digital progenitors. There are key differences in the ways we view those colors.

19.2.1 Color Model

A color model is a way to abstractly describe colors by way of sets of numbers. The main color models that are applicable to document examination are grayscale with two values, RGB with three, and CMYK with four.

The *RGB model* uses the *additive* primary colors of red, green, and blue, and these are the colors that make up the light-emitting picture elements (pixels) on a modern computer monitor or television. The *CMYK model* uses the *subtractive* colors cyan, yellow, and magenta for the dyes and pigments of inks, with black (K) added to improve darker tones and solitary use. The letter K is used because it represents the Key channel and is used for printing registration marks. Inks absorb certain wavelengths such that the remaining wavelengths are transmitted to the substrate, usually white itself, which reflects them back to the viewer. Cyan absorbs red light, transmitting green and blue; magenta absorbs green light, transmitting red and blue; and yellow absorbs blue light, transmitting red and green (see Figure 19.1).

Grayscale is not a color model, but since it is situated alongside RGB and CMYK in Adobe Photoshop, it is suitably discussed here. Grayscale is a gradient describing the intensity of light, from black at the darkest to white at the brightest. There is no color information beyond that. This is the basis for digital imaging sensors in digital cameras since a bare sensor only captures grayscale information. With a special Bayer filter in place over the sensor, RGB colors are filtered to each sensor pixel to create the captured color image we see.

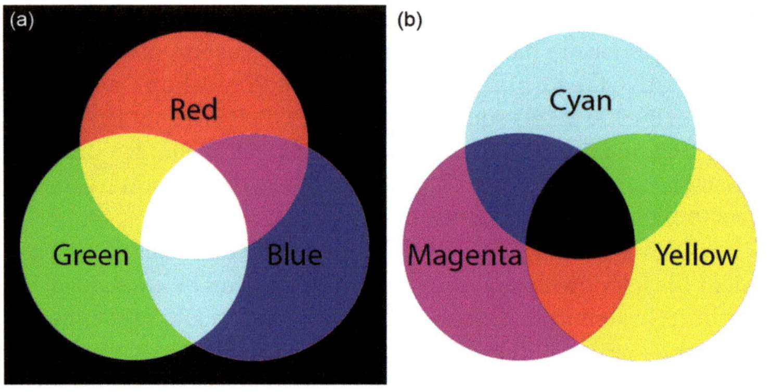

Figure 19.1 The additive RGB color model (a) used in light emission and subtractive CMY color model (b) used in dye and pigment absorption of light.

19.2.2 Color Space

A color space objectively maps a range of colors from light, pigments, or dyes as they are registered by the human eye in the visible part of the electromagnetic spectrum. Understanding color spaces is beneficial when comparing colored inks and their digital representations on a computer monitor.

A color space is a standard that defines a specific set of colors. The *CIE 1931 RGB* standard was developed in 1931 by the International Commission on Illumination (CIE) to describe the sensitivity of human eye cone cells to the three primary colors (RGB). Wavelengths marked around the curved boundary are in nanometers, and color appearance is dependent on the viewing medium[7] (see Figure 19.2).

The *CIELAB* or *CIEL*a*b* color space* was developed in 1976 to be device-independent for the hardcopy printing of computer graphics as it includes both the RGB and CMYK color models. The three channels are L* (lightness, from darkest black to brightest white) and color channels a* (from green to red) and b* (blue to yellow). These channels can be viewed in Adobe Photoshop's LAB Mode.

In 1993, the International Color Consortium (ICC) began to arrange a color management system that was not dependent on any one manufacturer. The ICC specification v4.3.0 (ICC.1:2010-12, also technically identical to ISO 15076-1:2010) allows for mapping color between disparate hardware and software. The *sRGB* (IEC61966-2.1) color space was defined by Microsoft and HP in 1996, and most computer monitors are capable of displaying these colors. The *Adobe RGB* 1998 color space encompasses the sRGB color space with the addition of more colors, and the *Pro Photo RGB* color space is larger yet.

19.2.3 Color Gamut

Gamut is the range of colors that a particular technology can produce. The gamut of a camera's sensor is different from the gamut a screen can display, which is different again from the gamut that a printer can print. Even paper and the eye have their own gamut.

When working with an image capture and output system (usually a camera-computer-printer combination), it is often desirable to ensure that the output accurately resembles the color and tone of the input through a calibration process. Because each component has its own gamut, it

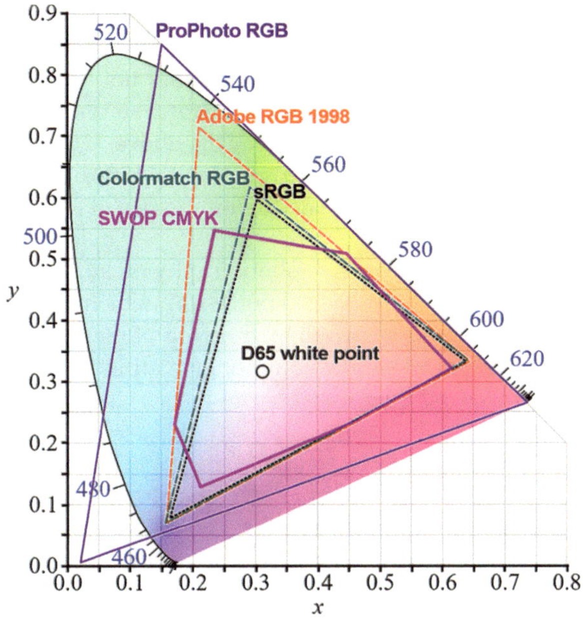

Figure 19.2 Various color spaces mapped onto the *CIE 1931 RGB* chromaticity diagram. (Retrieved from Wikipedia. Used per Creative Commons 3.0, posted by Authors *BenRG* and *Cmglee*. Image has not been modified.)

is unwise to rely on the factory settings and hope they are accurate. Instead, an external device with a close-contact camera can measure the brightness and hue of a color, compare it to a standard target, and direct the person to adjust the device's settings to render the proper display. This is done for the computer monitor and the printer. When the printer is calibrated, it must take into account the paper medium used to print upon, and thus a custom profile can be generated for each paper type that the operator expects to use. The gamut of a glossy photo paper can vary greatly from that of a standard office paper. By using a custom profile, the most accurate image can be printed on each. Many printers have an embedded color profile that needs to be disabled before using a custom or external color profile.

19.2.4 Digital Imaging in FDE: Cameras

The resolution for a digital camera is generally described as the total count of pixels on a sensor and is given in megapixels (MP). This is entirely dependent on not just the sensor size (APS-C vs full-frame) but also the size of the individual pixel. So, two cameras, a Nikon D7200 (APS-C) and a Nikon D780 (full-frame) can both have the same number of total pixels at 24 MP, but the pixel size must differ between the sensors. The latter sensor has larger pixels, allowing each to capture more light than the former, which boosts its sensitivity (ISO).

When a digital image is captured, it has a set number of pixels that must be displayed on a screen, and the resolution is described in pixels per inch (ppi). This is different than the printer resolution of an output image, which is described in dots per inch (dpi), though they are often used interchangeably.

A digital imaging sensor, however, is sensitive to all wavelengths of visible light and also IR light. Since camera manufacturers design products for the nontechnical photographer, consumer digital cameras are sold with an IR-blocking filter (IR-cut or hot mirror filter). Installed in front of a sensor to remove the IR wavelengths, it renders a captured image similar to that detectable to the human eye. Such a filter blocks out wavelengths above 720 nm. By removing this filter, a camera sensor can be made to detect wavelengths up to 1200 nm. The Bayer mosaic filter is required by the sensor to accurately determine the intensities of each channel of red, green, or blue to fall on a sensor pixel cavity.

Specialty DSLRs that allow for IR-sensitive photography include the FujiFilm X-T1 IR, which is available to law enforcement only, and the Nikon D810A, which caters to astrophotographers and thus is sensitive above 656 nm for stellar hydrogen alpha emission. The LifePixel website has a section devoted to DIY modification of common consumer digital cameras to allow for IR photography, in addition to offering their own conversion services.[8]

19.2.5 Digital Imaging in FDE: Scanners

A desktop scanner can be a very useful tool to the FDE during an examination. Due to fixed hardware parameters (lighting, focal distance, etc.), scanning can be more consistent between items than can be accomplished with camera-based photography. A flatbed scanner can be used to image a document submitted as a case item at a low or very high resolution. Because the scanner head travels across the flattened document, all portions of the page are in focus, and thus there should be little to no geometric distortion. The saved image can then be immediately imported into software for processing (such as Adobe® Photoshop®) or comparison (such as Pikaso's Write-On). It should be noted that even with the high resolution obtained by scanning, original documents should be optically examined when they are available.

The resolution of a scanned image, like a camera-obtained image, is described in pixels per inch, but the term megapixels is not used when discussing scanners. A simple record image for a case can be acquired at 300 ppi, while the closeup of a signature can be done at 600 or 1200 ppi. Such resolution is sufficient for observing ink effects and line intersections, but if additional magnification is required, a microscope is the better option. Scanner lighting is quite uniform, which is good for a record image. If other variants of lighting like oblique or coaxial are needed, a camera is more suitable, with or without microscopic magnification.

There are two main variants of flatbed scanners available, a contact image scanner (CIS) and a charge coupled device (CCD) scanner. A CIS scanner has a less expensive but platen-wide CMOS sensor, illuminated by LEDs and positioned directly beneath the glass platen, allowing for a thin case and low power consumption.[9] A CCD sensor is found in larger, more expensive flatbed scanners and uses mirrors to reflect the image of the document into the sensor array through a folded light path. A high-quality scanner like the Epson V850 Pro has a maximum optical resolution of 6400 ppi meant for scanning film negatives and slides. Even its lower-end sibling, the Epson V550, can obtain the same optical resolution, which far-surpasses what an FDE may require to obtain a decent scanned image of a document. In addition, the V850 has a dual lens system, one for each of 4800 and 6400 ppi maximum resolutions, and frames to hold negatives.

The geometric distortion of a scanner can be tested by scanning the document in the traditional way, then rotating the document through 90° and scanning it a second time. Then, in Photoshop, the second image is de-rotated (as a layer) back to the original orientation and overlaid with the first image. Reducing the transparency of the upper layer allows for comparison of the geometric superimposition of the two images. The horizontal pixel dimension is determined by the density of sensor elements, and the vertical pixel dimension is determined by the carriage transport stepper motor.[10]

19.3 HARDCOPY PRINTING DEVICES

Despite the threat of the paperless society over the past two decades, printers for producing hardcopy information remain abundant. Beyond the desktop printer, receipt printers and label makers share similar technologies. New products flaunted at trade shows such as Drupa in Dusseldorf, Germany, have shown that inkjet technology is a major focus for development in the industrial sector. eBook sales peaked and have dropped in recent years as readers return to printed text, which can now be ordered and printed-on-demand using electrophotography. Herein are some of the digital factors that affect how a page is printed from a computer to a physical medium.

A *Page Description Language (PDL)* is a programming language in human-readable text that describes the printed appearance of a page rather than a simple raster image. Full-page bitmap "images" are produced when a page is sent from the computer to the printer's print controller chip, which can then determine how the print mechanism is controlled.

The concept of *PostScript (PS)* as a PDL was first introduced by Adobe in 1982. It was a method of printing graphics whereby text and illustrations were handled separately, as opposed to the output of a single bitmap image of all components. Apple made PostScript a production reality in 1985 as an accurate standard for creating a high-quality print. It is so complex that it can be considered its own programming language, being capable of outputting to not just a printer, but any device, like a monitor.

There are three levels of PostScript:

Level 1. Released in 1985, this was the first version on the market.
Level 2. Released in 1991, it was faster, more reliable, and supported image compression and multiple fonts
Level 3. Released in 1997, it had better color handling

Since Adobe designed both PostScript and the PDF format, conversion between the two is relatively simple. Photoshop, Illustrator, and Acrobat are optimized for PostScript. Given the close relationship between Apple and Adobe, PostScript is native to the MacIntosh but also compatible with Windows.

Printer Command Language (PCL) was developed in 1984 by HP specifically for dot matrix and inkjet printers. PCL is a PDL that creates commands (escape codes) that are added to the print job on its way from the computer to the printer. *Epson Standard Code for Printers (ESC/P or Escape/P)* is a PDL developed by Epson for dot matrix printers, but later variants also found use in inkjet and thermal receipt printers. Although it saw widespread use while dot matrix printers were more prolific, it is not as common in units manufactured today as are PS and PCL. For pen plotters, *Hewlett-Packard Graphics Language (HP-GL)* has become a standard since its introduction in 1977.

19.3.1 Impact Printers

A *Pen Plotter* is a device that operates an inked pen stylus, drawing a vector graphics file from a computer aided design (CAD) program to a substrate by assembling pen lines into a diagram. Once used extensively in architectural and engineering design work, pen plotters came in multiple designs, including a stationary substrate bed with an XY armature for the stylus, or a mobile substrate that moved in one axis while the stylus moved in the perpendicular axis, much like a desktop inkjet printer. In the latter design, however, the substrate could move in a bidirectional manner, being fed forward and backward, so that a line could be drawn quickly and parallel to the feed direction by a temporarily stationary stylus before being relocated to draw another portion of the file. Because of the limitation to line drawing, cross hatching fills were more practical than a solid color fill for a larger area. Although modern wide-format inkjet plotters bear the plotter moniker, they use a fundamentally different technology, usually inkjet.

A *Single Element* type printer contains all printable typefaces on a single ball, cylinder, cone, basket, or disc/wheel, which is rotated to present the desired character to the substrate. This is accomplished by either striking the whole element against the page (as with the typeball) or by actuating a stationary hammer and forcing the individual character element against the substrate (as with the typewheel). In all cases, the replacement of the elements means the replacement of the entire character set because they are all bound to a common carrier. This is quite unlike a repair to a typebar typewriter in which a single character could be replaced. This also means that a single element typewriter or printer could allow for the rapid replacement of an entire typeface with a different one. Impact printing is a candidate for advanced analysis using 3D mapping via interferometry or confocal laser scanning microscopy (CLSM) to compare subtle typeface defects with topographical printing characteristics (see Figure 19.3 for an example).

The linear *Dot Matrix* printer was a mainstay of 1980s and 1990s computers at home and in business after the introduction of the IBM 2213 and the Centronics 101, both in 1970. Printing is accomplished by way of a vertical row of pins, each actuated separately and combined to produce

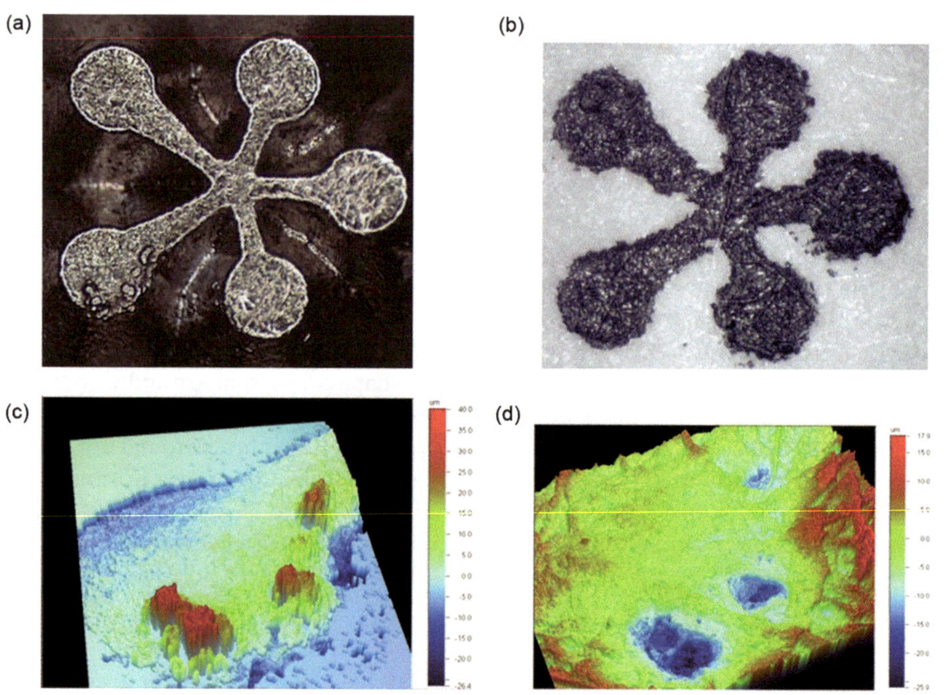

Figure 19.3 A 3D comparison of impact printing features. (a) Asterisk typeface on Selectric typeball, (b) typed character in mirror image (oriented to align), (c) height profile of defect on typeface, and (d) depth profile of impression in paper (oriented to align). (Images courtesy Andrew Barton.)

the portions of a single vertical line.[11] The printhead is moved horizontally across the page, with the necessary pins actuated at each vertical line-width. Paper was generally tractor-fed, perforated, continuous form paper.

The common 9-pin printer used the top two pins for lowercase letter ascenders, the bottom two pins for the descenders, and the remaining five pins for the body of the character. A 7-pin printer such as the Commodore MPS-801 might be able to print the core and ascenders of a character but not the descenders, so the lowercase characters were raised higher than the baseline. Otherwise, the descenders would be absent in the output. An 18-pin printer had two parallel banks of 9 pins that allowed for higher density dot formation and, therefore, a higher quality. A 24-pin printer also had two parallel banks, but they each contained 12 pins for taller characters. The second bank of pins was aligned to the gaps in the first bank, so a higher print resolution was attained. Larger graphics could be printed using multiple passes (see Figure 19.4). Color could be printed using a 4-color ribbon in some models, although it might be RGBK instead of CMYK.[12]

Early and low-end models printed in one direction, left to right, but others made use of bidirectional printing, increasing the output speed. Of the various modes of operation, Draft Mode is the fastest, printing a minimum of information with no concern for quality. Some models allowed the user to select the font style with a front panel control button for normal or italics. Near Letter Quality (NLQ) increased the quality of screen-displayed fonts at the expense of speed by printing dots on a second pass in the gaps between the dots of the first pass. The increase in quality was especially evident for 9-pin printers. Line feed offered the ability to advance the page one line at a time and form feed, one page at a time.

Impact printers are still in use today, well into the 21st century, to print multipart forms and shipping labels because their impact force can print through multiple layers of NCR or carbon paper.

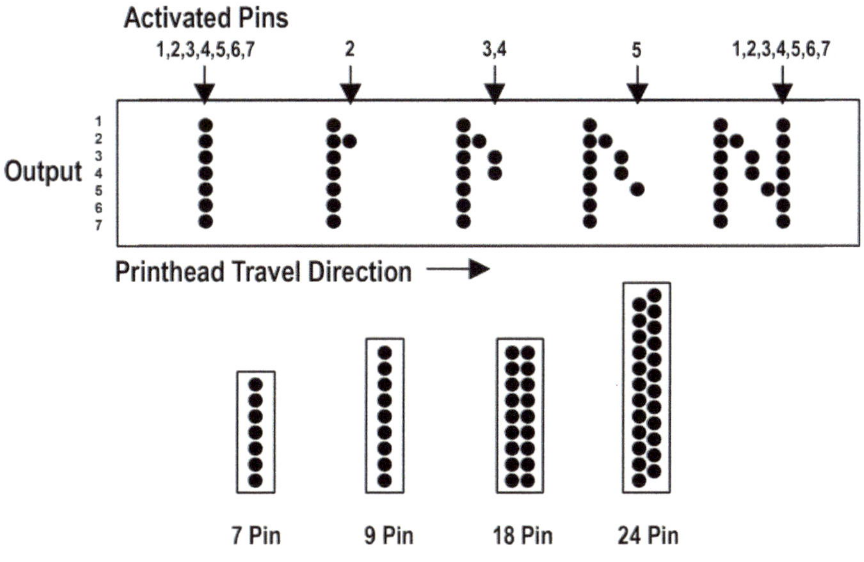

Figure 19.4 Wire dot matrix printing process and various printhead arrangements. (Upper portion of the image adapted from Wikipedia image uploaded by user *Pluke*; released to public domain. Lower portion of image adapted from an image in the Computer Desktop Encyclopedia, © 1998 The Computer Language Co., Inc.)

19.3.2 Nonimpact Printers

Inkjet printing gained mass market appeal in the late 1980s and 1990s as an economical alternative to laser printing (electrophotography). It produces a higher quality output on plain paper than its predecessor dot matrix, which was saddled with tractor feed paper, lower quality, and noise.

The HP Thinkjet was the first commercial inkjet printer, debuting in 1984. It was only capable of printing in black ink at 192 × 96 dpi. The first HP color printer was introduced in 1987 as the HP PaintJet, an inkjet device that produced a 180 × 180 dpi output on proprietary paper, though fanfold paper was acceptable as well.

There are two primary types of desktop inkjet printer technology, thermal and piezoelectric. Both are considered drop-on-demand, as ink is only ejected when called for. Thermal printheads heat the ink until a bubble forms, which ejects a droplet from the nozzle. The piezoelectric printhead vibrates the wall of the ink reservoir to eject the droplet.

As the printhead moves across the width of the page, ink is deposited in a banded fashion such that one band may be printed in part during one pass, with the rest of the band printed on a second pass. In some cases, the alignment of the two passes might not be perfect, resulting in a stitching effect where the separation of passes can be seen. Satellite droplets are a characteristic of inkjet printing and occur when an ejected drop breaks into two or more smaller droplets. The last droplet to reach the substrate lands in the direction of printhead travel. As such, the direction of printing can be determined. This is especially apparent when a line exhibits stitching from bidirectional printing, where the satellite droplets are pointed in opposite directions between the top and bottom of the character.

The standard desktop inkjet printer has a CMYK color space, but increasingly, printers with additional colors are appearing that increase the color gamut. Additional colors might be pastels in one model, fluorescents in another, or various intensities of gray in yet another.

Liquid inkjet inks may be dye-based or pigment-based. Dye-based inks have very small (~2 nm) molecules that are water-soluble. Pigment-based inks have larger particles (10–100 nm) that are not water soluble and can sediment out in solution. Low magnification of printed ink will probably not be sufficient to discern between dye- and pigment-based inks. Only at 200× or higher magnification will differentiation become possible, as the higher density of a pigment-based ink obscures the paper fibers below without mixing of the colors. Dye-based ink is absorbed, with its colors blending and leaving the fibers much more visible. When printed onto coated photo paper, pigments appear granular within the ink drop, which has a noticeable edge. In contrast, dye ink is diffuse.[13]

Liquid ink cartridges have a poor reputation for quickly depleting due to the repetitive printhead cleaning cycles that are required. If a printer sits unused for a period of time, the nozzles have a tendency to clog, requiring a large quantity of ink to be run through them to clear the blockage. Third party cartridge refilling is available for people who continue to use cartridges but wish to refill them with ink. This typically involves injecting fresh ink into the cartridge with a syringe, much to the chagrin of manufacturers who install memory chips onto individual cartridges to deter the practice through ink level monitoring. The most recent models of printers have ink tanks instead of replaceable cartridges that allow for easy and economical tank refilling. Examples are the Canon MegaTank and Epson EcoTank systems.

Solid inkjet printers were introduced with the Dataproducts SI-480 monochrome printer in 1986 but didn't gain widespread acceptance until the Textronix PhaserJet PXi color printer in 1991. Textronix was later purchased in 2000 by Xerox. Solid ink printers use ink that is a waxy pellet or block at ambient room temperature. The blocks of a Xerox ColorQube are roughly 1 inch^3 in size and are loaded as a stack into a hopper for dispensing. The blocks may have differing shapes between colors that prevents loading ink into the wrong hopper. The ink is heated into a liquid state and ejected as droplets via a piezoelectric printhead. It is not placed directly onto the substrate but onto a rotating intermediate transfer drum in a spiral fashion (unlike the linear electrophotographic method described below) until the full image is developed. The drum rotates against the substrate much like an offset press. The ink then instantly solidifies on the substrate.

Continuous inkjet (CIJ) printing is used in industrial applications to apply batch numbers, serial numbers, or best before dates to products moving rapidly past a stationary inkjet head. The stream of ink drops is deflected rapidly between the substrate and a waste receptacle for reuse of ink. CIJ is generally monotone and exhibits a noticeable dot matrix-like appearance. The technology is particularly suited to printing on nonplanar surfaces, like the curved neck of a plastic bottle. An example is seen in Figure 19.5.

As consumers realized that physical printouts of their personal digital photographs were still preferable to viewing on a monitor, photo printing on desktop inkjet printers at home using coated paper became common. But issues with the high price of ink cartridges and the propensity for clogged nozzles on inkjet printheads gave rise to disillusionment. There has since been a resurgence of the commercial photo labs in drugstores and department stores that print digital images onto high quality continuous-tone photographic paper, providing a quality that inkjet cannot replicate. Paper bearing silver halide or silver gelatin emulsion is exposed to the digital image by a laser or LED light source and developed through a chemical process like a traditional film print. Examples are the Durst Lambda, Océ LightJet, and the ZBF Chromira.

Thermal Wax Transfer printing involves a polymer ribbon with a wax coating that spans the width of the substrate and is heated by a stationary printhead. The ribbon is advanced in lockstep with the substrate, be it paper or plastic card. Individual printhead elements are rapidly turned on and off, producing heat when on and melting the wax such that it migrates to the substrate. The spent ribbon has an appearance much like a typewriter ribbon, whereby the printed information is left behind as a negative image and can be recovered through photographic means. Thermal wax transfer printing has been used extensively in facsimile machines and label makers.

Thermal Paper is similar in concept to thermal wax transfer in that a stationary printhead with heating elements is used, but in this case, the paper itself is thermally responsive. There is no ribbon. Thermal paper is used extensively in point-of-sale (POS) receipt printers and is subject to post-output thermal darkening, such as when placed into a bag with hot food. The infamous chemical component Bisphenol-A is present in thermal paper and has received public attention for its health implications.

Dye Sublimation, also called *Dye Diffusion Thermal Transfer (D2T2)*, makes use of the same printhead technology as thermal wax transfer. The ribbon is composed of distinct panels, one for each of the CMY colors and a black wax panel. Especially suited to the personalization of plastic identification cards, dye sublimation did not gain a strong foothold for letter-sized documents. The panels are generally arranged on the ribbon so that the yellow panel is printed first, then magenta, cyan, and finally black. It is labeled as YMCK. The three colors are used to print

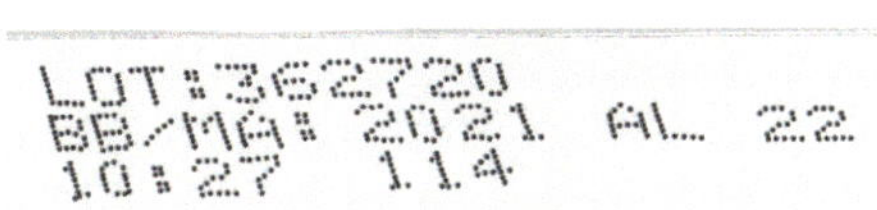

Figure 19.5 Continuous inkjet printing on a food package. The wavy appearance is due to a non-flat substrate at time of printing.

graphics and photographs. The benefit to black being printed last is that, due to its opacity, text can be printed over colors and be legible, which is especially important when barcodes are printed. Beyond the YMCK panels of the ribbon, a thin clear topcoat panel may be added for UV protection, as well as a thicker clear overlay that may contain a security hologram.

As in thermal transfer, a negative image of the printed areas remains on the ribbon. The black printed text can be recovered in the same way as a thermal ribbon, but the printed color panels may need to undergo additional processing via scanning and importing into Adobe Photoshop (or similar program), then recombining through layering the negative images, thus achieving a composite. The United States Secret Service developed an instrument for this purpose called the Thermal Ribbon Analysis System (TRAP) that operates similarly to the Ribbon Analysis Workstation (RAW) designed for typewriter ribbons.[14,15]

Electrophotographic printing applies dry toner "ink" (liquid toner is less commonly used) and fuses it to the substrate through heat and/or pressure. The printed image is drawn onto a photoconductor drum or belt by a laser that scans the length of the drum. As the drum rotates, a new line is scanned, sensitizing the image areas by altering the electrical charge to that opposite the charge of the toner. Some printers do not use a laser as the excitation source but instead employ an LED array across the width of the photoconductor, reducing the number of mechanical components. In this way, the LED printer is very much like the page-wide inkjet printer in that the printhead is stationary, and any defects will be replicated in a linear fashion down the travel path of the page. The detailed mechanism of electrophotographic printing is discussed elsewhere in this book.

HP Indigo is a modern liquid electrophotographic (LEP) system that uses encapsulated pigment particles approximately 1 μm in size. The encapsulation removes barriers of ink specificity to the common liquid carrier due to individual chemical composition. The ink is deposited onto a laser-charged photoconducting drum, as in traditional electrophotography, but transferred to a heated blanket roller where the ink is melted into a single sheet before application to a substrate of any type.

Indigo allows for a vast array of ink types and colors and has since spurred the CMYK+ printing market which expands beyond the standard 4-color printing methods, including dry toner EP. Specialty inks include metallic colors, white for highlights and colored substrates, clear inks to add dimension and texture, and invisible inks that allow covert security printing visible only under UV lighting. Xerox offers the printing of gold and silver metallic dry toner with a quick swap 4-specialty color Vivid kit, allowing for a total of eight different toners to be printed on a single document.

19.4 DATA ENCODING OF PHYSICAL MEDIA

There has been a plethora of schemes, both overt and covert, used to record information on a physical document, but only some of the more commonly encountered methods are discussed here.

19.4.1 OCR-A and -B

Two monospaced alphanumeric fonts were designed in 1968 to be computer readable with minimal incorrect character identifications, such as B for a 3, I for a 1 or l, or 0 for O. OCR-A, by American Type Founders, has a strange, angular appearance and is common in North America, where it can be found on financial institution documents such as checks. OCR-B was developed in Europe by Adrian Frutiger for Monotype and is easier for human readability, resembling less

TABLE 19.1 MAGNETIC STRIPES (ENCODING HAS DATA "..." SEPARATED BY CONTROL CHARACTERS)

Track	Standard Developer	Capacity	Encoding
1	International Air Transport Association (IATA)	76 alphanumeric	% ...^...?
2	American Bankers Association (ABA)	37 numeric	;...=...?
3	THRIFT Savings Industry	104 numeric	;...=... =...?

the harsh appearance of OCR-A and more a traditional typographic appearance. Indeed, OCR-B is the standard font directed by the International Civil Aviation Organization (ICAO) for use on the Machine-Readable Zone (MRZ) of travel documents.[16]

19.4.2 Magnetic Stripe

The magnetic stripe is the ubiquitous dark horizontal line seen on the back of plastic cards worldwide. It carries information that may or may not appear in readable text on the card face itself, and it is used to interact with a computer, often a point-of-sale (POS) terminal. The ISO/IEC 7811 and 4909 standards lay out the specifications for using magnetic stripes on a plastic card. As shown in Table 19.1, there are three types of stripes, called Track 1, Track 2, and Track 3, in various strength of magnetism (coercivity).

The base material is a magnetic tape, not unlike that from a reel-to-reel music cassette, and it can be applied to the substrate in one of two ways. In the first method, individual printed cards follow one another lengthwise through a transport mechanism, and a heated roller fuses the magnetic tape onto the card, where it adheres to the outermost layer of plastic, usually the laminate. Another means of application has the magnetic stripe embedded into the sheet of raw laminate that is baked onto the sheet of printed substrate before the cards is cut from the larger sheet. The two methods of application can be differentiated in that the former can be felt with the fingernail as a slight ridge above the laminate, whereas the latter cannot be discerned as separate.

The resistance of a magnetized material to a change in polarity can be described by its coercivity. A high coercivity (HiCo) material requires a stronger field to change the magnetization than does a low coercivity (LoCo) material. Generally, a LoCo stripe is used on a card that requires frequent changes to the information it carries, such as a declining value store gift card, but it is

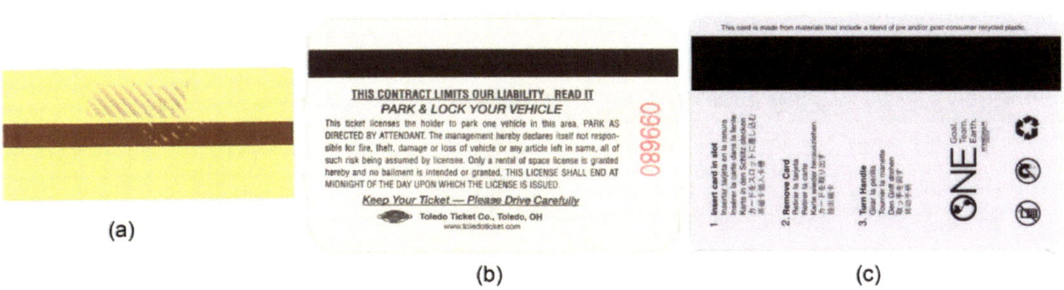

Figure 19.6 Track 1 (LoCo) stripe on a 1992 Paris metro ticket (a), Track 2 (LoCo) stripe on an automobile parking lot pass (b), and Track 3 (HiCo) stripe on a hotel room card (c).

also the most commonly seen on credit and debit cards. As such, the data it carries is also easily corrupted by stray magnetic fields. Alternately, HiCo is not easily corrupted and therefore more suitable for a card that carries information that is written once and never to be changed, such as a driver's license. Discerning between a LoCo and HiCo stripe is fairly easy on the basis of color. LoCo tends to be brown and HiCo tends to be black.

19.4.3 Barcodes

A barcode is a feature that facilitates the optical reading of data that may or may not be visually present elsewhere on the document. Whereas the term *font* refers to the appearance of text and numbers, a particular encoding method is called a *symbology*. It is an alternating set of black and white lines or squares, and it is usually printed in solid black ink as opposed to a CMY composite gray. This provides high contrast against white paper to ensure readability. Different symbologies generally have similar components such as start and stop sequences, data sequences, and error correction sequences, but they vary in the way encoded information is presented.

A 1D or Linear barcode is the simplest type of code, consisting of vertical bars only, oftentimes with a human-readable line of text nearby. *Code 39* is a simple and common alphanumeric symbology, often seen on identification cards such as workplace or library cards. It lacks a computed check digit, which is used to detect data entry errors, unlike most other symbologies. Because it requires no additional mathematical processing, it is easily printed as a standard computer font. Other examples of 1D symbologies are *Code 128*, *Interleaved 2 of 5*, *EAN 8*, *EAN 13*, and *ISBN*. See Figure 19.7.

A Universal Product Code (*UPC-A*) is a numeric-only barcode most commonly found on consumer trade items as a means of simplifying inventory control and price tabulation at the cashier. It consists of 12 digits with a human-readable line positioned below. Digits 2 to 6 identify the manufacturer, and 7 to 11 are the product identifier. A start and end digit, which is a check digit, are positioned on either side of the barcode itself. Guard patterns are found between digits 1/2, 6/7, and 11/12.

There are other variants of UPC-A, designated UPC-B through UPC-E, UPC-2, and UPC-5. The latter are supplemental barcodes that are printed following UPC-A for magazines and books to indicate volume, issue number, or price. *UPC-E* is a 6-digit format equivalent to UPC-A that allows placement in physically small spaces.

Postal services use special 1D barcodes such as *Royal Mail 4-State Customer Code (RM4SCC)* in the UK, *PostBar* in Canada,[17] or *Intelligent Mail (IM) Barcode* in the United States (see Figure 19.8). These symbologies use bars of different heights to encode information in four different positions. The barcodes contain addressing as well as customer-specific information.

Figure 19.7 Barcode 39 (a) is identifiable by its identical start and stop sequences; ISBN (b) is a variant of EAN-13 specifically for books. An add-on EAN-5 code for pricing sits adjacent. (Courtesy Wikipedia.)

(a)
Wikimedia Foundation Inc.
PO BOX 78350
SAN FRANCISCO CA 94107-8350

(b)
1000010298-L3P8A2-BR01

(c)
Lloyds TSB Bank plc
CREDIT CARD SERVICES
BOX 1
BX1 1LT

Figure 19.8 4-state postal barcodes, IM (USA, a), RM4SCC (UK, b), and PostBar (Canada, c).

Postal Numeric Encoding Technique (POSTNET) and *Postal Alpha Numeric Encoding Technique (PLANET)* were fully supplanted by IM barcode in the United States in 2013. Other postal barcode symbologies are *Facing Identification Mark (FIM)* and *CPC Binary Barcode*.

PDF417 (Portable Data File, 4 bars/spaces 17 units long) is a stacked linear barcode that appears as essentially a series of 1D barcodes positioned one atop another and can be read by a traditional laser scanner or newer image-based scanner. It can encode alphanumeric characters in as few as three rows or as many as 90 rows and is found on numerous government-issued identification cards, such as driver's licenses and health cards. It has no relationship to the Adobe PDF file format.

In 2005, PDF417 was adopted by the International Air Transport Association (IATA) for worldwide use on aircraft boarding passes[18] (see Figure 19.9). In 2008, Aztec, Datamatrix, and QR codes were approved for mobile phone, digital-only boarding passes. The initiative was completed in 2010, when older magnetic stripe boarding passes were phased out. The American Association of Motor Vehicle Administrators (AAMVA) specifies the use of PDF417 for North American driver's licenses and identification cards.[19]

Another stacked linear barcode is the *GS1 DataBar*. It was developed as an extension to UPC when UPC became too limiting for grocery store coupons. GS1 DataBar can be seen extensively on produce stickers and lend well to cashier scanning of fresh food (see Figure 19.9).

A 2D matrix barcode records information not only in a horizontal direction, like a 1D barcode, but also in a vertical direction, forming two axes of encoding in a grid pattern for some, circular patterns for others. Much more information can be recorded in a 2D barcode than a 1D barcode, and they have become common in product packaging as well as advertising. Error correction has been built into many 2D barcodes such that a sizable portion of the code may be damaged or absent, and the code will still scan properly.

The *Quick Response (QR) code* originated in 1994 for tracking automotive parts in Japanese production lines, and so they store not only alphanumeric and binary but also kanji data. ISO/IEC 18004:2015 sets the specifications of the symbology, allowing the ability to store a maximum

(a) (b)

Figure 19.9 PDF417 barcode (a), thermal-printed in green, covered in protected clear tape reducing the contrast, is still readable. GS1 DataBar (b) is from a fresh produce label. (Courtesy Wikipedia.)

Figure 19.10 A QR code on a Canadian passport application form, blank (a) and partially completed (b).

size of 177×177 squares encoding almost 7100 numeric-only characters and almost 4300 alphanumeric characters. With the ballpark figure of 3,000 typed characters per page in a book, equal to approximately 1.5 pages of material, it can handle significantly more than a UPC code. As such, the QR code has become popular for many uses, including internet website addresses (URLs) on print advertising and digital tickets for events and aircraft boarding passes. It is easily identifiable by the nested squares located in three corners.

The Canadian passport application is available as a fillable-PDF with a dynamically generated QR code that changes and grows as more information is entered. The QR code pictured in Figure 19.10a is from a new, empty application form. The QR code in Figure 19.10b is on the same document after personal information has been added to the PDF.

The *Data Matrix* code appears similar to a QR code, but it is recognizable by the finder pattern of two adjacent solid black lines along its sides and a timing pattern of alternating light and dark cells along the other two sides. Over 2300 alphanumeric characters can be stored. Its ability to be read at a low contrast ratio, along with a variable size down to the micrometer scale, it lends itself well to the barcoding of small items. Other 2D symbologies include MicroQR, Aztec, MaxiCode, and SPARQCode (Figure 19.11).

A 2D color barcode can hold even more information by encoding in a third mode. This is achieved in a virtual sense where instead of binary white or black units, multiple color units are introduced. The *High Capacity Color Barcode (HCCB)* from Microsoft, *CRONTO*, and *Just Another Barcode (JAB)* codes are examples, as seen in Figure 19.12.

Traditional barcode scanning hardware consists of a laser that scans in a line across a 1D barcode, recognizing the light and dark patterns and decoding it before passing the value onto a

Figure 19.11 2D barcodes Data Matrix (a) and Aztec (b). (Courtesy Wikipedia.)

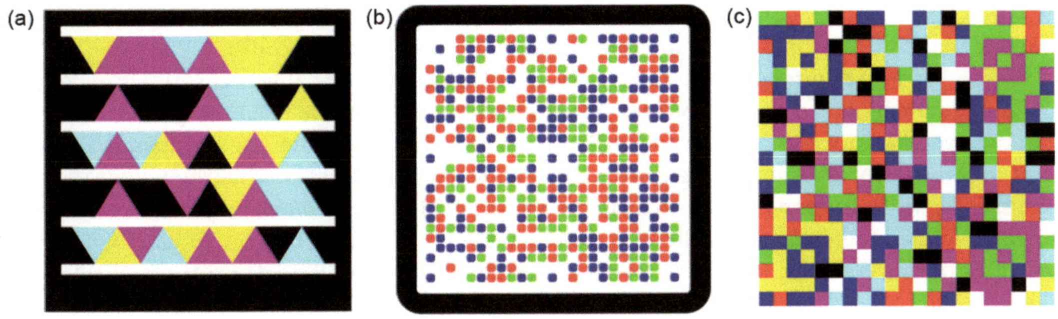

Figure 19.12 2D color barcodes: HCCB (a), CRONTO (b), and JAB[20] (c). (Retrieved from Wikipedia. Used per Creative Commons 3.0, author is *Dr. Georg Fischer*, edited by *Calypso10*. Image has not been modified.)

computer. In this way, it functions very much like a keyboard or mouse as a simple input device. The work is done within the scanner, and no additional software is required. Some types of scanners were enhanced such that a linear scanner could now also decode a stacked linear barcode like PDF417. In order to scan 2D barcodes, however, units that use image scanning (i.e. take a photo) are required.

Scanning a barcode has become a trivial task since the availability of free software applications (apps) for common smartphones. These apps make use of the smartphone's camera as an image scanner in the same way that a modern dedicated barcode scanner does. In this way, not only are 1D and stacked linear barcodes available to be scanned by anyone, but so are most complex 2D barcodes like QR codes.

19.4.5 Counterfeit Protection System (CPS)

A CPS code is a covert series of yellow toner dots, imperceptible to the unaided eye, that are added to a document bearing color (CMY) electrophotographic printing. It is a repeating pattern, where each unit is composed of a matrix of dots whose design is particular to the printer manufacturer (see Figure 19.13). Within the unit is encoded, at a minimum, the printer make and model. Additional information that may be encoded is the date, time, and serial number. The concept of a CPS code was a product of the agreement by various manufacturers to implement an anti-counterfeiting scheme to their printers, which were newly capable of accurately replicating colors and designs

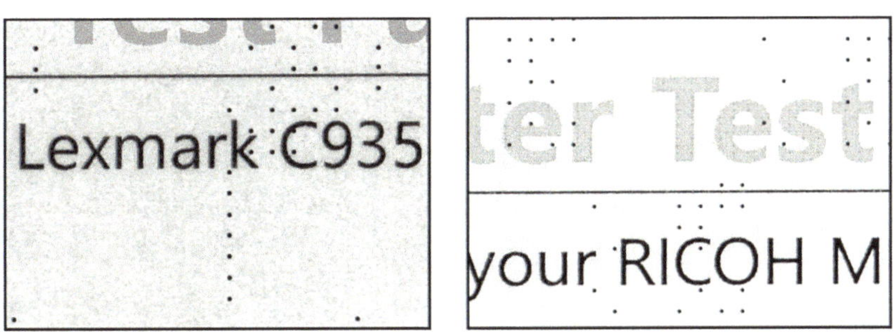

Figure 19.13 CPS codes on Windows 10 printer test pages from the same computer on two different color laser printers (codes enhanced for clarity).

such that there was a possible threat to the security of international banknotes. Efforts have been made in academia to employ manual[21] and automated[22] methods of decoding CPS codes.

CPS codes are a fantastically useful tool for the FDE. Meant to be able to discretely encode the make and model of a color laser printer or photocopier, they can be used for quick discrimination between two documents. If they were printed on separate printers, the code matrix will be of a fundamentally different configuration, discounting any contention that they share the same origin *in color printing mode*. Be aware that this says nothing about *black-only* toner printed text. Since the code is not printed in black-only mode, it is possible that two documents with different CPS codes were refed through a common printer for the black text. Features of refeeding, like smeared toner streaks, might be evident to suggest such action. It has been noticed in some instances that CPS codes can be reproduced directly from a color printout onto a photocopy, such that they are visible to the naked eye.[23]

19.4.6 Eurion Constellation and Anti-Counterfeiting Printing

The Central Bank Counterfeit Deterrence Group (CBCDG) is a consortium of 32 banks and note printing authorities who consult and produce anti-counterfeiting technologies such as the EURion (aka Omron) Constellation, named for its resemblance to the Orion constellation in the night sky. An overt scheme to prevent the photocopying of Euro currency initially, five small circles are printed in a specific pattern and repeated across a banknote at various orientations. It has since been adopted for use among the banknotes of many other countries. The presence of the circles alone is sufficient, but some currency designs integrate them into a less obvious graphical feature such as musical notes or flowers.

Like the EURion Constellation, other designs may trigger the detection system, such as the US Department of the Treasury seal on US banknotes. This has previously caused problems when attempting to photocopy non-currency casework items, where an organization's logo bears a passing resemblance to the seal, for example. The resulting output from a photocopier is a color copy of the item but composed of nonprinting lines in a regular pattern. The offending symbol can be detected by covering the item with a sheet of paper, copying first one half then the other, to determine which portion triggered the system. The technique is repeated on one half, then again until the smallest area possible is found. Then a Google Image Search can be conducted to determine similar designs, with the Treasury Seal being the example in Figure 19.14. A grayscale copy does not invoke the system and is printed as normally expected.

Some digital printers such as the Toshiba eStudio series have the capability to print, on demand, a covert security pattern with embedded text onto a document. The pattern is

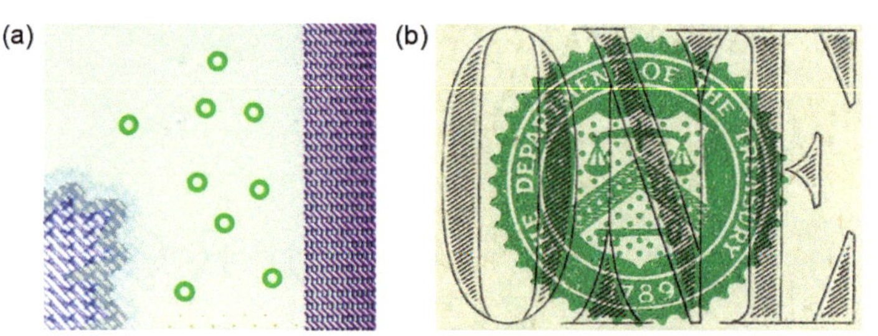

Figure 19.14 Anti-counterfeiting features on banknotes: EURion constellation (a) and seal of the US Treasury Department (b).

made apparent when the document bearing the embedded security pattern is copied and is intended to deter replication of documents deemed confidential. It functions best when the same machine is used for both production of the original and copying. The pattern can be chosen from a list of preset options or be generated by the user, as can the embedded string of text.[23]

19.5 CONCLUSION

The methods for printing from a computer discussed above are but a small sample of the total possibilities, but they are common enough that the information should be helpful to the FDE. Knowledge of archaic as well as modern printing practices helps elucidate where we have come from and are going to. The casework possibilities for the FDE are varied because the next case examination could involve a historical investigation into misdeeds of decades past, or it could be the most advanced conspiratorial fraud involving the latest equipment of today. Computer printing is an aspect of forensics that appeals to everyone's inner nerd.

REFERENCES

1. Julien, A., 2012. *Digital Fonts – The Complete Guide to Creating, Marketing and Selling*, Thames and Hudson, London.
2. Parker, Matt, 2016. "Stand-up comedy routine about spreadsheets," YouTube channel "standup-maths," https://youtu.be/UBX2QQHlQ_I, accessed February 5, 2019.
3. Field, G.G., 2004. *Color and Its Reproduction: Fundamentals for the Digital Imaging and Printing Industry*, GATF Press, Pittsburgh.
4. Miller, Matthew, 2019. "What does an unprocessed RAW file look like?" PetaPixel, accessed November 1, 2019. https://petapixel.com/2019/07/15/what-does-an-unprocessed-raw-file-look-like/
5. Borstein, R., 2016. *Acrobat for legal professionals blog*, http://blogs.adobe.com/acrolaw/
6. Adobe, 2017. "Font embedding and substitution," accessed November 1, 2019. https://helpx.adobe.com/acrobat/using/pdf-fonts.html
7. Kipphan, Helmut, 2001. *Handbook of Print Media – Technologies and Production Methods*, Springer, Berlin, 1207 p.
8. Unknown, 2019. "Do it yourself infrared camera modification tutorials." LifePixel.com, accessed November 1, 2019. https://www.lifepixel.com/tutorials/infrared-diy-tutorials
9. Gervais, Robert, 2017. "A study of photocopier distortion through interactive animations," *Journal of the American Society of Questioned Document Examiners*, vol. 20, no. 1 (June): 23–31.
10. Gervais, Robert, 2016. "Adobe photoshop and illustrator in forensic document examination – a workshop," *provided to CBSA FDE Section*, December 2016.
11. Webster, E. 2000. *Print Unchained – Fifty Years of Digital Printing, 1950-2000 and Beyond, a Saga of Invention and Enterprise*, DRA of Vermont. 37–38.
12. Williams, Richard A. 1988. "Wire Matrix Printing" in Durbeck, R.C. and Sherr, S., *Output Hardcopy Devices*. Boston, Academic Press Inc.
13. Fauser, R. and Rottes, T., 2014. "The Individuality of Inkjet Printing," *workshop provided to CBSA FDE Section*.
14. Stephens, J.C., Geiman, I., Rohde, S.M., and Rohde, M.M., 2016. "Thermal ribbon analysis platform (TRAP): The validation of a new instrument for recovering images on ribbons." *Journal of the American Society of Questioned Document Examiners*, vol. 19, no. 1 (June): 17–24.
15. United States Secret Service (USSS), undated. "Thermal ribbon analysis platform," accessed November 1, 2019. https://www.tswg.gov/ISF/Thermal_Ribbon_Analysis_Platform.html

16. International Civil Aviation Organization (ICAO) 9303 2015. "Machine Readable Travel Documents, Seventh Edition, 2015 Part 4 - 4.2 Machine Readable Zone," accessed November 1, 2019. https:/www.icao.int/publications/Documents/9303_p4_cons_en.pdf
17. Canada Post Corporation (CPC), 2005. "Canada Post 4-state bar code handbook." https://web.archive.org/web/20060321110734/http://www.canadapost.ca:80/common/offerings/address_management/pdf/dbc_handbook-e.pdf33, accessed October 2019.
18. International Air Transport Association (IATA), 2010. "Press release no. 58 - Airlines complete move to bar-coded boarding passes." December 15, 2010, accessed October 4, 2019. https://www.iata.org/pressroom/pr/Pages/2010-12-15-01.aspx
19. American Association of Motor Vehicle Administrators (AMVAA), 2016. "DL/ID card design standard – Personal identification – AAMVA North American standard – Annex D." accessed November 1, 2019. https://www.aamva.org/DL-ID-Card-Design-Standard
20. German Federal Office for Information Security (Bundesamt für Sicherheit in der Informationstechnik), 2016. BSI TR 03137 – Part 2: JAB Code (just another bar code), color bar code symbology specification, accessed October 2019. https://www.bsi.bund.de/EN/Publications/TechnicalGuidelines/TR03137/BSITR03137.html
21. Buck, P., 2018. "Printer steganography – Reverse engineering the machine identification code." Thesis, Saxion University of Applied Sciences, June 13.
22. Van Beusekom, J., Shafait, F., and Breuel, T.M., 2013. "Automatic authentication of color laser print-outs using machine identification codes." *Pattern Analysis and Applications*, vol. 16, no. 4: 663–678. DOI: 10.1007/s10044-012-0287-5.
23. Campbell, T., Pajos, P., and Osmond, J., 2014. "Unexpected introduction of tremor into photocopied handwriting on a xerox WorkCenter 7545," *presented at the American Society of Questioned Document Examiners annual conference*, Honolulu, HI.

Chapter 20

Radiography

Tobin Tanaka

CONTENTS

20.1 INTRODUCTION

Radiography offers insight into the inner structures of materials that may not be visualized under other conditions. It permits a range of noninvasive and nondestructive views of objects that is taken for granted in the modern context. Document examination is an area of forensic science where the application of radiography has found success for a variety of problems.

20.2 IONIZING RADIATION TYPES

Although radiography imaging is generally associated with x-rays, it should be kept in mind that other types of ionizing radiation may be used.[1] This includes gamma rays (γ-rays) and neutrons. In this chapter, the focus will be on the use of x-rays, particularly x-ray cabinets that provide rapid radiographs. As ionizing radiation may pose health hazards if not properly utilized, users are urged to consult with the appropriate authorities who can advise on the regulatory environment in their respective jurisdictions.

20.3 BASIC ATOMIC STRUCTURE

In nature, the chemical elements that make up all materials are composed of an atomic nucleus orbited by negatively charged electrons. The atomic number for an element is defined as the number of protons (positively charged) in the nucleus and is abbreviated as *Z*. For example, nickel has atomic number 28 ($Z = 28$) and may also be represented by the elemental symbol ($_{28}Ni$), whereas iron has atomic number 26 ($Z = 26$ or $_{26}Fe$). Within the atomic nucleus there may be neutrons which are neutral, i.e. with no electrical charge. Neutrons are close to the mass of protons and account for the different isotopes that may exist for an element. In other words, the same element may have different masses. The different isotopes of an element are designated by superscripted masses, for example $^{14}_{12}C$, where 14 refers to the isotope and 12 refers to the atomic number. For brevity, the reference to isotopes may sometimes omit the atomic number, for example ^{14}C.

Some isotopes are radioactive and may be referred to as radioisotopes. Radioisotopes are materials that emit radiation into their surroundings due to the unstable atomic nucleus. What is emitted as radiation depends on the radioisotope; some of them are present in nature whereas others are synthetically made. Some radioisotopes are high energy and may be used for industrial radiography purposes such as inspection of welds in metals. Other radioisotopes are lower energy and may be suitable for low density objects encountered in document examination.

However, the suitable lower-energy radioisotopes, such as tritium ($^{3}_{1}H$) and carbon-14 ($^{14}_{12}C$) in plate/sheet form, are neither easily acquired, nor are they simply used as successful radiographs may require several exposure trials to optimize the exposure. Film cassettes are also of a special type and require careful handling and long exposures from tens of minutes to hours. The application of radioisotopes for radiography in forensic document examination is nontrivial.

20.4 X-RAYS

Röntgen was the first to observe the physical phenomena that occurred when high voltage electrons strike a metal target.[2,3] Expressed in a different way, x-rays are generated when high speed electrons collide with specific types of matter. The resulting effect is the production of Röntgen rays or what has become known as x-rays. The full application of x-rays to a wide variety of medical, industrial, conservation, nondestructive examination, and forensic applications followed rather rapidly. It was not fully understood what x-rays were at first, but with further investigation it became clear that x-rays are part of the electromagnetic spectrum. X-rays have wavelengths that range approximately between 10^{-9} and 10^{-12} m. The distribution of wavelengths is not monochromatic, i.e. one wavelength, but is a range of wavelengths. The energy output for each of the wavelengths also differs.

The x-rays travel in straight lines and are not influenced by any other magnetic or electrical fields. As is well known, x-rays will reveal the inner structures of materials as they penetrate them. The degree to which this penetration occurs depends on the types of material and their thicknesses. X-rays are commonly made when high speed electrons collide with specific types of metals. This may be described as a continuous spectrum that is a result of energy released when the electrons rapidly decelerate after traversing through the electron's cloud that surrounds atomic nuclei in the material being subjected to x-rays. The German term *Bremsstrahlung*, which loosely translates to "braking radiation," is sometimes used to describe this process.

As for all electromagnetic radiation, the emitted radiation may be expressed as either frequency or wavelength, with higher frequencies having greater energy. The relationship between wavelength and frequency is:

$$\nu = c/\lambda$$

Where ν = the frequency, c = the speed of light (2.9979×10^8 m/s), and λ = the wavelength

Even though many radiography configurations are possible, the focus of this chapter will be on x-ray cabinet types of devices. X-ray cabinets are very safe to use and do not require specialized shielding beyond that provided by the cabinet. In addition, there are safety switches that stop the production of x-rays if doors are opened or ajar.

Other types of radiography with x-rays, such as auto radiography, use high-energy x-rays that are attenuated with lead sheets. As the high energy x-rays encounter the lead sheets, electrons are liberated from the lead atoms, which in turn may react with the object to be radiographed. Operation of this type of equipment needs special skills that are unlikely to be in the domain of most forensic document examiners (FDEs). As a result, no additional information will be provided on x-ray radiography outside of that for cabinet x-ray systems.

20.5 GAMMA RAYS (γ-RAYS)

Gamma rays are very high energy photons that are of shorter wavelengths than x-rays. In radiography applications, such radiation is commonly produced by synthetic isotopes of ^{60}Co and ^{192}Ir. The energy and penetration depth of such radiation is much greater than that needed for document examination except under unusual circumstances.

20.6 NEUTRON RADIOGRAPHY

Neutron radiography is a specialized technique where high velocity neutrons are used to create the radiograph. Its application is most useful when organic-based materials that are within inorganic surroundings must be differentiated. Plastic or leather components that are encased in heavy metal containers are examples. Attenuation by organic materials is greater than that for inorganic materials, resulting in organic materials becoming visible on neutron radiographs. However, this method requires specialists who are familiar with the techniques and have access to such equipment. Unlike x-ray radiography, this method may make the object subjected to neutron radiography radioactive for a short period of time.[4] Except for very limited instances, the application of neutron radiography to document examination is not practical.

20.7 RADIOGRAPHY APPLIED TO DOCUMENT EXAMINATION

The document examination literature describes the use of x-rays for examinations back to the works of Harrison and Conway.[5,6] Earlier publications in the mid-1940s refer to the use of x-rays for the examination of postage stamps and related materials.[7–14] More recently, several publications document the use of radioisotopes to successfully create radiographs. Harris outlined the use of radiography for passport examinations[15] and for lottery ticket examinations.[16] Mercer outlined the use of Beta radiography, where the carbon-14 radioisotope plate emits Beta particles which are energetic electrons, for visualizing the watermark on pages in a disputed will.[17] This technique was also described by Sehgal and Aggarwal for the examination of Reserve Bank of India banknotes.[18] Into the 1980s, several developments using tritium (^{3}H) radioisotopes were successful. A significant drawback to the use of these radioisotopes was the need for long exposure times ranging from 3 hours to 90 hours, depending on the film used.[19,20]

When considering radiography for document examination problems, the similarities to applications of the conservation community are apparent. Several resources within this community may reveal insights into how to approach similar types of materials, namely paper and related materials of low density. Conservationists often attempt to image similar features, such as watermarks on paper or construction of a multilayered document such as a book cover. Lang and Middleton provide an excellent overview of theory and practical application of radiography in conservation and cultural matters involving paper examination.[21] The recording of historical watermarks in paper by radiography is an area that is of great interest in the conservation field.[22] Ambitious efforts have been proposed for a database of paper watermarks by the Conservation Unit and the Institute for Image Data Research, University of Northumbria at Newcastle.[23] Other conservation-oriented research has highlighted the improvements in recording watermarks in paper.[24]

Lower energy x-rays are all that is needed to differentiate the features of interest for nearly all document materials. Historically, nearly all radiography work in documents was conducted on thin paper-based documents as single sheets, with the exception of items such as passports. In more recent times, the wide use of documents with different materials, such as plastic cards, laminated papers, and multi-material cards, have proliferated for many uses: payment cards, access cards, memberships, loyalty cards for merchants, among other uses. Many of these may have embedded antennas or electronic circuits which may be used with contactless readers. The contactless readers can read the data or authenticate some nonhuman readable information to grant access or confirm a transaction such as a financial payment.

In such cards, the antenna or electronics may become damaged from wear, abuse, or manufacturer defects. As such, cards are typically laminated plastic layers that cannot be delaminated without resorting to destructive testing. But even when the antenna or electronics are in a clear or transparent window, as in some passports, the advantage of radiography is that it has the potential to detect small scale breaks or fractures in materials, as well as cut marks, hollowed-out cavities, or other signs of density differences.

Recent improvements in x-ray technologies have increased the potential for high-quality radiographs from x-rays that can be obtained rapidly without needing a specialist in radiography. The high-quality radiographs are not solely due to the digital nature of detectors but the x-ray beam size that can be focused to narrow beams. Wider x-ray beams tend to have a decrease in image sharpness on radiographs which creates a *shadow effect* that is technically described as penumbra. This effect is minimal for thin, flat objects such as documents. However, for objects of a significant size in all three dimensions such as thick books or large packages, the effect may become noticeable. Taller or thicker irregularly shaped objects will tend to have greater geometric distortion as some portions are much closer to the x-ray source. Accordingly, interpretation of the features of thick objects on radiographs will require consideration of this geometric distortion. It may require multiple radiographs of the same object taken with different orientations.

When operating an x-ray cabinet, the practical considerations include the magnification, x-ray tube voltage, x-ray tube current, and exposure time. The magnification is determined by the position of the object relative to the x-ray source; the closer the object is to the source, the greater the magnification. Within a cabinet x-ray, there may be preset distances where a shelf is positioned to the desired magnification as shown in Figure 20.1.

When using x-ray equipment, the wavelengths are not selected, but the x-ray tube voltage in kilovolts (kV) determines the energy of the generated x-rays. Note that the x-ray tube does not produce a monochromatic wavelength of x-rays but a broad range of wavelengths. This is akin to the visible light that is emitted from a tungsten light that emits white light, i.e. a broad range of wavelengths from blue to red that appears to be white or nearly white. Increasing the voltage

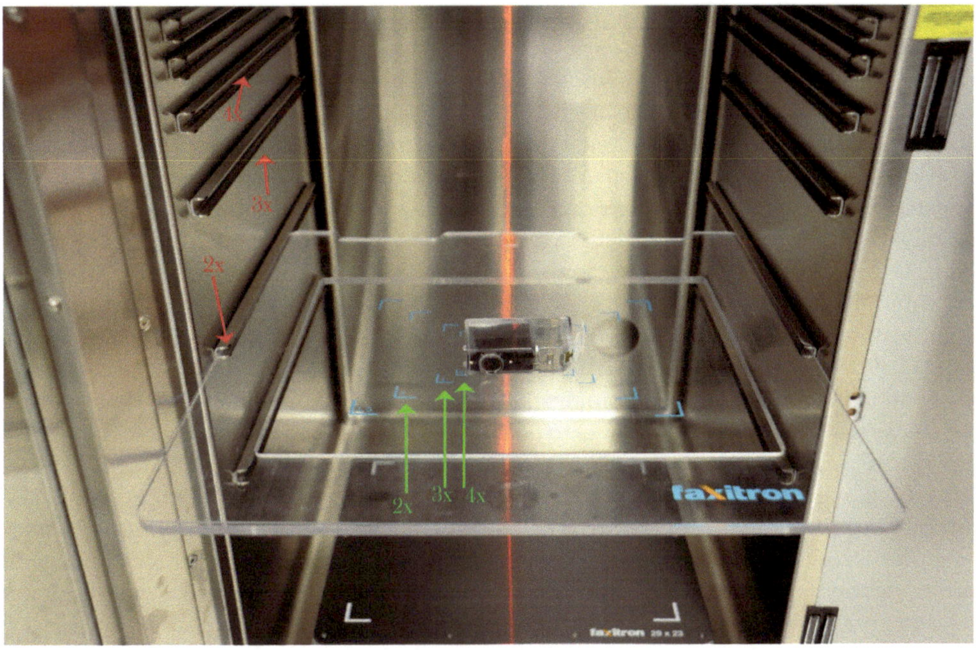

Figure 20.1 Inside of x-ray cabinet. Higher magnifications are achieved by positioning the transparent shelf closer to the x-ray tube, i.e. at higher positions in the cabinet. In the example here, the shelf positions for (2×, 3× and 4×) are shown with the red arrows. The green arrows indicate the area that is radiographed, higher magnifications result in smaller areas that are radiographed.

results in more energetic x-rays which in turn have greater penetration depth into materials. When the tube voltage is lower, the x-rays may be described as "soft x-rays" or Grenz rays from the German *Grenzstrahlen*, which translates into borderline rays. For low density, low atomic number items encountered in many document examination situations, such low energy x-rays have many applications.[25,26] This may be an important limitation as some equipment is not capable of producing low energy x-rays suitable for many materials encountered in document examination.

Low energy x-rays are appreciably attenuated by the air and, as a result, it may be necessary to place the object with the x-ray equipment in a partial vacuum. When the tube voltages are in the range of 2–5 kV, there is significant reduction in strength.[27] However, most document examinations do not require such low energy x-rays.

Current for the x-ray tube, stated in milli-Amperes (mA), determines the number of electrons per second that are directed to the metallic target to generate x-rays. Increasing the current only increases the number of electrons per second, it does not result in higher energy x-rays. Higher current should require less exposure time to acquire a radiograph if the other settings of tube voltage and exposure time are kept constant.

Exposure time refers to the length of time that the x-rays are generated, and the detector records the differences in x-ray attenuation. As the x-rays interact with the object, the differences in density should be recorded by the detector. The length of exposure is typically set in seconds (s), and the exposure settings are often quoted in milli-Amperes*seconds (mAs), which is simply the product of the tube current and exposure time. For example, if the tube current was 0.30 mA and the exposure time was 3.5 s, then exposure may be stated as 1.05 mAs.

A consideration for any radiograph is scatter of radiation. As is the case for all electromagnetic radiation, the interaction of x-rays with matter will result in differing degrees of scattered radiation. This is a complex phenomenon which may have a significant influence on the quality of radiographs, more so when there are heterogeneous types of materials or they are very thick or have geometries that tend to increase scatter. Fortunately for many document examination applications, this is less of a concern. Many items do not have characteristics that tend to have high scatter, and they are not living organisms where exposure to multiple sessions of ionizing radiation is undesirable.

Modern digital x-ray systems have several options for radiograph file format. In addition to the common image formats of TIFF, BMP and JPEG, there is the option of Digital Imaging and Communications in Medicine (DICOM) format. The DICOM format is meant to provide compatibility of data between a variety of medical hardware and software. Data that describes the equipment, exposure settings, and other related information is kept within the file.[28] DICOM format images can be converted to other image formats to permit inclusion into reports and notes. Software such as ImageJ can be used for viewing and conversion of radiograph files in DICOM format.[29,30]

X-ray images are grayscale images and often provide greater bit depth; more grayscale values permit greater differentiation of a variety of densities. For example, the radiographs shown in this chapter were recorded with a cabinet x-ray that stores the images as 14-bit (16384 levels) grayscale radiographs. Note that denser areas on the radiographs are lighter (higher grayscale value), and areas of lower density are darker (lower grayscale value).

The clarity of watermarks in paper can be improved with x-ray radiography. Interference from other printing or markings may be transparent in x-rays and may not be observed on the resulting radiograph. In Figure 20.2, the radiograph of a page with toner shows the watermark very clearly with no interference from the toner, such as is seen in Figure 20.3. This radiograph was

Figure 20.2 Radiograph of document with laser printing (nonmagnetic toner).

El Salvador (enforced disappearances, crimes against humanity and war crimes during the time of the civil war, *circa* 1979-1992),

Chile (enforced disappearances during the time of Augusto Pinochet; *circa* 1973-1990),

Uganda (crimes against humanity, enforced disappearances & genocide during the time of Idi Amin's presidency; *circa* 1971-1979).

In some cases the downfall of those in positions of power either led to amnesty under a reconciliation agreement or other measure; in other instances those who could be investigated and/or tried fled (Khmer Rouge leaders after 1979).

For General Augusto Pinochet, the hand of international justice took some years to take effect. The principle of universal jurisdiction was invoked in an attempt to have him brought to justice on a variety of violations of human rights law. In the United Kingdom in October 1998, at the request of Spanish prosecutors General Pinochet was taken into custody on charges of torture during his time as president of Chile. He claimed immunity as a former head of state, but the House of Lords ruled that this was not a valid claim and in the end General Pinochet returned to Chile due to declining health.[20]

The end of the Cold War in the early 1990s opened the possibility for some of these situations to see international justice slowly work its way through the investigations phase and onto the possibility of trials. It also was the decade that saw some of the worst human rights violations on such a widespread scale since World War II.

***Ad hoc* International Tribunals from the events in the former Yugoslavia and Rwanda & Special Court for Sierra Leone**

The events that took place during the breakup of Yugoslavia, the genocide in Rwanda in 1994 and the events during the civil war in Sierra Leone were some of the most challenging for the international community. Some of the issues that were faced during the time of the events could only be partially addressed. In the aftermath, it was recognised that there was a need to bring those

Figure 20.3 Transmitted illumination image of the same page as used for Figure 20.2. The toner present results in a loss of discernible detail.

taken at 2× and, as described in Figure 20.1, the four edges and numbers (3–6) are the marking points that show the area on the shelf that will be visible at different magnifications.

Book covers are typically made with a variety of materials. In the radiograph shown in Figure 20.4, the right side of the radiograph which is very dark shows the cover of a book with different densities of materials detected by radiography. Denser or very thick materials are lighter in intensity on radiographs. The left side of Figure 20.4 is lighter due to the thick bundle of paper and left side of the cover.

FDEs may encounter plastic cards with internal antennas or metallic components within. As there are significantly different materials within these types of cards, different exposures are needed to properly visualize them (see Figures 20.5 and 20.6). Fortunately, with modern digital x-ray cabinets, such multiple exposures are rapidly and easily done within a few minutes.

Radiography may be used to reveal hidden documents within larger objects. Low energy x-rays and sufficient magnification are needed for successful results (see Figures 20.7 and 20.8).

20.8 SUMMARY

These examples provide some insight into the application of radiography to document examinations. Although FDEs will not usually have ready access to x-ray cabinets, there may be opportunities to make use of equipment from other specializations such as the conservation sciences or dentistry.

Figure 20.4 The central portion shows the binding of the book. A lower density portion (in darker shades) is visible to the right of the central spine.

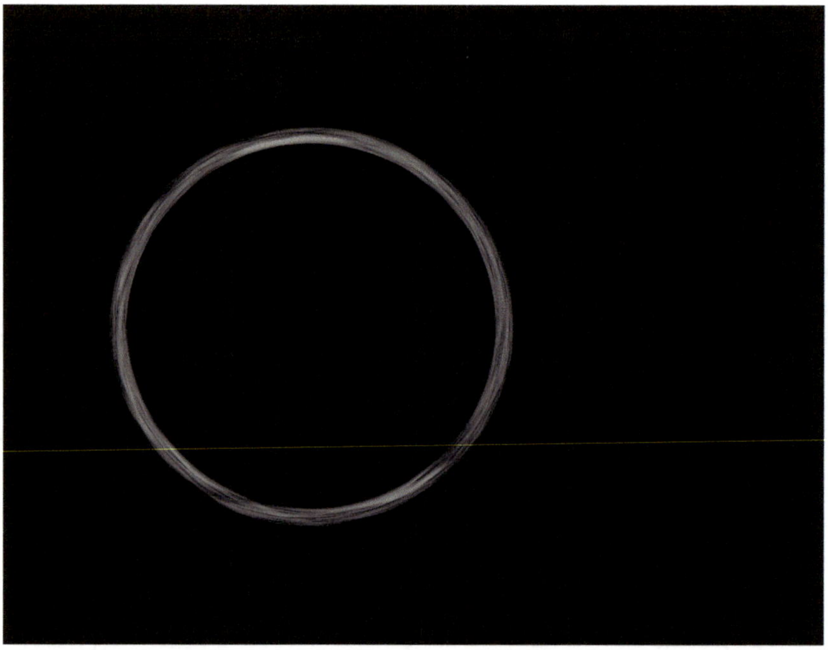

Figure 20.5 Automatic mode differentiates the large coil of internal wire embedded in a card; however fine details are not seen (44 kV, 0.25 mA, 5.11 s, 1.28 mAs).

Figure 20.6 The same card as in Figure 20.5, radiographed with manual settings (27 kV, 0.40 mA, 3.04 s, 1.21 mAs).

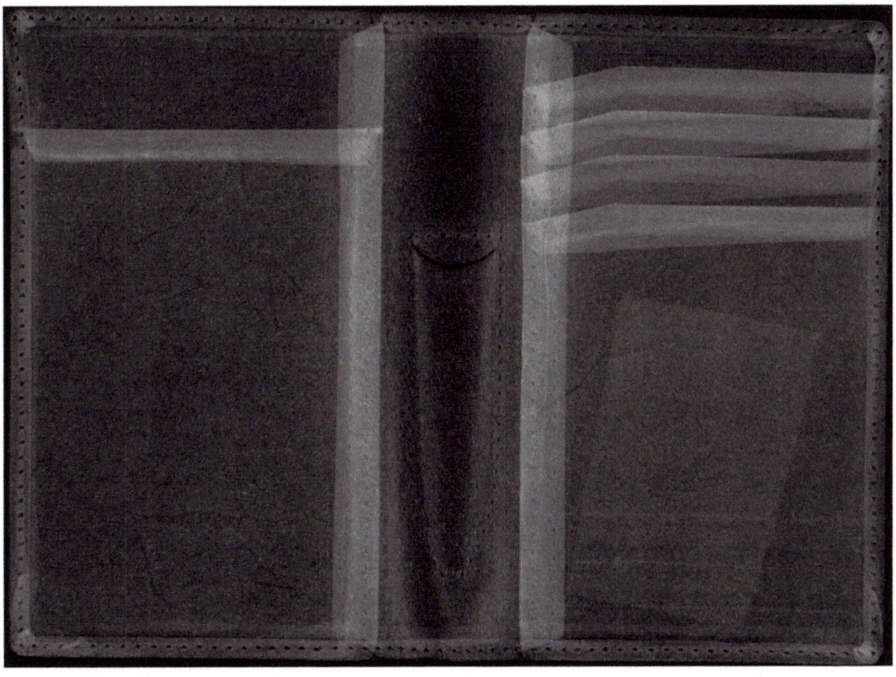

Figure 20.7 Leather wallet with rectangular-shaped embedded paper on the right side.

Figure 20.8 Plastic toy with paper instructions in sealed package can be easily visualized. Note the lack of sharp edges for some parts that are thicker.

REFERENCES

1. A. Middleton and J. Lang, Radiography: Theory. *Radiography of Cultural Material*, Second Edition, J. Lang and A. Middleton, Eds., Amsterdam: Elsevier Butterworth Heinemann, 2005, pp. 2–5.
2. W. K. Röntgen, "Über Eine Neue Art Von Strahlen," *Sitzungsberichte der Physikalisch-Medizinischen Gesellschaft zu Würzburg*, vol. 9, pp. 1320–1341, 1895.
3. W. C. Röntgen, "On a new kind of rays," *Nature*, vol. 53, pp. 274–276, 23 January 1896.
4. A. Middleton and J. Lang, Radiography: Theory. *Radiography of Cultural Material*, Second Edition, J. Lang and A. Middleton, Eds., Amsterdam: Elsevier Butterworth Heinemann, 2005, pp. 3–4.
5. J. V. P. Conway, *Evidential Documents*, Springfield, IL: Charles C Thomas, 1959, p. 187.
6. W. R. Harrison, *Suspect Documents Their Scientific Examination*, Chicago, IL: Nelson-Hall Publishers, 1981 (reprint of 1958 edition), pp. 84–85.
7. H. B. Tuttle, "From a photographer's notebook," *Identification News*, p. 5, November 1953.
8. W. H. S. Cheavin, "Photographing stamps by means of X-rays," *London Philatelist*, vol. 54, pp. 130–132, December 1945.
9. W. H. S. Cheavin, "Philately and X-rays," *Philately*, vol. 1, pp. 149–151, November-December 1947.
10. H. J. Lambot, "Determination of "loading" in paper by microradiography," *Nature*, vol. 159, p. 676, 17 May 1947.
11. J. D. Pelgroms, "Study of the structure of paper by means of "soft" X-rays," *Paper Trade Journal*, vol. 134, pp. 25–32, January 1952.
12. H. C. Pollack and C. F. Bridgman, "X-ray in philately," *Radiology*, vol. 62, pp. 259–261, February 1954.
13. H. C. Pollack, C. F. Bridgman and H. R. Splettstosser, "The X-ray investigation of postage stamps," *Medical Radiography and Photography*, vol. 31, pp. 74–78, 1955.

14. W. H. S. Cheavin, "Philately and scientific methods," *London Philatelist*, vol. 55, pp. 76–78, July 1946.
15. J. Harris, "Radiography and passport examinations," *Canadian Society of Forensic Science Journal*, vol. 23, no. 1, pp. 25–37, 1990.
16. J. Harris, "Radiography and the "scratch and win" lottery ticket," *Canadian Society of Forensic Science Journal*, vol. 22, no. 4, pp. 321–334, 1989.
17. C. Mercer, "A Futuristic Will Beta Radiography Revisited," in *American Society of Questioned Document Examiners*, Long Beach, 1994.
18. V. N. Sehgal and H. R. Aggarwal, "Modified method for beta ray radiography using C-14 methacrylate sheet," *International Criminal Police Review*, vol. 325, pp. 54–57, February 1979.
19. F. M. Kerr, "Isotopic radiography of documents," *RCMP Gazette*, vol. 47, nos. 7 and 8, pp. 15–16, 1985.
20. F. M. Kerr and J. L. Gallant, "Large area tritium sources for forensic document radiography," *Forensic Science International*, vol. 28, pp. 221–228, 1985.
21. A. Middleton and J. Lang, *Radiography of Cultural Material*, J. Lang and A. Middleton, Eds., Amsterdam: Elsevier Butterworth Heinemann, 2005, pp. 1–189.
22. C. F. Bridgman, "Radiography of paper," *Studies in Conservation*, vol. 10, no. 1, pp. 8–17, 1965.
23. A. J. E. Brown and R. Mulholland, "Using microfocus X-radiography and other techniques to create a digital watermark database," *Studies in Conservation*, vol. 47, no. Sup3, pp. 21–26, 2002.
24. J. van Aken, "An improvement in Grenz radiography of paper to record watermarks, chain and laid lines," *Studies in Conservation*, vol. 48, pp. 103–110, 2003.
25. D. Graham and J. Thomson, *Grenz Rays*, Oxford: Pergamon Press, 1980.
26. D. Graham, *The Use of X-Ray Techniques in Forensic Investigations*, Edinburgh: Longman Group Limited, 1973.
27. D. Graham, *The Use of X-Ray Techniques in Forensic Investigations*, Edinburgh: Longman Group Limited, 1973, pp. 110.
28. Faxitron Bioptics LLC, *Ultra Focus User's Manual (v01)*, Tucson, AZ: Faxitron Bioptics LLC, 2013.
29. National Institute of Health, "ImageJ," [Online]. Available: https://imagej.net/Welcome. [Accessed 10 October 2019].
30. C. A. Schneider, W. S. Rasband and K. W. Eliceiri, "NIH image to ImageJ: 25 years of image analysis," *Nature Methods*, vol. 9, no. 7, pp. 671–675, 1 July 2012.

Chapter 21

Digital Examination Techniques and Considerations

Mark T. Goff

CONTENTS

This chapter is designed to assist the Forensic Document Examiner (FDE) with examinations using digital image technology. The areas discussed are hardware and software considerations, imaging, direct examinations, comparative examinations, and demonstratives. Many of the techniques covered will be familiar to FDEs. Digital examinations are conducted in a similar method to physical examinations, but they can clarify observations or provide information not readily available in a physical exam. Before an FDE embarks on a digital examination, there are some considerations that should be made.

FDEs should familiarize themselves with two standards that describe the basics of forensic imaging: Standard for Use of Image Capture and Storage Technology in Forensic Document Examination and Standard Guide for Forensic Digital Image Processing.[1,2] Compliance with these standards ensures the FDE does not introduce undesired variables into an examination due to improper image handling.

21.1 HARDWARE AND SOFTWARE CONSIDERATIONS

In order to conduct digital examinations, FDEs need to ensure that they have the appropriate resources to adequately comply with the standards. Foremost in consideration is access to an advanced raster image editor, such as Adobe® Photoshop® or GNU Image Manipulation Program (GIMP), that allows for image editing using layers. The use of raster image editors will be discussed more in-depth later in this chapter. Complementary to the imaging software is the imaging hardware. The FDE will need to have access to advanced image capture devices, such as a scanner and digital camera capable of capturing high resolution, and a computer with sufficient memory, processing power, and storage space.

All digital examinations start with capturing an image of the physical items to be examined. This is accomplished with either a scanner or camera. Both devices capture images using similar technology, but they both have strengths and weaknesses, depending on the needs of the examination. The image scanner provides benefits over the digital camera in that it can capture the examination item with greater detail and provides the FDE with a true-to-life size (1:1) image. The digital camera is most useful when capturing items that are not suitable for the image scanner such as large, fragile, or hazardous items or when attempts to scan the examination items yield undesirable results. Advancements in digital cameras are narrowing the gap in resolution between scanners and digital photography.

21.1.1 Scanners

The two types of scanners commonly used are Charge-Coupled Device (CCD) scanners and Contact Image Sensor (CIS) scanners, commonly called LED scanners. Both types of scanner operate similarly: an image is captured by illuminating the items to be imaged, and the reflected light values are recorded with electronic sensors. While the images captured on both scanners are good quality, the CCD scanner has a greater depth of field, allowing for better image capture for items that may have a 3-dimensional quality such as wrinkled documents or pages of a book. CCD and CIS image scanners can be flatbed scanners, where the imaging sensor moves along the length of the item to be imaged, or sheet fed scanners, where the document is moved past a stationary imaging sensor. Caution should be exercised when using a scanner with an Automatic Document Feeder (ADF) because thin or fragile paper can be damaged. Additionally, an ADF can impart transport markings in paper that could have detrimental effects on future printer or copier examinations.

When capturing an image using an image scanner, the FDE should ensure the image is captured at a minimum of 300 pixels per inch (ppi) and stored in a lossless format, typically TIFF. A TIFF file (.tif) is a graphics file format for storing raster images that supports color depths up to 24-bit color, depth-perceptible to the human eye. Although 300 pixels per inch is the minimum acceptable scanning resolution, consideration should be given to scanning examination items at the optical resolution of the image scanner, typically 600 ppi for CCD scanners, to avoid image interpolation when the resolution is increased or the combining of pixel information when the resolution is reduced. Scanning an image at a resolution higher than the optical resolution of a scanner does not yield more detail, it only results in a larger image (Figure 21.1).

21.1.2 Digital Photography

Digital cameras use Complementary Metal–Oxide Semiconductor (CMOS) image sensors that capture the light values reflected from the examination items that have been focused through the camera lens. The choice of lens can have a considerable effect on the digital image by changing the depth of field or introducing distortion. Although this lens distortion can be corrected using digital image processing software, the FDE should attempt to mitigate this distortion at the time the image is captured to accurately reflect the examination item as it was photographed. When capturing an image of examination items with a digital camera, the FDE should

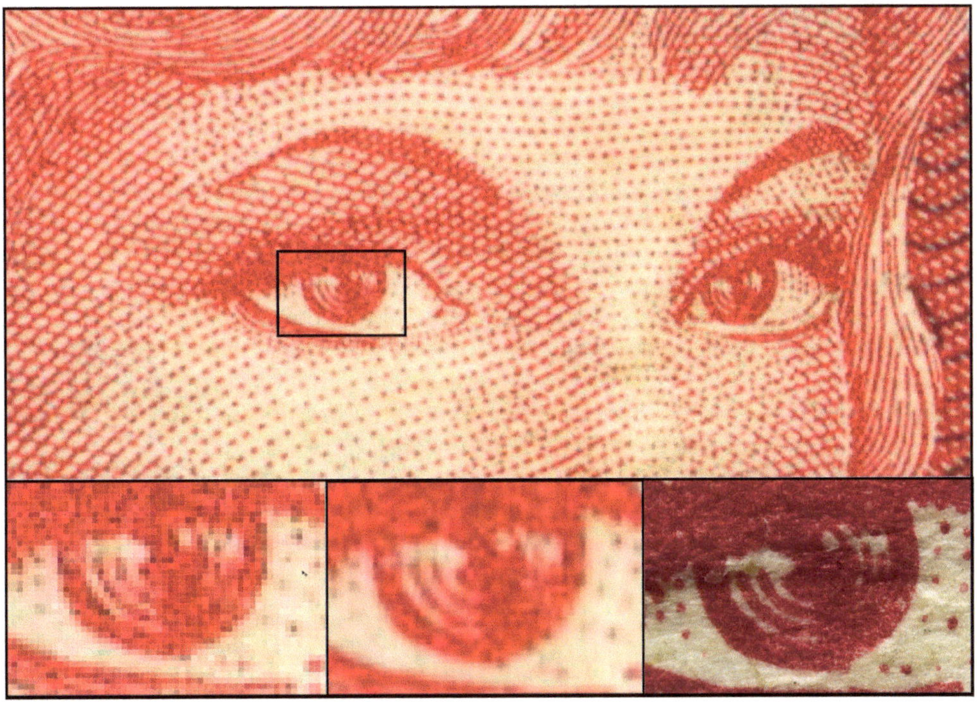

Figure 21.1 A comparison of images scanned on a CCD scanner at 600 ppi maximum optical resolution (left) and 2,400 ppi software interpolated resolution (center). Although the edges of the images appear smoother on the 2,400 ppi image, notice that they both have the same lack of fine detail, especially when compared to photomicrography (right) of the same area.

capture the image in raw image format. These files can be proprietary to a camera manufacturer; however, they all work in the same manner. The raw image file is the unprocessed data captured by the camera's image sensor at the time the photograph is captured. When compared to traditional film photography, this raw image is similar in concept to the negative.

21.1.3 Equipment

The transition to digital examinations brings with it some additional equipment requirements, particularly sufficient computing power to process large image files. When examining or comparing multiple images, the computer needs to have enough system memory, not only to accommodate large image files in excess of 1 GB in layered images, but also to run the operating system, the image editing software, and any other programs that may be running in the background. The addition of a performance processor will speed the execution of a task, but a performance Graphic Processing Unit (GPU) is not necessary for the types of comparisons usually conducted by the FDE. Its primary function is to assist the computer to process images with filters and 3D images. However, the addition of a discrete GPU can accelerate some image processing tasks, especially for 4k displays. The last equipment consideration is image storage. Large cases with multiple digital images can easily reach sizes of more than 1GB and up to 10 GB or more. FDEs conducting digital exams will need to decide on storage solutions that suit their environment, whether it is local storage, network storage, or return of the digital images to the submitter. If the FDE chooses to maintain local or network storage of examination images, it is beneficial to establish a retention schedule to keep from having to maintain a large amount of data in perpetuity.

21.2 DIRECT EXAMINATIONS

Direct examinations involve the use of image editing software to obtain a result that may not be visible to the FDE without the aid of editing software or other imaging equipment. When any image adjustments are made, it is important to follow best practices: Always conduct adjustments on a copy of the original image, work in nondestructive adjustment layers when possible, maintain the integrity representative of the original examination item, and document the steps taken in the history log to ensure results are demonstrable and repeatable. When processing an image, the goal is to clarify information that is in the image without changing the content.

A strength of image editing software is the ability to view and manipulate the different color channels of an image. These color channels consist of RGB (Red, Green, Blue), CMYK (Cyan, Magenta, Yellow, Black) and LAB (Luminance, a = green/red, b = blue/yellow). RGB color defines an intensity value of 0–255 for each color. The combination of the intensity values for each color channel can create up to 16.7 million colors. CMYK mode is primarily used in printing but can give an additional benefit in examining digital images because of the ability to render 100 million different colors. LAB color mode works by separating the color channels into a Lightness channel and two color channels that are independent of lightness. A way to imagine a color in LAB mode is to compare it to a 3-dimensional plot where the *a* channel is the x-coordinate, the *b* channel is the y-coordinate, and the lightness (*L*) channel is the z-coordinate. The ability to view colors in such a wide array allows the FDE an opportunity to visualize minor color differences that may not be readily visible or to eliminate colors that may be obscuring the examination item. We will make use of the properties of these various color spaces in the following examination techniques.

21.2.1 Background Color Removal

When an FDE encounters documents with interfering colors, such as checks with colored backgrounds or stamped impressions, it can be helpful to remove or isolate these colors. A simple method to accomplish this is to convert the image to the different color modes and view the separate color channels. Often, this is enough to separate the interfering colors. However, there are times when the colors may be too similar to separate with these broad methods. In these instances, the FDE should select the color channel in the color space that gives the best result, then use the channel mixer in an adjustment layer to fine-tune the selection.

21.2.2 Ink Differentiation

Some examinations require the FDE to attempt to differentiate inks, whether to determine if more than one writing ink was used to produce the writing in question or to visualize obliterated writing. One method is to use a video spectral comparator to attempt to separate the inks, using a combination of bandpass and barrier filters. However, when that method is unsuccessful, an image editor may be used to attempt to separate colors as they were recorded by a camera or scanner by use of LAB color mode.[3] This method expands the color channel to differentiate some inks and other obliterating substances and can be used to visualize writing that has faded or been obliterated.

21.2.3 Obliterated Writing

When altering the color values of an image does not work, the FDE can still use image editing software to visualize obliterated writing (for example, writing obliterated using the same writing instrument). In the following method, the FDE creates a layer mask that covers the obliteration with the color of the document background, leaving the obliterated writing to show through as demonstrated in Figure 21.2.

1. Open a working copy of a digital image containing the obliterated writing.
2. Create a new masking layer above the background layer.
3. Sample an area of the background color using the eyedropper tool.
4. Fill the masking layer with the color sampled from the background.
5. Change the transparency of the masking layer to 50% or less to allow the obliterated writing to be seen through the masking layer.
6. Set the brush width on the eraser tool to approximately the width of the written line.
7. Trace the obliterated written lines, words, and letters on the masking layer with the eraser tool.
8. Change the masking layer back to full opacity, and only the obliterated writing will be visible with the obliterations masked.
9. Save this layered document illustrating the visualized writing.

This same technique can be used to visualize erased writing that is difficult to see. After step 8, insert a new layer between the image layer and the masking layer, and fill this layer with a color that contrasts with the masking layer to visualize the erased writing.

Figure 21.2 The above entries illustrate how obliterations made with the same ink can be differentiated using layer masks. The top image shows the obliteration, the middle image shows the masking layer at 50% opacity, and the bottom image shows the obliteration completely masked at 100%.

21.2.4 Digital Examination of Charred Documents

This section will not explore the handling and preservation of charred documents but will instead focus on the examination of images captured during this process. Digital image examination of charred documents exploits the differences in the way materials react to heat. When exposed to heat, paper will blacken and become brittle. However, the inks on the document, being made of a different substance, normally will not behave the same as the paper. The paper can darken or char to black, but the inks on the document may char to a gray or blacken to a different shade of black than the paper substrate.

An effective method of visualizing machine printing or writing on charred paper is infrared photography. Infrared photography differentiates the ink from the paper by visualizing the difference in reflectance in the infrared spectrum. This can be done with a video spectral comparator or with an infrared camera, and the images can be quite clear. When this method does not work or provides less than optimal results, such as inks that become transparent when viewed in infrared, digital image processing may be able to visualize machine printing or writing present.

The digital imaging method used to visualize charred writing or machine printing relies on the previously mentioned difference in black values between the charred paper and the ink. For this task, the Levels adjustment tool in Adobe® Photoshop® can be used. Levels adjustment expands the tonal range between the black values of the charred document, increasing the contrast. The digitally captured image has brightness values between 0 (absolute black) and 255 (absolute white), but much of the image will be toward the zero end of the scale as the charred item is likely black. Using the Levels tool, we can remap the absolute black and white input values that are present to output values that allow the image to show more contrast between the black levels. When a Levels Adjustment layer is added, the histogram of a charred document (without

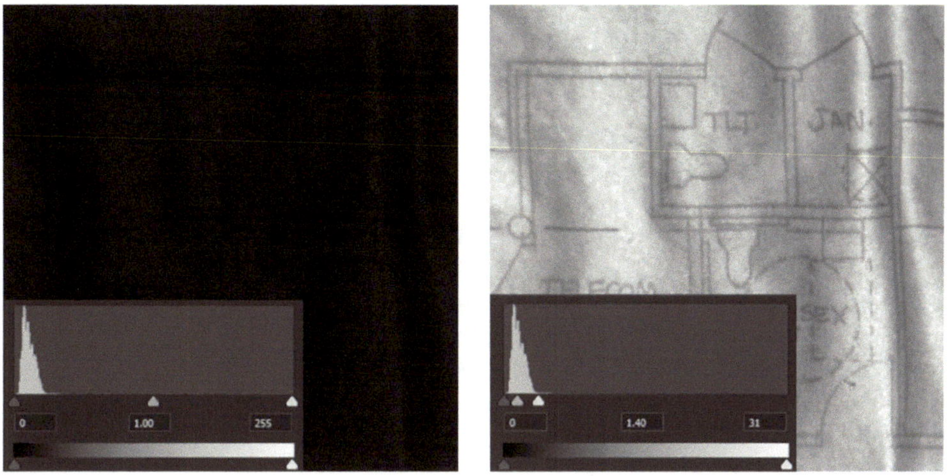

(a) (b)

Figure 21.3 The above images illustrate the histograms associated with the related images. In (a), the color values extend from 0 to 255. In (b), they extend from 0 to 31, creating more space between the black values.

any background visible) will appear as a steep slope that starts high in the black values (0) and descends steeply toward the white values (255) without reaching all the way to 255. If the sliders at the base of the histogram are adjusted inward toward the slope, the Levels tool will stretch the histogram slope, remapping the points designated as 0 and 255 respectively in the output levels and allowing the FDE to visualize the differences in black levels between the document and the writing or machine printing. Additionally, the gray value slider in the center can be moved left or right, compressing the black or white values for greater contrast (see Figure 21.3).

21.2.5 Deciphering Carbon Paper

Digital image processing is a modern solution to an old problem. Although the examination of carbon paper is infrequent, there is a process that will aid in the speed and accuracy of the examination. A scanned image of the carbon side of used carbon paper can be reversed to make the typing right-reading. Then the image is inverted to make the black area white and the typed entries black. The resulting image can be used to make the typing in the carbon paper easier to read and creates a good base layer for a digital overlay if it is to be compared to a typed document. A similar process can be used with carbon typing ribbons without the need to invert the image.

21.3 COMPARATIVE EXAMINATIONS

Much of an FDE's work involves the comparison of handwriting, and there are a couple of options to make this work more efficient. These options include Adobe® Photoshop® for building comparison charts and Pikaso's Write-On 3® software for conducting searches.

An effective way to create charts in Adobe® Photoshop® combines Adobe® Bridge® and Adobe® Photoshop®. Once the documents are scanned, the Batch Rename function can be used to name and consecutively number documents. Bridge® can then be used to Load Files into Photoshop® Layers. This will open a new Photoshop® canvas with all the selected images stacked in layers, preserving the original file name for each layer. Then the FDE crops the layers, preserving the writing, either one layer at a time if the writing is in different locations, or as an entire image stack if the writing is in the same location, such as request writing samples. With the writing appropriately cropped, the layers can be exported into individual files containing just the writing, preserving the layer name as the file name. Returning to Bridge®, the cropped writing can be combined into a handwriting chart using the output function. The result is a nicely formatted handwriting chart with each writing sample labeled with the original image name. With practice, handwriting charts can be created in this manner within a matter of minutes. These handwriting charts can be annotated in Adobe® Photoshop® or printed and marked up with a pen.

Write-On 3® is software specifically designed to assist the FDE in searches of writing samples for like characteristics to make handwriting comparisons more efficient. Scanned images of the writing to be compared is imported into the software where the user associates the image of the writing with typed text. Once all of the writing is associated, searches can be conducted of words, combinations of words, segments, and individual letters to ensure the FDE accounts for all instances of characteristics searched. Images from these searches can be exported to a comparison chart for further markup or as a demonstrative.

21.3.1 Overlays and Grids

Image editing software can be used to construct overlays for various types of comparison examinations encountered by the FDE. In the following examples, the images to be compared will be stacked as individual layers in Adobe® Photoshop® and rendered transparent by various means to allow lower layers to be visible through the upper layers, then aligned to conduct comparisons.

21.3.1.1 Changing Layer Opacity

In this method, the layered image file is created with the item(s) in question as the base layer, and the layer(s) of the comparison document(s) above. The opacity of the uppermost layers is adjusted to allow the lower layers to show through. A disadvantage of this method is that the comparison item becomes transparent also and may make the comparison more difficult.

21.3.1.2 Multiply Layer Blending Mode

Changing the blend mode for the upper image layers allows the base layer to show through. In this method, the layered image file is created with the item(s) in question as the base layer, and the layer(s) of the comparison document(s) above. In Adobe® Photoshop® the *Multiply* blend mode looks at the color information in the selected layer and blends it with the layer below. When the blend layer is white, it allows the lower layer to show through. This renders the white areas of a source document transparent, allowing the visible writing or machine printing to be aligned. This method is limited to documents that have a white or light-colored background. As the background of a document is not completely white, the blend mode can cause the slight darkness of the white values to build up over many layers and obscure areas of the base layer.

21.3.1.3 Layer Transparency

In this versatile method for comparing layered images, the layered image file is created with the item(s) in question as the base layer and the layer(s) of the comparison document(s) above. A layer mask of the comparison item is created by deleting all of the information in that layer that is not going to be compared, typically the background of the document. This method allows for the assembly of transparent layers for a wider range of test items. As the comparison areas are completely transparent, multiple image layers can be stacked without loss of transparency.

There are numerous comparisons that can benefit from digital image transparency methods outlined above.

21.3.2 Tracings and Copied Signatures

Image layer overlays can be an asset to illustrate a tracing or signatures that have been copied from another document. Using one of the methods listed above, the comparison signature(s) can be positioned over the questioned signature(s) to show precise alignment. In instances where the questioned signature has been resized, the comparison image can be transformed to resize the signature appropriately. If the questioned signature has been distorted, the comparison signature can be free transformed to align with the questioned signature. Caution should be exercised when distorting the comparison signature to align with the questioned signature to ensure that the change is applied to the signature as a whole, and not individual line segments. Applying the distortion to the whole signature mimics distortion that can occur during imaging or signature placement, whereas distorting individual characters and line segments reforms the signature and is an inappropriate use of this tool.

21.3.3 Typewriting

Digital layer overlay techniques can be used in a variety of typewriting exams, including alignment, font comparisons, damage comparisons, and ribbon/typeface/printed character comparisons. Digital layer overlays mimic the use of a comparison microscope, where the image of the questioned character/document is overlaid with the comparison character/document. Capturing an appropriate image is important when using digital overlays. A high-resolution scan can be used to illustrate similarities in margin settings, line spacing, font size, and can even be used as a screening tool for individual character comparisons. However, when conducting a final comparison of typeface damage, carbon ribbon fracture, or minor differences in type font design, the FDE should use photomicrographs of the comparison images taken at the same magnification. The process is the same for creating overlays, but the results will illustrate much finer detail for comparison and ensure the images have sufficient detail for a meaningful comparison.

21.3.4 Impression Comparisons

The comparison of impressions developed with an Electrostatic Detection Device (EDD) using digital image layers is an extension of the practice of comparing the physical transparent lift with the documents suspected of being the origin of the impressions.[4] In the physical comparison method, the impressions are developed with toner on transparent imaging film and encapsulated with a transparent fixing film. This encapsulation commonly called a *lift* is then overlaid on the document containing the writing, typing, or other markings thought to have imparted the impressions. While this works well for single-source impressions, it has some limitations. If the questioned document contains impressions from multiple sources, it may be difficult to keep track of and account for all of the impressions. Common practice is to make notations on a photocopy of the EDD lift. With extensive text or complex impressions, this can be labor intensive and difficult to achieve complete confidence in accounting for all impressions. Another limitation of this method is difficulty in decipherment of unsourced indentations intermingled with sourced impressions and embossing (developed images from the reverse of the document). A limitation of the physical overlay method is the possibility of cross contamination when comparing questioned items to other questioned items that will be processed for DNA. Research[5] has shown that cellular material on a document can adhere to the imaging film of an EDD lift. A physical overlay of an EDD lift from one questioned item with another questioned item could cross contaminate that item by introducing cellular material from one questioned item to another.

Closely mirroring the physical comparison method, a digital overlay is conducted by overlaying a transparent image of the comparison writing over a digital image of the impressions developed with EDD using one of the overlay methods described earlier. If there are multiple sources associated with one EDD image, multiple digital image layers can be stacked on top of the EDD image as the base layer. These layers can be color coded to associate impressions from the same source and rotated to show the orientation of the source writing when the impressions were imparted to the document. For a few layers with white backgrounds, the *multiply layer blending mode* method in Section 21.3.1.2 method works well. However, the *layer transparency* option described in Section 21.3.1.3 should be selected to overlay many layers.

Using multiple image layers to account for impressions of known writing will leave any unsourced impressions unaccounted for and easier to locate. These impressions can be highlighted with the brush tool on a separate layer for clarity, and if the unsourced impressions appear on other documents, this layer can be applied as an overlay to the EDD image to show a common source for the unsourced impressions.

21.3.4.1 Mask Embossing and Interfering Impressions

A slightly different approach to visualizing impressions is using digital image layers to mask embossed writing or interfering known impressions from unsourced impressions. In this method, the FDE creates a digital image transparency of the known writing and uses the Fill tool to paint the writing with a pattern of the EDD image background pattern. With the known writing or embossed impressions blending in with the EDD background pattern, the unsourced impressions can be more easily read (see Figure 21.4).

21.3.4.2 Recover Missing Pages

Building on the method to mask known writing and embossing, the same process can be used to recover information from a missing page in a journal, as an example. Writing from the front of the missing page may be impressed in the front of a succeeding page, and the writing on the back of the missing page may be impressed in the back of the preceding page. Therefore, if both pages before and after the missing page are processed with an EDD, and the interfering impressions and embossing are masked with digital image layers, the written text of the missing page may be read in its entirety.

21.3.4.3 Non-Contemporaneous Entries

Impressions developed with an EDD can show non-contemporaneous entries. An example is impressions that should align if they were purportedly entered in one sitting that do not align with the visible writing when overlaid. This misalignment of writings illustrates the document

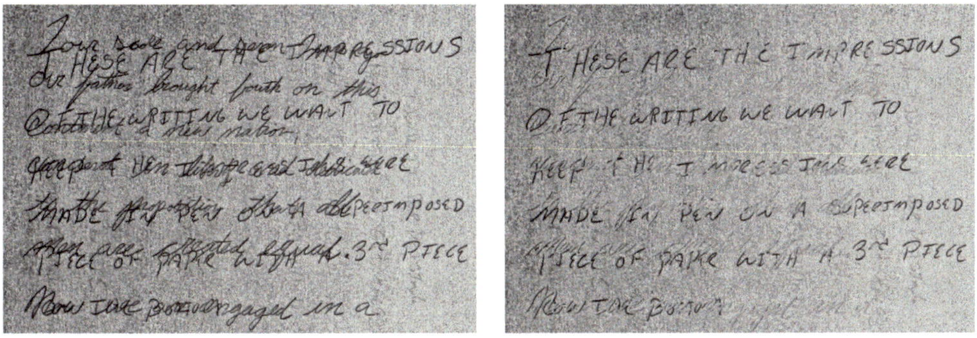

(a) (b)

Figure 21.4 (a) Developed EDD impressions with interfering indentations. A layer mask of the cursive writing from a document bearing visible writing was made from the background pattern of the EDD image. This layer mask was overlaid on the EDD impressions and conceals the interfering indentations, leaving the manuscript printing more easily deciphered, as seen in (b).

was repositioned before the entries, that are out of alignment, were made. A change of alignment can be demonstrated with digital image layers by making duplicate layers of the visible writing, rendering them transparent, and orienting individual layers to align with each change in alignment of the impressions. The individual layers can be turned on and off to show the changes in orientation or left transparent to show orientation relative to other layers.

21.3.5 Stamped Impression Comparisons

Like typewriter comparisons, stamped impression comparisons require high-resolution images for reliable results. When imaging the test items for comparison, the questioned and known items should be imaged with magnification, or macrophotography if the stamp is large. These images can be used to assemble an image overlay comparison using one of the methods previously described.

21.3.6 Photocopier/Printer Comparisons

Digital image overlay examinations of photocopiers and printers fall into two categories: the comparison of the printed image and the comparison of paper transport indentations. The comparison of the printed image uses digital image overlays to compare trash marks on questioned items to trash marks present on comparison items and a digital image of the glass platen of multifunction printers. To compare the trash marks, the images of the questioned item and comparison item can be overlaid with the comparison layer rendered partially transparent. The trash marks on the comparison item are aligned with the questioned item, and corresponding trash marks can be noted on a separate layer. The same overlay technique can be used for trash marks, trash mark constellations, and line marks.

Another comparison method is to overlay trash marks on the questioned item with a digital image of the glass platen or slit glass if the trash mark causing debris is still present. For this comparison, it is important to capture the images of the glass and the document containing the trash marks on the same plane at the same settings or to ensure that the questioned and comparison images are rendered as 1:1 (same size and resolution) images prior to conducting the overlay.

Digital image overlays of paper transport indentations can be done by comparing scanned EDD lifts or digitally photographed images of the developed EDD indentations. For this comparison, the FDE overlays the images and offsets them without rendering the comparison layers transparent. The digital images are then aligned along the paper transport indentations to illustrate how the various lines and markings correspond. This can also be illustrated by comparing the scanned or photographed EDD indentations to 1:1 images of the mechanical portions of the printer believed to be imparting the paper transport marks.

21.3.7 Altered Documents

The possibilities for the alteration of documents is limited only by the imagination. This section will attempt to cover the usage of digital image overlays for some of the more common methods that do not intersect with other methods previously described in this chapter.

Many types of alterations are accomplished by copy and paste of lines or signatures from a genuine document or by the addition of text or dates to alter the intent of the document. An indicator of this type of manipulation is that the added information does not conform with the formatting and alignment of other areas of the document. For a single page, the FDE can overlay a grid on the document to show any departure from alignment or margin formatting. For a precise display, the Ruler tool can be used to horizontally straighten the image. In the Photoshop® preference menu, the grid size should be changed to the same size as the document's vertical line spacing. The measurements for the grids can be inches, centimeters, millimeters, points, picas, percent, or pixels. Selecting *Show Grid* from the *View* menu displays a grid on the document. This grid cannot be saved as a layer with the document, but a screen capture will preserve an image showing the grid and the portions of the document that are not in alignment.

In a multipage document, a digital image overlay using one of the previously described methods can be created to show where areas of the questioned document may differ in horizontal alignment or margin formatting from the rest of the document.

Some additional methods of comparison to demonstrate alterations are digital image overlays of staple holes or other binding devices or markings and overlays of text size or font changes using one of the overlay methods listed previously.

21.4 DEMONSTRATIVES

Digital examinations lend themselves to dynamic court demonstratives. Most courts have the ability to show digital demonstratives, whether on a projector or large screen televisions. A common way to display demonstratives is with the use of Microsoft PowerPoint® presentations. While this is a good tool for demonstratives, the FDE needs to plan accordingly.

Each slide should be numbered and labeled with case information to ensure that printed versions are presented in their entirety. Also, to ensure that printed versions are representative of the presented slides, image transitions or animations that obscure an image or information should be avoided. Each item depicted should be labeled with item numbers and exhibit numbers if they are known in advance. When adding images, they should be properly sized to see the characteristics being explained from a distance. Screen captures of images can be added to the slide instead of importing full resolution images. This will help to keep the presentation size manageable. The format of the presentation should be considered. The 16:9 (widescreen) format is the default format for modern monitors and projectors, but many courts may still have older 4:3 (standard) format projectors. If the presentation is created in 16:9 format, and the court displays it in 4:3 format, the presentation will be laterally compressed, and the presentation can be negatively affected.

If the size of the presentation is prohibitive to being sent by email, providing the document using cloud storage or on physical media (e.g. flash drive, optical disc) can be considered. If the presentation is provided on physical media, it should be noted that many modern notebook computers no longer have an optical drive. Also, the FDE may need to surrender the physical media to the court as an exhibit, so it may be beneficial to use inexpensive media.

21.4.1 Live Demonstrations

Many methods discussed in this chapter are conducive to live presentations. When explaining how writing impressions are sourced to multiple documents, it is informative to show the overlay images. Likewise, when the FDE is explaining similarities or dissimilarities of writing characteristics, displaying searches in Write-On 3 ® can be equally powerful. These options have some special requirements for the FDE to consider if being used as a live demonstration.

To do a live demonstration of a digital image overlay or a character search, the FDE will need to bring his or her own computer to ensure the appropriate software is present and that the computer has sufficient resources to process complex images. This also requires that the computer is able to interface with multiple displays, including HDMI, DVI, and RGB.

When creating digital image demonstratives, the same overlays and comparisons used to form the conclusions should be used. The FDE must be able to explain the steps taken to create the visual comparisons, including how the images were captured, the tools used to process the images, how the tools work, and how the images are representative of the evidence as it was submitted. If the questioned evidence existed in digital format only, the FDE should be prepared to demonstrate how the underlying evidentiary image is unchanged and how any information developed is through the use of nondestructive image layers.

When conducting live character searches in Write-On 3®, practice beforehand is necessary to ensure the results display appropriately. How the characters are associated and how the searches are conducted needs to be explained. Also, the opposing counsel may request additional searches and to know what the potential results of those searches will reveal.

Finally, it is recommended that extra copies of the demonstratives be made in case they need to be provided to the opposing counsel or entered as an exhibit.

21.5 CONCLUSION

In our modern society, physical documents are being replaced by digital representations of documents. This is also true in document comparisons. Where comparisons used to rely on trying to explain notes and precise measurements to demonstrate similarity or dissimilarity, digital image comparisons can quickly and easily demonstrate these characteristics visually. Using digital image examinations and comparisons that conform to best practices and forensically acceptable techniques, the FDE can have confidence that the methods used in the physical examination of questioned documents can be replicated using digital images and, at times, provide superior results.

REFERENCES

1. ASTM International Standard Guide E2765-11. "Standard for Use of Image Capture and Storage Technology in Forensic Document Examination," ASTM, West Conshohocken, PA, 2003.
2. ASTM International Standard Guide E2825-19. "Standard Guide for Forensic Digital Image Processing," ASTM, West Conshohocken, PA, 2003.
3. Hammond, Derek. "Validation of LAB Color Mode as a Nondestructive Method to Differentiate Black Ballpoint Pen Inks." *Journal of Forensic Sciences*, vol. 52, no. 4 (July 2007): 967–973.
4. ANSI/ASB Standard 044. "Standard for Examination of Documents for Indentations, First Edition," ASB, Colorado Springs, CO, 2019.
5. Holt, Melanie J. "Sequencing ESDA Examinations with the Recovery of Trace DNA from Questioned Documents." Master's thesis, University of Canberra, 2013.

Chapter 22

Computational Analysis of Documents

Timothy A. Campbell

CONTENTS

22.1 INTRODUCTION

Artificial intelligence (AI) is a general term that encompasses all means in which a computer uses modern methods to not just execute a specific action that a programmer has decided, but to teach itself how to conduct a task. Thus, the computer learns sometimes in the way a human might. The scenario portrayed in popular media, such as C-3PO of Star Wars, Data of Star Trek: TNG, or HAL 9000 of 2001, is a general AI, one that would mirror human thought in all aspects. But this is not yet a reality and so not the type of AI that is applicable in the forensic context. Instead, specific AI that is task-dependent is of import. A particular action is desired with an expected outcome, and the task required to achieve that outcome is learned and conducted.

The insertion of AI presence into our daily lives has been seemingly innocuous, through mobile devices, streaming music and video services, and self-driving cars. But it can also be found in our professional lives. AI is now being used to determine which records are used as evidence in litigation and even being tested for use as a replacement for the trier-of-fact, the judge, in low-level cases.[1]

Just as previous human generations have undergone technological revolutions in the modern age, so too are we currently faced with inevitable change. As society progresses through technologies, the FDE has kept pace through means of training and research and adapted from the steel nib

TABLE 22.1 ADVANCES IN TECHNOLOGY (INCLUSION DOES NOT NECESSARILY IMPLY THE INVENTION OF A PARTICULAR TECHNOLOGY, BUT ITS EXPANSION AND PROLIFERATION)

Revolution	Time Range	FDE-Relevant Technologies
1st	1760 to c. 1840	Fourdrinier machine, graphite pencil
2nd	Late 19th to WWI	Electrification, typewriter, telegraph, wood-based paper, fountain pen
3rd	c. 1950s to present	Transistor, digital computing, desktop printer, email, internet
4th	Present to beyond	AI, 3D printing, robotics, nanotechnology, quantum computing

dip pens and iron gall ink of the past to the toner or inkjet printing of the present (see Table 22.1). Advances in imaging have likewise changed from film-based to digital capture. This has affected the way evidence is presented in court, from a large comparison chart on an easel to a real-time display of related handwriting associations on the court's television system.

Machine assistance in the forensic examination of documents began in the 1980s, when FDEs began discussing methods of analysis with computer programmers in Pattern Recognition (PR). Initial attempts were made to use live video sources to image documents and were met with limited success. In 1998, Lecun et al.'s work on the MNIST database with Convolutional Neural Networks was a turning point, leading to much new research done on handwriting.[2,3] Figure 22.1 depicts an example from the database. Significant advancements were made by researchers in the early 2000s, coinciding with the rise of commonplace digital imaging, big data (the internet), and more recently with the massive increase in computer power available.

In 2020, digital imaging sensors have matured and become advanced enough to capture images that far exceed that of film-based photography in the past. Not only has the quality of imaging increased, but also has the rate and ease at which imaging may be done such that it becomes feasible to acquire gigabytes of imagery within a single examination case. What to do with all this imagery? Possible future uses of machine learning could be specific applications for examination of handwriting, machine printing identification, CPS codes identification and decipherment, photocopier trash marks, etc. The value of such assistance would be best seen in very large cases or across disparate cases to obtain forensic intelligence.

Figure 22.1 Instances of the numeral *8* from the MNIST dataset.[4]

Academically, basic research could support fundamental axioms, such as "no two people write alike," by allowing a computer to process large amounts of data that would otherwise require an inordinate number of person-hours to analyze. The former facet has been met with success only recently. The latter facet remains elusive, and this is where the true expertise of the forensic expert lies. As such, it is not expected that the expert analyses conducted by the FDE would be supplanted by AI but augmented. Menial repetitive tasks are perfect for automation, and an AI could possibly function in a triage role, selecting likely contenders for examination that are then passed on to the FDE to conduct the in-depth evaluation. While this may not be required for a case with a small number of items submitted, it could be a boon for the examination of large, complex cases such as those found in revenue or transnational organized crime files.

As far as the application to non-handwriting examinations, machine learning begins to approach that of other domains such as identification of dog breeds from images or diagnoses of malignant tumors in radiograms. As such, identification of print processes, latent handwriting impressions, or printer make and model determination are only the tip of the iceberg.[5] However, as with handwriting, it is one thing to identify a method of production or technology used, it is quite another to interpret what that might mean in a legal context.

Other uses include digital archiving of historical writings (e.g. the READ project),[6] optical character recognition (OCR) and post-OCR verification, correction of geometric distortion, torn document reconstruction (DARPA Shredder Challenge),[7] and forensic intelligence.

In June 2019, the District Attorney for San Francisco, California, announced that prosecutors would be implementing an algorithm developed at the Stanford Computational Policy Lab to mitigate bias derived from police reports, prior to charges being laid, by way of redacting any racial context that might taint impartiality in the decision as to whether or not to lay charges.[8,9] Such a tool could easily be extended into the forensic realm to aid in the masking, and later sequential unmasking, of possibly-biasing information within a case, upstream before the forensic scientist encounters it.

22.2 MACHINE LEARNING

AI is an umbrella term that includes machine learning and within that, in turn, we find discrete algorithms as well as the technique called Deep Learning, whereby a computer figures out its own way of reaching a conclusion rather than being explicitly programmed how to do so by a discrete algorithm.

22.2.1 Visualizations

Principal Component Analysis (PCA) and t-Stochastic Node Embedding (t-SNE) are techniques to visualize data that use a dimensionality reduction technique. That means they can take high dimensional (multivariate) data, of which handwriting and document examination has in abundance, and distill it down to low dimensionality, simplifying the data for understanding. PCA has been used for thin layer chromatography (TLC) of pen ink in 2008 and in the hyperspectral analysis of written ink lines.[10] In 2018, researchers used t-SNE to analyze the spectra from the nondestructive Raman analysis of the CMY components of inkjet printed documents in order to generate a distinctive chemical signature.[11]

22.2.2 Predictive Coding

Predictive Coding (PC) is a machine learning technique that has been used in e-disclosure/e-discovery of massive legal case files. With a government or large corporation possessing a wealth of electronically stored information on their servers (such as word processing documents, spreadsheets, emails, databases, and media files), the task of producing relevant documents to a legal team is a daunting task for humans to sort though. For instance, email is 90% of corporate communications now, but because an email chain can consist of the same message repeated any number of times, only one instance of each message is required to obtain the textual information it contains for disclosure. Using PC, the volume of redundant information is reduced through deduplication, redundancy suppression, and data filters, greatly simplifying the effort required by humans involved. A lawyer can train the algorithm on a small batch of documents (4,500–6,000) which takes upwards of a week's time. Afterward, the computer does all the work, achieving a 98%–99% accuracy while humans are only 60%–70% accurate. The threshold for PC is around 50,000 documents, so a lawyer working on only 6,000 documents at most is a significant saving. The limitations of PC are that the documents must be text-based, so non-OCR'd images are not of use, and there must be a clear understanding of relevant information. On February 16, 2016, Master Matthews of England approved its use for a disclosure of some 3 million documents.[12]

What this means to the FDE is that if there are digitized scans of documents, then pertinent forensic information may be overlooked and excluded. The FDE could ask if such a process was used upstream before case receipt in order to understand the context of the documents being examined.

22.2.3 Deep Learning and Neural Networks

Deep learning is a class of machine learning that deals with the ability of a computer to learn, that is, to teach itself a new previously unknown task, as opposed to the above-mentioned methods which are designed and task-specific.[13]

Learning of a neural network (NN) may be supervised, whereby a human assists the NN by directing its learning, or it may be unsupervised, in which it is unassisted or unlabeled, or a combination thereof. In supervised learning, the ability to classify data is the goal, whereas in unsupervised learning, pattern analysis is achieved by the computer, though what that pattern is may be difficult to express. For instance, one might wish to know how many groups exist in a dataset, even if the meaning of the groups is unknown.

Beginning in the mid-2010s, the PR community focused on documents began seriously working on newer methods involving artificial NNs, leaving the previously used attempts of task-specific models and classifiers behind. An NN is inspired by the low-level synaptic connections of neurons in the human brain, produced virtually in the computer. As such, an NN can begin very simply and progress to something very complex.

Training always involves using a set of data, learning what it is that is of interest in that data, then testing what the NN has learned on a test set of data. After the NN has been verified to operate within acceptable parameters, it may be employed in analysis of actual data. This is very similar to how the standard FDE training program is conducted. The FDE begins training, is tested on what he or she has learned, then is permitted to conduct casework.

An NN works in a nonlinear layered structure such that an Input Layer (questioned item) produces an Output Layer (conclusion) by way of multiple Hidden Layers (analyses and comparisons) in between.[14] Each successive layer uses the output from the previous layer as input for the next. Like a black box, data is fed into it at the start, and a result is reached by way of various processes that may or may not be knowable. This is similar to the process an FDE uses to come to a conclusion but using different criteria (see Figure 22.2). Although FDEs may be called on to explain how they arrived at a conclusion, it is oftentimes a very simplified explanation of a much more complex process. An NN has similar complexity in its hidden layers.

Backpropagation is the core function behind how NNs learn. It allows an NN to calculate the difference between an actual outcome (i.e. conclusion) in a run of a single set of training data and the expected outcome of the ground truth. By nudging the weights and biases through repetitive training, the NN increases its accuracy with the expected outcome by averaging the cost of all those adjustments.

A large dataset is required for training to ensure accuracy, and in order for that to be done, the ground truth is required within that dataset. So real people are initially required to identify what the expected outcome is for each datum so that the NN has something to work toward. The MNIST database of handwritten digits is just such a database and has been used by academics to research handwriting recognition since 1998.[14] A large set of handwritten digits have been identified, isolated to one digit per image. In such a scenario, a single image is the "unknown" input layer, and the output layer is the conclusion of which value, 0–9, is represented.

If the input layer is the pixels' values of the input image, each pixel value is an activation, and the activations in one layer determine the activations in the next layer, from the input to the output. This is analogous to how some biological neurons in the human brain cause other neurons to fire. The path between layers and activations is weighted, determined by the NN. If an erroneous

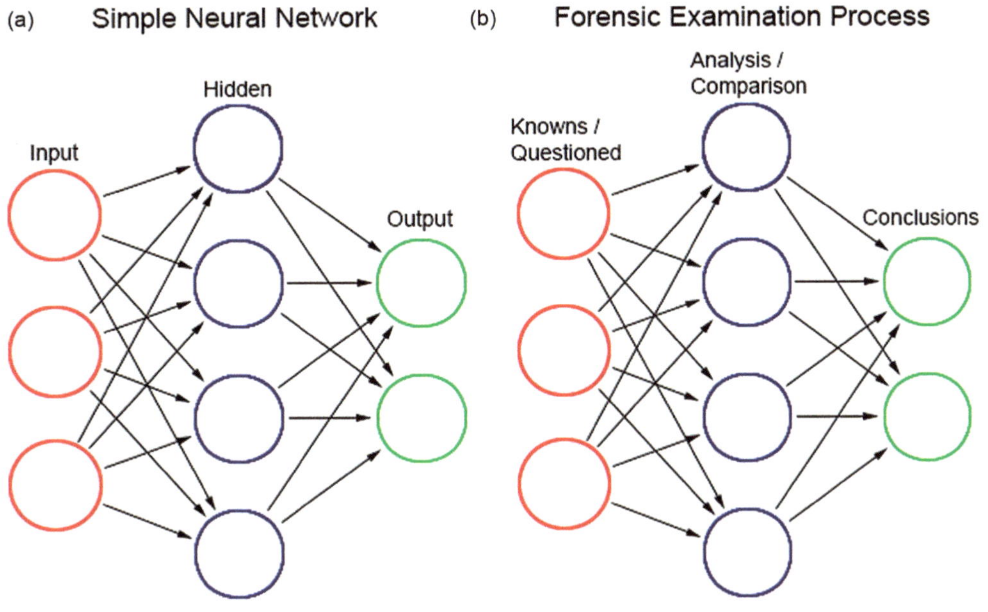

Figure 22.2 An NN (a) operates in a roughly analogous manner to that of the examination process (b), multiple layers (illustrated here in columns of same-colored circles) are in operation in each scenario. There are inputs (evidence and exemplars), work done (analysis), and outputs (conclusions in a report). The middle layers in each paradigm are fairly opaque to the outside observer, but can be probed if required, such as explanatory text in a report, or courtroom testimony. In an NN, they are generally the hidden layers and unseen.

(a)

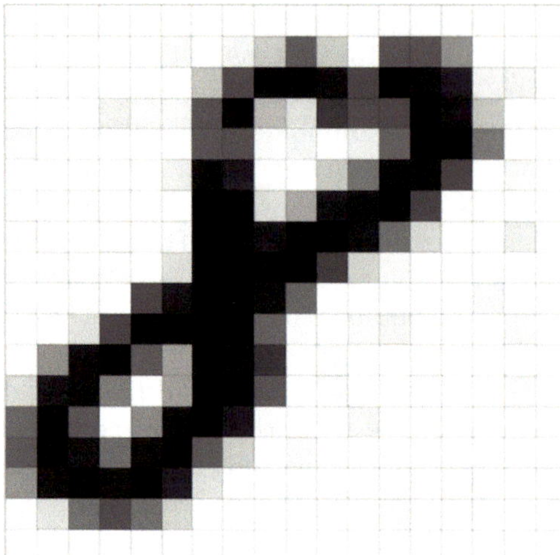

(b)

0	0	0	0	0	0	0	0	0	0	0	0	0	0	0	0	0	0
0	0	0	0	1	12	0	11	39	137	37	0	152	147	84	0	0	0
0	0	1	0	0	0	41	160	250	255	235	162	255	238	206	11	13	0
0	0	0	16	9	9	150	251	45	21	184	159	154	255	233	40	0	0
10	0	0	0	0	0	145	146	3	10	0	11	124	253	255	107	0	0
0	0	3	0	4	15	236	216	0	0	38	109	247	240	169	0	11	0
1	0	2	0	0	0	253	253	23	62	224	241	255	164	0	5	0	0
6	0	0	4	0	3	252	250	228	255	255	234	112	28	0	2	17	0
0	2	1	4	0	21	255	253	251	255	172	31	8	0	1	0	0	0
0	0	4	0	163	225	251	255	229	120	0	0	0	0	0	11	0	0
0	0	21	162	255	255	254	255	126	6	0	10	14	6	0	0	9	0
3	79	242	255	141	66	255	245	189	7	8	0	0	5	0	0	0	0
26	221	237	98	0	67	251	255	144	0	8	0	0	7	0	0	11	0
125	255	141	0	87	244	255	208	3	0	0	13	0	1	0	1	0	0
145	248	228	116	235	255	141	34	0	11	0	1	0	0	0	1	3	0
85	237	253	246	255	210	21	1	0	1	0	0	6	2	4	0	0	0
6	23	112	157	114	32	0	0	0	0	2	0	8	0	7	0	0	0
0	0	0	0	0	0	0	0	0	0	0	0	0	0	0	0	0	0

Figure 22.3 An enlargement of a numeral *8* from the MNIST set (a). The greyscale intensity value of each pixel from 0 to 255 is shown, 0 being white and 255 being black (b).[4]

outcome is achieved, the NN will adjust the weighting of each path separately until a correct result is obtained. Once that is done to a satisfactory level, the NN is considered "trained," and the unknown test data can then be analyzed.[15]

The values in Figure 22.3 comprise an input node of the NN. The output would be a value describing the probability that the input either is, or is not, an *8*. The brightness of each pixel in the image is a pattern of activations that causes some pattern in the activations in the next layer (a hidden layer). This occurs again in a successive hidden layer and again finally in the output layer where the brightest neuron is the NN's choice of ten possibilities (digits 0–9). This is a very simple example of how a NN can recognize a single handwritten digit. It is a much more complex task to extend this further to the determination of writership of a handwritten sample.

22.2.4 Uses and Limitations

Computational science excels at multivariate analyses such as handwriting examination, which is composed of multiple features: letter designs, slant, skill, fluency, alignment, proportions, among others.

Machine learning (ML) is especially suited to the analyses of large volumes of multivariate data, such as large, complex cases that might be seen in a long-term financial investigation. There are others that are not, such as small cases of only a few items that are easily done by a human expert. But when cases become large or incredibly complex, ML may have a role to play to assist the effort of the FDE.

It should be noted that disguise was rarely considered to be a relevant factor by PR researchers. In addition, test datasets are generally quite clean, with text isolated from the background and with good contrast, unidirectional writing, lack of overwriting, and so on. Actual casework is dirty and presents many additional problems for PR researchers to overcome, not the least of which is originality of a document. So, ML success does not equal expert human analysis to date, but for how long? A groundswell of research has arisen, with many people interested in the technical details but without consideration of regulation and oversight in AI research. Decisions made by algorithms are much less transparent than those by humans because the logic of the algorithm cannot easily be discerned. To the outsider, it is a black box of data coming in and, hopefully, the correct result going out.

22.3 ORGANIZATIONS, CONFERENCES, AND MEETINGS

The *International Association of Pattern Recognition (IAPR)* is the overarching organization that coordinates researchers across many domains of PR. Within the IAPR are technical committees, and it is TC-11 (Reading Systems) that deals with the computer recognition of documents.[16] There are three primary conferences that the TC-11 organizes:

The *International Conference on Document Analysis and Recognition (ICDAR)* meets in alternating odd years and sees attendance of over 400 participants. ICDAR is the larger meeting and encompasses the researchers of both handwriting and non-handwriting (i.e. document) domains.

The *International Conference on the Frontiers of Handwriting Recognition (ICFHR)* meets in alternating even years and is more focused on the handwriting domain.

Document Analysis Systems (DAS) meets in alternating even years and is the reciprocal of ICFHR in that its focus is only on the document domain.

Handwriting recognition is a staple area of research, with minor inroads made into writer identification, which remains elusive. In terms of research conducted into document analysis (i.e. non-handwriting), there is a wealth of work done, including a worldwide effort to digitize and make searchable the historical volumes of archives and libraries.

The *Automated Forensic Handwriting Analysis (AFHA)* team was a group of PR researchers who were organized by FDEs acting in guidance for a forensic context. Involving FDEs from the Netherlands Forensic Institute (NFI) and Canada Border Services Agency (CBSA), the AFHA attended meetings coinciding with ICDAR conferences and once with the American Society of Questioned Document Examiners (Honolulu, 2014).

Two meetings, in 2007 and 2009, preceded the AFHA proper, which then met in Beijing, China (2011) and continued until Nancy, France (2015). Researchers participated in competitions prior to the meeting and then presented their results. In some cases, results reached the ability of a human examiner, but only with sterilized datasets that did not take simulation or disguise into account. Unfortunately, the AFHA ceased meeting before these variables could be tackled with fervor.

The US National Institute of Standards and Technology (NIST) held *the Measurement Science and Standards in Forensic Handwriting Analysis Conference* over June 4–5, 2013, which was well attended by FDEs and academic researchers.[17] Presentations were given by many originators and collaborators of the software described later in this chapter. John Paul Jones II presided over the meeting and discussed the proliferation, or lack thereof, of analytical software tools in practical use. Few FDE laboratories were likely to have investigated such programs, let alone use them in live casework. About this time, NIST was forming the Organization of Scientific Area Committees (OSAC) to spur interdisciplinary discussion in the forensic community and to identify areas for research and facilitate the development of standards.

TABLE 22.2 HANDWRITING DATASETS (THE TERMS *ONLINE* AND *OFFLINE* AS USED IN THE PR COMMUNITY REFER TO THE TERMS *DIGITAL* AND *PHYSICAL* IN THE CONTEXT OF WRITINGS AS USED BY FDES)

Dataset Name	Description
4NSigComp2009	NFI Online and NFI Offline DBs
4NSigComp2010	1 author test, 7 contestants, 2006 Latrobe University Set (first publicly available with disguised signatures)
4NSigComp2011	Dutch and Chinese signature sets, online and offline
4NSigComp2012	3 author tests, 5 contestants, 2001/2004/2005 Latrobe University sets
SIGWICOMP2013	Dutch and Japanese Sets
DIBCO2013	Dataset of 8 handwritten docs, 8 machine printed docs
SIGWICOMP2015	Bengali and Italian offline signatures, German online signatures, English handwriting
SIGCOMP2019	Online and offline Hungarian signatures

22.4 COMPETITIONS AND TEST DATASETS

The PR research community generally operates by running competitions of all kinds (i.e. recognition of cursive, printing, numerals, signatures, different scripts), whereby competitors will be presented with a dataset for training and testing an algorithm (see Table 22.2). Such datasets are generally digital and easily accessible on the internet.

One of the earliest and most interesting datasets to FDEs is the MNIST (Modified NIST) dataset. It is a composite dataset of numerals aggregated by Yann LeCun in 1998. It includes two earlier datasets compiled by NIST in 1995. One was a training set with handwriting taken from American Census Bureau employees, and the other was a test set taken from high school students. To adapt them for a machine learning environment, LeCun mixed the two sets and then created a combined set that did not separate the different groups of writers. MNIST now has a training set of 60,000 examples and a test set of 10,000 samples. All samples have been normalized to represent one numeric digit per 28×28 pixel grayscale image.[18]

The FDE community can be a great resource for providing expertise and datasets with forensic relevance. FDEs can draw from the datasets for training and testing purposes as well. The datasets that PR researchers have worked with in the past have been of low quality, much lower than what an FDE would typically encounter in casework. This is one area where a dialogue between the FDE and PR researcher could improve the quality of datasets. Other issues include adding a variety of document types, varying levels of copy quality, and color vs. grayscale.

22.5 SOFTWARE

Below are synopses of various software programs that are geared toward FDE examinations, primarily in the realm of handwriting. Inclusion here does not imply that the software has been properly evaluated, but the information is provided so that an FDE can investigate the software's efficacy.

Write-On is a Windows-based program designed specifically for FDEs by Pikaso Software of Ottawa, Canada. Written by Pierre Gaudreault, it was initiated and developed with close FDE

TABLE 22.3 TIMELINE OF WRITE-ON SOFTWARE RELEASES

Month/Year	Version
Approx. 1997	Write-On conceived
Early 2000	Write-On v1 release date, simple image display only
November 2007	Write-On v2 release date, added indexes, charting (reports), 300 ppi images and comparison
October 2018	Write-On v3 release date, added use of full-resolution TIFFs, notetaking, UNICODE multiple script support enabling Arabic, Chinese, Cyrillic, Greek, Hebrew, Japanese, etc., backwards compatibility with v2

Source: Gaudrealt, P., 2019. Write-On 3 change log and personal communications.

input.[19] Write-On contains no machine learning capability at present, but it is discussed here amongst such advanced methods because of its tailored utility for the FDE (see Table 22.3).

Currently in its version 3 iteration, Write-On is a powerful application that the FDE can use to assist in the examination of not only handwriting but all other aspects of document examination as well. At its heart, Write-On is a sophisticated method of tagging or labeling regions of interest in images and arranging those regions of interest (ROI) in juxtaposition through indexed searching (see Figure 22.4).

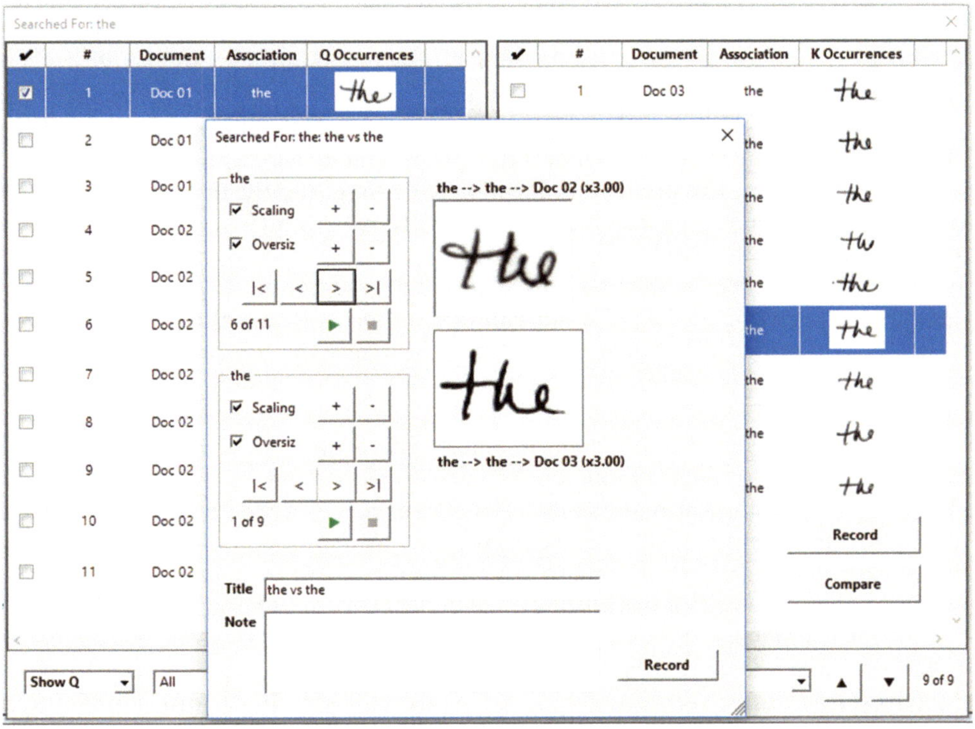

Figure 22.4 Each instance of a word in Write-On v3 can be displayed for an on-screen side-by-side comparison. Statistics of indexed writing can be used to determine frequency of occurrence.

Despite the name, Write-On can be used by the FDE for more than just handwriting examinations. As it is an image tagging program that can extract a document element and juxtapose it with one from another document, it can also be used for signatures, hand stamp impressions, dry seals, and typescript. In Logographic Mode, each character can be independently associated to a single transcribed character. This is a powerful tool for pulling out each instance of a typed or printed character.[19] The mode was created with the intention to be used on scripts like Chinese characters, but typescript can benefit in the same way for a typographic comparison. Using the Features filter, a document may be labeled with any term (e.g. "magnetic toner" or "rubber stamp") that is not associated with any written text on the item so that it may be searched for among large numbers of documents for a non-handwriting-based comparison

Write-On is used as a demonstrative aid in courtrooms by interfacing with existing viewing monitors when present. Due to the indexing of all typed text, it is possible to determine the presence of any desired letter or word, thus producing accurate statistics of the total occurrence found within the set of documents. As live searching for comparable forms is a quick task, the need for poster-sized courtroom charts that FDEs have used in the past can be dispensed with.

Masquerade is currently offered by Natural Intelligent Technologies (N.I.Te) in Italy. It bears some minor similarity to Write-On but employs some machine learning in that it automatically segments words into individual units and measures handwriting features, including dynamic movement. This includes a skeletonized wireframe of the writing stroke direction and continuity, as well as air strokes (pen lifts), much as an FDE would do in the course of a traditional microscopic examination. After completion of the analysis, a report that details measurements such as spacing, proportions, and slant for both a single word and a whole document can be generated.[20]

CedarFox is an application that was developed in conjunction with the US Postal Service (USPS) to recognize handwritten addresses on envelopes so that letters and parcels may be automatically routed to the correct destination. Such a format is highly structured because an address tends to only contain certain information, is ordered in a logical fashion, and is located on the face of the envelope in a predictable location. This simplifies the task, relatively speaking, and leads to high accuracy rates meeting or exceeding those of humans, where the sole purpose is to recognize and read the handwriting.[21]

The Center of Excellence for Document Analysis and Recognition (CEDAR) is located at the State University of New York (SUNY), Buffalo campus and led by Dr. Sargur Srihari. Srihari noted that a trained and skilled FDE could be expected to exceed the limitations of the CedarFox software when documents contain unstructured writing, as is commonly seen in casework documents.

iFox (Interactive Forensic Examination) is a 2013 follow-up work that involved FDE input and sought to associate numeric probabilities to the observations made by the FDE.[22] While CedarFox is devoted to the Latin alphabet/script, *CedArabic* was produced to conduct similar examinations of handwritten text in Arabic script.

Forensic Language Independent Analysis System for Handwriting Identification (Flash ID) by Gannon Technologies (now Sciometrics, LLC) of the US was developed in close collaboration with the FBI. It is language- and script-independent because it breaks down characters into graphemes, the components that make up a single character. It measures nearly 200 features, including distances, edges, vertex angles, and curvature. It uses linear discriminant analysis (LDA) to determine which features are most relevant to describe the writer's habit. The statistics from a document are used to compare against a reference database and retrieve similar pieces of writing, ranked using a likelihood ratio approach.[23]

Development of the *Forensisches Informations System Handschriften (FISH)* by the German Bundeskriminalamt (BKA, Wiesbaden) began in 1975.[24] It was deployed for active use by 1990 and was adapted by the US Secret Service to examine threatening letters sent to government officials. FISH operates on a standalone database, isolated from other installations, and searches for similar handwriting across documents based on extracted handwriting features using either automatic or interactive modes. In the latter, six descriptors are used: height, width, slant, ascenders, descenders, and loops.[25] In 1997, FISH contained 77,000 documents in its database. The underlying algorithm of FISH has also been adapted for use with automatic classification and identification of typescript with the system *Automatische Klassifizierung und Identifizierung von Maschinenschriften (AKIM)*.[26]

Development of *WANDA* from 2002 to 2005 was led by Katrin Franke at the Fraunhofer Institute (FHI), with collaboration from the German (BKA), Netherlands (NFI), and US governments. It involved contributors from more than ten organizations[27] and was intended to be a replacement for FISH. The name WANDA is a tribute to the movie *A Fish Called Wanda*. WANDA took a whole-case approach to FDE in that it proposed to not only invoke measurement of handwriting and elements of ML into the examination but also conduct administrative tasks such as report writing, data storage, and allow clients network access to their case. WANDA is no longer in development.

22.6 OPTICAL CHARACTER RECOGNITION

Optical Character Recognition (OCR) is used to convert scanned hardcopy documents into editable and searchable digital documents. It has been a mainstay in the digitization of typed documents since the 1980s and has become quite robust as newer algorithms are developed and become more accurate.[28] However, it should not be confused with Handwriting Recognition (i.e. text that is not typed), which is a much more recent issue tackled.

The first method for OCR is based on Matrix Matching, whereby a scanned image of text is compared to a stored glyph via PR. The second is Feature Extraction, where a glyph is reduced to lines, loops, stroke direction, and intersections, increasing the efficiency of the process. The nearest match to a stored vector-based glyph is then chosen.[25]

Character substitution has been observed on some photocopiers. For example, in the process of scanning to PDF on the Xerox WorkCenter 7545, one character was mistaken for another character during the JBIG2 compression phase of OCR. This happened with *stress* documents, those of low quality that push the limits of the scanning system.[29]

To increase the accuracy of OCR, the scanned document should be at least 300 dpi, 50% brightness with good contrast, exhibit little to no skewing, and in RGB if it is an older degraded document. Other factors affecting OCR accuracy are older texts, inconsistent typeface/font, and damage to the paper.

22.6.1 OCR Software Applications

Adobe Acrobat Pro is a pervasive PDF creation program that is available, with cost, for all common computing platforms. It has OCR ability upon scanning or after the PDF has been created. The ubiquitous Acrobat Reader is free to use but does not contain OCR capability.

ABBYY FineReader is an OCR system available since 1991, available for Windows and Mac computers, that can recognize and process 190 languages, with full dictionary support for

48 languages. It has been implemented into many commercial and desktop scanners/copiers, even smartphones, for seamless OCR of freshly scanned files in popular formats like PDF and MSWord.

Tesseract operates as a command-line interface for Mac, Windows, and Linux, and it is regarded as a highly accurate open source program, supported by Google. It uses a two-pass approach, but determines characters recognized on the first pass at a high degree of confidence to aid in better recognition of lower-confidence characters on the second pass. This is called Adaptive Recognition and is suited to complex documents with multiple columns and tables. Tesseract only works on existing image files and does not fit into the scanning workflow as FineReader or Acrobat Pro do.[30]

22.7 CONCLUSION

The topic of AI and machine learning has received little attention in the FDE community to date. It is hoped that this chapter has shed some illumination on a relevant mainstay of the 21st century that will come to affect most facets of society, if it hasn't done so already. AI has indeed been present as a tangential tool for the FDE through software such as OCR and more directly in FDE-specific handwriting applications like FISH and FLASH ID and reconstruction of shredded documents. It is the future course of directing what documents may be submitted for analysis, via predictive coding. It serves the FDE well to, at the very least, be aware of the presence and possible influence of AI in the sphere of forensic examinations, or at best, be involved in assisting in the direction of relevant research.

REFERENCES

1. Niiler, E., 2019. "Can AI be a fair judge in court? Estonia thinks so," *WIRED*, March 25, accessed October 29, 2019. https://www.wired.com/story/can-ai-be-fair-judge-court-estonia-thinks-so
2. LeCun, Y., Bottou, L., Bengio, Y., and Haffner, P., 1998. "Gradient-based learning applied to document recognition," *Proceedings of the IEEE*, 86(11):2278–2324.
3. LeCun, Y., Cortes, C., and Burges, C.J.C., 1998. "The MNIST database of handwritten digits," accessed October 29, 2019. http://yann.lecun.com/exdb/mnist/
4. Geitgey, A., 2016. "Machine learning is fun! Part 3: Deep learning and convolutional neural networks," https://medium.com/@ageitgey/machine-learning-is-fun-part-3-deep-learning-and-convolutional-neural-networks-f40359318721
5. Silburt, A., Ali-Dib, M., Zhu, C., Jackson, A., Valencia, D., Kissin, Y., Tamayo, D., and Menou, K., 2018. "Lunar crater identification via deep learning." arXiv:1803.02192v3.
6. READ Project, 2018. "Recognition and enrichment of archival documents," accessed October 29, 2019. https://read.transkribus.eu
7. DARPA, 2011. "DARPA Shredder challenge," accessed October 29, 2019. https://web.archive.org/web/20140611065615/http://archive.darpa.mil/shredderchallenge/index.html
8. Barba, M., June 12, 2019. "San Francisco DA announces AI tool from Stanford to avoid racial bias in prosecutions," San Francisco Examiner. https://www.sfexaminer.com/the-city/san-francisco-da-announces-ai-tool-from-stanford-to-avoid-racial-bias-in-prosecutions
9. Gascon, G., June 12, 2019. "DA GASCÓN leans on artificial intelligence to remove potential for bias from charging," San Francisco District Attorney's Office Press Release. https://sfdistrictattorney.org/da-gasc%C3%B3n-leans-artificial-intelligence-remove-potential-bias-charging
10. Schuler, R.L., Treado, P.J., and Nelson, M.P., 2008. "Chemical Imaging of TLC Plates of Closely Related Ballpoint Inks: A Blind Study." ChemImage Corporation, 7301 Penn Avenue, Pittsburgh, PA 15208, USA.

11. Buzzini, P., Curran, J., and Polston, C., 2018. "The Application of t-Stochastic Node Embedding and Random Forest Statistical Methods to Classify Raman Spectra of Inkjet Printer Inks for Purposes of Identification and Production of Investigative Leads," *presented at the American Academy of Forensic Sciences (AAFS) 70th Annual Scientific Meeting*, Seattle, WA.
12. Master Matthews, 2016. "Pyrrho Investments Limited (and another) v. MWB Property Limited (and others) [2016] EWCH 256(Ch)," Royal Courts of Justice, UK.
13. Nielsen, M.A., 2015. "Neural Networks and Deep Learning," Determination Press. http://neuralnetworksanddeeplearning.com/chap1.html
14. Rashid, T., 2018. "Make Your Own Neural Network," http://makeyourownneuralnetwork.blogspot.com
15. Santos, L.A., 2017. "Artificial Intelligence," accessed October 29, 2019. https://leonardoaraujosantos.gitbooks.io/artificial-inteligence/content/chapter1.html
16. International Association for Pattern Recognition (IAPR) Technical Committee Number 11, 2019. "IAPR-TC11: Reading Systems," accessed October 29, 2019. http://www.iapr-tc11.org/mediawiki/index.php?title=IAPR-TC11:Reading_Systems
17. National Institute of Standards and Technology (NIST), 2013. "Measurement Science and Standards in Forensic Handwriting Analysis Conference," Gaithersburg, MD, accessed October 29, 2019. https://www.nist.gov/news-events/events/2013/06/measurement-science-and-standards-forensic-handwriting-analysis
18. Yadav, C. and Bottou, L., 2019. "Cold Case: The Lost MNIST Digits," https://arxiv.org/abs/1905.10498
19. Anderson, C., Agius, A., and Storey, G., 2017. "Utilizing data from Write-On™ 2.0 to provide a stronger scientific basis for handwriting examinations," *Journal of the American Society of Questioned Document Examiners*, vol. 20, no. 2, pp. 31–36.
20. Parziale, A., Senatore, R., Marcelli, A., Rizzo, A.P., Molinari, C., Cappuzzo, A.G., and Fontana, F., 2017. "Combining FHE features with machine decision making for automatic writer identification," *Proceedings of 18th IGS Conference*, June, Gaeta, Italy, pp. 153–156. https://www.nitesrl.com
21. Srihari, S., Cha, S., Arora, H., and Lee, S., "Individuality of handwriting," *Journal of Forensic Sciences*, vol. 47, no. 4, 2002, 856–872.
22. Srihari, S. and Singer, K., 2014. "Role of automation in the examination of handwritten items," *Pattern Recognition*, vol. 47, no. 3, 1083, 2014.
23. Walch, B. and Gantz, D., 2013. "The Forensic Language-Independent Analysis System for Handwriting Identification (FLASH-ID)," *presented at the Measurement Science and Standards in Forensic Handwriting Analysis Conference*, Gaithersburg, MD. http://sciometrics.com/flashid.html
24. Hecker, M. and Eisermann, H.W., 1986. "Forensic Identification System of Handwriting (FISH)," *presented at the 44th meeting of the American Society of Questioned Document Examiners*, Savannah, GA.
25. Maquire, K. and Moran, T.L., 1996. "Identification of Written Text Writings by the Forensic Information System of Handwriting," *paper presented at the 54th meeting of the ASQDE*, Washington, DC.
26. Bundeskriminalamt, 2019. "Der Computer als Kommissar: Spezielle Informations- systeme (FISH AKIM)," accessed October 29, 2019. https://www.bka.de/DE/UnsereAufgaben/Ermittlungsunterstuetzung/Technologien/SpezielleInformationssysteme/spezielleInformationssysteme.html
27. Franke, K., Schomake, L., Veenhuis, C., Taubenheum, C., Guyon, I., Vuurpijl, L., van Erp, M., and Zarts, G., 2003. "WANDA: A generic framework applies in forensic handwriting analysis and writer identification," In: Abraham, A., Koppen, M., Franke, K. (eds) *Design and Application of Hybrid Intelligent Systems (HIS 2003)*, pp. 927–938. IOS Press, Amsterdam.
28. Markoff, J., 1988. "Business Technology; Now, PC's That Read a Page and Store It," *New York Times*, August 17, accessed October 29, 2019. https://web.archive.org/web/20121112010926/https://www.nytimes.com/1988/08/17/business/business-technology-now-pc-s-that-read-a-page-and-store-it.html
29. Campbell, T., Pajos, P., and Osmond, J., 2014. "Unexpected Introduction of Tremor into Photocopied Handwriting on a Xerox WorkCenter 7545," *presented at the American Society of Questioned Document Examiners Annual Conference*, Honolulu, HI.
30. Illinois University Library, 2019. "Introduction to OCR and Searchable PDFs: An Introduction to OCR," accessed October 29, 2019. https://guides.library.illinois.edu/OCR/intro

Index

Note: **Bold** page numbers refer to tables and *italic* page numbers refer to figures.